SYRIA AND IRAN

In memory of my father, Mohsen Goodarzi, patriot, diplomat, and above all, humanist.

SYRIA AND IRAN

*Diplomatic Alliance and Power Politics
in the Middle East*

Jubin M. Goodarzi

TAURIS ACADEMIC STUDIES
LONDON·NEW YORK

Reprinted in 2007 by Tauris Academic Studies
an imprint of I.B.Tauris & Co Ltd
6 Salem Road, London W2 4BU
www.ibtauris.com

In the United States and in Canada
distributed by St Martin's Press
175 Fifth Avenue, New York NY 10010

First Published in 2006 by Tauris Academic Studies
Printed and bound in India by Replika Press Pvt. Ltd
Copyright © 2006 Jubin M. Goodarzi

Library of Modern Middle East Studies 55

ISBN 978 1 84511 127 4

A full CIP record for this book is available from the British Library
A full CIP record for this book is available from the Library of Congress

Library of Congress Catalog card: available

Typeset in Berkeley Oldstyle by Oxford Publishing Services, Oxford

Contents

Acronyms and Abbreviations

ABC	American Broadcasting Corporation
ACC	Arab Cooperation Council
ADP	Arab Democratic Party
AFP	Agence France-Presse
AMU	Arab Maghreb Union
AWACS	Airborne Warning and Control System
CAIS	Centre for Arab and Iranian Studies
CENTO	Central Treaty Organization
CIA	Central Intelligence Agency
DFLP	Democratic Front for the Liberation of Palestine
DPA	*Deutsche Presse Agentur*
EC	European Community
GCC	Gulf Cooperation Council
GDP	gross domestic product
IAEA	International Atomic Energy Agency
ICP	Iraqi Communist Party
IDF	Israeli Defence Forces
IISS	International Institute for Strategic Studies
INA	Iraqi News Agency
IPC	Iraq Petroleum Company
IRGC	Islamic Revolutionary Guards Corps
IRNA	Islamic Republic News Agency (formerly Pars Agency)
IRP	Islamic Republican Party
IUF	Islamic Unification Front
KDP	Kurdistan Democratic Party
LCP	Lebanese Communist Party
MNF	Multinational Force
NAM	Non-Aligned Movement
NATO	North Atlantic Treaty Organization
NSA	National Security Agency
OIC	Organization of the Islamic Conference

OPEC	Organization of the Petroleum Exporting Countries
PBS	Public Broadcasting Service
PLA	Palestinian Liberation Army
PLO	Palestine Liberation Organization
PNSF	Palestinian National Salvation Front
POW	prisoner of war
PSP	Progressive Socialist Party
PUK	Patriotic Union of Kurdistan
RASD	*Republica Arabe Saharaui Democratica* (Saharan Arab Democratic Republic)
SAM	surface-to-air missile
SANA	Syrian Arab News Agency
SAVAK	*Sazeman-e Ettela^cat va Amniyat-e Keshvar* (Shah's secret police)
SDC	Supreme Defence Council
SEAL	SEa, Air and Land
SLA	South Lebanon Army
SSNP	Syrian Social Nationalist Party
SWB	Summary of World Broadcasts
TWA	Trans World Airlines
UAE	United Arab Emirates
UAR	United Arab Republic
UKP	United Kurdish Party
UNIFIL	United Nations Interim Force in Lebanon
UNRWA	United Nations Relief and Works Agency for Palestine Refugees in the Near East
USAID	US Agency for International Development
USS	United States Ship
USSR	Union of Soviet Socialist Republics

Introduction

Alliances are central to any analysis of Middle East politics. Tribes, clans and small communities have found security in them since the dawn of civilization. Indeed, for thousands of years, since the ancient empires of the Egyptians, Hittites, Assyrians and Persians, alliances have been a common feature on the Middle East's political landscape.[1] Recurrent struggles between various regional, and later extra-regional, powers like the Greeks, Romans and Mongols determined the course of Middle East history for more than two millennia until the rise of modern nation-states in the region during the early half of the twentieth century.

In the decades just before and after the Second World War, the rise of modern nationalism in the region, the gradual retreat of Britain and France and the onset of the cold war ushered in a period of intense political and ideological rivalry among the various radical and conservative states in the Middle East. The newly-created state of Israel's defeat of the Arabs in the 1948 Palestine War, the appeal of radical Arab nationalism, and archaic political systems exacerbated and polarized the situation. Also, the region's vast oil reserves and geopolitical importance – at the crossroads between Europe, Africa, Asia and the Indian subcontinent – increased the Middle East's significance to the superpowers and led to continued outside inter-ference in the area. Concomitantly, in jockeying for influence and aid to boost their own regional and international power and position, many regional actors wanted to exploit the bipolar system by cultivating close ties with either Washington or Moscow. Others tried to enhance their security by forging alliances with regional actors that wanted to minimize the foreign presence in the Middle East. The volatile and precarious conditions in the region led to the formation of many short-lived alliances.

In a landmark study on alliance theory and alliance formation in the Middle East, Walt identified 33 different alliances in the region from 1955 to 1979 alone.[2] The general trend has been for regional actors to form alliances to diminish a threat posed by another regional power or alliance. They will overcome their ideological differences in the face of an immediate threat, for such factors assume more significance in the absence of a security challenge. However, there is clear evidence that they are more likely to form alliances with extra-regional actors that are willing to support their political objectives. Interestingly, as the record during the cold war clearly demonstrated, ideological factors were more salient in alliances between Middle Eastern states and their superpower patrons.

In the 1950s and 1960s, conservative, pro-Western monarchies formed defence pacts against the radical, nationalist, republican governments that emerged in Syria, Egypt and Iraq. The latter prematurely attempted to form political unions and assumed a confrontational stance against Israel and its allies. However, the Arab defeat in the 1967 Six Day War discredited the radical camp, diminished the importance of ideology and regime structure in alliance formation, and eventually gave way to more pragmatic alignments against common threats. This was epitomized by the formation of the short-lived 'Arab Triangle' consisting of Egypt, Syria and Saudi Arabia in the early 1970s, and its bid to demonstrate Arab dissatisfaction with the post-1967 *status quo* and US policy by launching the 1973 October war. The emergence and evolution of the Syrian–Iranian axis over the past quarter century is a fascinating and rare example of an enduring alliance. After the overthrow of the Iranian monarchy in 1979, the new revolutionary Islamist regime and the secular Arab nationalist government in Syria cultivated close bilateral relations and eventually formed an alliance in response to the direct challenges posed by Iraq, Israel and the USA in the Levant and Persian Gulf during the 1980s and beyond.

The Syrian–Iranian axis is one of the most intriguing developments in modern Middle East politics. In the turbulent 1980s, the nature and longevity of the Tehran–Damascus partnership baffled many scholars and observers. Many were quick to write it off as a short-term, opportunistic alliance against Iraq, or describe it as a marriage of convenience that would dissolve rapidly once Iran ceased to deliver oil to Syria. Pointing to many differences in their respective ideologies, as well as their social and political foundations, most analysts expressed surprise at how a revolutionary, pan-Islamic theocracy like Iran could form an alliance with a secular, pan-Arab socialist republic like Syria.[3] Moreover, while Ba'thist Syria claimed to be an ardent supporter and the rightful leader of the pan-Arab cause, revolutionary Iran advocated Islamic universalism and, during the Khomeini era, purportedly rejected the concept of the nation-state.[4] Also, although Syria traditionally maintained strong ties with the

USSR and was a primary recipient of Soviet military aid in the 1980s, Moscow's relations with Tehran's ruling clerics were strained intermittently after the establishment of the Islamic Republic.[5]

In this book, I aim to provide an in-depth analysis of the forces that led to the emergence and consolidation of the Syrian–Iranian alliance during a turbulent decade in the modern history of the Middle East. The alliance between the two states, which has lasted for more than 25 years, has been an enduring feature of the political landscape of this troubled region. Moreover, since its inception, it has had a significant impact on moulding events and bringing about major changes in the contemporary Middle East. I show that, contrary to prevailing views (formed by the Syrian and Iranian regimes' authoritarianism and unpopularity in the West and in parts of the Arab world), the alliance between them has been essentially defensive and emerged in response to acts of aggression orchestrated by Iraq (1980) and Israel (1982), in both cases with the prior knowledge and tacit support of the USA. Because my research revealed three distinct phases in the evolution and institutionalization of the Damascus–Tehran axis, I devote one chapter to each of these stages.

In this brief introduction, I provide a general conceptual framework for understanding the genesis and longevity of the Syrian–Iranian nexus. In Chapter 1, which covers the emergence of the alliance between 1979 and 1982, I show that while the initial impetus for the relationship came from the overthrow of Iran's conservative, pro-Western monarchy in 1979, Iraq's invasion of Iran in September 1980 brought Syria and Iran closer together, with Syria providing valuable diplomatic and military aid to help Iran stave off defeat and expel the Iraqi invaders. In Chapter 2, I examine the period between 1982 and 1985 when Israel invaded Lebanon for a second time and challenged Syria in its backyard. Here, in 1983–85, Iran lent support to Syria by mobilizing Lebanon's Shiites to drive out Israeli and Western forces. In Chapter 3, I cover a critical and problematic phase in the development of the alliance when the two allies developed conflicting agendas, which by 1985 had created tensions between them. However, by the late 1980s, through continued bilateral consultations in which they were able to prioritize their respective objectives without impinging on the interests of the other, they were able to redefine the parameters of cooperation and consolidate their relationship on a more mature basis. Finally, in the fourth and concluding chapter, I look at the reasons why the alliance lasted beyond the 1980s into the twenty-first century.

Although Agha and Khalidi (1995) and Ehteshami and Hinnebusch (1997) shed light on certain aspects of the alliance, they focus primarily on its continued importance in the 1990s and provide only a general overview of the formative years of the Tehran–Damascus nexus. I, however, aim to trace in detail the origins and development of the strategic partnership between Damascus and Tehran from the toppling of Mohammad Reza Shah in early 1979 until the Syrian–Iranian intercession to halt Amal–Hezbollah clashes in Beirut and the end of the first Persian Gulf war in mid-1988. Besides providing an empirical survey with a chronology of events, through analysis, I intend to distinguish three phases in the evolution of the alliance and explain their significance both in terms of how they affected bilateral relations between the two states, as well as their regional implications in the volatile environment of 1979–88.

In my research I relied mostly on secondary sources (books, periodicals, newspapers), transcripts of radio broadcasts, official government statements, and personal interviews with former government officials and Middle East experts. Given the closed and often secretive nature of decision making in the Syrian Ba'thist and Iranian Islamist regimes, and the importance and sensitivity of cooperative ties between them, it is improbable that responsible officials would have engaged in frank discussions on these matters or provided first-hand knowledge about bilateral relations between the two states. Indeed, inaccessibility to primary sources and interviews with current government officials in Damascus and Tehran remain the main obstacle to a complete and accurate picture of the nature and extent of Syrian–Iranian collaboration during the first decade of the alliance. The opacity of political decision making among these regimes' key figures and bodies poses a formidable challenge to any outsider trying to understand the inner workings of these authoritarian governments. I try to compensate with an exhaustive survey and analysis of the available secondary sources and attempt to fill in some of the gaps and clarify certain inconsistencies by obtaining first-hand information from former senior government officials. These include former Iranian president Abolhassan Bani-Sadr's account of Syrian military aid to Iran in the early years of the Iran–Iraq hostilities (1980–81) and Tehran's policy on the Syrian Muslim Brethren (Chapter 1); and former US assistant secretary of state (1981–89) Richard Murphy's insights on the degree of Syrian–Iranian involvement in attacks on US assets in Lebanon in 1983–84 (Chapter 2).

My focus on the genesis and development of the Tehran–Damascus

nexus during this decade may give the impression that the maintenance and augmentation of their strategic bilateral links was the main
foreign policy consideration of Syrian and Iranian leaders between
1979 and 1989. In some respects, this was the case for both partners,
especially Iran. The Iranian militants' seizure of the US embassy in
Tehran in 1979 (which plunged US–Iranian relations into an abyss
and led to Iran's international isolation), and the Iraqi invasion of
Iran in 1980 meant that Khomeini's regime became extremely dependent on Hafez Assad's diplomatic and military support. This was
needed to stave off defeat and avoid regional isolation at a time when
Saddam Hussein held the initiative, occupying large swathes of
Iranian territory and trying to depict the war as an Arab–Persian
conflict. With the expulsion of Iraqi forces from most of the areas
they held in Iran by mid-1982 and the concurrent Israeli invasion of
Lebanon, the pendulum swung the other way, with Syria requiring
Iranian assistance to keep Iraq in check and mobilize Lebanon's
Shiites to expel Israeli and Western forces from its backyard between
1982 and 1985. As the Israeli threat receded with the withdrawal of
Tel Aviv's troops to the self-declared security zone in mid-1985, and
Arab disenchantment grew as Iran continued the Gulf War, Iran once
again became dependent on Syrian cooperation and goodwill to
maintain a foothold in the Levant and avoid total regional isolation.
This situation continued until the cessation of hostilities with Iraq in
1988. Overall, Tehran valued its strategic alliance with Syria more
between 1979–82 and 1985–88, particularly against the backdrop of
the poor state of US–Iranian relations throughout the 1980s and the
erratic nature of its ties with the USSR and western Europe during
that period. For Syria, the years from 1982 to 1985 represented the
height of its reliance on Iran to undo the achievements of its foes in
Lebanon. At the same time, at the international level, Syria continued
to place great emphasis on its close links with the USSR in the first
half of the 1980s because of the latter's status as a superpower and as
its main provider of military and economic assistance. However, with
the rise of Mikhail Gorbachev in 1985 and the gradual cooling of
Soviet–Syrian relations in the second half of the 1980s, a subtle shift
occurred in Syrian perceptions of Moscow. Damascus realized that it
would have to diversify its political and economic ties internationally
and, at the same time, rely more heavily on regional allies and proxies
such as Iran and Lebanon's Shiites to achieve its strategic and military
objectives and to keep Israeli and Iraqi power in check. While my
main focus is on the evolution of the Syrian–Iranian alliance, I also

attempt to locate the bilateral relationship within the context of the changing regional and international environment of the 1980s. I show how Syrian and Iranian policymakers viewed the situation evolving around them and how they tried to utilize their strategic partnership to achieve their objectives.

During 1980/1 and 1986/7 there were differences of opinion within the Iranian leadership about the extent and use of cooperative ties with Syria and, by 1984, Rif'at Assad had serious reservations about the strategic alliance with Iran. However, for three reasons, I decided not to concentrate on domestic factors. First, it is clear from the available evidence that throughout the 1980s and beyond, most key political decision makers in Tehran and Damascus firmly believed that perpetuating and strengthening the alliance was central to their foreign policies. Second, secretive decision making even now makes it difficult to ascertain what various members of the Syrian and Iranian leadership really think. Information on the main rifts or differences of opinion that were ultimately reflected in their domestic or regional policies are based on interviews and press accounts that appeared at the time in the Middle Eastern and Western media. Third, the available evidence and the authoritarian nature of the Syrian Ba'thist and Iranian Islamist systems suggest that domestic opinion was never taken into account. In fact, it was a non-issue, particularly for the Syrian government. Despite disapproval in the Syrian Ba'th Party and among the Syrian masses of the policy to support non-Arab Iran during its eight-year war with Arab Iraq, Hafez Assad and his inner political circle saw no need to alter their position to gain party approval or win domestic support.[6] When the Iranian Islamist regime began to deliver oil to Syria and to expel the Iraqi army from much of its soil in 1982, the public gradually began to question the wisdom of crude shipments to Syria at a time when the Iraqi threat seemed to have receded and also opposed the continuation of the Gulf conflict. By the mid-1980s, with Syria failing to make timely payments for its oil purchases and the acute economic situation in Iran, some Iranian MPs became quite vocal in their opposition to continued shipments and to the logic of the alliance with Syria. However, despite some tensions in bilateral relations, Khomeini and his lieutenants would not be swayed and were determined to preserve links with their only significant Arab ally.[7] Such is the nature of authoritarian doctrinaire regimes. Overall, my emphasis here is on the output and policies that emerged from the black box of Syrian–Iranian decision making.

In general, there is a wealth of information and analysis on the evolution of the Syrian–Iranian alliance during its first decade. Through careful research and analysis, I try to put the various pieces together and to shed new light on linkages between major events and crucial decisions that were made in Tehran and Damascus during one of the most turbulent periods in the contemporary history of the Middle East – especially those that regional analysts and scholars have overlooked or ignored. For example, in Chapter 2, I put the case that the Israeli invasion of Lebanon on 6 June 1982 and the subsequent Syrian–Iranian consultations (7–17 June 1982) had a direct bearing on Tehran's fateful decision to continue the Persian Gulf conflict and invade Iraq in the weeks that followed. In Chapter 3, I show how US–Iraqi military operations against Iran in the Persian Gulf during the spring of 1988 (designed to turn the tide of the Gulf conflict) prompted Tehran to throw its weight behind Lebanon's Hezbollah in its violent confrontation with the rival, pro-Syrian Amal movement (albeit in a calculated and limited manner) and to try to maintain its precarious foothold in Lebanon. This bloody affair put the Syrian–Iranian alliance to the test since Tehran was overtly defying Damascus in its own backyard.

Before delving into the specific aspects of the genesis and development of the Syrian–Iranian alliance, it is useful to identify and elaborate on several general concepts and theoretical explanations to understand the strength and longevity of the cooperative ties between revolutionary Iran and Ba'thist Syria. First, the alliance consists of only two members: it has never been a broad coalition of states with various and divergent interests. Since it is small, it is more viable.[8] In the words of Holsti et al., 'the smaller the alliance, the more cohesive and effective it is, and the more important the contribution of each member.'[9] Second, it has primarily been a defensive alliance aimed at neutralizing Iraqi and Israeli offensive capabilities in the Gulf and Near East, and thwarting American encroachment in the Middle East. In general, alliances with set and limited objectives are more stable and durable.[10] Both Liska and Walt see defensive alliances as less fragile than offensive ones. In the latter case, once the opponent has been attacked and vanquished, the rationale for maintaining the alliance ceases to exist for the members, and they subsequently fall out over the fruits of their victory.[11] Third, the two partners' priorities differ in the two arenas in which they cooperate. The Gulf region is the main area of concern for Iran, whereas for Syria it is the Levant. Over time, by continually consulting and modifying their aims, the two allies have come to recognize this reality and, in the process, have tried to coordinate their policies and accommodate one another while still furthering their own interests.[12] In other words, between 1985 and 1988 Iran finally acknowledged that Syrian interests took precedence in the Arab–Israeli theatre, and Syria in return deferred to its Iranian partner when vital matters regarding Gulf security were at stake for the Islamist government. Though not all their interests converged, through consultation Tehran and Damascus gradually harmonized their positions as far as they could. As Liska posits in *Nations in Alliance*, the more complementary the interests of alliance members, the more easily intra-alliance compromises can be achieved.[13] Furthermore, the fact that Syria has carried the greater part of the burden in checking Israeli power, and Iran's main role has been to serve as a bulwark against Iraqi expansionism in the Gulf and beyond, has meant that the two partners fulfil different functions, thus reinforcing the rationale and utility of their strategic links. In other words, the more pronounced the differentiation of functions of the members, the more cohesive the alliance.[14] Fourth, the mere fact that the alliance has endured for so many years (especially by Middle East standards), gives it considerable weight and importance. Interestingly, in *Alliances and Small Powers*, Rothstein argues that 'once an alliance has been created, there is positive value placed on continuing it, even if it seems to perform very few functions.'[15] Furthermore, Kaplan builds on this point by postulating that longstanding alliances are characterized by greater unity and legitimacy.[16] It is also worth noting that if a member wishes to abandon an alliance that has become institutionalized, it is prudent to find another viable arrangement that has at least equal utility. In other words, the member will pay an opportunity cost unless it joins or forms an alternative arrangement that is at least equally useful as the previous alliance.

Finally, another general point needs to be made about the role of ideology in maintaining an alliance. Ironically, a crucial factor in the longevity of the Syrian–Iranian axis is that the states have different ideologies; herein lies the paradox. Quite often, alliances between states that espouse the same transnational universalistic ideology are less likely to endure than those in which ideology plays a minimal role. This is particularly true of the Middle East where authoritarian regimes predominate and frequently use ideology as a tool to boost their political legitimacy and base of support domestically and in neighbouring countries. Revisionist ideologies such as pan-Arabism and Islamic fundamentalism have frequently been quite divisive because they are used to project power and influence and to destabilize rival states. In the Middle East, the record clearly shows that states sharing a common ideology compete for the mantle of leadership rather than form durable alliances. Each state may claim to be the legitimate leader, and demand others to relinquish their rights and sovereignty to form a single political entity. The most poignant example of this phenomenon was the failure of the various unity schemes during the 1950s and 1960s involving Nasserite Egypt, and the radical regimes in Syria and Iraq. Walt supports this view in *The Origins of Alliances*. He asserts that alliances among Arab states and communist countries that have sought to form a single centralized movement have been unstable and short-lived. In the final analysis, common ideologies have often served as an obstacle to unity, prompting states to compete with one another rather than form durable alliances.[17] Iklé also recognized this point in *How Nations Negotiate* when he opined that in certain instances, alliances not characterized by doctrinal unity will more easily resolve internal differences without disrupting the partnership.[18]

In studying the Syrian–Iranian alliance it is apparent that Iran (a non-Arab nation) is not trying to champion Arab nationalism, unlike its Syrian partner, which considers itself 'the beating heart of Arabism'. Syria, for its part, is not vying to lead the Islamic revivalist movement in the Middle East or elsewhere. Moreover, Iran refrained from supporting the Syrian Muslim Brethren in their ill-fated effort to overthrow the Ba'thist regime in Damascus during the early 1980s. In general, there has been neither ostensible competition on an ideological level (except in Lebanon during 1985–88) nor fear that one partner might upstage the other precisely because of their distinctly different ideological platforms. According to Dinerstein, 'ideological dissimilarities will not disrupt alliance cooperation if none of the members is intent on political revolution in the others.'[19]

Both Ba'thist Syria and Islamic Iran have been fiercely independent states and, throughout the years following the toppling of the Pahlavi dynasty in Iran, found it expedient to cooperate to thwart Iraqi and Israeli designs in the region and to frustrate US moves that implicitly or explicitly supported Tel Aviv and Baghdad. In addition, Damascus and Tehran were wary of Washington's attempts to advance its own agenda and make inroads in the Middle East at their expense. During 1982–85, Syrian President Assad was determined to resist the Reagan administration's effort to bring Lebanon within the US–Israeli orbit and to push for a piecemeal approach to resolve the Arab–Israeli conflict. Khomeini's Iran shared Syria's concerns in the Levant and sought to punish Iraq for its invasion of Iran in 1980 and, after 1982, much to the consternation of Washington and its Arab allies, tried to oust Saddam Hussein from power. Moreover, since the end of the cold war, US hegemony in the Middle East has reinforced the logic of an alliance between Syria and Iran. Deep-seated concerns in Tehran and Damascus over US adventurism and the occupation of Iraq in 2003 have strengthened their resolve to stand together and thwart US ambitions in the region.

In the following chapters, I will demonstrate that Syrian–Iranian cooperation during the formative years of the alliance had a major impact on shaping the course of events in the Middle East and transformed the region. The joint policies pursued by Tehran and Damascus also had a profound effect on the actions of the superpowers in the Middle East. Not only did Assad and Khomeini succeed in inflicting one of the very few foreign policy defeats that Reagan experienced during his two terms in office, but they also proved adept at enlisting Soviet support on a number of occasions to attain their objectives. Furthermore, they frustrated Saddam Hussein and Menachem Begin's designs in the region. Careful, well-crafted strategies eventually led to the expulsion of the Iraqi army from Iranian territory by 1982, the withdrawal of US troops from Beirut in 1984, and the retreat of Israeli forces from most of the Lebanese territory they occupied by 1985 (and indeed the self-declared security zone by 2000). At the same time, despite their impressive achieve-ments, there were limits to the Syrian–Iranian power in the region. As two middle powers that did not enjoy the backing of most regional states, and only received some qualified support from the USSR (until its demise in 1991), they were unable to alter the regional *status quo* in their favour, or determine the outcome of events on their own in the Levant and Persian Gulf. Although the Syrian–Iranian axis possessed limited offensive capability in regional terms, let alone on the international level, it was nonetheless a force to be reckoned with during the 1980s and beyond – one that has left an enduring mark on Middle East politics.

Chapter 1

The Emergence of the Syrian–Iranian Axis, 1979–82

The 1979 Iranian revolution was one of the most important milestones in modern Middle Eastern history. The overthrow of the Pahlavi dynasty not only brought major changes to Iran, but also ushered in a new era of politics at the regional level. The new regime under Ayatollah Khomeini's leadership radically altered the content and form of Iranian foreign policy. Overnight, imperial Iran, which had once pursued a strongly pro-Western *status quo* foreign policy, was transformed into a new republic committed to a purportedly universalistic religious ideology and bent on changing the political map of the Middle East.

The revolutionary changes in Iran during 1978/9 sent tremors throughout the region, particularly the Arab world. While they alarmed many regimes that had previously enjoyed close ties with the imperial government, many non-aligned and pro-Soviet governments welcomed it enthusiastically. Moreover, it gave a major boost to and served as a powerful source of inspiration for various Islamic, Third World and revolutionary movements and political parties in the region and beyond.

The overthrow of the Pahlavi throne naturally brought with it a reversal in the pattern of Iran's alliances and enmities. At a stroke, the country's new leadership terminated Iran's long-standing alliances with the USA and Israel. Consequently, though not inevitably, Iran's relationship with the pro-Western Arab states suffered. As a result of the changing nature of Arab–Iranian relations, inter-Arab political configurations and alliances were reconsidered and reshaped to meet the requirements or challenge of Iran's new Islamic revolutionary ideology and foreign policy.

Prior to the Shah's fall, most Arab governments viewed the political order in the Middle East as predominantly Arab. Non-Arab actors like Israel and Iran were confined to the margins of mainstream Arab politics, particularly during the heyday of Arab nationalism in the 1950s and 1960s when Nasser was in power. Then, Tel Aviv and Tehran saw radical Arab nationalism as a major threat to their national security and existence, and joined forces to counter the 'progressive Arab Front' under Nasser's leadership. But the devastating Arab defeat in the 1967 Arab–Israeli war and Nasser's demise three years later sounded the death knell of the radical period in mainstream Arab politics and the beginning of a new era of political pragmatism. This was clearly exemplified by the ascendance of new leaders such as Anwar Sadat in Egypt and Hafez Assad in Syria, who placed less emphasis on the role of ideology and made *realpolitik* a hallmark of their diplomacy in the decade that followed.

When the revolt against the monarchy erupted in Iran, the Arab political order was weak and in a state of disarray. The failure to derive any tangible benefits from the limited success of the 1973 Arab–Israeli war, the impasse over Palestine, the lingering domestic conflict in Lebanon, incessant inter-Arab feuding and Egypt's 'defection' with the signing of the Camp David accords in March 1979, had thrown the Arabs into total confusion. It was within this context that the Iranian revolution occurred.

As a major watershed in the history of the Middle East, the Iranian revolution and unique circumstances in the Arab world at the time dramatically altered the course of events in the Middle East. Revolutionary Iran's ideology and new foreign policy brought challenges or opportunities to a number of Arab regimes, particularly Iraq and Syria. The interplay between events in the Arab world and Iran in fact heavily influenced Saddam Hussein's decision to go to war against Iran in September 1980. Ironically, what was expected to be a swift Iraqi victory turned into one of the bloodiest and longest wars in modern Middle Eastern history. At the same time, the conflict turned the emerging Syrian–Iranian entente into a formal alliance – probably one of the most durable regional alliances – that has lasted to this day despite all odds and predictions to the contrary.

With the outbreak of the first Gulf war on 22 September 1980, many observers expected Syrian President Assad to join ranks with the other Arab leaders who rallied to aid Iraqi strongman Saddam Hussein in his effort to deliver a major blow to non-Arab Iran and blunt the intrusive edge of its Islamic revolution. At the very least, after the recent break in Syrian–Iraqi relations and the looming possibility of a serious confrontation with Israel in Lebanon now that Egypt was no longer a frontline state, Assad was expected to declare his neutrality. Indeed, in view of its precarious regional position, Damascus could have chosen to avoid having enemies on both its eastern and western flanks. Such expectations were partly based on the structural and ideological similarities between Assad's and Hussein's regimes. Both leaders had come to power through Ba'th Party orchestrated military coups in their respective countries and both espoused a pan-Arab socialist ideology. However, to the dismay of many, by 1982 the war had led to the consolidation of the emergent Syrian–Iranian axis.

There has been a great deal of debate among scholars and analysts over what prompted Damascus and Tehran to seal their 'unholy alliance' in spring 1982. Many observers put it down to their common hostility to Iraq. Although this was no doubt an incentive, it would be a gross oversimplification to regard it as the only important factor in developing the Syrian–Iranian alliance. Careful analysis reveals that, despite their differences and certain discrepancies, the birth of the Syrian–Iranian entente between 1979 and 1982 can be viewed as much more than an alliance of convenience against Iraq.

In this chapter, I aim to provide an accurate chronology of events and in-depth analysis of the chain of events and forces that moulded and influenced the start and eventual formalization of the relationship between the winter of 1979 and spring of 1982. It is important to note from the outset that Syria's decision to mend fences with Iran after the success of the Islamic revolution, must be observed through the prism of inter-Arab politics, Assad's leadership ambitions, and revolutionary Iran's new foreign policy orientation and ideology.

Syrian–Iranian relations before the 1979 revolution

Under the Shah, bilateral relations between the two states had been anything but cordial. Despite a brief thaw in the mid-1970s, their relations had fluctuated between outright hostility and cold peace throughout much of the 1960s and 1970s. Pahlavi Iran perceived Ba'thist Syria, with its close ties with the USSR and support for radical Arab movements, as a menace in the region. Moreover, Syria's vociferous claims that the Iranian province of Khuzestan (historically and more accurately known by Arabs as Arabestan) was 'an integral part of the Arab nation' because of its indigenous Arab population, and that the Gulf had an 'Arab character' greatly disturbed Iranian officials.[1] The Shah perceived radical Arab nationalism as a major threat to Iran's regional interests and national security.

Syria's Ba'thist leaders (who first seized the reins of power in 1963) saw imperial Iran as a source of instability in the Middle East and a

dangerous enemy of the Arab nation. They resented the Shah's close
ties with Israel and conservative pro-Western Arab regimes. From
their viewpoint, the Shah served as an instrument of US imperialism
in the region by thwarting Arab aspirations and, more specifically, by
impeding efforts to liberate Palestine from the Zionists.

Since full diplomatic relations were established in 1946, a striking
and recurrent feature of modern Syrian–Iranian relations has been
that the tightening or loosening of bilateral ties depends largely on
the state at the time of Syrian–Iraqi and Iranian–Iraqi relations and
the regional environment.[2] This was evident in the mid-1950s, but
became more pronounced after the creation of the UAR in February
1958.[3] Both Hashemite Iraq and, to a lesser extent, Pahlavi Iran were
alarmed by the union between Egypt and Syria. King Faisal of Iraq
subsequently visited Tehran to resolve outstanding differences with
the Shah over their common borders and other issues. Indeed,
Iranian–Iraqi relations improved noticeably during February–July
1958, prior to the overthrow of the Iraqi monarchy.

In July 1960, when the Shah stated at a press conference that Iran
already recognized Israel, UAR President Nasser severed diplomatic
ties with it.[4] It was thus no surprise that when Syria left the UAR in
September 1961, the Shah welcomed the event and moved to restore
full diplomatic relations with the new government in Damascus.
However, following the Ba'thist seizure of power in Iraq and Syria in
February/March 1963, and the ensuing tripartite negotiations in
Cairo in March/April, Iran was extremely concerned about the prospect of a union between Egypt, Syria and Iraq. Despite the collapse of
this initiative by mid-1963, Iran remained uneasy as the Syrian and
Iraqi Ba'thists subsequently took steps to create a union between their
two countries. This process came to an abrupt end when Abd al-
Salam Arif ousted the Iraqi Ba'th Party in November 1963.

It is noteworthy that when Baghdad and Cairo drew closer after the
Cairo summit of January 1964, and strengthened their political and
military ties, Iraq's relations with Syria and Iran deteriorated. Nasser
and Arif were both dismayed to see the Syrian Ba'th Party strengthen
its grip on power and stabilize the situation. The Syrian Ba'thists, for
their part, fearing being trapped between a 'hammer and anvil',
launched an intensive propaganda war against Arif and the Syrian
news media's attacks on Iran ceased. Damascus seemed to have
modified its policy on Tehran to avoid needlessly alienating it in view
of the emergent Iraqi–Egyptian alliance. Both Damascus and Tehran
became concerned about the visit of the Egyptian chief of staff

Marshall Abd al-Hakim Amer to Amman in mid-1964 in a bid to draw Jordan into the Iraqi–Egyptian orbit.

Although Syrian–Iranian relations never improved markedly, by 1965 significant shifts had occurred in the Syria–Iraq–Iran triangle. As the Shah and Arif tried to ease tensions and reach a *modus vivendi* in the Gulf, Syrian–Iranian relations plunged to an all-time low when, in an unprecedented move, Prime Minister Yusuf Zu'ayyin's militant Ba'thist government called for the 'liberation' of Arabestan from 'Iranian occupation' and printed official maps designating it as part of the Arab homeland.[5] Iran's riposte was to lodge an official protest with the Syrian government and withdraw its ambassador and most of its diplomatic staff from the country, leaving only one official representative in Damascus.

There was some improvement in bilateral relations after the June 1967 Arab–Israeli war when Iran's Red Lion and Sun Society (renamed Red Crescent Society after the 1979 revolution) sent medical personnel and humanitarian aid to assist the Syrian wounded and refugees displaced by the fighting.[6] While diplomatic relations were upgraded to the chargé d'affaires level and trade links improved, there were intermittent tensions. In 1969, the situation again degenerated when the Syrians uncovered an Iranian espionage network in their country and the number of staff in their respective embassies was reduced.

In 1970, as the Jordanian–Palestinian confrontation erupted during Black September, with Syrian and Israeli military intervention in Jordan, Iran sent munitions and weapons to the Jordanian army[7] and the Shah mediated between King Hussein and the Israelis. Through Iran's good offices, the Jordanian monarch obtained guarantees from Tel Aviv that its military intervention was only intended to crush the Palestinians, and would not aim to destabilize the Hashemite regime.[8] Hafez Assad's successful coup in November 1970 brought no noticeable improvement in Syrian–Iranian relations. In July 1973, Assad condemned the ill-fated, Iranian-backed attempt by Iraqi intelligence chief Nadhim Kzar to topple the rival wing of the Ba'th Party in Baghdad on 30 June 1973.[9]

Bilateral relations between Syria and Iran improved during the 1973 Arab–Israeli war and its aftermath. During the conflict, Iran provided logistical, medical and non-military assistance to the Arab combatants.[10] In the period that followed the war, Iran gave some financial assistance and relations warmed up to some degree. Within two months of the cessation of hostilities, in December 1973, the process of

upgrading relations to ambassadorial level began with the appointment of a new Iranian ambassador to Damascus.[11] In 1974, after several
ministerial-level exchanges, Iran agreed to provide a US$ 150 million
loan and a US$ 50 million grant to finance a number of industrial and
agricultural development projects in Syria. High-level exchanges
between the two erstwhile foes continued, and in 1975 Iran gave an
additional US$ 300 million in loans to Syria. The warming of rela-
tions between Syria and Iran and the simultaneous deterioration of
Syrian–Iraqi ties in the period following the 1973 Arab–Israeli conflict,
prompted Hafez Assad to undertake his first state visit to Iran in
December 1975 to consolidate what seemed to be an emerging friendship with Iran. He was also determined to avoid being outmanoeuv-
red by the Iraqis, who had concluded the Algiers accord with Iran in
March 1975 and were in the process of mending fences with their
Iranian neighbour.[12] Assad's four-day state visit (28–31 December 1975)
paved the way for further ministerial-level exchanges to expand
political, economic and cultural ties between the two countries. However, the process is best described as a limited *rapprochement*.

With warmer Egyptian–US relations, Sadat's decision to pursue a
separate peace with Israel and the Shah's close ties with Cairo and
Washington, Assad had hoped to convince the Shah to use his influence to persuade the Americans to assume a balanced approach in
their attempts to resolve the Arab–Israeli conflict. Much to Assad's
chagrin, the Iranian monarch refused to accommodate his request.[13]
The Shah instead encouraged Anwar Sadat's peace initiative towards
Israel.[14] Consequently, by the late 1970s, the rift between Tehran and
Damascus seemed irreparable. It was therefore quite understandable
that when the Shah was deposed in February 1979, Assad saw the
change in government as a positive development and deemed it
necessary to establish cordial ties with the new revolutionary government, which seemed sympathetic to the Arab cause and the plight of
the Palestinians.

The Syrian experience in the regional context

Syria's motive for establishing close links with the new clerical regime
can be partially understood in the context of inter-Arab and internal
Syrian politics. Assad's bitter experiences of dealing with other Arab
states between 1973 and 1979 had by 1979/80 prompted him to re-
evaluate his regional policies.[15] Egypt's betrayal in the 1973 Arab–
Israeli war and its unilateral efforts following the war to work out a
separate peace agreement with Israel, which eventually resulted in the

signing of the Israeli–Egyptian Sinai agreement of September 1975, had outraged the Syrians. With Egypt out of the picture, the efficacy of any military action on the part of the Syrians in response to Israeli aggression was greatly reduced.

Concurrently, in March 1975, Iraq signed the Algiers accord with Iran, which settled the border disputes between the two countries and implicitly recognized Iran's superiority in the Gulf. With its eastern borders and outlet to the Gulf now secure, in April 1976, after failing to reach an agreement with Syria on transfer fees (for exporting Iraqi oil via the trans-Syrian pipeline), Iraq informed Damascus that it would cease to use the trans-Syrian pipeline. Iraq's decision brought huge financial losses to Syria, which helplessly watched the deterioration of economic and political conditions at home and the decline of its power and prestige abroad.[16]

The evolution of the US-approved Saudi–Iranian–Egyptian axis, Sadat's historic visit to Jerusalem in November 1977 and the Camp David accords in March 1979 further isolated Damascus. Syria was even sidelined at the November 1978 Arab summit held in Baghdad to create a united front against Egypt's warming relationship with Israel and, to its disappointment, witnessed the formation of the Saudi–Iraqi–Jordanian entente.[17]

Between October 1978 and July 1979 a *rapprochement* between Syria and Iraq seemed a distinct possibility. This was partly because of the need to forge a credible military alliance to keep Israeli power in check on the western front, thus relieving Syria of some pressure and bolstering Iraq, which was uneasy about the chaos in neighbouring Iran and its potential impact on its own Shiite population.[18] A Syrian–Iraqi partnership did not, however, materialize. Mutual distrust and irreconcilable differences eventually brought the bilateral negotiations to a screeching halt in the summer of 1979 when Iraq accused Syria of involvement in a coup attempt to topple the Ba'thist regime in Baghdad, despite Syrian denials. Damascus was again isolated and placed in a vulnerable position *vis-à-vis* Israel and a hostile Iraq. It was thus no surprise that by 1979/80, the betrayals and disappointments of the past had killed any lingering Syrian hope of relying on fellow Arabs.[19] Assad subsequently continued to cultivate even closer relations with the new revolutionary government in Tehran and watched events unravel in Iran with great interest.

Syrian–Iranian *rapprochement*: February–July 1979

Immediately after the collapse of the monarchy, on 12 February

1979, Assad sent Khomeini a telegram congratulating him for his triumph over the Shah. In his message, he praised the 'Iranian people's victory', and went on to say: 'we proclaim our support for the new regime created by the revolution in Iran. This regime is inspired by the great principles of Islam. The creation of this regime is in the Iranian people's greatest interest, as well as that of the Arabs and Muslims.'[20] In fact, Syria was the first Arab country to recognize the new regime in Iran, though Libya, Algeria, South Yemen and the PLO also expressed strong support for the new leadership in Tehran. Conversely, Iraq, Saudi Arabia, Jordan and Egypt reacted cautiously. Iraq's foreign minister, for example, on hearing of the Shah's overthrow, only went so far as to say that 'Iran's internal affairs concern the Iranian people only.'[21] However, it was clear, even during the winter of 1978/9, that the Iraqi Ba'thists were very concerned about the opposition movement in Iran having assumed a religious character. Baghdad was wary of a Shiite revival and its potential repercussions on Iraq. Even before the toppling of the Pahlavi throne, the Shah's close ally, King Hussein of Jordan had gone on record as denouncing Khomeini as a heretic.[22]

Straight after the revolution, Hafez Assad's brother, Rif'at, sent envoys to Tehran to discuss ways of cooperating between the two countries, particularly against Iraq. Tehran followed up on these contacts by dispatching emissaries to Damascus to explore various options to lend support to the Iraqi opposition, particularly in the Shiite south. Rif'at, who served as commander of the Syrian defence brigades (*Saraya al-Difa'*), apparently opposed the Syrian–Iraqi unity talks, for he feared that they might benefit his leading rival for succession to his brother, former air force and intelligence chief, Na'ji Jamil, who had close ties with the Iraqi Ba'thists.[23]

In March, the first senior Syrian official, information minister Ahmad Iskandar Ahmad, visited Iran where he met Ayatollah Khomeini in Qom and presented him with an illuminated Quran as a gift from Hafez Assad.[24] Apart from bilateral relations between the two states starting on the right footing, the regional foreign policies of both were strikingly similar. Damascus and Tehran perceived and interpreted various regional developments in the same manner. This trend reinforced the growing cooperation between the two states. In Iran's case, relations with Arab states that had enjoyed close relations with the *ancien régime* (Morocco, Egypt, Saudi Arabia and Iraq) gradually deteriorated. Conversely, Arab governments and movements that had been hostile to the Shah began to seek favour with revolutionary Iran. Close ties were cultivated with the Polisario Front, Libya's Muammar Qadhafi and Shiite movements in both Iraq and Lebanon. It also came as no surprise in early May when Khomeini instructed the foreign ministry to sever diplomatic ties with Egypt 'bearing in mind the treacherous treaty between Israel and the Egyptian Government's unreserved obedience to the USA and Zionism'.[25]

Syria also found itself with few reliable allies as events unfolded in early 1979. With Egypt out of the equation in the Arab–Israeli conflict, Syria initially pinned its hopes on the unity scheme with neighbouring Iraq. Indeed, some progress was made towards implementing the scheme in the winter of 1978/9. However, by April 1979, it had become clear that the leadership of the two rival wings of the Ba'th Party had incongruent visions about what unification would entail. As progress in the negotiations became painfully slow and finally grinded to a halt, Assad began to give careful consideration to the next viable option – an alliance with Iran to outflank Iraq, bolster his position vis-à-vis the Gulf Arab sheikhdoms and strengthen his hand among the Lebanese Shiites.

Following a referendum on Iran's future form of government, Assad sent another congratulatory message to Khomeini on the Iranian people having finally achieved their aspirations. He also expressed confidence that their bilateral relations would continue to grow and flourish at the official and popular levels. Their *rapprochement* in the spring and summer of 1979 coincided with a marked deterioration in Iran's relations with Iraq and the Gulf Arab states. While Tehran encouraged the Iraqi Shiites to defy the government in Baghdad, Iraq also conducted a wide range of activities to support centrifugal forces on the periphery of Iran, including Kurdish and Arab movements that demanded autonomy or independence from the Iranian state. By late spring, a major insurrection had broken out in Iranian Kurdistan, while in the oil province of Khuzestan (Arabestan) local resistance movements had begun to oppose the regime by attacking oil installations and government facilities. The Iraqi Ba'th Party did its utmost to encourage the unrest in these regions in order to pin down Iranian security forces, thereby weakening the Iranian state to the benefit of Iraqi power and influence in the Gulf region.

One should note that Iraq's campaign was not totally offensive: it was partially a defensive attempt to neutralize and deter Iranian interference in Iraq's domestic affairs by levelling the playing field. By June 1979, a propaganda war was in full swing with the media of each side denouncing the other. Tehran portrayed Iraqi leaders as unbelievers belonging to a 'Takriti clique', while Baghdad depicted the clerics as 'turbaned shahs' with pre-revolutionary ideas of Persian racial superiority and intent on expanding Iran's 'lebensraum' in the Gulf region at the expense of the Arabs.

In an editorial on 14 June in the Iraqi daily *Al-Thawrah*, the author severely criticized the theocratic regime in Tehran and belittled the past achievements of Persian civilization, by arguing that:

> Persia was liberated from the tyranny of emperors only twice in thousands of years. The first time was by the Muslim Arabs who bravely fought Anoushiravan, defeated his army and demolished his empire – which was built on tyranny and corruption – and spread Islam, the religion of right and justice, in Persia. The second time the Iranians were only able to rid themselves of their tyrannical emperor, Mohammad Reza Pahlavi, through Islam – for whose advancement and spread among nations, including the Persian nation, primary credit should go to the Arabs.

As early as June that year, Tehran radio's Arabic service called on Iraqi people to unite and topple the tyrannical regime that was oppressing them.[26] Then, statements by some prominent clerics with no official status in the regime further tarnished Arab–Iranian relations. The most notable instance occurred at a press conference in Qom on 15 June, when Ayatollah Sadeq Rouhani declared that Bahrain was an integral part of Iran. His statement, which Baghdad and Cairo sharply rebuked, provoked a strong reaction throughout the Arab world. By July, Iran's relations with Iraq and many other conservative Arab states had degenerated to such a degree that two distinct camps with conflicting positions on Iran had crystallized in the Arab world. The battle lines of the Persian Gulf War had been drawn.

Before looking at the numerous developments in Syrian–Iranian and Arab–Iranian relations in the year preceding the outbreak of the Gulf War, it is necessary to present a brief overview and analysis of Iran's new foreign policy after the toppling of the Pahlavi throne and the Syrian reaction.

New Iranian foreign policy and the Syrian response

Once in power, the new regime in Tehran followed up on the policies of Shahpour Bakhtiar's government, which had been in power for the last 37 days of the imperial regime, which broke off diplomatic relations with Israel and South Africa, withdrew from CENTO and announced that Iran would no longer assume the role of the West's policeman in the Gulf. With respect to the Arab–Israeli conflict, Tehran turned over the former Israeli embassy to the PLO as an expression of its solidarity with the Palestinian cause. Iran not only became an enemy of Israel but also identified with the position of the Steadfastness Front.

In the light of Iran's new political posture and Egypt's banishment from the Arab fold, Syrian officials argued that losing Egypt to Israel could be offset by forging an alliance with Persian Iran. As they saw it, nurturing an Arab–Iranian friendship would strengthen the Arab camp. Despite Egypt's absence, a powerful new ally like non-Arab Iran would enhance the ability of the Arab states to undermine Israeli power in the region. Moreover, with the loss of Iran being one of the greatest setbacks suffered by the West and Israel since Nasser's rise in Egypt almost a quarter of a century earlier, the Arabs would be foolhardy not to exploit this new opening.[27]

On changing Tehran's foreign policy, the Iranian authorities took measures to bring public opinion in the country in line with the state's new international political orientation. Unlike the Shah, who tried to generate a chauvinist ideology by glorifying Iran's pre-Islamic history, and to purify Persian culture by ridding it of outside influences (particularly Arab), the revolutionary regime downplayed Iran's Persian heritage to emphasize its Islamic character. The Iranian authorities made systematic efforts to stress the commonality of interest, history and culture between Persians and Arabs within the framework of the Islamic *ummah* (community). The increase of Arabic language instruction and Arab studies in the curricula of schools and universities reflected this trend.[28] Some Iranian officials stated that the Persian Gulf should be called neither 'Persian' nor 'Arabian' but the 'Islamic' Gulf.[29] The Iranian foreign minister, Karim Sanjabi, announced that Prime Minister Bazargan's provisional government would reconsider the fate of the three Gulf islands Iran had occupied since November 1971 (Greater Tunb, Lesser Tunb and Abu Musa) and would possibly turn them over to the UAE. Politically, Iran's newfound flexibility on issues pertaining to the Gulf and its security were part of an overall effort to show friendliness to the Gulf Arab states. From the ideological perspective of the Islamic universalist approach, it was felt that territorial disputes and names of bodies of water should not drive a wedge between Muslim peoples, regardless of their nationality.

The Syrians, for their part, tried to convince their fellow Arabs that the Islamic revolution provided 'a unique opportunity to end the historic Arab–Persian animosity' and bring Iran into the Arab camp.[30] On the other hand, they knew quite well that if the Arabs took a hostile stance towards Iran, there was a distinct possibility that Tehran would renew its links with Tel Aviv and Washington.[31] They also knew that Iran's revolutionary ideology contained internationalist and indigenous ideas that were incompatible – namely an Islamic universalist ideology on the one hand versus Iranian nationalism influenced by Ithna Ashari (Twelver) Shiism on the other. Historically, these two contending positions had presented Iran policy makers with a major dilemma. Like other revolutions that occurred in a specific national and international context, the foreign policy of the Islamic Republic could be interpreted as the product of a dialectical relationship between Iran's affinity with Arabs because of its Islamic faith versus Iranian nationalism, which differentiates Iran from its Arab neighbours.[32]

Many Arab states, including Saudi Arabia, Jordan, Egypt and Iraq, felt threatened by the vitriolic rhetoric emanating from Tehran and so did not share Syria's enthusiasm for the Iranian revolution. They did not see the revolution as an opportunity to end the Arab–Iranian rift, but rather as an event that could spark domestic unrest in neighbouring states and threaten regional stability. As it turned out, Iranian–Iraqi relations, for instance, were marked by tension and distrust from almost the very beginning.

It is important to note that the failure of the Syrian–Iraqi unity talks corresponded in time with the emergence of the Islamic Republic in Iran. In fact, the 1979 Iranian revolution sharpened already existing antagonisms and introduced new stumbling blocks on the path to reconciliation. On almost every issue to do with Iran, be it the Shah, Khomeini, Shiite fundamentalism or Arab–Iranian relations, Damascus and Baghdad had conflicting views. While Iraqi–Iranian relations steadily improved under the Shah between 1975 and 1979, Syrian–Iranian ones deteriorated over the same time period. In the 1970s, Syria had provided a safe haven to the Shah's opponents, while Iraq had expelled Khomeini at the Shah's request in October 1978.[33] Assad welcomed the Shiite awakening in the Middle East after the Iranian revolution, while Baghdad feared that Iran would incite the restive Shiite population in southern Iraq to rebel against it.

Overall, while Syria saw revolutionary Iran as a powerful new ally of the Arabs in the struggle against Israel, Iraq viewed it as a major threat to the security of the eastern flank of the Arab world and the sheikhdoms of the Gulf. In 1979/80, Syria and Iran drew closer to one another, while Iraq distanced itself from both and assumed a more militant posture *vis-à-vis* Iran as tensions between the two states escalated.

The Syrian–Iranian entente and the road to war (1979–80)

A month after the Syrian–Iraqi negotiations collapsed amid accusations of Syrian involvement in the alleged coup attempt, Syrian foreign minister Abd al-Halim Khaddam was sent to Iran as part of a major diplomatic initiative to expand relations between the two states. Khaddam held talks with Iranian foreign minister Ebrahim Yazdi and Prime Minister Bazargan on increasing political and economic cooperation between the two countries. He also met Khomeini in Qom where he declared that Iran's Islamic revolution was 'the most important event in [our] contemporary history'. He proudly stated that Syria had assisted the forces that participated in the Iranian revolution 'prior to its outbreak, during it and after its triumph'.[34] On the Arab–Israeli conflict and Egypt's defection from the Arab camp, he pointed out that the revolution was considered to be a positive 'step in restoring the balance in the area against the Zionist enemy'.[35] Furthermore, in subsequent meetings between Syrian information minister Ahmad Iskandar Ahmad and his Iranian counterpart, Dr Minachi, it was agreed that SANA would set up an office in Tehran and, similarly, Iran's Pars news agency (later renamed IRNA) would open up an office in Damascus.

When Syria began to make serious overtures to Iran, the latter could respond positively because of the rapid deterioration of Arab–Iranian relations in the Gulf. Tehran thus gradually began to put more emphasis on its friendship with Damascus. The tensions in the Gulf were to a large extent an outgrowth of the escalating crisis between Iran and Bahrain.

Deterioration of Iranian–Gulf Arab ties and the Syrian mediation effort

Although the appointment of an Iranian ambassador to Manama partly allayed Bahraini concerns, the detention of a prominent Bahraini Shiite cleric, Muhammad Ali al-Akari, on his return from a visit to Iran sparked demonstrations and unrest. Iran accused Bahrain of persecuting its Shiites and demanded the immediate release of all political detainees. The escalating cycle of tension continued with Iran (intentionally or inadvertently) conducting naval manoeuvres in the Gulf, which Bahrain interpreted as Iranian muscle-flexing. By September, Saudi Arabia had dispatched two army brigades to the island at Manama's request. Ayatollah Rouhani subsequently added more fuel to the fire by warning the Emir of Bahrain that unless he stopped oppressing his people, Iran would encourage the Bahrainis to demand unification with the Islamic Republic of Iran.[36]

Iran's behaviour drew harsh criticism from different corners of the Arab world. Apart from sharp words from Bahrain and Kuwait, as a sign of things to come, the Iraqis and Egyptians were only too happy to denounce Iranian behaviour and express readiness to protect Arab interests in the Gulf. Egyptian Vice-President Mubarak stated that Egypt would, if asked, provide military support to Bahrain or any other Arab state that was the victim of foreign aggression. Iran, in turn, lashed out accusing Baghdad and Cairo of blowing the matter out of proportion to justify trying to fill the vacuum left by the Shah as the new policemen in the Persian Gulf.

The struggle in the Tehran government between pragmatic and radical elements over whether to export the Islamic revolution or to pursue its goals at home had a direct impact on the country's foreign relations. Iran's neighbours, in particular, were disturbed rather than soothed by the mixed signals emanating from Tehran. Coupled with historical Arab–Persian and Sunni–Shiite prejudices, the stage was gradually being set for a full-scale war. The Kuwaiti and Iraqi news media at the time accused Iran of using religion as a front to establish a new Persian empire and to create schisms among the Sunni and Shiite Arabs in the area.

Although Iran's image was becoming sullied in much of the Arab world, Syria and other members of the Steadfastness Front maintained their loyalty to the Iranian revolution. In September, Foreign Minister Yazdi stopped off in Damascus on his way back from an NAM summit in Havana. In his meeting with Assad, he extended an invitation to the Syrian leader to visit Iran in the near future. This was followed up by the visit of Iranian deputy prime minister Dr Sadeq Tabatabai in early October to discuss the rift between Iran and its Arab neighbours. After meeting Assad and other senior officials, he explained at a press conference that revolutionary Iran's foreign policy was based on the principle of non-interference in the affairs of its Arab neighbours. However, Iran would not sit idly by in the event of a conflict between the Arabs and Israel. With regard to Bahrain, he emphasized that neither Khomeini nor any other Iranian official had ever claimed Bahrain to be part of Iran. He went on to attack Egyptian President Sadat as a traitor to the Arab cause who was attempting to fan the fires of hatred in the Gulf in order to re-enter the Arab fold in a circumspect manner. Tabatabai also held discussions with the grand mufti of Syria who praised the Iranian revolution, stressed the need for Islamic unity and declared that there was no difference between Sunnis and Shiites.

To defuse the situation in the Gulf, of which Iraq and Egypt were taking full advantage, a few days later, Tabatabai and the Syrian foreign minister Khaddam flew to Manama to speak to the emir of Bahrain, Shaykh Isa Bin Salman Al-Khalifah. There, they had a joint meeting with the emir, prime minister, foreign minister and heir apparent (who was also the defence minister). Despite the joint Syrian–Iranian initiative to calm tensions, and subsequent Syrian claims that their mediations had bridged the differences between the Gulf Arabs and Iran, relations between the two sides continued to be uneasy.

Iraqi–Iranian relations then sank to new depths in autumn 1979. A cycle of mutual recriminations, continuous border clashes, incessant interference in the affairs of the other and calls to overthrow the other regime led to the closure of Iranian consulates in Basra and Karbala, and Iraqi consulates in Khorramshahr and Karbala. However, a major confrontation with the USA after Islamic militants seized the US embassy in Tehran on 4 November 1979, temporarily eclipsed the growing tensions with Iraq.

Iran's confrontation with the USA and Iraq, and Syria's role

In the immediate aftermath of the embassy takeover, Syria declared its support for the Iranian action and called on other Arab states to throw their weight behind Iran. The Syrians even suggested that the Arab League take up the issue at its summit in Tunis in late November. Foreign Minister Khaddam stated that 'the Iranian revolution gave appreciable help to the Palestinian cause and it is normal that it should be backed by the Arabs.'[37] Libya insisted that the Arab League take up and challenge the Carter administration's decision to freeze Iranian assets in US banks, but the Arab League's foreign ministers rejected the request outright. In the meantime, a flurry of diplomatic activity ensued. Iran's new foreign minister Bani-Sadr held extensive talks with Syrian ambassador Ibrahim Yunis on how to broaden the scope of political and economic cooperation between the two

countries, while an Iranian delegation was dispatched to Tunis to galvanize Arab support for Iran's case against the USA. Iranian represen-
tatives subsequently held a series of meetings there with Syrian
President Hafez Assad, Lebanese Prime Minister Selim Hoss, PLO
Chairman Yasser Arafat, Libyan Foreign Secretary Jallud and the
Algerian delegation. Again, only Syria and Libya were out front
demonstrating their solidarity with Iran. On 26 November, a joint
Libyan–Iranian statement confirmed the need for 'Arab–Iranian
fraternity' and the two parties reiterated their support for Islamic and
Arab liberation movements in 'their struggle against colonialism,
imperialism and Zionism'.[38] Then, a few days later, an official Syrian
government statement supported the Iranian cause and expressed
concern over the US naval build-up in the Indian Ocean and Mediterranean Sea in response to the hostage crisis. At the same time,
another Iranian delegation led by Dr Mohammad Ali Hadi was dispatched to various foreign capitals to win Arab backing for Iran's
position. The delegation's first stop was Damascus, where it held
meetings with Assad and Khaddam.

Two days before the Iranian delegation arrived in Damascus,
Brigadier-General Mohammed al-Khouli (chief of Syrian air force
intelligence, director of special operations in the Middle East and a
close aide of Hafez Assad) arrived in the Iranian capital. While in
Tehran, he delivered a message from Khaddam and held extensive
talks with Sadeq Ghotbzadeh. According to Western intelligence
reports, during his visit the two sides secretly agreed to conduct joint
covert operations against Iraq to destabilize Saddam Hussein. Al-
Khouli held talks with several of Khomeini's advisers. Apparently, the
main outcome of the meetings was closer collaboration between the
Syrian and Iranian intelligence services to assist the activities of the
Shiite opposition in southern Iraq. In the course of his meetings and
deliberations, it was agreed that Ayatollah Montazeri's son would
serve as the main liaison with Damascus on the anti-Iraq operations.
Immediately after al-Khouli's visit, two Syrian intelligence teams were
dispatched to Iran to establish a permanent base of operations.[39]

Harmonizing Syrian–Iranian policies in November and December
coincided with the erosion of Iran's relations with its two most
important Arab neighbours, Saudi Arabia and Iraq. In late November,
when Saudi Shiites in the oil-rich Hasa province tried to commem-
orate the holy day of Ashura, which the authorities had banned,
clashes with security forces resulted in a number of deaths. The
incident sparked off demonstrations and unrest throughout the prov-

ince. Saudi authorities quickly rushed in 20,000 troops to restore order. Although Shiites were traditionally a repressed minority in the Saudi kingdom, the victims of discrimination and poor treatment and therefore with legitimate grievance against Riyadh, the evidence suggests that, as the Saudis have charged, Iranian ayatollahs like Khalkhali and Rouhani were trying to encourage Shiite opposition to Riyadh. Iran subsequently denounced the 'barbaric repression' of the Shiite minority as clear proof of the tyrannical and ferocious nature of the Saudi regime.[40]

Amid continuous border clashes between Iran and Iraq, and repeated calls from senior officials on both sides for the removal from power of their rivals across the border, on 1 November, Iraq's ambassador to Lebanon held an interview with the Lebanese daily *Al-Nahar* in which he bluntly stated that, as far as Iraq was concerned, relations with Iran could only improve if Tehran agreed to revise the 1975 Algiers accord (relinquishing joint sovereignty over the Shatt al-Arab), granted the Kurdish, Arab and Baluchi minorities in Iran autonomy, and withdrew from the Tunb and Abu Musa islands in the Persian Gulf. His comments prompted a swift response from Tehran that accused Baghdad of serving the goals of Western imperialism by refusing to participate in the Steadfastness Front against Israel and the unity scheme with Syria. Iran also moved in November to restore full diplomatic relations with another of its staunch Arab allies, Libya. Ties between the two had been broken nine months earlier by Iranian suspicions that Qadhafi was responsible for the disappearance of the prominent Lebanese Shiite cleric, Ayatollah Musa Sadr.[41]

It is worth mentioning that during a three-week period in the month of December, unidentified gunmen (probably Iraqi-backed) twice attacked Syrian diplomatic representations in Tehran. In the first instance, they attacked the Syrian consulate general, and in the second, they assaulted the Syrian ambassador's residence. In the latter incident, at least one Iranian Revolutionary Guard assigned to the premises was shot.

In early 1980, unrest in Saudi Arabia's Hasa province, intense Iranian propaganda against the House of Saud and a realization in Baghdad and Riyadh that Iran's revolution threatened their national security prompted both sides to coordinate their policies more closely. This in turn brought further attacks from the Iranian news media, which portrayed the Saudi–Iraqi *rapprochement* as part of a grand scheme to safeguard the West's interests in the Gulf in the absence of the Shah; Iraqi–Saudi relations had grown more cordial since the November 1978 Baghdad summit. Moreover, the failure of the Syrian–Iraqi unity scheme in mid-1979 and Iran's provocative behaviour in the area had given extra impetus to the reconciliation between Saddam Hussein and King Khaled. As early as November 1979, Saudi Arabia and Iraq had reportedly begun secret negotiations about collective security arrangements in the Gulf. During these talks, Riyadh apparently agreed to the stationing of Iraqi forces in Bahrain and Oman to prevent any unrest instigated by Iran and to serve as a springboard for military action against the latter.[42] Before the Iranian revolution, Iraq had been seen as the main revisionist power in the area bent on upsetting the existing *status quo*. With the toppling of the Pahlavi throne, and the emergence of a revolutionary regime in Tehran, the general view among the Arab sheikhdoms was that Saddam Hussein had now assumed the Shah's mantle as the guarantor of the *status quo* in the Gulf. Tehran, for its part, did not hesitate to take advantage of every opportunity to denounce the Saudi royal family as puppets of the USA, and the Iraqi Ba'thists as atheists who adhered to a godless ideology.

The Iraqi propaganda war and Syria's utility for the Islamic Republic

A gradual change in Iraqi propaganda against Iran accompanied the deterioration in Arab–Iranian relations. By early 1980, subtle changes were noticeable in the statements of Iraqi officials who had previously alluded to 'turbaned shahs' when trying to tarnish the clerical regime. Instead, they also described it as un-Islamic and presented the rivalry between Iran and Iraq as an extension of the age-old conflict between Persians and Arabs. Between January and September 1980, the Iraqis' verbal attacks on the Iranian regime were extended to the Persian people, which, at an ideological level, made it imperative for Iran's ruling clerics to cultivate close ties with as many Arab states as possible. They concentrated on those that would counter the Iraqi challenge and allow Iran to join in the Arab–Muslim battle against Israel in the Levant. By those criteria, and in the light of Tehran's warm relations with Damascus, Syria was the ideal candidate.

Responding to Iranian denunciations of the Iraqi Ba'thists as not only reactionary but also un-Islamic, Saddam said in an interview with the Paris-based *Al-Watan al-Arabi* that it was wrong of the Iranians to think that there was a contradiction between an Islamic and an Arab revolution. He held that 'the mere supposition or expectation that such a conflict or contradiction is inevitable, makes the Iranians the enemies of the Arab nation'.[43] Just over a week later, on

8 February, Saddam issued his pan-Arab declaration in which he advocated close collaboration among Arabs against foreign enemies, and stressed the need for all Arab states to support an Arab country engaged in war against a non-Arab one. By spring, there was every indication that Baghdad had come to the conclusion that war with Iran was the only viable way in which it could neutralize the Iranian threat and assert its position in the region, especially in the Gulf and vis-à-vis Syria. The Iraqi leadership had by then become extremely sensitive to the attitude of other Arab countries towards the Iranian revolutionaries, interpreting any Arab sympathy for the clerical regime as a betrayal of greater Arab and Iraqi interests. Syria, on the other hand, continued to cultivate strong ties with Tehran, despite the increasing disillusionment with its policies among the majority of its Arab neighbours. Senior officials like the information minister Ahmad Iskandar Ahmad articulated the Syrian position and stressed in an interview that:

> We appreciate the role of the Iranian revolution and we are establishing the closest possible relations with it in various fields. … We believe that establishing good relations with the Iranian revolution and supporting that revolution so it can settle down and devote time to help the Arabs liberate their occupied territories is the duty of every Arab who believes that Israel and US imperialism are the danger to be faced.[44]

Even in the light of Iran's increasing isolation brought about by the continuation of the hostage crisis and the imposition of economic sanctions, the Syrians seemed adamant about preserving their ties with Iran and, if the opportunity arose, helping to resolve the dispute with the USA.[45]

In mid-March, Iraqi–Iranian relations reached a new low when both countries were forced to reduce their embassy staffs at the request of the host government and their ambassadors were declared *persona non grata*; relations continued at the chargé d'affaires level. Baghdad blamed Iran for an attempt on the Iraqi foreign minister's life on 1 April and, from then on, Iraqi statements assumed a distinctly racist tone. For example, in a speech about the incident, Saddam evoked the 1400 year-old battle of Qadisiyah between the Persian Sassanid and Arab armies.[46] A subsequent political commentary said Khomeini had a distorted understanding of Islam and used it against the Arabs to achieve 'racist, decadent, and Shu'ubi' objectives. It went on to accuse him of wanting to dominate the Arabs to avenge a 1400 year-old Persian inferiority complex. It continued to say that Khomeini wanted to 'kill all that is neither Persian nor Islamic in his devious fashion, is a racist lunatic. Were Khomeini's regime in a position to begin [this] war, it would not hesitate to do [so], despite its consequences. ... They are sick with their Persianism.'[47] The intensification of the propaganda war coincided with an outright statement of solidarity for Iraq by Jordan's King Hussein, and a visit by the Jordanian chief of staff to Baghdad to assess the military situation.[48]

These events happened at the same time as a meeting between Khomeini and Syria's ambassador to Iran, Yunis, who conveyed a message of support for Iran from Hafez Assad. Khomeini for his part, asked for Syrian cooperation with Iran in its struggle against imperialist and anti-Islamic forces like the USA and Iraq. Escalating tensions between Iran and Iraq were revealed in different ways throughout the region. In Lebanon, there were periodic armed clashes between the Shiite Amal militia against the pro-Iraqi Arab Liberation Front and elements of the Lebanese Ba'th Party sympathetic to Iraq.

In the aftermath of the failed attempt to rescue the US hostages (April 1980), in which eight US servicemen died, the Syrian government was quick to condemn the action as 'an act of piracy aimed against Iran and its people'.[49] Following the debacle in the Iranian desert, the Syrian regime received Iranian Foreign Minister Ghotbzadeh on the first leg of an Arab tour to win support for Iran. Ghotbzadeh met Hafez Assad, Khaddam and Rif'at Assad. He briefed them on the details of the US rescue attempt and other regional developments. During his meeting with the Syrian leader, the latter reiterated his support for Iran's stance against Washington and Tel Aviv. Another topic high on the agenda, according to diplomatic sources, was the growing tension between Iran and Iraq and the need for further Syrian assistance. After two days of talks, a joint communiqué was issued condemning the US operation as a clear violation of Iran's territorial integrity, independence and sovereignty, and a threat to international peace and security. At another press conference on 1 May, Khaddam criticized the US onslaught on Iran, emphasizing that any effort directed against the Iranians would be considered to be against the Arabs also. He accused Washington of trying to impose its will on the Arab world.[50]

By mid-spring, Syria had started a major airlift of Soviet-made arms to Iran to replace the latter's stocks of Western-supplied arms, which were rapidly becoming depleted, and to assist Iran's military operations on the frontier with Iraq. Syrian Antonov An-12 cargo planes ferried the arms from Syria's stockpiles to Iranian airfields. The weapons included 23-mm anti-tank guns, mortars, artillery pieces, anti-tank missiles, anti-aircraft missiles and ammunition. Damascus had apparently agreed to provide military help during a secret visit by a personal representative of Iranian President Bani-Sadr in April. The emissary had submitted to Assad a detailed list of weapons, ammunition, spare parts and medical equipment that Iran urgently needed to counter a possible Iraqi attack.[51] In addition to the arms airlift, Syrian military personnel were sent to Iran to train and familiarize the Iranian troops with the military equipment.[52]

Syria's quest for regional allies and inter-Arab politics

Besides their mutual hate of Iraq, Syria had other reasons to cultivate close ties with Iran. Its relations with Saudi Arabia and Morocco deteriorated badly in mid-1980 when the Saudi and Moroccan monarchs expressed regret that the Steadfastness and Confrontation states had recognized the RASD at their meeting in Tripoli. The growing friendship between Iran and Syria alarmed the Saudis, which, given the poor state of Iranian–Gulf Arab relations, enabled Syria to play its 'Gulf card' in the arena of inter-Arab politics. Damascus, on the other hand, was livid when Saudi Prince Fahd expressed Riyadh's willingness to help bring about a settlement of the Arab–Israeli conflict within the framework of UN Resolutions 242 and 338, which in effect undermined the PLO and Syrian positions.

Syrian motives at the time were defensive and offensive. With Egypt out of the picture in the Arab–Israeli conflict, the possibility of an alliance with Iraq ever more remote, and Saudi and Iraqi ambivalence about the Camp David accords, Assad decided to bolster his position in the Levant and Gulf by befriending Khomeini's Iran. He saw a Syrian–Iranian axis in the region as strengthening his hand, thus giving him the leverage he needed to deal with Baghdad, Riyadh and Tel Aviv from a position of power.

Another bone of contention between the Syrians and Saudis was the inclusion of South Yemen as a confrontation state at the Tripoli conference. Much to the Saudis' chagrin, the Syrians subsequently went so far as to say that an attack on South Yemen would be regarded as a betrayal of the Palestinian cause. Assad's main reason for stressing the importance of friendship with Aden and Moscow was to irritate the Saudis and Iraqis. Riyadh, for its part, disapproved of Syrian efforts to push the Soviets centre stage as the Arabs' loyal patron. Furthermore, it viewed the prospects of an emergent Syrian–Iranian–South Yemeni entente with deep consternation. By August, several operating axes had appeared in the Middle East, a Saudi–Iraqi–Jordanian axis, a Syrian–Iranian–Palestinian axis, a Syrian–Soviet–South Yemeni axis, and an Omani–Egyptian–American axis.[53]

When the Syrian ambassador and his staff were expelled from Baghdad on 18 August and Damascus retaliated in kind three days later, Syrian–Iraqi relations reached a nadir. Surprisingly, this row gave Syria a new opportunity to diversify its relations and seek a new ally when Qadhafi sent a message to Saddam and Assad pleading for reconciliation between the two Ba'thist regimes and unity in the Arab world. In early September, Damascus responded positively to the Libyan call by proposing a union between Syria and Libya. Assad eventually undertook an official state visit to Libya where the two leaders held extensive talks, which culminated in a declaration of unity under the terms of which the two states would take simultaneous steps towards forming a single political entity ruled by a single executive body and revolutionary command.

Qadhafi's decision to call for a union between the two states was primarily politically motivated, whereas Assad hoped that the merger would bring economic benefits. The Libyan leader wanted finally to legitimize his dubious claim that his country was a confrontation state. Ever since Israel and Egypt had signed the Camp David accords, he had consistently argued that nothing stood between Israel and Libya, and Syrian–Libyan unity seemed to be an effective way of lending credibility to his position. From Assad's viewpoint, the alliance would allow him to secure Libyan petrodollars to finance his arms build-up to check Israeli power. After Camp David, Qadhafi had, after all, promised to foot a billion dollar bill for Soviet-made arms for the Steadfastness Front. Moreover, it was hoped that the union with Libya would translate into a reliable source of oil for Syria, which no longer considered it prudent to rely on Iraq and Saudi Arabia given the poor state of relations between those two countries. Both parties also believed that a union between them would strengthen their bargaining position with Moscow, thereby enabling them to persuade the Soviets to upgrade their military assistance to the new state.[54]

Following the declaration of unity, Iran's government expressed support for the alliance and a willingness to cooperate with the new united front against Israel and the supporters of Camp David. On 11 September, Iran's prime minister Raja'i sent messages to Assad and

Qadhafi conveying his delight at their moves towards unity and the hope that they would support the Iranian revolution and other progressive movements against foes like 'the bloodthirsty Iraqi Ba'thi regime'.[55] Baghdad, on the other hand, ridiculed the Syrian–Libyan unity attempt, stating that it would inevitably fail, for neither party was sincere in its unionist intentions. The Iraqi media also denounced Damascus and Tehran as enemies of Arabism and criticized them for supporting the Amal militia in Lebanon.

Iraq, for its part, was also at this time engaged in intense diplomatic manoeuvring and discussions with prospective allies as it prepared to go to war with Iran. In summer 1980, Iraqi foreign minister Tareq Aziz had secret talks in Jordan and Saudi Arabia with US officials, and told them of Baghdad's plan to invade Iran in the autumn. Given the abysmal state of US–Iranian relations at the time, the USA expressed no objection to the Iraqi plan.[56] Subsequently, in early August, Saddam flew to Taif where he spoke to the Saudi monarch and informed him of his decision to invade Iran.[57] The following month, the Iraqi leader received the Bahraini prime minister, Shaykh Khalifah bin Salman al-Khalifah, and later on the Qatari foreign minister. Both expressed their support for Iraq's policies in the Gulf and condemned Iran's behaviour. Finally, on 17 September, Saddam Hussein convened an extraordinary session of the Iraqi national assembly, where he announced the abrogation of the 1975 Algiers accord with Iran, thus setting the stage for the invasion of Iran five days later.

Syria and the Persian Gulf war

A few days before the Iraqi invasion Iranian president Bani-Sadr sent a special envoy to Damascus to seek diplomatic and military assistance: having come to the conclusion that all-out war with Iraq was imminent, he asked for public statements of support for Iran's position, additional arms, and for Syria to hold manoeuvres on the Iraqi border to divert Iraqi forces from the eastern front. After prolonged talks and consultations, the Syrian leader refused to give Iran public support or to conduct military exercises in the east, for fear of the political repercussions it would have on the regime both domestically and regionally. However, Assad agreed to resume arms shipments to Iran as soon as possible. Within a few days of the war starting, the Syrians began to airlift weapons, medical supplies and teams of ordnance experts and physicians to Iran. The arms shipments consisted primarily of SAM-7 ground-to-air missiles, Sagger anti-tank missiles and RPG-7 anti-tank rockets.[58]

Immediately after the hostilities began, most Arab leaders declared their support for Iraq, most notably King Khaled of Saudi Arabia who stated that his country stood 'with Iraq in its pan-Arab battle and its conflict with the Persians, the enemies of the Arab nation'.[59] In Amman, King Hussein convened an emergency meeting of the council of ministers who subsequently released a statement urging a united Arab stand in support of 'fraternal Iraq'. Only Qadhafi and Arafat sent messages to both Baghdad and Tehran expressing regret and pleading for an end to the war, since it only served US and Israeli interests. Although Syria remained silent, Assad spoke on the telephone with the Saudi and Jordanian monarchs on 25 September in the hope of finding a way to stop the hostilities as soon as possible. He subsequently sent his minister of state for foreign affairs Faruq al-Shara to Taif to confer with King Khaled. However, all indications seem to suggest that the mission was in vain.

Despite Arab support for Iraq, Baghdad made three major mistakes when it decided to launch a full-scale war. It not only miscalculated its own military capability and the resilience of its revolutionary foe, but also failed to secure its western flank by mending fences with Damascus before setting out to deal with Iran. And, with Assad's hopes for a ceasefire and quick end to the fighting dashed, the spectre of a triumphant Iraq prompted him to take drastic measures to help avert an Iraqi victory and ensure Iran's ability to fight on. The Syrian regime feared that if Iraq decisively defeated Iran, it would come under a direct threat from Baghdad. Furthermore, a victorious and confident Iraq would be in a favourable position to assist the Syrian Muslim Brethren openly and challenge Syrian interests in the region.

While the war produced no new alignments, it crystallized the already emerging rival camps, thereby polarizing the Arab world even more. The most important axes in the early phase of the conflict were the Syrian–Iranian–Libyan and Saudi–Iraqi–Jordanian ones. In the former, Syria proved to be Iran's most valuable ally, while Jordan played a critical role in aiding the Iraqis by letting them station their military aircraft at Jordanian air bases out of harm's way. The Mafraq air base in eastern Jordan was in effect handed over to the Iraqis. Jordan also put its port facilities at Aqaba at their disposal, and mobilized a fleet of trucks and transport vehicles to take the cargo to Iraq. Furthermore, in early October, a 40,000 strong Jordanian force was reportedly moved to the Jordanian–Iraqi border, ready to intervene in the Gulf War if the need arose.[60]

Syria, for its part, remained silent about the war for the first two weeks as it anxiously waited to see if Iran would survive the Iraqi onslaught. In the first week of October, when it became clear that Iran had absorbed the initial blow and was rolling with the punches, Damascus finally broke its silence and condemned the Iraqi invasion as 'the wrong war against the wrong enemy at the wrong time'.[61] Baghdad's attempts to depict the conflict as an Arab–Persian war and a defence of the Arab homeland against 'fire-worshipping racist Persians' were severely criticized.[62] In a speech, Assad made a thinly veiled attack on Saddam's 'hollow heroics' and stressed that Syria had the 'capacity to inflict fierce punishment' on imposters.[63] Damascus claimed that fighting Iran would divide the Arab ranks and needlessly divert their attention at a time when they should be concentrating their energies on defeating the true enemy, Israel. It clearly stated that the war was neither in the interest of Iran nor Iraq and the Arab nation.

According to the Syrian daily *Al-Ba'th* of 5 October, 'fighting the Iranian revolution will only make Iran join the camp against the Arabs', but 'we want Iran to join Arab ranks that are hostile to imperialism and Zionism; we want Arab Iraq to remain an additional strength for Arabs against imperialism and Zionism, and not against the Iranian revolution'.

Meanwhile, Iraq continued its intense propaganda against Syria, accusing it of betraying the pan-Arab cause by sending troops and weapons to Iran. Despite Iraqi claims that Syrian and Libyan soldiers were captured in the fighting, no convincing evidence was ever produced.[64] Baghdad's campaign to discredit its neighbour prompted Syrian assistant foreign minister Nasir Qaddur to summon the Iraqi chargé d'affaires in Damascus on 6 October to lodge a formal protest against the Iraqi accusations.

Two days later, Assad flew to Moscow to sign a friendship and cooperation treaty with the USSR. This was part of a strategy to bolster his position in the region (particularly vis-à-vis Israel and Iraq) by securing Soviet military and economic assistance and thus bring his superpower patron in on the side of Iran.[65] On concluding the treaty, Assad and Soviet premier Leonid Brezhnev issued a joint communiqué indirectly rebuking Iraq by supporting 'Iran's inalienable right to determine its destiny independently and without any foreign interference'.[66] The negotiations included arrangements to have Soviet arms delivered to Iran. The Kremlin also approved the shipment of Soviet-made arms from Syria, Libya and other countries to Iran. Subsequently, Iranian military transport planes began continuous flights to Syria and Libya, carrying Soviet-made weapons back to Iran.[67] Iranian air force Boeing 707s, 727s, 747s, and Lockheed C-130s flew to Damascus and Tripoli carrying arms and ammunition back to Iran. Furthermore, some C-130s brought Iranian casualties to Damascus for treatment in Syrian hospitals.[68] The Syrians played a critical role in maintaining the flow of arms from various Arab states to the Islamic Republic. Soviet-made equipment from Libya was shipped by sea to Syrian ports, and then transhipped by land via Turkey.[69] Algeria also commenced arms transfers to Iran in May 1981, after having decided to aid the Iranian war effort. These weapons were first sent by ship to the Syrian port of Tartus, where the cargo was unloaded and subsequently flown to Iran.[70]

Besides providing war material, the Syrians passed on valuable intelligence on Iraq's capabilities and plans. Their ambassador to Tehran, Ibrahim Yunis, assiduously relayed useful intelligence to Iranian officials, and Moscow too used him as a conduit of information.[71] To improve the coordination of the joint Syrian–Iranian effort to stem the Iraqi onslaught, General Ali Aslan, the Syrian deputy chief of staff and head of operations, travelled to Iran to consult his Iranian counterparts. He discussed the military situation with the joint chief of staff, General Valiollah Fallahi, and with General Javad Fakuri, the defence minister and air force commander. As part of their overall effort to aid Iran, the Syrians agreed to try to procure US-made spare parts in Europe for Iran's Western-equipped arsenal.[72]

The war quickly brought the rifts in the Arab world into sharper focus and deepened existing cleavages. In 1980, relations between members of the pro-Iraqi camp and Iran's other valuable Arab ally, Libya, deteriorated dramatically. Qadhafi was quick to criticize Riyadh's decision to allow a US military presence (AWACS early-warning aircraft) in the kingdom and to side with Iraq in the war. In a telegram to King Khaled, he stressed that it was 'an Islamic duty for [them] to be allied with the Muslims in Iran in this confrontation in order to face the crusade instead of fighting them in place of America'.[73] On 11 October, Baghdad severed its diplomatic ties with Damascus and Tripoli, accusing them of having erected an air bridge to Tehran to supply the 'Magi racist clique' with arms to continue their aggression against Iraq. The Iraqi foreign ministry declared Syrian and Libyan embassy staff *persona non grata* and gave them 48 hours to leave. A statement released by the foreign ministry asserted that the rulers of the two countries were devoid of any Arabism.[74]

Interestingly, Syria and Libya both denied giving Iran military assistance, even after the Iraqi announcement. Assad and Qadhafi were clearly aware of the public mood about the Gulf War both within their countries and in the Arab world. In their riposte, the Syrians accused Saddam of serving US interests by starting the war, characterizing it as Saddam's 'crazy and condemned war against revolutionary Iran and against its principled stand with the Arabs'.[75] Qadhafi's sermons on the 'liberation' of Mecca from US occupation prompted Riyadh to break off diplomatic relations with Tripoli in late October. The Saudis warned Qadhafi to stay out of their internal affairs and (instead of supporting Iran) to remain neutral or side with Iraq in the war. The intense inter-Arab squabbling in October clearly demonstrated that the Arab world was more divided than ever. The eruption of the Gulf War alone was not cause enough for two mutually hostile camps to emerge, but with the plethora of other politically divisive issues confronting the Arabs, the conflict caused even the most ardent pan-Arabists to drop any illusion of existing Arab unity.

While Jordan and Saudi Arabia threw their weight behind Iraq, Iran, with Syria's help, tried to secure as many regional allies as possible. In late October, Prime Minister Raja'i visited Algeria and Libya on his way back from a trip to the UN in New York. On 30 October, Ayatollah Montazeri, Khomeini's designated successor, met the Syrian, Libyan and Algerian diplomatic heads of mission in Qom, where he expressed 'gratitude for the Islamic and revolutionary stance adopted by [these] fraternal states and their support of Iran's Islamic revolution'.[76]

Despite Amman and Riyadh's efforts to help Baghdad diplomatically, economically and militarily, the Saudi–Iraqi–Jordanian axis could not meet all Iraq's military needs and requirements. Baghdad eventually had to compromise its pan-Arab stand by dispatching a military delegation to Cairo to buy spare parts and ammunition for its rapidly depleting Soviet-made arsenal. Worsening Iranian–Gulf Arab relations following the Islamic revolution and the outbreak of the first Gulf War finally gave the Egyptians a back door through which to improve their relations with Iraq, but more importantly through which to re-enter the Arab political arena.

Similarly, the Syrian–Libyan–Iranian axis failed to meet many of Tehran's expectations of military help. While the Syrian armed forces had a Soviet-manufactured arsenal, the Iranian equipment the clerical regime inherited from the Shah consisted mainly of US arms. Second, there were limits to how much military hardware Syria could spare for its Iranian ally because, for its own security, it needed to deploy troops against Israel along the Golan Heights in Lebanon and in Syria too at a time when the Muslim Brethren were escalating their campaign of terror against the Ba'th regime in Damascus. Third, deploying troops along the Syrian–Iraqi border to ease Iraqi military pressure on revolutionary Iran was bound to evoke a harsh response from many Arab capitals. Thus, Iran was forced to compromise its political stand by approaching Israel for spare parts and equipment to maintain its Western-equipped armed forces. However, while Tel Aviv may have made temporary inroads by re-establishing contacts in Tehran, Egyptian collaboration in the Iraqi war effort was to have a far greater and more lasting impact on inter-Arab politics.

Despite limitations on Syria's ability to help Iran militarily, it played an important role in preventing the formation of a united Arab front against Iran in November 1980 by provoking a major diplomatic crisis and military confrontation with Jordan in the lead-up to the Arab summit meeting that had been scheduled to begin in Amman on 25 November.

The Syrian–Jordanian confrontation and the Amman summit

By the autumn of 1980, differences on a whole range of critical political issues had brought Syrian–Jordanian relations to an all-time low. The Syrian Ba'thist regime was fighting for survival against an unrelenting campaign orchestrated by the Muslim Brethren with the aid of Iraq and Jordan. In addition, with a new US administration scheduled to take office in two months, Jordan's King Hussein intended to resuscitate the Middle East peace process by putting himself in a politically advantageous position to persuade Washington to include the Hashemite kingdom in a new peace initiative. Still infuriated by Sadat's defection, the Syrians were intent on preventing such a development, which would further sideline and weaken their position. Iraq's invasion of Iran also drove a wedge between the two states as Jordan very quickly became Saddam Hussein's staunchest supporter in the conflict, while Syria lent valuable assistance to Iran, albeit in a discrete manner whenever possible.

With the domestic confrontation with the Muslim Brethren coming to a head, and Jordan planning to use the Arab summit scheduled to begin in Amman on 25 November to rally support for its position in the Gulf War and Middle East peace process, Damascus set out to thwart the Jordanian monarch's efforts, using all possible means on every possible front. Shortly after the Gulf War began, Hafez Assad authorized the chief of Syrian military intelligence General Ali Duba, and head of air force intelligence General Mohammed al-Khouli, to intensify their campaign to subvert the Iraqi regime and to start targeting Jordanian officials in retaliation against their support for the Syrian brethren.[77] Also, in mid-November, the Syrians sponsored the formation of a united front of Iraqi opposition groups committed to overthrowing the rival Ba'thist regime in Baghdad. The front, named the National Democratic and Patriotic Front in Iraq (*Al-Jabhah Al-Wataniyah Al-Qawmiyah Al-Dimuqratiyah Fi Al-Iraq*) consisted of dissident Iraqi Ba'thists, the Iraqi Communist Party, the Patriotic Union of Kurdistan, the Arab Socialist Movement, the People's Liberation Army Organization, and the Democratic Independent Movement. The front's charter reflected the diverse goals of its members, such as improved relations with the USSR and Iran, autonomy for Iraqi Kurdistan, democratic reforms in Iraq, and active participation in the struggle against Israel.[78]

Two weeks before the Amman summit, Damascus made known its reluctance to attend the meeting when Foreign Minister Khaddam urged the secretary-general of the Arab League, Chedli Klibi, to postpone the conference. Khaddam warned that at a time of many 'disputes and deep divisions' among the Arabs, holding a summit would be futile because it would only underline the 'failure and fragmentation' of the Arab nation.[79] Iran also demonstrated its displeasure at Jordan's stance on and conduct in the Gulf War when the SDC secretary announced that Tehran had decided to downgrade its diplomatic presence in Jordan from the ambassadorial to the chargé d'affaires level. Two days later, on 17 November, Syria and Iran's other ally, PLO chairman Yasser Arafat, embarked on a tour of several Arab countries to persuade them to support Syria's position on the postponement of the Amman summit.

At the same time, Iraq's other Arab ally, Saudi Arabia, reacted swiftly to prevent the political gulf widening even further among Arabs by dispatching its foreign minister, Prince Saud al-Faisal, to Damascus. On his arrival, he tried to persuade Assad and Khaddam to drop their request to postpone the summit meeting. However, the Saudi foreign minister failed to sway the Syrian leaders who subsequently exacerbated the situation by accusing Jordan of mistreating Syrian citizens at border crossings between the two states. An incident in which a member of the Syrian Muslim Brethren was assassinated in Amman and the two killers apprehended and executed by the Jordanian authorities further heightened the tensions.[80]

On 18 November, though, Foreign Minister Khaddam travelled to Amman to take part in a plenary meeting of Arab foreign ministers and to set the agenda for the summit. However, the discussions degenerated into a row when the issue of postponing the summit was put forth. The meeting apparently came to an abrupt end amid confusion and sharp exchanges between Syrian and Iraqi representatives. Khaddam, adamant that inter-Arab differences should be resolved at foreign ministers' meetings before the start of the actual summit, warned that 'if this summit takes place over our objections, it may be the last summit held by the Arab League.'[81] He explained that 'unless the present Arab situation were treated seriously, it was difficult to imagine the summit achieving anything and its convocation might be a catastrophe'.[82] He later added, 'we want to purify the Arab atmosphere and to achieve a concerted Arab situation, capable of confronting the challenges threatening the Arab nation from Zionism and imperialism. ... There can be no talk of our participation in the summit before the purification of the Arab atmosphere.'[83]

Syrian officials then held a joint strategy session in Damascus with representatives from Algeria, Libya, South Yemen and the PLO, and travelled to Amman to persuade other Arab foreign ministers to postpone the conference. The Syrians announced that they wanted comprehensive talks on all inter-Islamic disputes, such as the Gulf War and their fallout with Iraq, before the summit convened. If their demands were not met, they would boycott the conference. Subsequently, the PLO stated its intention to follow suit if other members of the Steadfastness Front also refused to participate. Damascus asked for a smaller-scale summit to be held in an Arab capital other than Amman, a request that came from the serious differences of opinion among the Arab foreign ministers over the exact agenda of the conference. King Hussein's main aim was to win a general Arab endorsement for Iraq's war effort, whereas Assad was determined to restrict the agenda to inter-Arab economic cooperation and the conflict with Israel.

In the meantime, as tensions mounted between Syria and Jordan, Iran made a serious effort to lobby members of the Steadfastness Front to back the Syrian position. In conjunction with the Syrian effort, the speaker of parliament, Ali Akbar Hashemi Rafsanjani, travelled to Algeria and Libya where he held discussions with government officials. On 23 November, two days before the summit, he flew to Damascus for talks with Syrian leaders. The next day, Libya, Algeria, South Yemen, Lebanon and the PLO announced their intention to boycott the Amman summit, which dealt a serious blow to King Hussein's prestige and plans. Furthermore, Syria had clearly succeeded in demonstrating that it possessed veto power on Arab

League deliberations. The PLO's decision to stay away from the conference further undermined the Iraqi–Saudi–Jordanian gambit to create a pan-Arab front not only against Iran but also against Israel. The absence of Syria, Lebanon and the PLO, three of Israel's major adversaries, and other members of the Steadfastness Front underlined King Hussein's failure to push forth his agenda, and the fact that the Arabs were suffering one of their most serious political crises in over a decade. As one observer put it, 'the withdrawal of the Syrians and their allies reduced the Amman summit conference to little more than a rump session.' Syria's information minister Ahmad Iskandar Ahmad boasted that without Syria and the PLO the conference was meaningless.[84] King Hussein had hoped to benefit from backing Iraq, which he perceived as the emerging dominant power in the Middle East. Although, Jordan's goal to draw up a joint Arab strategy against the 'Zionist entity and the Persian enemy' had been gravely compromised, thereby forcing the participants to concentrate on a joint Arab economic development policy, Assad did not stop there.[85]

Early on, Assad decided to avoid the Arab summit for fear of being castigated by the majority of the participants as 'un-Arab' for siding with Persian Iran and 'un-Islamic' for defending the Soviet occupation of Afghanistan (a price he had to pay for consolidating his friendship with Moscow). Moreover, he refused to sit at the same table as King Hussein and Saddam Hussein, two of the Syrian Muslim Brethren's main supporters.[86] Five days before the summit began, Assad ordered the first Syrian armoured division to be deployed near the town of Dar'a, five kilometres from the border with Jordan. As the summit approached, more armoured units were gradually dispatched to the area. By the second day of the summit, 20,000 troops and 400 tanks had been deployed.[87] Once the build-up was confirmed, the Jordanians quickly moved their twelfth mechanized division stationed in the northwestern region bordering Syria and Israel eastward to counter the Syrian concentration. As a precaution, the fifth armoured division based northeast of Amman was moved 16 kilometres north to the border to cover the twelfth's right flank. When both sides had completed their deployments, 24,000 Hashemite troops were facing more than 30,000 Syrians.[88] To intimidate the Jordanians further, Syrian warplanes crossed into Jordanian airspace and overflew the Mafraq air base in the northeastern part of the country.[89]

Referring to the looming crisis, King Hussein declared during the summit that, if necessary, his country would use all possible means to defend 'every last inch of its territory' against Syrian aggression.[90] On

the last day of the summit, in his concluding address at the conference, King Hussein rebuked Assad for his actions by stating that 'an
Arab must not support a non-Arab in a dispute with another Arab
brother. It is a shame indeed that Iraq, which is fighting to regain
both Arab rights and its own rights and sovereignty over its territory
and waters on the eastern flank of the Arab homeland, is stabbed in
the back by an Arab hand.'[91] He went on to warn that 'we must all
stand against this, for it establishes a new and dangerous trend for the
first time among the Arab states. This can bring us damaging consequences.'[92] Damascus immediately lashed out by denouncing the Jordanian monarch's comments and threatening to attack Syrian Muslim
Brethren camps, which it alleged had been set up inside Jordan.

The imminent threat of hostilities between Jordan and Syria was
enough to prompt Riyadh to send Prince Abdullah, the kingdom's
deputy prime minister and commander of the National Guard, as a
mediator to defuse the crisis on 30 November. After several rounds of
talks in Damascus and Amman, in early December Prince Abdullah
announced that the Syrians had agreed to a gradual withdrawal of
forces, which was completed by the middle of the month. Amman
also ceased its sabre-rattling and dispersed its troops. Although the
Saudis claimed credit for ending the showdown, it is doubtful that
Assad ever wanted to go to war. In all fairness, however, Saudi efforts
did reduce tensions and made it easier for both parties to climb down
the ladder of escalation in a face-saving manner.[93]

The impact of the Gulf War on Syrian–Iranian relations

The Syrian–Jordanian confrontation was a poignant example of
Assad's willingness to take extreme measures – to go almost to the
brink of war to derail the diplomatic efforts of Iraq's staunchest Arab
ally. Tehran undoubtedly appreciated Syria's instrumental role in
convincing six key Arab players to stay away from Amman and
militarily intimidating the host. The Iranians greeted the Arab
participants' failure to take decisive steps to resolve inter-Arab feuds
exacerbated or produced by the Gulf War with a sigh of relief. On all
levels, political, military and ideological, Syria's moves and the outcome of the summit were a major gain for the Damascus–Tehran axis.
Moreover, to an unprecedented degree, the outcome of the events
demonstrated that non-Arab actors now could play a role in the arena
of inter-Arab politics. By the end of 1980, the Syrian–Iranian–Libyan
axis had become as much a part of the Middle Eastern and Arab
political landscape as the Saudi–Iraqi–Jordanian camp confronting it.

The continuation of hostilities between Iran and Iraq consolidated some trends in Arab–Iranian relations and introduced others. Fear of Iran's brand of Islamic fundamentalism and a sense of Arab solidarity prompted Jordan, Egypt and the Gulf Arab states to throw their weight behind Iraq. Conversely, the war facilitated the transformation of the Syrian–Iranian *rapprochement* into a formal alliance.

At a time when many of its Arab neighbours were overtly siding with Iraq and the situation at the war front was anything but favourable, Iran clearly valued its friendship with Syria. Besides the vital role Damascus played in brokering the Iranian military resupply effort, Tehran considered it vital to cultivate a close friendship with the Syrian Arab Republic to prevent the formation of a hostile Arab union against Iran. Iranian policy makers feared the possibility of regional isolation. Also, they realized that strong ties with Syria would add a whole new dimension to Iran's foreign policy, enabling it to play a more active role in inter-Arab affairs.

Indeed, maintaining and expanding cordial relations with as many Arab states as possible was vital for depolarizing the situation and dispelling any notion that the Gulf War was an extension of the historical Arab–Persian conflict. This particular objective was also of great ideological significance to Iran's religious leaders who firmly believed that an alliance with Syria would lend credibility to their claim that revolutionary Iran was at the forefront of all progressive anti-imperialist movements internationally, regardless of their national or religious character.

In an official statement in the aftermath of the Amman summit crisis, Iran's prime minister Mohammad Ali Raja'i expressed gratitude at Syria's unwavering support for the Iranian revolution, and described bilateral relations between the two states in very favourable terms. It is interesting that on the subject of the Syrian Muslim Brethren's aims and activities, he condemned them as 'a gang which masqueraded under the guise of religion and was supported by the Jordanian and Iraqi regimes'.[94]

A series of events in early 1981 drove Damascus and Tehran even closer together, and made the strengthening of bilateral relations a primary goal of both Syrian and Iranian diplomacy. During a brief hiatus in the Syrian–Jordanian confrontation (December 1980 to January 1981), Assad travelled to Tripoli to explore avenues for closer collaboration with Qadhafi. But in early February, the Syrians came to the bitter realization that their hopes of a union with Libya had been dashed. Qadhafi, having buttressed his position through substantial Soviet arms deliveries and recent military gains in Chad, demanded the dissolution of the Syrian Ba'th Party and its replacement with Libyan-style popular committees. For the leadership in Damascus, with the memory of the dissolution of the Syrian Ba'th and the painful experience of the union with Nasserite Egypt still in their minds, this was one pill they refused to take for the sake of so-called 'unity'. Thus, relations between Tripoli and Damascus cooled to some degree.

Meanwhile, there was a second crisis in Syrian–Jordanian relations when 20 armed men from a Syrian-backed Palestinian group called the Eagles of the Revolution Organization abducted the Jordanian chargé d'affaires in Beirut, Hisham Moheisen, after a 30-minute gun battle with security forces in which at least two Jordanian embassy guards died and three others, among them Lebanese policemen, were wounded. Amman accused Assad's brother Rif'at and Syrian military intelligence of the kidnapping. The arrest in Jordan five days earlier of a team of Syrian agents who were planning to assassinate Prime Minister Mudar Badran preceded the incident. Amman made the plot public only after the incident in Beirut, and once again implicated Rif'at Assad. By the end of the month, a propaganda war between the two sides was in full swing, with the Syrian press even calling for the overthrow of the Hashemite monarchy.[95]

Iran's relations with several Arab countries also took a turn for the worse during this period. In January, Tehran finally severed diplomatic ties with Amman and Rabat because of their pro-Iraqi stance in the Gulf War and at the Islamic summit in Taif. Saudi–Iranian relations also deteriorated the following month when Iran accused Riyadh and Kuwait of collusion with Baghdad by agreeing to boost their oil production to 1.8 million barrels per day in the run up to the invasion of Iran to aid the Iraqi war effort. Moreover, there were reliable reports that Saudi ports had been used to ship 100 Soviet-made T-54/55 tanks to Iraq.[96] Subsequently, Iraqi first deputy prime minister Taha Yasin Ramadan flew to Saudi Arabia to discuss the Gulf War and Saudi–Iraqi ties with King Khaled. During his visit, Riyadh publicly reiterated its support for the Iraqi position. In late February, an Iranian delegation headed by Jalaleddin Farsi arrived in Damascus and held talks with their Syrian counterparts.[97]

Amid a growing sense of regional isolation, the urgent need to forge closer bilateral links was driven home in Tehran and Damascus, and reinforced in early April, by revelations about the extent of Iraqi–Egyptian military cooperation in the Gulf War. After months of repeated denials by Egyptian officials, President Sadat finally admitted that an initial agreement worth $100 million had been reached in December between the two parties. Under the terms of the agreement, 4000 tons of ammunition, spare parts, missiles and rockets were delivered to Iraq while another 8000-ton shipment was being prepared to be sent later via Jordan.[98]

The raid on Al-Walid

Perhaps the most notable instance of Syrian–Iranian cooperation against the Iraqi war effort in the early stages of the conflict occurred in spring 1981. On 4 April, eight Iranian F-4 Phantom fighter bombers took off from Nojheh (formerly Shahrokhi) air base near Hamadan. The aircraft carried full payloads of bombs. Their mission was to attack the Iraqi military and petroleum complex at Al-Walid (also known as H-3), which consisted of four installations. This was the first such raid against Al-Walid, which, unlike all other Iraqi air bases had not been the target of any Iranian air attacks so far. The base was in the westernmost region of Iraq, situated only 50 kilometres east of the Iraqi–Jordanian border (just west of the town of Al-Rutbah). Until then, the base had been effectively out of range for Iranian aircraft. The main significance of Al-Walid at the time, which made it a high priority target, was that it was the home base for the bulk of the Iraqi strategic bomber force (Tupolev TU-16 Badgers, TU-22 Blinders) and transport aircraft (Ilyushin Il-76s, Antonov An-12s).[99] In the first phase of the war, the Iranian air force had succeeded in achieving air superiority by launching an intensive air campaign against Iraqi air bases and flying air superiority missions. Unable to make effective use of its bomber force, and fearing their destruction in bases in eastern Iraq, the Iraqi high command had moved them to Al-Walid out of harm's way, to be utilized later at an opportune moment.

To ensure that the Iranian warplanes reached Al-Walid, during the planning of the operation, the Syrians consented to allow them to fly over Syrian airspace where they would be refuelled in the air on both legs of the mission by Iranian air force Boeing 707 and 747 tankers. The Iranian Phantoms flew at low altitude over Iraqi airspace near the Turkish border, attempting to evade Iraqi radar, crossing then into Syria and proceeding southwest towards the Iraqi panhandle, where they re-entered Iraqi airspace flying at low levels to escape detection. The attack succeeded in catching the Al-Walid defences off guard.[100] During the course of the attack 46 Iraqi aircraft were destroyed on the ground.[101] After discharging their payloads they returned to Iran by flying the same route back. Iraqi anti-aircraft fire damaged one of the Phantoms during the raid. It was forced to make an emergency landing at a Syrian air base near Dayr al-Zawr, from where the two-man crew was taken to Damascus and on to Tehran.[102]

The raid on Al-Walid was significant in several respects. Militarily, in a single stroke Iran was able to annihilate most of Iraq's strategic bombers without incurring any losses. Furthermore, the loss of those aircraft meant that in one operation approximately 15 to 20 per cent of the Iraqi air force had been destroyed. Politically, the attack showed the lengths to which the Syrians were willing to go to help the Iranian war effort against Iraq without directly involving their own military personnel in an attack on a fellow Arab country. The operation would have been unfeasible without Syrian collaboration. The raid on Al-Walid was a one time shot, for the Iraqis quickly learned from their mistakes and took steps to ensure that they would never again incur losses of such a magnitude. However, both militarily and politically the raid was extremely important and an impressive feat, but one that is often ignored or downplayed in Arab and Western circles because of the authoritarian nature and unpopularity of the Syrian Ba'thist and Iranian clerical regimes.

Stalemate, power struggle in Tehran, and regional developments

By spring 1981, despite sporadic fighting and occasional incidents like the Al-Walid raid, the situation at the war front had reached an impasse. The Iraqis were unable to advance further and were trying to consolidate their gains from their initial offensives in late 1980. Iran had tried an ill-conceived offensive in January to push the Iraqi forces back, but the operation turned out to be a disaster because of Iraqi military preparedness and political bickering between Iran's president Bani-Sadr and the IRP radical clerics. In the spring and summer, the political power struggle between the two factions intensified, resulting in no further military operations at the front and very few important diplomatic initiatives because the future course of Iran's revolution was being fought out among the leadership in Tehran.

Irrespective of the political power struggle, the continuation of the war led to close cooperation among members of the pro-Iraqi bloc in the Arab world and a greater effort on Iran's part to preserve close relations with its Arab allies, particularly Syria and Libya. In April, Saudi Arabia and Kuwait announced that they had agreed to lend Iraq $6 billion for reconstruction of war ravaged areas. This seems to have been part of a larger $14 billion aid package put together by the Gulf

Arab states.[103] The pro-Iraqi bloc continued to be very critical of Iran and its main Arab allies, Syria and Libya.

In the aftermath of the Al-Walid raid, numerous reports were circulated in the Arab and Western media about a secret agreement between Syria and Iran on the conduct of the air war against Iraq. According to the reports, during a secret visit by the Iranian defence minister to Damascus, an understanding was reached to put Syrian airfields at the disposal of Iranian warplanes to conduct raids into Iraq, and for Syrian MiG-23 aircraft to provide close air support for Iranian planes on bombing missions. Overall, these reports seem suspect. The evidence indicates that although Iranian warplanes used Syrian air bases on some occasions, it is highly improbable that Syrian warplanes provided support for the Iranian air force sorties inside Iraqi airspace, which, in the event of a Syrian plane being shot down would have had huge repercussions for the Assad regime at home and in the Arab world. Furthermore, with the exception of Al-Walid, most of Iraq's airfields were located in the eastern part of the country along the Tigris–Euphrates valley, much closer to the Iranian border. It would make very little sense for Iranian warplanes to take a longer route from Syria without escaping detection to raid Iraqi military installations in the east. The only plausible case would be for Iranian warplanes to use air bases in northeastern Syria near the adjoining Turkish–Iraqi border to attack Iraqi strongholds in Iraqi Kurdistan.[104]

Syria's continued support for Iran and incessant Arab criticism of its stance and conduct in the Gulf War at a time when the Syrian Muslim Brethren were intensifying their campaign within the country meant that Iranian officials occasionally, albeit somewhat reluctantly, also had to take a stand on the unrest in Syria by making public statements expressing their 'wholehearted solidarity' with Hafez Assad. The Iranian state-controlled media in general refrained from providing any coverage of the events in Syria.[105] In late April, the leader of the Islamic Republican Party (IRP), Jalaleddin Farsi, told a SANA correspondent that the IRP could not condone the actions of the Syrian Brethren against the Syrian Ba'thists at a time when Assad was trying to confront imperialist agents in the region such as Israel, Egypt and Jordan. Farsi praised Syria's ardent support of the Iranian revolution against the Iraqi aggression.[106]

Despite the mutual animosity of both Tehran and Damascus towards Baghdad, this did not prevent them, at least officially, from condemning the Israeli raid on the Iraqi nuclear reactor site at Osiraq on 8 June 1981. In a public statement, Iranian President Bani-Sadr posited that 'the uncompromising opposition to the Iraqi regime and the brave and intense battle with the aggressor does not stop the Muslim nation of Iran from seriously condemning the airstrike by Israel.'[107] At the same time, the Syrian foreign ministry issued a statement declaring that 'the Syrian Arab Republic was not taken by surprise by the criminal operation suffused with treachery and rancour which was carried out by the Israeli air force against the Iraqi centre for generating nuclear energy for peaceful purposes.'[108] However, Iran's relations with most of its Arab neighbours remained tense. Iranian air attacks in Kuwaiti territory in mid-June, which the Iraqi media was quick to depict as part of the 'Zionist–Persian' conspiracy in the light of the Osiraq raid and the appearance of various press reports about Israeli arms shipments to Iran, and their public denunciation by Iraqi and Jordanian officials throughout this period, further exacerbated the situation.

Furthermore, in mid-June, a heavy earthquake struck the town of Golbaf in the Kerman region resulting in a serious loss of life and extensive damage. Syria and Algeria responded by sending the victims food and medical supplies. Assad also sent a message of sympathy to Ayatollah Khomeini. Once the political power struggle in Tehran had come to an end with the overthrow of President Abolhassan Bani-Sadr and the election of Mohammad Ali Raja'i as the country's new president in early August, Assad congratulated him wholeheartedly, expressing his conviction that the ties between the two states would be strengthened 'in the interest of the two peoples' struggle against imperialism and Zionism'.[109]

Iran's autumn offensives and Syria's assistance

With the power struggle in Iran now settled, the new leadership set out to expel the Iraqis from occupied territories and expand cooperation with Syria. Regular contacts between Syrian and Iranian officials were resumed to coordinate their activities on political and military matters.

A series of events in the inter-Arab arena and the Gulf War in the autumn of 1981 gave further impetus to the need for increased contacts and collaboration between Tehran and Damascus. Iran's unprecedented involvement in inter-Arab politics was highlighted in September by its presence at the Steadfastness Front conference in Benghazi as an observer and guest of Qadhafi's Libya. At the same time, as the war dragged on, the pro-Iranian camp appeared to be gradually coming apart. Against the outspoken support of Syria and

Libya, Algeria was more low key, while South Yemen and the PLO distanced themselves from their earlier position. These noticeable shifts made it imperative for the Islamic Republic to maintain cordial ties with its two most valuable Arab partners, Syria and Libya (particularly the former) at a time when it finally seemed that a continuation of the hostilities would be to Iran's advantage.

In late September, the Iranians had their first major battlefield success when elements of the 92nd and 16th armoured divisions pushed the Iraqis back across the Karun River, thereby breaking the siege of Abadan. This breakthrough could partly be attributed to help from the Syrians who provided five French-built Aerospatiale CT-20 airdrones. Being able to photograph the disposition of Iraqi forces in the Abadan area before the start of the operation significantly enhanced Iran's reconnaissance capability.[110] Some of the pro-Iraqi camp, notably Saudi Arabia, went so far as to credit the lifting of the siege mainly to Syrian and Libyan military help. According to the available sources, this would seem to be an exaggeration of the extent of their involvement and importance in the battle for Abadan.

Tehran's newly regained confidence was also reflected in the bombing of Kuwaiti oil installations. Despite Iranian denials, this action was clearly intended to intimidate Kuwait (seen as the weak link among Iraq's Gulf Arab allies who were bankrolling the Iraqi war machine). Kuwait reacted by recalling its ambassador to Tehran. Baghdad, Amman, Cairo, San'a and Abu Dhabi condemned the Iranian action as further evidence of the clerical regime's anti-Arab disposition. The Saudis also denounced the Soviet–Iranian *rapprochement* that had been evolving for some time with Assad's blessing. The pro-Iraqi media again turned up the pressure on Syria by claiming that Iranian warplanes were being stationed in Syria 'to stab Arab Iraq in the back'.[111] Recurrent accusations in the Arab media and by Iraqi officials like information minister Latif Nassif Jasim aroused sensitivities in Syria, which responded by calling for an Arab military commission of inquiry to investigate the Iraqi charges.

With respect to the Arab–Israeli dispute, Tehran and Damascus greeted the news of Anwar Sadat's assassination with enthusiasm. Moreover, they deplored Saudi Prince Fahd's eight-point peace plan, which Hafez Assad made sure did not get off the ground at the Arab summit at Fez in November. The ruling clerics in Tehran greatly appreciated Syria's successful drive to frustrate the Arab initiatives undertaken by members of the pro-Iraqi camp. At this juncture, Iran's denunciation of the continued presence of US AWACS aircraft on

Saudi territory, the Fahd initiative and Riyadh's staunch support for Saddam Hussein plunged Saudi–Iranian relations to new depths. These points of contention inevitably led to a dramatic escalation in the war of words between the two sides. Tensions finally reached new heights in December with the uncovering of an Iranian-sponsored coup attempt to unseat Bahrain's ruling al-Khalifah family. Manama immediately expelled the Iranian chargé d'affaires. The North Yemenis followed suit as a gesture of support.

In response to the menacing threat originating from across the Gulf, Riyadh took a series of decisive measures to protect the Gulf Arab states and strengthen ties with members of the pro-Iraqi bloc in an effort to isolate and deter Iran. When news of the coup attempt broke, the Saudi minister of interior Prince Nayif Bin Abdul Aziz declared that 'the Kingdom of Saudi Arabia considers the security of Bahrain and the Gulf countries the security of the Kingdom'.[112] The Saudis followed through on their words by signing a bilateral agreement on internal security cooperation with Bahrain on 20 December. Similar agreements were concluded with Oman, Qatar and the UAE in the weeks that followed. On sealing the agreement with Bahrain, the Saudi interior minister berated the Iranians severely by stating that 'after their revolution, they [the Iranians] did not want to be the policeman of the Gulf, they have become the terrorists of the Gulf'.[113] He added that 'our stand must be an Arab stand in support of Iraq; at the same time we must work to bring about an end to the war.'[114] The Gulf Arab states, led by Saudi Arabia and Kuwait, subsequently embarked on an all-out effort to buttress the Iraqi position. Within a week of the Saudi–Bahraini security accord, Riyadh had signed an agreement with Baghdad resolving a 60 year-old border dispute and settling differences over their 500-mile common frontier.[115] Kuwait also announced a $2 billion loan to Iraq, bringing the total Gulf Arab contribution to Iraq to at least $16 billion by the end of 1981.[116]

Having suffered a number of recent setbacks, Iraq tried to take full advantage of these events. In late November, the Iranians successfully launched Operation Tariq al-Quds, primarily to recover the key border town of Bostan. However, to enrage Arab opinion, Baghdad played up allegations of Iranian atrocities against Iraqi prisoners in the aftermath of the battle. Increasingly, Iran's most ardent supporter, Syria, found itself in a very difficult position, struggling to defend its stance in the conflict.

In the second half of 1981, both Syria and Libya continued to provide Iran with various kinds of military assistance. In the summer, the first group of Iranian tank crews returned home from being trained to operate Soviet-made tanks in the Libyan desert. Shortly after their return, a shipment of 190 Soviet-built T-54s, T-55s and T-62s arrived in Bandar Abbas from Libya.[117] By December, 250 Iranian tankmen had received training in Libya and 300 Soviet-made tanks had been shipped to Iran.[118] Libya and Syria continued to airlift east bloc weaponry to Iran. The Syrians especially played a vital role in transhipping weapons to Iran throughout the year. Syrian and Iranian intelligence services in Lebanon collaborated to weaken Iraqi power and influence as much as possible. As part of their overall strategy, a number of pro-Iraqi Ba'thists and Iraqi diplomats were assassinated. However, the *coup de grâce* came on 16 December when a car bomb totally demolished the Iraqi embassy in Beirut, killing 30 embassy employees including the Iraqi ambassador.[119]

The defection of Arab states to the pro-Iraqi camp, a continuing struggle against the Muslim Brethren and the looming crisis with Israel had, by the end of the year, led Assad to the conclusion that serious efforts should be made to diffuse the situation in the Gulf and that he should ask for Arab support against Israel. He thus took it upon himself to visit the Gulf sheikhdoms in late December to ask for help, but the Gulf Arab leaders made their assistance conditional on Syria abandoning its pro-Iranian stance in the conflict. Following his visit to the Gulf states, the Syrian and Kuwaiti governments announced a joint initiative to end the Gulf War. Damascus radio announced that the opportune moment had arrived to end the hostilities between Iraq and Iran 'in the interest of conserving Arab and Islamic energies to counter Israel's expansionist designs'.[120] During his meetings with Saudi officials, Assad also agreed to Prince Fahd's plan to resolve existing differences between Syria and Iraq. Furthermore, Fahd was given the green light to mediate between Syria and Jordan.

Tehran responded to these developments and to the Arab states' diplomatic posturings by dispatching foreign minister Ali Akbar Velayati to Damascus on 30 December to hold talks with Assad and Khaddam. Once the negotiations were concluded, it became apparent that the Iranians had rejected any attempt to intercede between the two combatants. They had decided to rebuff the Syrian–Kuwaiti initiative and to determine the outcome of the war on the battlefield.[121] By the beginning of the new year, Tehran undoubtedly believed that the scale had tipped in its favour. Between 12 and 16 December, Iran had launched its third consecutive offensive in a three-month period, this time near Qasr Shirin. The operation, codenamed Matla al-Fajr, resulted in the recovery of 100 square miles of Iranian territory.[122] At a press conference on 1 January, after his deliberations with the Syrian leadership, Velayati explained that 'the fate of the Iraqi-imposed war on Iran will be determined by the corps and combatants of Islam on the battlefronts'. He denied that the issue of mediation between Iran and Iraq was ever raised in his meetings in Damascus. Velayati enumerated Iran's conditions for the cessation of hostilities: (1) unconditional withdrawal of Iraqi forces from Iranian territory, (2) determination of the aggressor by a competent and impartial international body, and (3) payment of war reparations by the aggressor to the victim of the aggression.[123] As a gesture of solidarity against Israel's annexation of the Golan Heights, Iran offered to send Revolutionary Guards to fight against Israel.[124]

Despite the failure of the Syrian–Kuwaiti initiative, Assad's moves in the Gulf had not been completely in vain. He managed to ease tensions with Riyadh after the debacle at the Fez summit when he obstructed any meaningful progress on Fahd's peace proposal. In addition, Assad was able to mend relations between Saudi Arabia and Libya, leading to the resumption of diplomatic ties between the two states on 31 December.

Iraq's 'pan-Arab struggle' and Iran's growing regional isolation

The Islamic Republic's outright rejection of the Syrian–Kuwaiti offer did not adversely affect its relations with Ba'thist Syria. Iran could ill afford to drive away its most valuable Arab partner at a time when it was clearly alienating many of its Arab neighbours and former allies. On 12 January, Khaled al-Hassan, a member of the PLO's central committee, criticized Iran's attempt to subvert the regime in Bahrain, calling it 'irresponsible' and underlining the poor state of Palestinian–Iranian relations.[125] On the same day, North Yemen expelled the Iranian chargé d'affaires in San'a, accusing him of involvement in subversive activities. Earlier in the month, Iraq and South Yemen agreed to raise their diplomatic ties to ambassadorial level. Iraq, in the meantime, lobbied aggressively in Arab circles for all Arab states to sever their diplomatic ties with Iran. It attempted to portray the Gulf War as a pan-Arab effort against 'Persian expansionism'.[126] To facilitate the Iraqi effort, King Hussein of Jordan announced that the Jordanian Arab Yarmuk forces would accept volunteers to fight against Iran. The response was overwhelming, with hundreds of young Jordanians filing into recruiting stations to enlist in the

Yarmuk forces. Syria and Libya were quick to denounce the Jordanian move. *Al-Ba'th* condemned the establishment of the force to wage war on Iran, pointing out Jordan's neglect of the threat emanating from Israel.[127] Damascus described King Hussein's decision as 'a worthless political stunt designed to distract attention from the Arab–Israeli conflict ... trying to provoke Syria and inventing a marginal battle useful only to the enemies of the Arab nation'.[128] Libya's leader Qadhafi adopted a similar line declaring: 'we thought that the call for volunteers by King Hussein would be aimed at liberating Palestine and Holy Jerusalem which is a stone's throw from King Hussein's residence, and not for the purpose of fighting against Iran'.[129]

Iran reacted to the Jordanian action swiftly by announcing the formation of a battalion of Iraqi volunteers and former POWs to be sent to fight against the Israelis. The unit would be called the Golan battalion. The Iranian foreign ministry issued a statement highly critical of the Jordanian decision, characterizing it as 'a direct and clear' proclamation of war against Iran.[130] With the intensification of the anti-Iranian camp's efforts to describe the war as an Arab–Persian conflict, and wean away pro-Iranian Arab states, Iran explored various options to convince the Arabs that the war was not about conflicting nationalisms but disparate ideologies with different visions of a 'just Middle Eastern Order'. To stress the importance of the Palestinian cause in Iran, and discredit the propaganda of the pro-Iraqi bloc, Iranian President Hojjatolislam Ali Khamene'i took the additional step of promising direct Iranian military intervention in the Arab–Israeli conflict once the war with Iraq had ended. In a message to Hafez Assad, the Iranian leader claimed on behalf of the Iranian people that the occupation of Jerusalem and the Golan was 'as an occupation of our lands'.[131] Concurrently, Iranian Foreign Minister Velayati toured Libya, Algeria and the Western Sahara to reaffirm Iran's friendship and desire for future cooperation with its North African Arab allies.

As Iraq's allies, especially Jordan, tried to arouse Arab patriotic and nascent anti-Persian sentiment, Iran's partners heightened their efforts to discredit them as tools of Zionism and Western imperialism in the region. Baghdad used every available opportunity to demonstrate that Arab states were backing the Iraqi war effort and showing solidarity. In late February, the North Yemeni President, Colonel Ali Abdullah Salih, made a state visit to Iraq. The Iraqi media gave the maximum possible coverage to this event, which included the inspection by the two heads of state of a battalion of North Yemeni volunteers at a training camp. During the tour of the camp, President Salih stated, 'the danger of intransigence would have never been stopped in the Arab homeland and the Islamic land had it not been for the steadfastness of Iraq, Iraq's army and its leadership.'[132]

The ever widening rift among Arab ranks came into sharper focus in this period. Iran's and Iraq's Arab allies took drastic measures to ensure that the combatants they supported would be able to prosecute the war at a time when it seemed that the tide of the war was finally turning in Iran's favour. A case in point was the Kuwaiti parliament's decision to cancel their financial contribution to the maintenance of the Syrian Arab deterrent force in Lebanon. The Kuwaitis angrily lashed out at the Assad regime, accusing it of pursuing its own agenda in Lebanon, carrying out repressive policies at home and betraying the Arab cause by backing Iran in the Gulf War.

For Hafez Assad, having just survived a major political confrontation with the Syrian Muslim Brethren, which culminated in the crushing of the fundamentalist opposition in the city of Hama, he now set out to deal a devastating blow to the Brethren's Arab backers, and assist the Iranians by cementing his budding alliance with Tehran. The Iranian military at this point in time was also planning a series of offensives in the early spring aimed at recovering the territories the Iraqi army occupied.

Formalizing the axis and Iran's spring offensives

Both sides stepped up their diplomatic efforts to seal the emergent Syrian–Iranian alliance. This process culminated in the visit of a high-ranking 48-man Syrian delegation headed by Khaddam (then deputy prime minister and foreign minister) to Tehran in March 1982.[133] The two sides signed many important agreements, including a trade protocol and oil deal. According to the terms of the latter, Iran would export nine million tons of oil to Syria annually. In return, Syria would provide 300,000–400,000 tons of phosphates (required for Iran's petrochemical industry) for one year. Afterwards, Syria would increase its annual phosphate exports to one million tons, an amount equivalent to Iran's domestic needs.[134]

At the time, Iranian officials stated that approximately 2.7 million tons of Iran's oil exports to Syria would be on a barter exchange basis, and the remaining 6.3 million tons would be paid for in cash.[135] However, one year later, Western sources revealed that Syria was importing 100,000 barrels a day of Iranian oil at the low rate of $28 a barrel, an additional 10,000 barrels a day in a barter deal, and 20,000 barrels a day for free. This was a time when the official OPEC price was still $34 per barrel.[136]

During his visit to Tehran, Khaddam reportedly also signed a secret arms deal with his Iranian counterpart. Reports show that in early April, several shiploads of heavy war material, including 130mm howitzers, ZSU-23 anti-aircraft guns, tank engines and ammunition left the ports of Tartus and Latakia bound for Iran. Furthermore, several planeloads of weapons also arrived in Iran from Syria. These deliveries coincided with a series of successful Iranian offensives in spring 1982, which resulted in the expulsion of Iraqi forces from much of the Iranian territory they had occupied.[137]

The bilateral agreements signed in Tehran formalized the Syrian–Iranian axis. The conclusion of the agreements and the setbacks the Iraqi army suffered on the battlefront encouraged Damascus to step up its efforts to assist the Islamic Republic. With the tide of the war turning and the possibility of the collapse of Saddam Hussein's regime on the horizon, Syria resorted to various means to put pressure on Iraq.

On 22 March, within a week of the conclusion of these agreements, the Iranian army launched Operation Fatah al-Mobin (Clear Victory) to drive back the Iraqis in Khuzestan province. The operation lasted only eight days, but the results were so spectacular that they exceeded even the best expectations of the Iranian high command. By 29 March, 850 square miles of territory had been liberated and three Iraqi divisions destroyed.[138] The Iraqi defeat sounded alarm bells throughout the region. The day after the operation ended, King Hussein arrived in Baghdad with his chief of staff to confer with Saddam Hussein. There was a great deal of speculation at the time that Amman might commit its own regular forces in the Gulf conflict. Though this never materialized, the Iraqi reverses were significant enough to warrant decisive action on the part of its allies. On the day King Hussein arrived in Baghdad, King Khaled telephoned Saddam Hussein to discuss the events at the battlefront. The gravity of the situation prompted the Saudi monarch to send his defence minister, Prince Sultan, to Baghdad to consult the Iraqi leader.

On 8 April, Syria closed its borders with Iraq. Two days later, having stored up 1.5 million barrels of Iraqi oil, Syria shut down the trans-Syrian IPC pipeline to Tripoli and Banias.[139] The closure had major economic repercussions and compounded Iraq's predicament at a time when the country faced mounting problems. Syria's action cut Iraqi oil exports by half to a mere 600,000 barrels a day, which translated into $17 million a day in lost revenue (approximately $6 billion a year).[140] Iraq's only remaining oil export route was the Kirkuk–Dortyol pipeline, which could carry up to 600,000 barrels a day.

The shutdown of the trans-Syrian pipeline heightened Baghdad's sense of insecurity: the Iraqis quickly realized that they were still vulnerable to Syrian economic warfare. To diminish their dependence on the Syrian pipeline, steps were taken to expand the Dortyol pipeline to a million barrels a day. Plans were also drawn up to have alternate pipelines built to link Iraqi oil facilities with the Saudi port of Yanbu and the Jordanian port of Aqaba.[141]

During April 1982, Syrian military units were deployed along the border with Iraq and Syrian military aircraft periodically violated Iraqi airspace.[142] This military activity along Iraq's western frontiers was part of an overall plan to put pressure on Ba'thist Iraq and compound its sense of insecurity. The spectre of Syrian military intervention forced Iraq to send military forces to its western borders.[143] The Syrian military deployment benefited Iran in several ways. At a military level, troops that could have been used to resist the Iranian offensives during this period were now tied down along the Syrian–Iraqi frontier. Furthermore, Syrian pressure had a profound psychological impact on the Iraqis, who feared the possibility of a war on two fronts and economic strangulation.

Syria's growing support for a number of Kurdish separatist movements and opposition groups operating within Iraq magnified Iraqi trepidations and concerns. The Syrians as well as the Iranians provided military and financial assistance to the National Progressive and Democratic Front, a coalition of various anti-Ba'thist organizations, which, as mentioned earlier, included the Marxist PUK, the UKP, the National Democratic Party, the United Kurdish Socialist Party and the ICP.[144] In fact, in early 1982, Iraq's oil export capability was temporarily crippled when Kurdish guerrillas blew up the Kirkuk–Dortyol pipeline. This was a serious blow for a country already $20 billion in debt.[145] Hafez Assad's assistance to the Kurdish rebels was intended to encourage the insurgency in the northern provinces and tie down additional Iraqi troops in this region.

Syria and Iran calculated that the combination of maintaining military pressure, waging economic warfare and aiding the Kurdish insurgency would lead to the deterioration of domestic conditions and the introduction of austerity measures by the regime. This would erode internal support for Saddam Hussein and the Iraqi Ba'th Party, eventually sparking domestic unrest and bringing about the overthrow of the government. The Iranians, in particular, believed that this would be the most practical way of scoring a political victory, without ever having to carry the war into Iraqi territory.

Iran's military successes in April and May 1982, which culminated in the recovery of the Iranian port city of Khorramshahr, strengthened Syria's resolve to stand by and cooperate with its Iranian ally. When it became evident that Iran would reject Arab peace offers and possibly invade Iraq, many Arab states called for a united stand against Iran. However, Damascus stopped an Arab summit being convened for this purpose in May 1982.[146] Iran's refusal to accept a negotiated settlement drew criticism from different corners of the Arab world, prompting even Algeria to distance itself from Tehran. As the Islamic Republic became increasingly isolated in the Middle East, Iranian officials started to place greater emphasis and value on their relationship with Syria. Although Damascus declared that it would not endorse an Iranian invasion of Iraq, and threatened to re-evaluate its stance on the Gulf War, no shift occurred in the existing alliance. In fact, after the Israeli invasion of Lebanon on 7 June 1982, and Iran's decision to carry the war into Iraq the following month, the Syrian–Iranian alliance entered a new phase, which would mark the zenith of Syrian–Iranian cooperation in the Middle East.

Conclusion

Despite ethnic dissimilarities and ideological incompatibilities, in the final analysis it was no surprise that on their ascent to power, Ayatollah Khomeini and his inner circle cultivated close ties with the Syrian Ba'thist regime. Because of the poor state of Syrian–Iranian relations in the last half of the 1970s, Assad had allowed the Shah's opponents to use Syria as a base for their activities. These included a number of individuals who eventually became some of Khomeini's close advisers and held senior posts in the revolutionary government. After the Shah's overthrow, the convergence of interests and striking parallels in the foreign policies of the two states gave further impetus to the Syrian–Iranian *rapprochement*. In a break from previous Iranian policy, the clerical regime drew closer to the radical Arab camp at a time when the Arab world was becoming more polarized and divided over issues like the Camp David accords and Iranian revolution. Similarly, Syria's relations with many of the moderate pro-Western Arab states suffered. The marked deterioration in both capitals' relations with the USA in 1979/80 further strengthened the links between Tehran and Damascus as they developed closer ties with the USSR.

The failure of the Syrian–Iraqi unity talks in mid-1979 and growing tensions between Iran and Iraq facilitated the emergent Syrian–Iranian alliance. From the perspective of officials in Tehran and Damascus, close coordination of their policies was essential if they were to contain Ba'thist Iraq. The showdown between Iran and Iraq, which eventually led to the first Gulf War in September 1980, was the single most important factor in formalizing the Tehran–Damascus axis in early 1982. The conflict also radically changed the balance of power within the relationship. While Syria had been more dependent on its links with Iran before the hostilities erupted, in the aftermath of the Iraqi invasion, Iran became more dependent than it had been on diplomatic and military assistance from Damascus.[147] Although the alliance became somewhat asymmetrical during 1980–82, the Israeli invasion of Lebanon in June 1982 brought about some shifts in the power relationship and enhanced the position of both states in the Middle East (see Chapter 2 for more details and analysis). However, by the spring of 1982, the Syrians had not only succeeded in determining the extent and limits of cooperation in most spheres of common interest, but had also managed to extract tangible economic and political benefits from the Islamic Republic to facilitate their realization of regional dominance. The Iranians, on the other hand, had an even stronger incentive for continuing their liaison with Syria. Syria had been instrumental in turning the tide of the war against Iraq by providing war *matériel*, intelligence and operational bases, and its assiduous diplomatic efforts and posturing had blocked the creation of a united anti-Iranian front. In addition, the alliance had provided them with greater access to the Arab–Islamic world, broadened their narrow constituency and enabled them to dismiss accusations that Persian or Shiite interests were the primary forces shaping their foreign policy.

Chapter 2

The Achievements and Limits of Syrian–Iranian Power, 1982–85

In late May 1982, the Syrian–Iranian alliance entered a new phase marked by close cooperation and intensive efforts to respond to new challenges not only in the Gulf, but also, and more importantly, in the eastern Mediterranean. This period can be delineated approximately from June 1982 to March 1985 – a three-year period that was one of the most critical in the modern history of the Middle East.

This particular phase can be characterized as both the zenith of the Syrian–Iranian axis in the region and, paradoxically, a time of lost opportunities in which the limits of its power were demonstrated and the seeds of its decline were sown. June 1982 was a critical month in the history of the contemporary Middle East: it was when Israel invaded Lebanon and engaged the Syrian armed forces in what became the fifth Arab–Israeli war, and when Iran, having turned the tide of the Persian Gulf war to its favour (with the expulsion of the Iraqis from most of its territory), decided to carry the war into Iraq.

Despite a wealth of literature on these two conflicts, very little research has been done on the connection between the events and decisions that were made in spring 1982 in Baghdad, Tel Aviv, Damascus and Tehran. I shall show in the following analysis that policymakers in Tel Aviv and Baghdad hoped that an Israeli–Syrian confrontation would diminish Syrian power in the region. Hafez Assad's brinkmanship in the aftermath of the Israeli invasion, however, not only thwarted Israeli and Iraqi calculations but also hindered the Reagan administration's policies in the Middle East. Therefore, much to his opponents' chagrin, Assad's prestige and influence grew noticeably. In addition to frustrating Israeli and US designs in the area, the Lebanon war drew Syria and Iran closer than before – contrary to the hopes and expectations of the Iraqi leadership. It is highly improbable that Iran would have altered its decision to invade Iraq in July 1982 had the Israelis not initiated hostilities in Lebanon. On the other hand, it shall be argued that had events played out differently, Tehran may have reconsidered the wisdom of continuing the Gulf War, and instead may have dispatched a sizeable military force to Lebanon to fight alongside the Syrians. In the words of Iran scholar, R. K. Ramazani, 'the truism that all things in the Middle East are interconnected is one that statesmen and scholars alike ignore at their own peril.'[1]

In this chapter, I give a detailed chronology of events and an in-depth analysis of the impact of the Lebanon war on the evolution of the Syrian–Iranian alliance. I explain how policymakers in Damascus and Tehran coordinated their policies as best they could and took up the challenge to expel Israeli and Western forces from Lebanon between 1982 and 1985. I also show that once the Islamic Republic of Iran carried the war into Iraq, it had only a brief window of opportunity in which to defeat its foe on the battlefield. I argue that through drastic shifts in the configuration of forces in the Middle East, this chance had been lost by early 1984. The US–Iraqi *rapprochement*, Egypt's re-entry into the Arab world and the emergence of the Baghdad–Amman–Cairo axis (all to varying degrees motivated by the success of the Syrian–Iranian axis and its potential to exert even greater regional power and influence) ensured that, at the very least, Iraq would be able to stave off defeat in the Gulf War. A lack of consensus among Iran's political and military leadership over the conduct and objectives of the invasion of Iraq also had a huge impact on Iran's failure to exploit fully Iraq's vulnerability between 1982 and 1983. By the time of Iran's first major offensive in February 1984, the balance of power had shifted in Iraq's favour. Although the constellation of forces arrayed against the Tehran–Damascus axis had succeeded in checking its power by 1985, the foundations and mechanics of the alliance were firmly in place. Both partners gave one another invaluable support in two consecutive crises – Syria helped Iran stem the Iraqi invasion of 1980, enabling its ally to turn the tables on the invader; then Iran collaborated with Syria to frustrate Israeli and US designs in Lebanon. So, despite the eclipse of the alliance and tensions between the two after mid-1985, the partnership was now firmly in place. Having withstood major challenges and the test of time, contrary to the expectations of many, it had been turned into one of the more durable features of the Middle East's political landscape. Overall, the Lebanon war served to expand and intensify Syrian–Iranian collaboration in the region with a view to thwarting Tel Aviv and Washington's designs.

Iraq tries to weaken the axis and the origins of the Lebanon war

By late May 1982, Iraq was in dire straits. Its gambit to defeat revolutionary Iran and become the Arab world's undisputed leader had failed miserably. The invasion of Iran in autumn 1980 had not only helped Khomeini's regime consolidate its position, but had also allowed the clerical leadership to mobilize the Iranian masses into ousting the Iraqis from much of the territory they had captured in the initial stages of the war. The liberation by Iranian forces of the key port city of Khorramshahr on 24 May marked the culmination of Iran's military effort to dislodge the Iraqis from their last major stronghold on Iranian soil. In just two months, the Iraqi forces in Iran had been decimated.[2] Saddam Hussein had very little to show for his efforts – his grand design had come to naught and now he had to brace himself for a possible Iranian invasion of Iraq. Baghdad's position became even more precarious when the Syrian–Iranian alliance was formalized two months earlier. The closure of the trans-Syrian IPC pipeline and Syria's support for the Iranian war effort and for Iraqi opposition groups had compounded Iraq's predicament. Baghdad looked for ways to prevent the Syrian–Iranian pincer from crushing it. The failure of the Iraqi-backed Muslim Brethren uprising in the Syrian city of Hama (February 1982) and Iran's success in routing the Iraqi army (March–May 1982) prompted Iraq to focus on Lebanon where the political situation was extremely volatile and ideal for foreign manipulation.

In the period leading up to June 1982, Prime Minister Menachem Begin's Likud government began to plan a huge military operation in Lebanon to expel the PLO, inflict humiliating defeat on the only remaining major Arab confrontation state, Syria, and create a new political order in Lebanon that would be willing to establish strong political links with Israel. However, to launch the invasion of Lebanon, codenamed Operation Peace in the Galilee, Tel Aviv needed internationally-recognized provocation. The excuse came on 3 June with an attempt on the life of the Israeli ambassador to Britain, Shlomo Argov. Ironically, the attempt was made by the Iraqi-backed Abu Nidal Organization, uncompromising foes of Yasser Arafat's PLO. In the past, the organization had primarily focused on eliminating high-ranking PLO officials, so the attempt on Israel's top representative in London was a major departure from its standard operational norms. In reality, Iraqi intelligence masterminded the attack to provoke an Israeli military response in Lebanon. Baghdad was aware of the Israeli plan to crush the PLO in the south. The Iraqis calculated that a major Israeli military incursion into Lebanon would be to the detriment of the Syrians, regardless of the course of action they adopted. From the Iraqi perspective, if Assad took up the gauntlet by challenging the Israelis militarily, his forces would be annihilated, and even if he did not confront the Israeli forces, he would lose face and credibility at home and throughout the Arab world. For Saddam Hussein, either scenario would be a source of great satisfaction. It also provided a way to settle the score with Menachem Begin for having ordered the bombing of the Osiraq reactor, just a year earlier.[3]

The regional environment and Israeli perceptions

According to some scholars, Israel's decision to invade Lebanon was based on new realities in the region and on the Reagan administration's foreign policy agenda (to check Soviet power and outmanoeuvre it in the Middle East). Defence Minister Ariel Sharon saw the toppling of the Pahlavi throne in Iran as a major loss for both Israel and the USA. However, the absence of a US foothold in Iran meant that Israel's strategic value had increased significantly in the eyes of US policymakers. In the aftermath of the Iranian revolution and Soviet invasion of Afghanistan, Washington hastily sought to create a new security framework in the region to hold the Soviets at bay. But the new US administration had few options, for it was highly doubtful that countries like Saudi Arabia could effectively fill the vacuum the Shah had left or would be willing to cooperate with Israel on regional security matters. Sharon apparently believed that in the final analysis, despite some reservations, Washington would not object to an invasion of Lebanon that would deal a severe blow to the Soviet-backed PLO and Syria, and at the same time lead to the installation of a pro-Western Maronite regime in Lebanon.[4] Such a move would not jeopardize the Camp David accords because the Israelis had completed their withdrawal from the Sinai in April 1982 and their southern flank was now secure.

Another argument to underline the link between the Lebanon War and the Gulf War is that events in the Persian Gulf even affected the timing of the Israeli invasion. The Israelis calculated that they could deflect attention in Washington and the Arab capitals from their operation if they made it coincide with the series of defeats the Iraqis were suffering in the Gulf and the imminent Iranian invasion of Iraq.[5]

Syrian–Iranian consultations on the Lebanon and Gulf wars

On 7 June 1982, the day after Operation Peace in the Galilee started, a high-ranking Iranian military delegation headed by defence minister Colonel Salimi, army commander Colonel Seyyed Shirazi and Revolutionary Guards commander Mohsen Reza'i arrived in Damascus to offer help against the Israeli assault on southern Lebanon. On arrival, the delegation held talks with Assad and delivered a message from Iran's President Khamene'i. The Iranian leadership expressed its readiness to dispatch forces to repel the Israeli invaders and assist in the struggle against 'Zionism, the battle to liberate the occupied territories, and the occupation of southern Lebanon'.[6] Apparently, an agreement was reached to have Iranian troops sent to Lebanon to participate in the fighting against the Israelis. Two days later, at a news conference in New York, Iranian foreign minister Ali Akbar Velayati stated that 'we consider this matter one of our foremost duties. It is part of the strategic aims of the Islamic Republic to fight against the Zionist regime. At present, the Defence Minister, the Ground Forces Commander and the revolutionary Guards Corps Commander ... are in Syria to assess the amount of assistance required and the mode of its dispatch. In this matter we shall not hesitate. If our brothers in Syria and Lebanon request it, we shall enter the war.'[7]

On 11 June, Iraq announced a unilateral ceasefire and said it would withdraw its forces to the international boundaries within two weeks. Then, on the Iranian military delegation's return from Syria, an SDC meeting was convened to discuss the Iraqi proposal and the situation in Lebanon. As a subsequent outcome of the deliberations among the Iranian political and military leadership, Tehran demanded free passage for its armoured units through Iraq to assist the Syrians in the mêlée as a new condition for ending the state of hostility between Iran and Iraq.[8] Iranian Prime Minister Mir Hossein Musavi described this stipulation in the light of the new circumstances in the Arab–Israeli conflict as 'one of the prime rights of an Islamic country'.[9]

Iraq's riposte, which came almost immediately, accepted the new Iranian demand and expressed readiness to discuss transit arrangements for the Iranian forces as soon as Tehran agreed to a ceasefire to end the hostilities between the two countries.[10] Curiously, for several days Iran did not respond at all to Iraq's proposal. There seem to have been fundamental differences of opinion within the regime about what to do next, over whether to accept the Iraqi ceasefire proposal, send an expeditionary force via Iraq to Lebanon and mend fences

with Baghdad, or to continue the Gulf War by launching an invasion
on Iraq and relegating the Syrian–Israeli conflict in Lebanon to a
secondary position (perhaps only sending a token force as a symbolic
gesture of solidarity). Various accounts suggest that Khomeini and
Rafsanjani favoured taking the war into Iraq, while Khamene'i,
Musavi and the top Iranian military brass were against prolonging the
conflict with Iraq. The latter group argued that the emphasis from
then on should be on rebuilding the country and safeguarding the
revolution at home.[11] While the debate brewed in Tehran, Iran
airlifted three contingents of volunteers to Damascus. Within a week,
several hundred volunteers had been flown to Syria.[12] By all accounts,
it was unclear exactly how many Iranians travelled through Syria to
Lebanon. Most reports suggest several thousand in three or four
contingents. Damascus only acknowledged the presence of 400, while
the Israelis and some foreign diplomats in the Syrian capital claimed
that the number was as high as 3000.[13] In a speech to a group of local
representatives from Tabriz, Rafsanjani boasted: 'Since the day our
forces arrived in Syria, the situation has changed. That is, the name of
the Islamic Republic of Iran and its youth have such a reputation that
according to Syrian and Lebanese assertions, the value of the few
planeloads of Iranian combatants is far more than if ten divisions had
come from the Arab countries.'[14]

Apart from dispatching fighters, Iran's Red Crescent Society shipped
substantial amounts of medical supplies and field hospitals.[15] While
popular sentiment and domestic pressure grew for a more active
Iranian role in the Lebanon war, the debate over the continuation of
the Gulf War and the scope of Iranian participation against the
Israelis remained unresolved within the Islamic regime. On 17 June, a
senior Iranian political-military delegation headed by foreign minister
Velayati and defence minister Salimi arrived in Damascus to explore
avenues of cooperation between the two allies in Lebanon. Discussions
were held with Syrian deputy prime minister and foreign minister
Khaddam, defence minister Mustafa Tlas, and the head of the political directorate of the Syrian armed forces Major-General Hassan al-
Turkumani. The Iranian delegation put forth proposals to help the
Syrian forces and the Amal movement in the Lebanese theatre of
operations. The Iranians apparently offered to send 40,000 regular
troops with heavy armour and 10,000 lightly-equipped Revolutionary
Guards and volunteers to fight in Lebanon under Syrian command.
The Iranian military had put forth a similar proposal a week earlier,
but on both occasions Assad flatly rejected them. It seems that offi-

cials in Damascus had been irked when Tehran initially criticized them for accepting the 11 June ceasefire.[16] But this does not explain why Assad turned down a generous Iranian offer at a time when the IDF had resumed the advance north towards Beirut and were engaging Syrian forces in the process. The answer lies in how the battle unfolded in the first week of the Lebanon war, the prospects for an Iranian invasion of Iraq, and Assad's interpretation of these two factors.

How Syria saw developments in Lebanon and the Gulf

While Damascus had anticipated an Israeli military incursion into Lebanon in the period leading up to 6 June, it had underestimated the scope and scale of the IDF attack. Up until the third day of the invasion, the Syrians believed that Israel's only objective was to destroy the PLO bases and infrastructure in south Lebanon. They assumed that the IDF thrust would not go beyond the south. However, by 8 June, it had become painfully clear that the Israeli scheme was more ambitious than previously thought. For the next three days, the Syrian forces in Lebanon engaged the IDF in the bloodiest fighting since the 1973 Arab–Israeli war. Despite the Syrian army's determined resistance, the Israelis inflicted heavy losses on their hapless opponent. On 11 June, when Begin's government announced a unilateral ceasefire on the Bekaa front, Assad eagerly accepted, for the brief respite it would give him to rush in more units from Syria and eastern Lebanon to beef up defences along the central and western parts of the front along the Beirut–Damascus highway and Shouf Mountains. The Israelis continued their advance towards Beirut, determined to annihilate any Syrian or Palestinian resistance they met. Though facing a larger, better-equipped force, and lacking air cover, the Syrian troops put up stiff resistance and made the Israelis pay dearly as they advanced towards Beirut in the two weeks that followed. By 25 June, the IDF had reached Beirut, and laid siege to the city. Although it took the Israelis less than three weeks to reach Beirut, within the first few days of the invasion, the Syrians had come to the bitter realization that their conventional forces could not conduct a convincing defensive action against the enemy, let alone counterattack and launch offensive operations to roll back the Israelis. In this context, one has a better understanding of why the Syrians turned down a generous Iranian offer at a time when their ally was still in a state of war with Ba'thist Iraq. Damascus knew that help from the Iranian forces would not be enough to tip the scale in their favour.

Moreover, an important prerequisite for major Iranian involvement in the Lebanese theatre was the cessation of hostilities between Iran and Iraq. Such a development would loosen the Syrian–Iranian noose around Saddam's neck and give him a new lease on life. From Assad's viewpoint, such a scenario was far from desirable because it would put him under pressure not only from the Israelis in the west, who had just decimated a good part of the Syrian armed forces, but also from his uncompromising foe to the east, Saddam Hussein. Given Iran's impressive military victories in spring 1982, Assad calculated that even if an Iranian invasion of Iraq would not result in the overthrow of his Ba'thist rival in Baghdad, at the very least the Iraqi military machine would be pinned down by his Iranian allies – preventing Saddam from focusing on his western flank.

While the Syrians were not keen on a large-scale Iranian military intervention in Lebanon, the Iranian 'doves' in the Gulf War debate apparently saw a limited Iranian role in the Lebanon war as a more secure alternative than an invasion of neighbouring Iraq. It would provide an outlet for the radical clerics' revolutionary fervour, entail fewer risks and allow the army to demobilize partially, thus enabling the regime to begin the reconstruction of the country. However, Assad's refusal to accept Iranian troops and his probable insistence on the continuation of efforts to unseat Saddam, undoubtedly weakened the position of the Iranian doves and strengthened the resolve of the hawks who were riding high on the wave of success and trying to build on the momentum that had started in March.

On 20 June, the Iranian military delegation returned to Tehran. The same day, Foreign Minister Velayati announced that Iranian forces already in Lebanon had completed reconnaissance missions there and would subsequently engage the Israelis. At the same time, Saddam Hussein declared the commencement of a unilateral Iraqi withdrawal from Iranian territory that would be completed in ten days to 'eliminate an important pretext being used by the suspect regime in Tehran to continue the war, and to put the regime to a decisive test to disclose the rest of its real intentions'.[17] Two days later, on 22 June, a meeting of the Iranian SDC was convened to discuss the course of action in the two wars. Afterwards, President Khamene'i stated that the leadership had decided not to send a sizeable military force to Lebanon until the war with Iraq was successfully terminated. The IRGC command issued a statement the same day that it was 'a binding duty to continue the war until the complete downfall of the Ba'thi–Zionist regime in Baghdad'.[18] In the end, Khomeini overruled the regime's more cautious members who included President Khamene'i, Prime Minister Musavi, Foreign Minister Velayati, high-ranking military figures like defence minister Salimi, armed forces chief General Ghassem Ali Zahir-Nejhad and army commander Colonel Seyyed Shirazi. The decision to cross into Iraq was also unpopular with the officer corps and conscripts who had hoped for early demobilization after the liberation of Khorramshahr.

Overall, those in favour of an invasion won out for several reasons. First, a string of impressive victories over the Iraqis between March and May exceeded the Iranian high command's most optimistic predictions. This boosted expectations about the efficacy of a future offensive, even if it meant invading Iraqi territory. Khomeini and his supporters smelt blood, believing that one more decisive battle in Iraq could bring down Saddam Hussein. Second, on the ideological level, with victory within grasp, the prospect of establishing an Islamic regime in Baghdad was quite attractive. Third, Khomeini's personal animosity to the Iraqi leader must have figured in his final decision.[19] Fourth, from an ethical standpoint, the continuation of hostilities made sense because the aggressor had not been punished. The war had assumed a moral dimension, portrayed as a 'just war' to secure peace in the future. Taking into account the recently consolidated Syrian–Iranian alliance, which now had an economic stranglehold over Iraq, and Assad's decision to refuse major Iranian participation in the Lebanon war, the resumption of offensive operations against the Iraqis seemed to be the logical plan of action both for pragmatic and ideological purposes. Syria's refusal to allow Iran to carry out an Islamic struggle against the Israelis in Lebanon meant that only through continuing the Gulf War would Iran have a means and outlet to export its revolution and channel its missionary zeal. Despite reports and statements by Syrian officials that they would reconsider their relationship with Iran if Arab Iraq were invaded, such declarations seem highly suspect. In all likelihood, they were hollow words to allay Arab fears that Damascus was supporting a non-Arab country's intention to invade another Arab state.

The Iranian invasion of Iraq and Syrian regional diplomacy

The available evidence clearly indicates that there were strong differences of opinion among the Iranian leadership about the wisdom of continuing the Gulf War. Furthermore, one can only speculate about the nature of the deliberations between Syria and Iran between 7 and 17 June, and the critical SDC meeting on 22 June. If

Damascus had consented to large-scale Iranian intervention in the Lebanon war, the position of the 'doves' in the Gulf War debate definitely would have been strengthened and the course of history in the region may have been totally altered. Moreover, given Hafez Assad's cool-headed and meticulous approach to formulating and implementing policy, even in times of crisis, he must have had strong reservations about the utility of Iranian participation in the Lebanon war, and knew that denying Tehran a prominent role in Lebanon would bolster the position of the Iranian hardliners who advocated toppling Saddam Hussein and the Iraq Ba'th Party. Interestingly, most of the statements Iranian officials made between 6 and 22 June about Tehran's position on Iraq and Israel were quite vague, but right after the crucial SDC meeting on 22 June, Iranian policy makers made numerous declarations explicitly stating and articulating their future policy in the Gulf and Lebanon.

On 29 June, Saddam announced that all Iraqi forces had been withdrawn from Iranian soil and had taken up defensive positions in Iraq. (In fact they still held at least 550 square miles of Iranian territory to prevent possible Iranian thrusts towards Baghdad and southern Iraq.)[20] On the same day, the Iranian foreign ministry issued a statement explaining that Iran would 'continue its honourable war against Saddam's regime ... until the sources of fire of the Iraqi forces are silenced and an honourable peace is secured'.[21] Following a meeting on the exact same day with Iranian Speaker Rafsanjani, the Soviet chargé d'affaires and the head of the Libyan People's Bureau, the Syrian ambassador in Tehran stated that, 'The President of Syria agrees with the recent remarks by the Imam [Khomeini] about the Iran–Iraq war, namely that the problem with Iraq should be sorted out first and then it will be the turn of the Zionist regime.'[22]

Preparations were already underway to launch a major offensive in southern Iraq. On 6 July, one week before the first major operation in Iraq, defence minister Mohammad Salimi declared that 'a push into Iraqi territory had become inevitable'.[23] In the light of events in Lebanon, Iranian deputy foreign minister Ahmad Azizi justified the decision by positing that the only way for Iranian forces to reach Lebanon and fight the Israelis was to cross Iraqi territory once the enemy had been defeated, thereby ensuring the security of Iran against any possible future aggression.[24] Echoing a view similar to that held by the Syrians, Azizi also severely criticized Soviet 'silence' and inaction towards the crisis in Lebanon.

As Iran prepared to take the offensive once again, there was a flurry of diplomatic activity in the pro-Iraqi camp to cement ties between Baghdad, Cairo, and Amman. On 5 July, Iraqi justice minister Mundhir Ibrahim al-Shawi paid a visit to Egyptian President Mubarak in Cairo. During their talks, the Iraqi envoy officially extended an invitation to the Egyptian leader to attend the NAM summit which was scheduled to be held in Baghdad between 6–10 September. Jordan's King Hussein flew to Baghdad a few days later to coordinate activities and improve avenues of cooperation with the Iraqis.

Finally, on 11 July, in a telling interview with the IRP daily, *Jomhuri Eslami*, Musavi clarified the official government position on the Gulf War by enunciating that:

> we have a right to take any measure deemed necessary to protect our country, create real security, and obtain reparations for war damages. It is a religious obligation for us to fight against injustice and aggression. If the Islamic Republic were to sue for peace at a time when none of our conditions are fulfilled, [it] would be like strangling the revolution with our own hands.[25]

Two days later, Iran launched its first major offensive into Iraq. Operation Ramadan was executed in three phases and lasted until 3 August. Its objective was to breach the Iraqi defences east of Basra, seize the key port city and count on a spontaneous Shiite uprising in the south against the Ba'th government. Despite inflicting heavy losses on the Iraqis and occupying 180 square miles in the south, the offensive was a disaster. The Iranians failed to overwhelm the Iraqis who stood their ground on the outskirts of Basra and repulsed the invaders. Apart from suffering substantial losses, Tehran's clerical establishment was very disappointed there was no Shiite rebellion.

When the offensive began in mid-July, Baghdad also reported border skirmishes between Iraqi and Syrian ground forces and renewed Syrian air force activity along their common frontier.[26] The failure of Operation Ramadan was a huge disappointment to officials in both Tehran and Damascus and prompted them to redouble their efforts to destabilize the Iraqi regime internally. To orchestrate their joint strategy, General al-Khouli, the chief of Syrian air force intelligence, and two high-ranking military intelligence officers were dispatched to Tehran to coordinate their activities with Iranian officials and representatives of the Iraqi Al-Dawa party. Al-Khouli's two companions remained in Iran to facilitate planning and cooperation with their Iranian counterparts and the Iraqi opposition.[27] This led to an intensification of sabotage and subversion in Iraq and abroad. In early August, the Iraqi ministry of planning in Baghdad was car bombed and the Iraqi embassy in Paris was attacked. A primary goal of this joint Syrian–Iranian effort was to create too unsafe an atmosphere in Baghdad to convene the NAM summit.[28]

Regionally and internationally, Operation Ramadan was a political watershed because it changed the nature of the conflict and how various actors perceived it. It demonstrated that the Islamic Republic was bent on exporting its revolution, toppling the Iraqi Ba'th Party in the process and radically altering the political map of the Middle East. It forced the moderate Arab states, France and the USA to throw their weight behind Iraq even more, and made the USSR critically reassess its pro-Iranian stance and realign itself in order to prop up Saddam Hussein. On the domestic level, Iran's failure to capture Basra clearly demonstrated the resilience of the Iraqi armed forces in rising to the occasion to defend the homeland, rallied popular support around the Ba'thists and showed that the Iraqi Shiites were unwilling to collaborate with their Iranian coreligionists in the conflict.

Khorramshahr's fall initially made Gulf Arabs and Egyptians reluctant to help Iraq or openly support their Arab brethren, but Iraq's successful defence of Basra changed the situation. In an interview in Riyadh with the London-based daily *Al-Sharq Al-Awsat* immediately after Iran's defeat in the first phase of Operation Ramadan, Kamal Hasan Ali, Egyptian deputy and foreign minister, said that Cairo would continue to give Iraq military hardware and supplies. He then criticized Syria's conduct in the Lebanon and Gulf conflicts.[29] As early as mid-July, Iraq's staunchest ally King Hussein of Jordan, referring to the Israeli invasion of Lebanon and the Iranian invasion of Iraq, called for an emergency Arab summit to discuss 'the fateful challenges facing the Arab nation'. He lashed out at Iran, accusing it of complicity with Israel. He denounced Iran's Operation Ramadan for giving Israel *carte blanche* to do as it wished in Lebanon.[30]

Indeed, Jordan and other Arab states concerned about Iran's intransigence were presented with a golden opportunity to voice their concerns and urge greater inter-Arab cooperation and solidarity at the Fez II summit in September. In the period leading up to the meeting, there was some diplomatic activity among members of the anti-Iraq bloc. A few days prior to the summit, Hafez Assad received Iranian deputy foreign minister Ahmad Azizi and discussed regional developments and bilateral ties. At the same time, Algerian foreign minister Dr Ahmed Taleb Ibrahimi arrived in Tehran for talks with Iranian officials. The purpose of these meetings seems to have been to harmonize positions on regional issues. Before discussing Syria's participation at the Fez conference and Syrian–Iranian cooperation in the closing months of 1982, it is necessary to look at Syrian policy in Lebanon during the summer.

Syria's confrontation with Israel and Iran's Lebanon policy

As mentioned earlier, though Damascus had seen the Israeli military build-up along the Lebanese border in the two months before the invasion, it was surprised by the scale and scope of the attack. Only on 8 June, the third day of Operation Peace in the Galilee, did the Syrians decide to take a stand against an advancing Israeli armoured spearhead at the strategically-located crossroad town of Jezzine (dominating the axes leading to the Shouf Mountains, the Bekaa Valley, Sidon and southern Lebanon). For the next three days there was intense fighting between Israeli and Syrian forces along the three major axes of the Israeli thrust north and in the air. By 11 June, when Menachem Begin finally accepted a US ceasefire proposal and subsequently announced a unilateral end to hostilities, the Syrian forces in Lebanon had suffered an enormous blow. Within a 72-hour period, the IDF had knocked out 400 Syrian tanks, 90 combat aircraft, 100 artillery/missile batteries, 70 armoured vehicles and inflicted about 1900 casualties.[31] Assad knew he was outmatched qualitatively and quantitatively. Despite heavy losses, the Syrians had not been routed. The bulk of their forces remained intact. Assad's decision to engage the Israelis had been a carefully calibrated response to avoid the two possible scenarios that Saddam Hussein had hoped would materialize. Avoiding a confrontation with the invading army would have allowed him to save most of the Syrian forces in Lebanon, but would no doubt have brought Syrian dominance over the country to an end and greatly diminished Assad's prestige and influence both at home and in the Arab world. Conversely, had he committed the majority of his forces to battle and waged total war against the Israelis (as the Iranian clerics advocated), the Syrian army would have been annihilated and lost its foothold in Lebanon permanently.[32] Moreover, the latter was not a viable option because all-out war could have led to an Israeli invasion of Syria through the Bekaa Valley and Golan Heights, with the loss of Syrian territory and the collapse of the Syrian Ba'th regime. Assad's Iranian allies initially advocated total war against Israel with Iranian participation.[33] Assad strenuously objected to such suggestions, and instead pursued an alternative course of action to preserve

Syrian interests in Lebanon as far as possible and deliver limited blows to the Israelis in the process.

The 11 June ceasefire gave Assad breathing space to regroup and reinforce his troops. The elite third armoured division, equipped with advanced Soviet-made T-72 tanks, was immediately moved into Lebanon to take up defensive positions in the Bekaa. Once the deployment was complete, the IDF never again attempted to make further advances along its eastern front. Furthermore, Syria's decision to bring crack commando battalions into the fray in the early days of the invasion stymied Israeli efforts to reach the Shouf and the Beirut–Damascus highway by the 11 June ceasefire. Overall, the IDF's inability to achieve its objectives rapidly and the Syrian defenders' unexpectedly stiff resistance, persuaded Israeli military planners to move their forces away from the east and concentrate on pushing towards Beirut and the Beirut–Damascus highway along the western and central axes. Between 12 and 25 June, the IDF resumed its advance towards Beirut and the international highway (on the pretext that the Palestinians and Syrians had violated the ceasefire) and eventually succeeded in gaining control of the highway and laying siege to the Lebanese capital. According to some reports, some Iranian soldiers were fighting alongside some Palestinian units in West Beirut.[34] There were claims by Tel Aviv that several hundred were also involved in clashes with the IDF in the Syrian-held Alei (Alayh) district, southeast of Beirut in the central sector.[35]

On 25 June, after pressure from the Reagan administration (when Tel Aviv had attained its operational objective of reaching Beirut), the Israeli government again announced a unilateral ceasefire. The primary goal now was to get rid of the PLO infrastructure in Beirut and facilitate the establishment of a Maronite government in Lebanon (freed from the shackles of Syrian and Palestinian dominance) that would be willing to sign a peace treaty with Israel. The IDF then started a siege and simultaneous bombardment of the city to achieve the desired outcome. Syrian troops, Shiite Amal militiamen and 14,000 Palestinian fighters were trapped in West Beirut. The Syrian forces were primarily composed of the 85th infantry brigade, and the PLA's Hittin and Qadisiyah brigades. Khomeini spoke out against the 'deadly silence' in the Arab world and the failure of many Arab states to send troops to stem the Israeli invasion. He called on them to join the ranks of Syria, Iran and the PLO to defend the dignity of Islam against the 'Zionist' onslaught.[36]

Despite massive Israeli artillery and aerial bombardment lasting until mid-August, the defenders put up an unexpectedly firm resistance. With a ceasefire in effect on all other fronts, Damascus took advantage of this period to rebuild and upgrade its armed forces with help from the USSR. In addition, Assad was content to see the IDF tied down in a brutal campaign to force the defenders to submit by destroying parts of the city and killing civilians – in the process bringing international condemnation of its actions. Finally, in mid-August, US envoy Philip Habib hammered out an agreement between the two sides to withdraw the Palestinians and Syrians from Beirut under the supervision of a multinational force comprised of Western troops. The evacuation began on 21 August and was complete by the end of the month. While most Palestinians left for other Arab countries by sea, the 6000 remaining Syrian and PLA soldiers withdrew via the Beirut–Damascus highway to the Bekaa and Syria.

By September, Assad's fortunes were at a low point; in three months his power and influence had plunged to new depths. Many Syrian units in Lebanon had been destroyed (demonstrating the inferiority of their conventional capabilities), large parts of the country had been lost to the enemy, and Syria's prestige and image had been severely tarnished. To make matters worse, on 23 August, the pro-Israeli Phalange Party leader Bashir Gemayel was elected as Lebanon's new president. Worse still, US President Ronald Reagan announced his Reagan Plan to create a Jordanian–Palestinian confederation that included the West Bank and Gaza Strip, with no mention of Syria or the Golan Heights. Having been rendered militarily impotent by the Israelis, faced with a political *fait accompli* in Lebanon and isolated in the Arab world, Assad set out to recoup his regional power and standing. The first step was to attend the Fez II summit in early September.

The Fez II summit and its consequences

As shown in Chapter 1, Syria boycotted the Amman summit in November 1980 and only sent a low-level delegation to the Fez I summit the next year. However, in its weak and vulnerable state after the initial phase of the Lebanon war, Assad felt obliged to attend Fez II to avoid the risk of even more criticism and isolation in the Arab world.[37] The highlight of the summit was a four-hour meeting on 8 September attended by Hafez Assad and Saddam Hussein at the behest of King Hussein, King Fahd, King Hassan of Morocco and the Emir of Kuwait, all of whom were present at the meeting. It resulted in Assad accepting a strongly-worded pro-Iraq resolution on the Gulf War and agreeing to meet the Iraqi leader again (in the Saudi mon-

arch's presence) within two months.[38] Syria's acceptance of the resolution reflected its weak and awkward position due to its painful predicament in Lebanon and 'deviant' behaviour in supporting non-Arab
Iran.[39] Although the Syrian and Iranian state-controlled media left out
all references to this particular section of the final statement, the
Iranian foreign ministry nonetheless condemned the Arab summit.[40]

Immediately after the summit, Assad dispatched his close aide and
political confidant Ahmad Iskandar Ahmad and deputy foreign minister Nasir Qaddur to Tehran to reassure the Iranian leadership of
Syria's commitment to the alliance and continued support for Iran's
'firm and principled stand'. They met President Khamene'i, Rafsanjani
and other officials over a two-day period. Ahmad defended Assad's
decision to meet Saddam Hussein by describing the meeting as mere
protocol and politically insignificant. In an official statement, before
his departure from Iran, he declared:

> We consider the Iranian revolution the most important event in
> the second half of the twentieth century. We also consider it a
> positive development in this age. This revolution has turned the
> Iranian people and capabilities from an alliance with Israel and
> enemies into an alliance with the Arabs, struggling with us
> against Zionism and US imperialism for the sake of liberating
> holy Jerusalem.[41]

The overall tone of his statement seemed apologetic. He admitted that
Iran was justified to denounce the Fez resolution and said that the
mutual animosity between Baghdad and Damascus left no room for
dialogue or compromise until one of the two Ba'thist regimes had
been overthrown.

Syria's handling of the Fez summit showed how much political
clout and room for manoeuvre it had lost since the defeat in Lebanon.
To prevent a further slide into isolation and perhaps banishment
from the Arab fold, at the very least, it needed to play an active role in
Arab politics. Its military inferiority and political isolation in the Arab
world meant that, to reverse Tel Aviv's gains in Lebanon, it now
needed revolutionary Iran more than ever. Political exigencies in the
region necessitated even closer cooperation with the Islamic Republic
now that it had taken the war into Iraq. Syria's collaboration with Iran
was no longer to enable the latter to stave off defeat in the Gulf War,
but to maintain pressure on Ba'thist Iraq and utilize Iranian support
and influence in Lebanon to thwart Tel Aviv's ambitions.

Syria's 'sword and shield' strategy in Lebanon

By September 1982 Assad was facing numerous insurmountable obstacles. After the bitter defeat in his military confrontation with Israel, waging a conventional war was no longer an option. Also, he now faced a large Israeli military presence in Lebanon, a new government in Beirut that did not share his goals, and a US administration that saw him as a Soviet puppet and vehemently opposed every aspect of his policy in the region. Despite the complexities of the situation, Assad devised a simple two-pronged strategy that would seek to minimize the risk of further escalation or a direct military confrontation with Israel and the USA, and simultaneously roll back the IDF. Assad's policy consisted of two components (one offensive and the other defensive), hereafter referred to as the 'sword and shield' strategy, which was highly dependent on the goodwill and help of Syria's two primary allies – Iran and the USSR.

The political linchpin of the 'sword and shield' strategy to buttress Syria's position in relation to the Bashir Gemayel regime, Israel and the USA was Syria's special relationship with its superpower patron, the USSR, and its main regional partner, Iran. From September 1982, the Syrians started to use Iran's influence over the Lebanese Shiite community to help their two Shiite allies wage a campaign of terrorism, subversion and guerrilla attacks against their mutual opponents. The use of unconventional warfare as an offensive instrument served as the 'sword' in Syria's strategy. Damascus took advantage of its role as Moscow's only major ally in the region to demand Soviet-made conventional arms to replenish its losses from the war, and achieve 'strategic parity' with Tel Aviv over the long term. Soviet replenishments would thus serve to build a conventional deterrent that would act as the 'shield' in the overall scheme. In addition to putting their ties with Iran and the USSR to good use, the Syrians also mobilized other political and sectarian groupings within Lebanon to wage war against the Israeli forces.

The first significant incident was on 14 September, when a tremendous blast ripped through the Phalange Party headquarters, killing President Bashir Gemayel and more than 30 of his associates. Subsequent events showed that a clandestine SSNP member, whom Syrian intelligence had activated, had planted the explosive. The assassination came as a huge shock to the Israeli leadership, which had pinned much hope on establishing a close working relationship with the new Lebanese president. At a stroke, one of the main pillars of the Pax Hebraica Menachem Begin had envisioned was dismantled.

Though not known for having pro-Israeli credentials, Bashir Gemayel's brother Amin, who was elected a week later, was the best the Israelis could hope for under the circumstances. The process of gradually denying the Israelis the fruits of their initial military victory had been set in motion. Syria's patient planning and close collaboration with Iran and the Lebanese Shiites, coupled with egregious acts committed by Israel and its allies, encouraged the Shiites to resist the imposition of an Israeli–Maronite diktat.

The Syrian–Iranian axis and the Lebanese Shiite community

Ironically, in the initial phase of Operation Peace in the Galilee, most Lebanese Shiites welcomed the expulsion of Palestinians from the south and indeed saw the Israelis as liberators. Palestinian heavy-handedness and arrogance over the years had alienated many of their Shiite 'Arab brethren' who by 1982 had lost sympathy for the Palestinians' plight. In fact, in the early days of the invasion, the mainstream Shiite Amal movement condemned the Israeli attack but did not call for a military confrontation or popular uprising against the IDF. Because of the destruction of the PLO's infrastructure in the south and the evacuation of its forces from Beirut in August 1982, the Shiite militias were able to strengthen their presence in West Beirut and other parts of the country. Amal, in particular, was able to maintain a powerful and disciplined force. Two developments in this period, however, turned the Shiite community against the IDF and Gemayel government. First, with Syrian and Iranian encouragement, local resistance slowly began to grow once it became clear that the Israelis intended to stay indefinitely, especially given their brutal conduct in the areas they occupied (which were predominantly Shiite).[42] Second, following the Israeli withdrawal from Beirut (which had been a precondition for the return of the multinational force) in late September, the US-supported Lebanese army entered West Beirut to reassert control of the remainder of the city. However, its mistreatment of the Shiite inhabitants led to ferocious clashes with Shiite militiamen. Guerrilla activity against the IDF began to increase in south Lebanon, the most notable instance being the destruction of the IDF staff headquarters in the southern city of Tyre on 11 November, when 67 Israelis were killed.

By now, it was in both Damascus and Tehran's interest to mobilize the Lebanese Shiite community against their pro-US Maronite overlords in Beirut and their Israeli occupiers. Syria's relationship with Iran began to pay dividends when the need to 'unsheathe the Lebanese Shiite sword' overlapped with Tehran's mission to export the Islamic revolution and deal a decisive blow to 'Zionism and American imperialism'.[43] At this time, 2000 Iranian Revolutionary Guards were reportedly stationed in Ba'albek in the Syrian-held Bekaa Valley. They made their presence felt when, on 22 November, 300 men took over the town hall in Ba'albek and attacked the Lebanese army garrison in the town. Lebanese foreign minister Elie Salem summoned Iranian ambassador Hojjatolislam Musa Fakhr-Rouhani and lodged an official protest demanding immediate Iranian withdrawal from the area and threatening to sever diplomatic ties.[44] The Iranian ambassador flatly denied involvement and Iranian President Khamene'i subsequently insisted the Revolutionary Guards remain in Lebanon. By now, the Iranian Revolutionary Guards had close links with radical Shiite groups in the area, particularly with Hussein Musawi's Islamic Amal. Musawi, a Lebanese of Iranian descent, had previously been the military commander of the parent Amal movement. In the aftermath of the Israeli invasion, he broke away and, with Syrian and Iranian support, formed his own group in the Bekaa. He differed from Amal leader Nabih Berri over the movement's ideological orientation. Berri espoused the traditional Shiite position of loyalty to the Lebanese state and religious plurality within the framework of the existing political system, while Musawi saw the Lebanese political structure as fundamentally flawed and artificial. Instead, he advocated mass mobilization of Shiites towards the fulfilment of an Islamic revolution and the emulation of the Iranian theocratic state model.[45]

Contrary to the Gemayel government's wishes, Tehran bolstered its presence by dispatching more Revolutionary Guards to the Bekaa via Syria; they set up a radio station and stepped up their efforts to proselytize and indoctrinate Lebanese Shiites. None of this could have happened without the tacit cooperation of Damascus. The Iranians and Islamic Amal also managed to spread their influence to West Beirut's Shiite neighbourhoods.

As Tehran sought to expand its foothold in Lebanon, with the help of the Syrians and Shiite radicals, Damascus mobilized many of the other political parties that could prove beneficial in the struggle against Begin's grand strategy. These consisted of some of the key players in Lebanese politics, such as the Druze PSP, the Lebanese Ba'th Party, the Lebanese Communist Party and various other Shiite groups. While the result of these efforts was not immediately noticeable, they would have an enormous impact on the course of the political struggle in Lebanon the following year.

Syrian–Iranian cooperation and the Persian Gulf war

Although Syria had warned its Iranian allies that it would not condone an Iranian invasion of Iraq, and would seriously reconsider its
ties with Tehran, Syrian policy did not change in the aftermath of
Operation Ramadan. In fact, Syria continued to send Soviet-made
weapons to Iran.[46]

In the aftermath of Fez II, which brought strong Arab condemnation of Iran, the clerical regime in Tehran continued to nurture its
friendship with Damascus despite its disappointment at Assad's impo-
tence and lacklustre performance at the summit.[47] From Iran's viewpoint, with victory within reach and Iraq's incessant attempts to depict
the war as a historical continuation of the Arab–Persian conflict, there
were strong ideological and practical reasons to maintain cordial ties
and a close working relationship with Arab Syria, especially given the
growing military cooperation between Iraq and Egypt, and the poor
state of relations between Iran and many Gulf states, particularly
Saudi Arabia. Saudi–Iranian relations suffered during the hadj season
when Iranian pilgrims were involved in clashes with Saudi security
forces in the holy city of Mecca. There were mutual recriminations,
and bilateral relations deteriorated even further.

In an attempt to advance towards the Iraqi capital after a two-
month lull in the war, Iran finally resumed the offensive on 1 October,
with the launch of Operation Muslim Ibn Aqil in the central sector
(near the town of Mandali). Again, the Iraqis held their ground and
blunted the Iranian assault. During the Iranian offensive, the Sudan,
Jordan, Saudi Arabia and North Yemen expressed solidarity and support for Iraq. Also, a high-level Jordanian delegation headed by King
Hussein visited Baghdad during the hostilities to discuss avenues of
cooperation between the two sides.[48] With Iran determined to prosecute the war to the bitter end and Israel's ostensible victory in Lebanon, in an article reflecting official government opinion on 25
October, the Amman daily *Al-Dustur* called for an end to Egypt's
banishment from the Arab fold because it was detrimental to Arab
interests and would only benefit the enemies of the Arab nation.

On 1 November, the Iranians undertook their last major offensive
of the year, in the south. Codenamed 'Muharram al-Harram', the
main objective of the attack was to cut the Baghdad–Basra highway
and establish a bridgehead to serve as a springboard for further offensives against Basra. Though capturing the Bayat oilfield and destroying an Iraqi armoured brigade, the attackers failed to attain their main
goal and advanced only five miles in seven days of heavy fighting.

Meanwhile, the war of words between Tehran and Riyadh intensified. In a broadcast from Riyadh on 10 November the commentator
tried to arouse nationalist and religious sentiments by arguing that:

> The only factor in the continuation of this war is Iran's insis-
> tence and stubbornness in continuing the fighting. ... Today,
> Iraq stands in firm confrontation with plans that have been
> made by the enemies of Arabism and Islam who have chosen the
> Iranian regime to implement them. There is no way to thwart
> those plans and foil them, except by supporting Iraq financially
> and militarily in order to destroy the Iranian war machine.[49]

Iranian ripostes broadcast on Tehran's Arabic service bitterly criticized Saudi Arabia's 'unlimited support' for Saddam Hussein, accusing it of being a US lackey in the region. A propaganda campaign was
also waged against the GCC states, claiming that since the outbreak
of the Gulf War they had given $45 billion in financial aid to
Baghdad.[50] An editorial in the Iranian daily *Ettela'at* on 1 December,
characterized the GCC as a military security pact for propping up
decadent, repressive regimes that served as a substitute to CENTO to
further the interests of Washington.

Tehran's growing isolation from its Arab neighbours in this period
necessitated it forging closer links with its two remaining Arab allies,
Syria and Libya. During a visit by Libyan secretary for foreign liaison
Abd al-Ati al-Ubaydi to Tehran in early December, he declared that
the 'least punishment appropriate for Saddam is his overthrow', and
that Libya would assist Iran in the war 'in any way necessary'.[51]

The impact of deteriorating Soviet–Iranian relations

As mentioned in Chapter 1, despite having an operative friendship
treaty with Iraq, the USSR opposed its invasion and occupation of
Iran in September 1980, and suspended arms shipments to Iraq soon
after the war began. The Kremlin also perceived this as a golden
opportunity to win over Iran, the key strategic prize in the Persian
Gulf. However, with the expulsion of Iraqi forces from Iran by mid-
1982, and the first Iranian offensive against Basra in July, Moscow
expressed its displeasure at Iran continuing the conflict. The Kremlin's subsequent failure to persuade Iran to accept a negotiated settlement led to a resumption of Soviet arms deliveries to Iraq. This
resulted in a marked deterioration in Soviet–Iranian relations. By the
autumn of 1982, Iraq had begun to fire Soviet-built Scud-B and Frog-

7 surface-to-surface missiles at Dezful, Ahwaz and other Iranian border cities. Iran's state-controlled media carried scathing criticisms of the Tudeh (the Iranian communist party) and Soviet foreign policy.

During the same period, the Soviet vice-consul in Tehran, Vladimir Kuzichkin defected to British intelligence with documents revealing the extent of Soviet and Tudeh penetration of Iran. The British subsequently gave this information to the Iranian government, which eagerly embarked on a massive crackdown to destroy the Soviet–Tudeh network. By February 1983, the entire leadership and hundreds of Tudeh members had been arrested and charged with spying for the USSR. In April, 18 Soviet diplomats were summarily expelled. By the following month, the Tudeh had been officially banned and the Soviet embassy staff reduced by half. In December, ten top Tudeh members were executed after being tried and charged with infiltrating the armed forces and providing military secrets to the USSR. Within a matter of a few months, the entire Tudeh infrastructure and Soviet network that had been painstakingly developed was destroyed. Besides the internal crackdown on pro-Soviet elements, the government continued its anti-communist media campaign, and started to provide substantial amounts of aid to Afghan guerrilla movements.

The marked deterioration in Soviet–Iranian relations at this time also affected Syria's ties with both its superpower patron and its Iranian ally. While Assad's dependence on Moscow grew noticeably in the aftermath of the defeat in Lebanon, he was able to strengthen his position vis-à-vis the Kremlin and demand extra military assistance because of the rupture in Soviet–Iranian relations at a time when Soviet–Iraqi ties were just starting to thaw. Furthermore, the Kremlin could ill afford to ignore the plight of its only major regional ally at a time when Washington was pursuing an activist policy in the Middle East and supporting Israel in order to diminish Soviet power and influence in the area.[52] The breakdown in cooperation between the USSR and Iran also increased the value and utility of the Syrian–Iranian axis from Tehran's viewpoint. Iranian enmity towards both superpowers meant that greater emphasis would have to be put on forging even closer ties with regional allies like Syria. Thus, Syria's role assumed even greater importance in both Tehran and Moscow since it could serve as an intermediary between the two parties.

Partly to avoid being trapped in an awkward position between their two closest friends, the Syrians undertook to stop any further worsening of Soviet–Iranian relations.[53] In fact, they attempted to effect a

Soviet–Iranian *rapprochement*. However, by March 1983, their efforts had fallen short of their initial expectations.[54] Syrian–Iranian relations became strained when Damascus granted some Tudeh members political asylum in Syria. Furthermore, the revolutionary clerics in Tehran disapproved of Moscow's attempts to reconcile existing differences between Syria and Iraq.[55]

The emergence of the Egyptian–Jordanian–Iraqi axis

By late 1982, there were definite signs of Egypt gradually making inroads into the Arab world. Major steps were taken to cement relations with Jordan and Iraq. On 9 December, Egypt's foreign minister Boutros Boutros-Ghali visited Amman bearing a message from Husni Mubarak for King Hussein. Then, on 28 December, in a statement in the Egyptian daily *Al-Ahram*, Iraqi foreign minister Tareq Aziz declared that 'the Arab structure could not be straightened without Egypt'. He went on to explain that the enemies of the Arab nation had failed in their efforts to isolate Egypt, and stressed Baghdad's willingness to restore diplomatic relations with Cairo. Aziz also announced that he would be prepared to meet high-ranking Egyptian officials in Cairo, Baghdad or anywhere else to discuss the resumption of bilateral relations. This elicited a positive response from the Egyptians. From their perspective, an Egyptian–Iraqi *rapprochement* was an important stepping stone towards their eventual reintegration into the Arab world.

Indeed, in the last half of 1982, the continuation of the Gulf conflict and Iran's incessant attempts to penetrate deep into Iraqi territory proved to be important catalysts for Egypt's gradual return to the Arab fold. Besides, with growing cooperation between Cairo and Baghdad and material assistance being given to Iraq, both sides tried to present their coordinated effort to thwart Iranian ambitions in terms of pan-Arab interests and condemned renegade Arab states like Syria for stabbing the Arab nation in the back. For example, in his Army Day speech, Saddam Hussein bitterly criticized Syria's 'collusion with the [Arab] nation's enemies' and warned that Iran's actions, which had prolonged the war, were 'not only a plot against Iraq, but against the Arab nation, Arab civilization and the Arabs' entire security and future'.[56] In an interview in the Arab press, Egypt's President Mubarak denounced Iran's Arab allies Syria and Libya. He singled out Syria in particular, saying that 'it is unbecoming of Syria to stand with Iran against Iraq. The Syrians at least, should have played the role of mediators.'[57] In mid-January, shuttling between

Baghdad and Damascus, Saudi Crown Prince Abdullah took the initiative to bring about a Syrian–Iraqi *rapprochement*. His objective was twofold. First, to convince Syria to change its stance in the Gulf War to one of benevolent neutrality, thereby reopening the trans-Syrian pipeline and boosting Iraq's position economically, and second, to deny Iran its most valuable Arab ally, thus inflicting a major psychological and political blow on Tehran. The Saudis calculated that delivering such a *coup de grâce* could induce Iran to accept a ceasefire.[58] In the meantime, King Hussein visited Iraq and other Gulf Arab states to rally support for Baghdad's cause, while Syria's foreign minister toured the Gulf sheikhdoms to prevent the emergence of a sizeable Arab bloc to neutralize the Tehran–Damascus axis. During talks with King Fahd, Khaddam flatly rejected the Saudi monarch's offer to mediate and arrange a meeting between the Syrian and Iraqi heads of state. Moreover, a generous Saudi offer of $2 billion in return for reopening of the trans-Syrian IPC pipeline was also turned down.[59]

Instead, to Riyadh's chagrin, in late January, Syria organized a high-level meeting in Damascus to rally Arab support for Iran's position in the Gulf War. On 20 January, Iranian foreign minister Velayati and Libyan justice minister Muhammad al-Zouai arrived in Damascus for a tripartite meeting to harmonize their policies and positions on a whole host of issues. On his arrival, Velayati immediately went into conference with Hafez Assad. Meetings were also held between Syrian foreign minister Khaddam, his Iranian counterpart and the Libyan emissary. On 23 January, after three days of talks, a joint Syrian–Iranian–Libyan communiqué was issued calling for Arab solidarity with Iran and the overthrow of Iraqi president Saddam Hussein.[60] Moreover, it reiterated Syrian and Libyan support for the Islamic Republic and stressed a need to reactivate the Steadfastness Front to 'confront instigations by imperialism and Zionism' and the vital contribution of Iran to its cause.[61] The strongly-worded communiqué also condemned the invasion of Lebanon and promised to provide financial and material support to the Lebanese resistance to end the Israeli occupation. The participants denounced 'all attempts aimed at forcing the PLO to make concessions diametrically opposed to the just struggles and legitimate objectives of the organization … [and] attempts by imperialism and Zionism to create a Baghdad–Cairo axis in order to confront the revolutionary forces in the region'.[62] The tripartite declaration opposed any actions to resuscitate the peace process as an extension of the Camp David accords, and any 'attempts to return Egypt to the Arab fold and Islamic organizations unless [it rejected] the treacherous Camp David Accords'.[63]

The tripartite meeting in Damascus must have been a major disappointment to Riyadh given its strenuous efforts to induce the Assad regime to abandon its alliance with Iran. However, from a Syrian viewpoint, it made sense to bolster its cooperation with Tehran and Tripoli. Support for Iran was necessary to check Iraqi regional ambitions and ensure that Saddam Hussein and the Iraqi Ba'th Party did not emerge unscathed from a conflict they had initiated in the first place. Furthermore, Assad was not about to allow Washington to regain the initiative by hammering out a peace treaty between Israel and Lebanon, and drawing the Palestinians and Jordanians into negotiations with Tel Aviv. He intended to erode Arafat's power base by propping up rejectionist factions within the PLO who were engaged in a power struggle with Fatah, obstruct US plans in Lebanon to secure a peace agreement between Beirut and Tel Aviv, and block or at least weaken the power and influence of the emergent Cairo–Amman–Baghdad axis, which had Washington and Riyadh's blessing.[64]

The Damascus tripartite communiqué drew harsh reactions from Baghdad and Amman. They accused Syria and Libya of betraying the pan-Arab cause and jeopardizing the security of the Arab nation by lending support and encouragement to 'a war of expansionist Iranian ambitions'.[65] Besides attacking Damascus and Tripoli's stance on the Gulf War, Iraq asked the Arab League in Tunis to punish Iran's two Arab allies for their collusion with the Islamic Republic.[66]

At a time when Iranian influence was waning in the Arab world, and more states were rallying to Iraq's support, the Damascus tripartite declaration represented a limited, but nonetheless important symbolic victory to the clerical regime in Tehran, giving it a psychological boost and enabling it to dismiss anti-Iranian Arab propaganda about the Gulf War being a continuation of the historical Arab–Persian conflict. Syria also took other measures to aid its Iranian ally to prosecute the war and preserve its growing presence in Lebanon. Damascus seems to have successfully mediated an arms-for-oil deal between Tehran and Pyonyang, and turned down a request by US envoy Philip Habib to expel the Iranian Revolutionary Guards operating in the Bekaa Valley region.[67]

Iran's winter offensive and Syria's role

By early 1983, the hardliners on Iran's SDC, led by Khomeini's representative Rafsanjani, were pressing for renewed military action in

Iraqi as soon as possible. Despite the military high command's strong reservations, the radical camp believed that one more decisive engagement would turn the tide of the war. The military commanders were loath to carry out an offensive in inclement weather and use unorthodox 'human-wave' tactics that would bring high casualties and possibly not yield any substantive results. The insistence of the hawks was largely based on domestic conditions within Iraq, which led them to believe that it was on its last legs.

Indeed, there was some merit to their arguments at the time. Inside Iraq, morale was low. The country had lost the initiative in a conflict it clearly could not win, and it was now stuck in an endless war against a relentless foe. With a population one-third the size of Iran's, it could not sustain high casualty rates. On the economic front, the destruction of its oil installations in the Gulf and the inoperability of the trans-Syrian pipeline meant that it could export only just over 600,000 barrels of oil a day, while Iran's production had bounced back to 3.2 million barrels in the winter of 1983.[68] In both Baghdad and Tehran, policy makers were convinced that time was on Iran's side. Therefore, once again, the hawks on the SDC prevailed over the better judgement of the military commanders and, on 6 February, the Iranians launched Operation Wal-Fajr (At Dawn) in an attempt to seize the southern town of Amara on the Basra–Baghdad highway. After several days of heavy combat, which cost both sides 7000 to 15,000 casualties, the fighting ended in defeat for the Iranians who failed to attain their objectives and incurred many more losses than the Iraqi defenders.[69]

The failure of Wal-Fajr was a significant turning point in this stage of the war, for the military now advocated ending major offensive operations and turning the conflict into a war of attrition. In subsequent SDC deliberations, the military commanders finally prevailed by arguing that exerting steady but limited pressure along the 650-mile front would force the Iraqis to overstretch their already scarce resources to breaking point. In the aftermath of Wal-Fajr, Tehran undertook other offensive operations during 1983, but on a more limited scale as the military had prescribed.

A few days before the Wal-Fajr attack, Syrian information minister Ahmad Iskandar Ahmad came to Tehran with a message from Hafez Assad to Ali Khamene'i and had talks with Prime Minister Musavi and Speaker Rafsanjani. At this juncture, to complement the resumption of military operations in early 1983, with Syrian help, Tehran initiated a diplomatic offensive. Following deliberations with Iranian officials, Syrian envoy Ahmad flew to Riyadh to reassure the Saudis that Iran's ambitions did not extend beyond toppling Saddam Hussein. Exporting the revolution to the Gulf sheikhdoms was not part of its plans. While Iranian envoys had assuaged the concerns of some Gulf states in recent visits, the Saudis had been particularly irked by Iran's policies in the Gulf and conduct in OPEC. In a speech reflecting the general Iranian position towards the Gulf states, Rafsanjani elucidated that:

> the Islamic Republic is generally against aggression against other countries, and particularly neighbouring Muslim countries. The concept of exporting revolution is not one of resorting to force to impose the revolution on others ... [The least we expect is for the Gulf countries] to maintain their neutrality if they do not want to defend justice ... so that we can justify our forgiveness of these sins.[70]

In the disappointing aftermath of Wal-Fajr, Tehran and Damascus continued to cooperate and try to coordinate their actions more closely to prevent further erosion of their overall regional position. In late February, President Khamene'i sent his deputy foreign minister Ahmad Azizi to Damascus for consultations with Assad. The following month, in the light of the rapid deterioration of Soviet–Iranian relations, reports indicate that Syria tried to mediate between the two parties, though its efforts proved to be futile.[71] With regard to military cooperation against Iraq, it is worth noting that by early 1983, Syrian military personnel had established a permanent presence in the general headquarters at the Iranian Ministry of Defence, where they gave advice and intelligence on Iraqi military strategy, tactics, planning, training and the use of Soviet weaponry.[72]

In early spring, Tehran and Damascus revitalized and intensified their collaboration in various ways. A new oil agreement was negotiated in early April in which Iran agreed to provide five million tons of crude oil to be paid for by a combination of hard currency and barter, and an additional one million tons of oil free of charge. Tehran justified the generous gift as a contribution to the Syrian confrontation with Israel in Lebanon. Although the original agreement negotiated the previous year had stipulated that Iran export eight million tons of oil to its Arab ally, Syria had been unable to keep up with the payments under the terms of the deal.[73]

Once the agreement had been concluded in Tehran, Iranian foreign minister Velayati flew to Damascus for talks with Assad on 'bilateral relations and issues of common interest'. Subsequent reports suggest that Syria allowed Iran to increase its presence in the Bekaa area.[74] By now, Assad was ready, with Tehran's help, to spoil the grand design that Washington and Tel Aviv had in mind for Lebanon. He was determined to resist what he perceived as a 'US–Israeli diktat' with the political backing of Iran and the military support of the USSR.

Changing balances of power and the limits of the alliance

While Iran sought to mend fences with the Gulf Arab states, Iraq and Egypt tried to consolidate their budding friendship. Baghdad lobbied to readmit Egypt into the Arab League, expressed willingness to recognize Israel under the terms of the Fez II resolution, and approved of PLO–Jordanian efforts to move the peace process forward. In a significant move on 7 January, the foreign ministers of Egypt and Iraq met for the first time in four years. After their discussions Iraqi foreign minister Tareq Aziz praised Egypt for its solidarity and support for his country in the Gulf War. A month later, Egyptian foreign minister Boutros-Ghali, and undersecretary and director of the president's office for political affairs Dr Usamah al-Baz, flew to Baghdad (on the last leg of a trip to Amman and Beirut) where Saddam Hussein received them. Boutros-Ghali conveyed a message from Mubarak 'expressing Egypt's solidarity with Iraq in its war against the Iranian regime's aggression, which [had] Iraq and the Arab nation as its target'.[75] Ironically, the more Tehran tried to pursue the military option in its war with Iraq, the more impetus it gave to the *rapprochement* between Egypt and Iraq, to the formation of the Egyptian–Jordanian–Iraqi axis and, consequently, to the gradual diminution of Syrian–Iranian power and influence in the Middle East.

Tehran's policy for the prosecution of the war after spring 1982 was tactically and strategically flawed. The government's radical faction led by Khomeini and Rafsanjani overestimated Iran's conventional military capability and its ability to score victories with unorthodox methods of warfare (such as human-wave tactics and tapping into the revolutionary fervour of volunteers and guards). They also underestimated the resilience and determination of the Iraqis to defend their homeland. Although one can only speculate in retrospect, if General Zahir-Nejhad's advice to launch offensive operations with conventional tactics only after proper training and careful planning had been heeded, the military situation in 1983 may have been very different. The hastily planned and poorly executed Iranian offensives between July 1982 and February 1983 not only proved futile, but also alerted the pro-Iraqi camp into taking drastic measures to avert an Iranian victory. Also, increasing Egyptian military assistance had a major impact on Iraq's military capability. Politically, the war provided the catalyst for Iraq, Jordan and, to a lesser degree, Saudi Arabia to put aside their differences with Egypt and coordinate their policies to meet the challenge the ascendant Syrian–Iranian alliance posed. By February 1984, when Iran had finally given up on the war of attrition and reverted to launching major offensives, the balance of power – both politically and militarily – had noticeably shifted in Iraq's favour. In reality, Iran's window of opportunity to deliver a decisive blow against its foe militarily in set-piece battles had been closed.

On the other hand, Syria learned from its costly defeat by the Israelis in June 1982. Between September 1982 and April 1983, Assad lay low, feigning total military and political paralysis. He rallied scarce resources and, with the aid of the USSR, gradually rebuilt his conventional forces to assume a credible defensive posture against Washington and Tel Aviv. At the same time, Damascus cultivated ties and formed links with various groups in Lebanon that shared its animosity to the USA, Israel and the Gemayel government. Many of these groups would, with Iranian support, eventually serve as the primary offensive instrument against their foes in Lebanon, without directly involving Syria or Iran in the tug-of-war that followed between 1983 and 1984. By spring 1983, Assad had strengthened his position enough to feel confident to pick up the gauntlet in Lebanon.

The Syrian–Iranian struggle in Lebanon

While the Gulf had been the main area of Syrian–Iranian cooperation between 1980 and 1982, by spring 1983, the focus of their activities against their mutual foes (the USA, Gemayel government, Israel and to a lesser extent France) had shifted to Lebanon. Although Syria's objectives in Lebanon were apparent, Iran's multifold ambitions were more complex and less tangible. From the outset of the Israeli invasion, Tehran had been eager to play an active role in the unravelling Lebanese state. The Islamic Republic saw the war-torn land as an appropriate theatre to which to export its revolution. There, it could convert the local Shiite population, fight Israel and its Western backers, cooperate meaningfully with its most valued Arab ally and improve its bargaining position with Syria (which became the more dominant partner in the alliance when Iraq invaded Iran). And, to bolster its ideological position and for propaganda purposes, it could explode the pro-Iraqi myth that the Islamic Republic was pursuing policies similar to those of Pahlavi Iran to subjugate the Arab nation.

The chief coordinator of Iranian activities in Syria and Lebanon was Tehran's ambassador to Damascus, Hojjatolislam Ali Akbar Mohtashami. His main Syrian contact was Brigadier-General Ghazi Kan'an, head of Syrian military intelligence (G2 section) in Lebanon. With Syrian acquiescence, Iran was able to keep 1500 Revolutionary Guards in the Bekaa Valley. The Iranian contingent worked intimately with local radical Shiite groupings like Hussein Musawi's Islamic Amal and Hezbollah (the Party of God) led by Abbas al-Musawi and Sheikh Subhi al-Tufayli. As well as paramilitary personnel, the Iranians brought clerics to the area to expose the local inhabitants to their brand of religious and ideological indoctrination.[76] Although Ba'thist Syrians did not share revolutionary Iran's vision of turning Lebanon into an Islamic republic, they were severely constrained after their military defeat by the IDF and therefore needed Iranian assistance to co-opt the largest sectarian group, the Shiites, as part of their strategy to wage a proxy war against the Israelis in Lebanon.

By March 1983, there were clear signs of Shiite activity brewing in the Bekaa. In one incident, Islamic Amal militiamen and Iranian Revolutionary Guards clashed with Lebanese troops in the town of Brital and four Lebanese soldiers, including a colonel, were wounded.[77] Iranian Revolutionary Guards and their Shiite Lebanese allies also attacked the Lebanese army barracks in Ba'albek. Some Iranian and Islamic Amal personnel infiltrated the Shiite suburbs of Beirut to mount operations against Western powers supporting the Lebanese regime.[78] There were intermittent skirmishes between pro-Iranian Shiite militiamen and MNF troops, particularly members of the US and French contingents. The number of these instances increased in March and April. The *coup de grâce* came on 18 April, when a truck laden with explosives blew up the US embassy in Beirut killing at least 63 people. Senior CIA Middle East expert Robert Clayton Ames (director of the CIA's office of analysis for the Near East and South Asia), the CIA station chief, his deputy, and other agency personnel and support staff were among the dead. A secret meeting of CIA officials and agents was apparently in progress when the blast occurred. In all, nine CIA personnel (virtually the entire intelligence team in Beirut) were annihilated at a stroke. Ironically, Ames, who had been a former CIA station chief in Beirut, was visiting

Lebanon to investigate the new phenomenon of Shiite political activism and terror and ended up as an unwitting victim of it.

Though an unknown group called Islamic Jihad claimed responsibility for the attack, the consensus in the diplomatic community in Beirut and Western capitals was that it had been perpetrated by radical pro-Iranian Shiites supported by the Syrian and Iranian governments.[79] Tehran was quick to deny involvement, but most of the evidence to emerge revealed that Iran had masterminded the operation with Syrian complicity.[80]

Though the bombing of the US embassy had no immediate impact on the course of events in Lebanon, symbolically and psychologically it unnerved the US government (and boosted the confidence of its foes). The incident clearly demonstrated that the main foreign benefactor of the Gemayel regime and Israel could not effectively protect its own interests in the war-torn land. The death of Robert Ames, who had been US secretary of state George Shultz's right-hand man on Middle Eastern affairs, was a major loss to the Reagan administration. Without his key adviser, Shultz was uncertain about how best to safeguard and promote US interests in the region.[81] While the Reagan administration's primary objective was to broker a bilateral peace agreement between Israel and Lebanon, Assad was determined to throw as many obstacles as he could in Washington's path to prevent the fruition of a deal. By now, the whole thrust of Assad's diplomacy – and Soviet Premier Yuri Andropov's, for that matter – was to force the USA and Israel to accept their view that peace could only be achieved through collective bargaining and a comprehensive settlement involving all parties, not 'piecemeal' measures like bilateral treaties.[82] Indeed, the US tendency to view regional developments through the prism of cold war politics and the fact that Washington went to such lengths to help the Israelis achieve their goals in Lebanon, coupled with Syria's military defeat at the hands of the IDF and the deterioration of Soviet–Iranian relations, prompted Andropov to take decisive steps to prop up his Arab ally militarily as the possibility of another Syrian–Israeli confrontation began to loom on the horizon.[83]

Assad reacted to the Israeli–Lebanese peace agreement of 17 May by raising the stakes in the conflict with Israel. Syrian ground forces held manoeuvres near the Golan Heights, and other units near the Israeli and Lebanese border were put on alert. In addition, the Syrian military presence in Lebanon and near the Bekaa was increased to 50,000 men. Damascus vehemently opposed the agreement, charging that it rewarded Israeli aggression in Lebanon by granting it political and security concessions.[84] Assad deliberately upped the ante by daring the Israelis to assault his new protective 'shield'. He then unsheathed the 'sword' by unleashing pro-Syrian Lebanese and Palestinian guerrillas against the IDF in Lebanon. There was a significant increase in the number of armed clashes between the Israelis and the pro-Syrian fighters in the month of May. Compared with the previous month, IDF casualties doubled from about 40 to 80. Assad was now fighting a war of attrition in Lebanon on his terms, determined to bleed the IDF gradually at a time when public opinion in Israel was becoming more and more disillusioned with the war and the wisdom of maintaining a military presence in Lebanon.[85]

As the proxy war intensified, in the summer, Syria took measures to form a political coalition opposed to Amin Gemayel. The National Salvation Front was created on 23 July and composed of Walid Jumblatt's Druze PSP, the Maronite ex-president Suleiman Franjieh and Sunni leader Rashid Karami. It would soon prove to be a vital instrument in Syria's bid to dislodge the Lebanese army from Mount Lebanon once the IDF had withdrawn from the region to the Awali River in the south.

The Israeli forces' inability to stop the outbreak of recurrent clashes between Druze and Christian militias in the Shouf Mountains and their failure to broker a ceasefire between the warring parties left Tel Aviv in early September with no recourse but to withdraw to more defensible positions 22 miles south of Beirut along the Awali River. Powerless to effect the outcome of the fighting or secure an agreement with the Druze for the pro-Gemayel Lebanese army to replace the IDF presence, Israel's decision to redeploy its forces signified the crumbling of another pillar of its grand strategy in Lebanon. The withdrawal also coincided with renewed attempts by the Gemayel regime to reassert its control over West Beirut and the suburbs in the south. These efforts were vigorously resisted by the Shiites who were subsequently joined by Druze and Sunni militiamen in fierce clashes with the US-backed army units. The fighting, described as the largest engagement in the history of the Lebanese army, lasted four days and resulted in the partial defeat of the anti-government militias. Although the army was able to restore control over the heart of West Beirut, it was unsuccessful in driving the Shiite fighters out of the southern sections and suburbs of the city. The Shiite Amal militia, which now boasted 10,000 seasoned fighters, was well-supplied with arms by Syria, Iran and, indirectly, the USSR.[86]

The battle for West Beirut marked a major turning point in the character of the conflict in Lebanon; the Shiites were now at the forefront of the struggle against the central government.

At this point, Assad clearly sensed that the tide was turning and seized the initiative to reassert control over Lebanon through his various proxies and allies. With the IDF withdrawal from the Shouf Mountains, the Druze launched a full-scale offensive to neutralize the Christian militias in the region (which the Israelis had armed during the occupation) and to re-establish control in an area they had traditionally viewed as part of their domain. The Druze, with the support of Palestinian, Syrian and Iranian fighters and heavy equipment provided to them by the Syrian army, were able to overwhelm the Christian militias very rapidly. The Lebanese forces of Samir Geagea (the Druzes' main opponents in the 'Mountain War') were forced to retreat in haste. The only serious effort to resist the Druze onslaught was at the town of Behamdoun, where again the positions of the Christian forces were quickly overrun.[87] Within a few days, the Druze and their allies had scored an enormous victory by seizing the Shouf and Alei regions (to the south and east of Beirut). Alarmed by the Druze victory, the government dispatched the predominantly Christian eighth brigade of the Lebanese army commanded by General Michel Aoun to hold the key town of Souk el-Gharb on the southeastern approach to East Beirut and the presidential palace at Ba'abda. Having reached the outskirts of the capital, the Druze subsequently provided artillery support for Shiite militiamen still fighting Lebanese army units in the city's southern and western districts. A convergence of interests, coupled with Syrian encouragement, very quickly led to the emergence of a Druze–Shiite alliance.[88] During the first week of September, Damascus raised the stakes by announcing its intention to call for a complete political, economic and military boycott of the Gemayel government at the next Arab summit.

As fighting intensified in early September, Druze artillery batteries shelled MNF positions in Beirut, killing four US and French soldiers. Paris reacted angrily, threatened to retaliate by striking at the Druze artillery emplacements in the mountains and accused Damascus of indirect involvement. Washington also expressed concern for the safety of its marines and accused the Syrians of fomenting hostilities against the MNF contingents. In the immediate aftermath of the shelling of the marine barracks at Beirut international airport, US navy ships off the coast of Beirut shelled Druze positions in retaliation on 8 September. This led to an escalating spiral of violence as

Druze batteries promptly responded once again by bombarding US Marine positions in the same area in the days that followed.

By the middle of the month, the fighting was mainly focused on the strategic town of Souk el-Gharb, which the Lebanese army still held. As the battle for this key position raged, with repeated assaults being repulsed by Lebanese government forces, the Druze were reinforced by pro-Syrian Palestinian, Iranian and Syrian fighters. In one particular clash, a much larger force of Syrians, Palestinians and Iranians overwhelmed a 90-man army unit of the crack 82nd brigade.[89] By the time the mêlée had ended, two-thirds of the Lebanese army unit had been wiped out. Reports that Syrian army troop carriers were transporting hundreds of these fighters from Ba'albek to the front lines to assist the Druze greatly alarmed officials in Washington and Paris who now were considering air strikes to prevent the fall of Souk el-Gharb.[90] Moreover, news that the Druze had penetrated the town's defences caused panic among US and Lebanese officials, prompting them to take drastic measures to prevent its capture.

After some ineffectual Lebanese air force strikes against Druze forces near Souk el-Gharb, between 17 and 21 September, US warships shelled anti-government strongholds in the same area. With the USA now a *de facto* co-belligerent in the conflict, tensions rose to new heights as Syria threatened to retaliate if US forces continued to attack its allies in Lebanon.[91] As the fighting in and around the capital intensified, the French joined the fray after six of their soldiers were wounded in two separate incidents. Super Etendard aircraft from the carrier *Foch*, off the Lebanese coast, bombarded artillery batteries behind Syrian lines. US warships continued to pound anti-government positions as they maintained their pressure on the Lebanese army and a US marine contingent near the airport. Eventually, through the mediation of Saudi envoy Prince Bandar bin Sultan, the escalating cycle of attacks and counter-strikes was broken. The cessation of hostilities on 25 September paved the way for the convening of the national reconciliation conference in Geneva.

In many respects, the three-week battle for the Shouf was a turning point in the Syrian struggle with Israel and the USA over the control of Lebanon. Unable to achieve its goals or stomach further losses, Tel Aviv's decision to withdraw from the region immediately created a political vacuum that Assad and his allies quickly exploited. By 24 September, pro-Syrian forces were in control of virtually the entire Shouf. The expulsion of the Phalange Party and the Lebanese forces from their strongholds in the area, and the Lebanese army's failure to tip the scale sounded the death knell of the US–Israeli scheme in Lebanon. Abandoned by Israel, the Gemayel regime was left to fend for itself in Beirut with partial MNF backing.[92] The Syrians took advantage of the ceasefire to reinforce their proxies in Lebanon.[93]

Hopes of national reconciliation were quickly dashed when former president Suleiman Franjieh made the cancellation of the 17 May Israeli–Lebanese agreement a precondition for attending talks between the warring factions. The other members of the pro-Syrian National Salvation Front, Walid Jumblatt and Rashid Karami, had only insisted the abrogation of the agreement be on top of the agenda, not a pre-requisite for peace talks. Then, in early October, there were renewed clashes in the southern suburbs of Beirut between the Lebanese army and pro-Iranian Shiite fighters.[94] The fighting intensified as the month progressed, with pro-Iranian militiamen targeting the Lebanese army and MNF troops. Recurrent attacks on US Marine positions at the airport resulted in nine US casualties in a period of four days. Now, both US Marine commander Colonel Geraghty and the Lebanese government pointed the finger at the pro-Iranian group, Hezbollah.[95]

On 17 September, when USS *Virginia*'s guns opened fire on pro-Syrian forces to avert the fall of Souk el-Gharb, US forces in effect became an involved party in the civil war. By this stage, Washington was no longer seen as an impartial mediator, but as one of the main architects of the treaty with Israel and the primary outside power try-ing to perpetuate Maronite domination in Lebanon.[96] The USA's active involvement in the conflict now provided Syria, Iran and their Lebanese allies with an irresistible opportunity to deliver a devastat-ing blow to US power and prestige in Lebanon, while at the same aggrandizing their position at their foes' expense. In the early hours of 23 October, when most troops were still asleep, a suicide bomber drove a truck filled with explosives into the US Marine compound at Beirut airport killing 241 US military personnel in what was later deemed to be the biggest non-nuclear explosion since the Second World War.[97] A few minutes after the blast, the French MNF force headquarters in Beirut were also demolished in similar fashion, taking the lives of 57 French paratroopers. Washington was quick to pin the blame on Tehran and Damascus. US defence secretary Caspar Weinberger suggested that 'there is a lot of circumstantial evidence … but there is much that points to the direction of Iran'.[98] US secretary of state George Shultz went a step further the day after the bombing when he told a closed-door Senate meeting, 'Iranian elements in Lebanon operate from behind Syrian lines and are allied with Syria.

Syria must bear a share of the responsibility for any Iranian actions in Lebanon whether or not Syria knew of any specific terrorist plans.[99] By the end of the month, President Reagan confidently declared: 'I think the evidence that I have is sufficient that this last horrendous act involved Iranian terrorists and they were facilitated in their entry and in the provision of munitions by the Syrians.'[100]

Iran and Syria were both quick to deny any involvement in the bombings and instead attributed them to the 'heroic resistance of the Lebanese people' against the US Marines and MNF who were waging 'a real war against the Lebanese national forces'.[101] Although the Islamic Jihad, which had bombed the US embassy, claimed responsibility for the two attacks, most observers were convinced that Hussein Musawi's Islamic Amal had orchestrated them.[102] Days after the incidents, US intelligence identified Islamic Amal as the main perpetrator with the backing of Syria and Iran. The Lebanese security forces then began a manhunt for the spiritual leader of the pro-Iranian Hezbollah, Sheikh Fadlallah, for he had reportedly blessed the two men who took part in the two suicide missions.[103]

Despite steadfast denials from Damascus and Tehran, subsequent revelations demonstrated that the two operations were planned and executed with Syrian and Iranian assistance. According to the information disclosed, the Iranian embassy in Damascus paid an obscure Lebanese courier named Hassan Hamiz $50,000 to finance the operations.[104] While the evidence indicated that the head of Syrian military intelligence (G2 section) in Lebanon, Colonel Ghazi Kan'an, was aware of the whole affair, one of his associates, Ahmed Diyab, was one of the overall coordinators of the attacks.[105] Three days before the bombings, a meeting was held at the Soviet–Palestinian Friendship House in Damascus where the details were discussed. One of those present was none other than Sheikh Fadlallah.[106]

Although intelligence on the Iranian connection in the matter was rather sketchy, several figures seem to have provided support for the activities of radical Shiite groups in Lebanon. Besides the instrumental role of Iran's ambassador to Damascus, Hojjatolislam Ali Akbar Mohtashami, in overseeing Iranian activities in Syria and Lebanon, deputy foreign minister Hussein Sheikholislam was involved in supervising the bombings of the US embassy and MNF barracks. It could not have been sheer coincidence that he appeared in Damascus two days before the the US embassy bombing in Beirut, and again four days prior to the attacks on the MNF contingents.[107] Although the official purpose of Sheikholislam's visit in October was to discuss the Syrian–Iranian oil trade, he is suspected to have gone to Lebanon to see the Iranian Revolutionary Guards and give Hussein Musawi final approval for the planned attack on the MNF forces, apparently with Syria's full knowledge and cooperation.[108] He was scheduled to stay in Syria until at least 24 October, but abruptly left for Iran on 22 October – a day before the Beirut bombings.[109] Reports also suggested that a shadowy Iranian figure who had been sent to Lebanon in 1982, codenamed 'Abu Muslih', engineered the suicide attacks with Syrian assistance.[110] Other Iranians who may have had a role in planning the explosions were Iran's military attaché in Damascus, Hussein Ahromizadeh, who served as the main liaison between the embassy and the Iranian bases in Ba'albek and Zebdani (the latter being in Syria), and Ayatollah Khomeini's personal representative in Syria, Seyyed Ahmad Fehri, who enjoyed close and intimate links with Syrian officials and Lebanese Shiite activists.[111]

An important Lebanese Shiite militant who played a key role in these activities was Abu Haidar Musawi (perhaps a relative of Islamic Amal leader Hussein Musawi). US military sources claim he had close links with Damascus and Tehran, and gave logistical support to the October attacks.[112] Not surprisingly, following the bombings, Hussein Musawi held a press conference at which he denied any role in the attacks but praised the two 'martyrs' for their actions against US and French forces.[113] Hezbollah leader Sheikh Mohammed Yazbek also saluted the suicide bombers for delivering a decisive blow against US and French might and arrogance.[114]

By early November, the political situation in Lebanon had come to a head, with some sort of military showdown inevitable. Syria's obstinacy on the need to abrogate the 17 May agreement, and indirect harassment of the MNF, prompted Washington to augment its naval force in the eastern Mediterranean to 30 warships and 300 carrier-based aircraft. Convinced that Musawi's followers had orchestrated the suicide bombings with Syrian and Iranian complicity, the Reagan administration now conferred with the Gemayel government and its other allies about various options for retaliating against pro-Iranian and Syrian forces in Lebanon.[115] With the prospect of a military confrontation with the USA seemingly imminent, Syria assumed a war footing by calling up its reserves as part of a general mobilization.[116] The Iranian foreign ministry also issued a statement underlining its support for Syria in the light of the overt threats made by the USA and Israel to use force in Lebanon. According to the statement:

Iran once again emphasizes its unstinting support for the fraternal country of Syria and all the Muslim and revolutionary
Lebanese and Palestinian forces, and announces that ... side by
side with her Syrian, Palestinian and Lebanese brothers, it will
defend their legitimate rights with all its power and remain at
their side until the last aggressive soldier has been expelled from
the region.[117]

In addition to the growing confrontation between the Syrian–Iranian
axis and the US–French supported Gemayel government, tensions
gradually rose to new heights in southern Lebanon between the
Israelis and the Shiites. A unique situation emerged from late 1983
onwards, which Damascus and Tehran again exploited to the full. As
the constellation of forces arrayed against the Gemayel government
and its backers gradually began to overwhelm them, the tide was also
turning against the Israelis in the south. On 16 October, while 50,000
Lebanese Shiites were commemorating Ashura (the martyrdom of the
Prophet's grandson Hussein) in the town of Nabatiya, violence
erupted when an IDF convoy made an ill-timed and clumsy effort to
cut through the enormous procession. The deaths of some of the
mourners at the hands of the Israelis only added insult to injury.
Incensed by the incident, the Shiites of the south stepped up their
guerrilla activities against the IDF in the weeks that followed, slaying
40 Israeli soldiers by the end of the year.[118]

In the most notable instance, a truck crashed through the gate of
the IDF headquarters in Tyre on 4 November and blew up the building, killing 29 Israeli soldiers. Again, pro-Iranian Shiite radicals
operating from behind Syrian lines were blamed.[119] Uncharacteristi-
cally, retribution did not follow swiftly after the attack. Tel Aviv
finally decided to conduct air strikes on 15 November against two
training camps in the Bekaa Valley used to train Shiite militants.[120]
The Israelis claimed that retaliatory raids were initially postponed
because of their assumption that the USA was planning to hit radical
Shiite strongholds to avenge the deaths of the US Marines.[121]

In the aftermath of the Israeli raids, US officials stated that they
were unlikely to take similar action because the Israeli operations
made the need for such measures by the USA superfluous. Moreover,
they tried to make an unconvincing case that Washington had no
prior knowledge of Israeli intentions, and that Tel Aviv was not partially acting on their behalf.[122] By all accounts, US inactivity at this
crucial point could be attributed to the divergence of views within the

US administration about the wisdom and efficacy of air strikes. Given the recent US invasion of Grenada, Washington's stance on deploying Pershing missiles in western Europe, and the growing involvement of the US MNF in the Lebanese civil war on the side of the Maronite-dominated central government, the doves had prevailed – at least for the moment – over the more hawkish elements who argued for launching air strikes. The administration did not want to give its Western allies the impression that it was all too willing to use military force in every international crisis, and furthermore did not want to give the Arab–Islamic world the impression that it was their primary enemy.[123]

Some 36 hours after the Israeli raids, 14 French Super Etendard and Crusader fighter-bombers from the carrier *Clemenceau* bombed the Sheikh Abdullah barracks on the outskirts of Ba'albek and the Khawwam hotel in the town housing Islamic Amal militiamen and Iranian Revolutionary Guards. Although Paris had vowed to avenge the deaths of its paratroopers immediately after the bombing of the French MNF headquarters, the French defence ministry justified the air strikes as a pre-emptive measure to deter further attacks on its forces in Lebanon.[124] Tehran subsequently admitted that 14 Revolutionary Guards had been killed in the Israeli and French raids. However, no accurate details were ever revealed about the number of Lebanese Shiite casualties.[125]

The escalating spiral of hostilities in the latter half of November only strengthened the Syrian–Iranian alliance, thereby hastening the formalization of a US–Israeli strategic partnership that had been underway for some time. Washington had initially hoped it could convince Lebanon's warring factions to accept the 17 May agreement and force the Syrians to withdraw from the war-torn land. In three months, there had been a dramatic reversal of fortune for Washington and its regional allies. With pro-Syrian Druze forces now controlling the Shouf, and the Shiites mounting a tough challenge to the Lebanese army in Beirut's suburbs and intensifying their efforts against the IDF in the south, the position of the Gemayel government and the MNF became more precarious as the days passed. By mid-November, the central government controlled less than 20 per cent of Lebanon, while 200 US marines were withdrawn from Beirut to naval vessels of the Sixth Fleet offshore. As the US position in the Middle East began to unravel, the administration scrambled to recoup its losses. Caspar Weinberger, the US secretary of defence, blamed much of the happenings in Lebanon on the Islamic Republic and Ba'thist Syria. On the subject of the attacks on US forces, he explained that those responsible were 'basically Iranians with the sponsorship, knowledge and authority of the Syrian government'.[126]

Indeed, as the crisis in Lebanon reached boiling point, Tehran became more vocal in its support for Damascus, and took substantive measures to harmonize policies between the two allies. At a press conference in Tehran on 21 November, the foreign minister Velayati stressed that 'we regard defending the people of Syria, Palestine and Lebanon in their fight against Israel and the imperialist forces as our duty and as one of the strategic objectives of our foreign policies.'[127] A few days later, a delegation headed by presidential adviser Mirsalim left for Syria and Lebanon to hold talks with Hafez Assad and leaders of pro-Iranian Lebanese groups.[128]

Washington's initial reluctance to risk a major confrontation with Syria, and the diminution of the Gemayel regime's power meant that a new formula would have to be adopted to offset the challenges posed to US policy in the region. The Reagan administration took decisive steps within a matter of weeks to restore its position.

The Syrian–Iranian challenge and US response in the Middle East

From the vantage point of US policymakers in the closing months of 1983, the situation in the Middle East was spiralling out of control. By late October, a number of developments had greatly alarmed the Reagan administration, now painfully aware of the limits of US power to influence events in Lebanon and the Persian Gulf. Syria's ability to frustrate US policy in the Levant, and Tehran's obduracy in continuing the war with Iraq, prompted the Reagan administration to reformulate certain aspects of its policy and to accelerate certain trends that had been underway for some time. In late 1983, Washington pursued a two-pronged approach by cementing ties with Tel Aviv and thawing relations with Baghdad in an attempt to confront and neutralize the Syrian–Iranian threat in the two political arenas.

However, when pro-Syrian forces overran the Shouf Mountains and Syrian–Iranian agents demolished the US Marine barracks, the Reagan administration critically reassessed its policy and adopted a more defiant political and military posture, confident that Syria and its allies would eventually back down. The new strategy (national security directive number 111) was the brainchild of secretary of state George Shultz and national security adviser Robert McFarlane. It was officially approved by Ronald Reagan on 29 October, despite objections from Caspar Weinberger and the joint chiefs of staff.[129]

It is important to recognize that in the light of the steady stream of advanced Soviet weaponry to Syria, the presence of 7000 Soviet military advisers in that country, and the Reagan administration's obsession with viewing the Lebanese crisis through the prism of cold war politics, US interests were now virtually identical to those of Israel.[130]

Not surprisingly, the first manifestation of the response was the signing of a memorandum of understanding with Tel Aviv on strategic and political cooperation on 29 November, while Israeli Prime Minister Yitzhak Shamir and Defence Minister Moshe Arens were visiting Washington. The agreement between the two long-time allies was mainly symbolic, aimed at demonstrating to Damascus the importance the USA attached to its special relationship with Israel. It was also an implicit signal that the Reagan administration was not about to back down from its previous position on the Israeli–Lebanese accord, and would not exert pressure on the Israelis to withdraw their forces from Lebanon before the Syrians, as stipulated in the agreement.[131] The visit by Shamir and Arens was immediately followed by the arrival of Amin Gemayel in Washington on 1 December. US officials could do very little directly to bolster Gemayel's position. By this stage, both parties had few cards to play to avert further setbacks. Indeed, it was little consolation for Gemayel to be informed that he should rely more on the IDF to extend his authority over other parts of Lebanon.[132]

To show US–Israeli resolve, within a week of signing the memorandum, on 3 and 4 December, Israeli and US warplanes bombarded Syrian troops east of Beirut. The Reagan administration denied any collusion with the Shamir government and justified the attack as an appropriate response to Syrian air defence units' attempts to shoot down US reconnaissance aircraft that had overflown the Syrian positions, but it was apparent from the sequence of events that Washington intended to provoke the Syrians and subsequently make a clear show of force to intimidate them.[133] The raids were meant to deliver a carefully calibrated blow to Damascus so it would bow to military force and accept the US–Israeli diktat in Lebanon.

While US aircraft involved in the attack hit their designated targets, the loss of two planes brought down by Syrian air defences and the capture of a US airman turned what was considered a successful military operation into a major political and psychological achievement for the Syrians. In fact, the incident signified a symbolic defeat for the USA. In its first direct military confrontation with the Syrians, US forces had incurred losses. Not since the Vietnam War had the USA lost combat aircraft in hostilities.[134] US vulnerability was further highlighted in the immediate aftermath of the attacks when Druze artillery shelled the US MNF compound, killing eight marines.[135] The loss of two warplanes, and an Israeli aircraft in an earlier incident, showed that Damascus had markedly improved its anti-aircraft capability with Moscow's assistance.[136] Subsequent reports revealed that US and NATO intelligence specialists had underestimated the efficacy of Syrian air defences.[137] By now, it had become apparent that Assad's 'shield and sword' strategy was paying significant dividends.

Despite heavy bombardment of Druze positions by US naval warships, the events on that fateful day revealed that Washington's gambit to raise the stakes in its confrontation with Syria and its allies had failed. The correlation of forces had shifted to Syria's advantage in almost every respect; offensive operations by pro-Syrian forces were slowly bleeding the Gemayel government and its backers, while Syria's conventional shield was now unquestionably operational. Moreover, Assad was willing to sustain more casualties than his opponents could stomach.[138] Politically checkmated and with no meaningful alternative course of action, the Reagan administration discontinued air attacks in Lebanon, limiting military operations to occasional naval bombardment of enemy strongholds.

On 12 December, a series of suicide bombings targeting the US and French embassies in Kuwait and a number of other installations alarmed and shook the USA. Again, a shadowy organization known as 'Islamic Jihad' claimed responsibility for the attacks.[139] Washington was quick to blame pro-Iranian Arab elements in Kuwait who opposed French and Kuwaiti support for Iraq in the Gulf war and overall US and French Middle East policy, particularly in the Lebanon war. It interpreted the bombings as part of a broad campaign waged by Tehran and Damascus to unnerve the allies of the Gemayel government and Ba'thist Iraq.[140] The day after the Kuwait bombings, Iran's ambassador to the UN, Said Raja'i-Khorrasani, bluntly stated that continued US involvement in Lebanon would bring 'further retaliations'. He squarely blamed Washington and Paris for the escalation of hostilities and emphasized that the two powers had 'lost whatever claim they had to maintaining peace and order there'.[141]

Buoyed by their recent success, the Syrians struck a more defiant posture, again firing on US reconnaissance aircraft overflying their positions in Lebanon on 14 December. US warships responded immediately by pounding Syrian anti-aircraft batteries for several days. In the meantime, Khaddam reiterated his government's demand that the 17 May Israeli–Lebanese agreement should be abrogated before political reconciliation could commence in Lebanon. Khaddam met twice with US envoy Donald Rumsfeld, who had been dispatched to defuse the potentially explosive situation and ease Syrian–US tensions. However, his efforts proved to be in vain. In a clear indication of the weakening of US resolve, Ronald Reagan stated for the first time in mid-December that US forces would be withdrawn if Amin Gemayel failed to end the factional strife in the country.[142]

The US overture towards Iraq in the overall equation

It is no coincidence that the event that provided the major impetus for the Syrian–Iranian *rapprochement*, the 1979 Iranian revolution, also helped bring US–Iraqi relations, which had been frigid since the 1967 Arab–Israeli war, out of the cold. Immediately after the overthrow of the Shah, Washington indicated its willingness to mend fences with Baghdad.[143] Subsequently, with the seizure of the US embassy in Tehran and the outbreak of the first Gulf War, both sides drew closer together. By the end of 1982, with the Iraqi regime locked in a struggle for survival with an intractable foe, the Reagan administration made palpable gestures by providing Baghdad with $480 million in agricultural credits and satellite intelligence on Iranian troop movements.[144] This was followed by a meeting between US Secretary of State George Shultz and Iraqi Foreign Minister Tareq Aziz in Paris in April 1983, where the latter urged greater US involvement in the Gulf to impede Iranian efforts to prosecute the war.[145]

By autumn 1983, Iraq featured prominently in the Reagan administration's Middle East policy. This renewed interest in Iraq can be attributed to a new conception and critical reassessment of US strategy in the region in the light of a series of major setbacks and alarming developments during this period. In the closing weeks of 1983, it had become painfully clear that Washington's bid to impose its own order in Lebanon had failed. The Gemayel regime seemed to be on the brink of collapse, Tel Aviv could do very little to alleviate the situation, and Washington now seriously began to look for a way to extricate itself from the Lebanese quagmire in a face-saving manner. Syria, with Soviet and Iranian assistance, had regained the initiative. US power and prestige had suffered a number of consecutive blows – the destruction of the US embassy in Beirut, the bombing of the US MNF compound and the loss of two warplanes.

While the Reagan government desperately tried to reformulate policy in the Levant, to its dismay, events in the Persian Gulf seemed to be taking a turn for the worse. With the delivery of French Super

Etendard aircraft to Iraq (equipped with AM-39 Exocet missiles, which the Argentine air force used to devastating effect against British vessels in the Falklands war), Iran (after repeatedly trying to persuade France to cancel the deal) threatened to close the Strait of Hormuz if Baghdad attacked Iranian shipping in the Gulf. In November, France confirmed that Iraq had received the warplanes the previous month. The prospect of the war spilling into the Gulf and disrupting the flow of oil to world markets unsettled the USA, and the Kuwait bombings reinforced the growing sense of helplessness and panic in official Washington circles. From a US perspective, Iraq could serve as a vital component in its overall Middle East strategy to check Iran's revolutionary expansionist tendencies, and simultaneously exert pressure on its Ba'thist rival, Syria. Baghdad's role in facilitating the reintegration of Washington's main Arab ally (Egypt) into the Arab camp, its endorsement of the Israeli–Lebanese agreement and its moderate take on issues pertaining to the Arab–Israeli peace process also made US officials amenable to a US–Iraqi *rapprochement*.[146]

Although the move puzzled some observers, it should have come as no surprise that, having failed to ease tensions with Syria after two days of talks in Damascus, US special envoy Donald Rumsfeld flew to Baghdad on 19 December to thaw relations with the Iraqi regime. On arrival, he immediately held talks with Tareq Aziz and subsequently delivered a written message from Ronald Reagan to Saddam Hussein. Rumsfeld expressed US readiness to re-establish full diplomatic ties with Baghdad.[147] Washington admitted that one of the aims of the visit was to wage 'discreet psychological warfare' on Syria, which was impeding the successful resolution of the Lebanese civil war.[148] In addition, the warming of US–Iraqi relations was intended to 'bring the Syrians a little closer to the edge of their seats'.[149] The move was also another way of increasing pressure on Damascus to withdraw its 40,000 troops from Lebanon, and to expand US influence among certain Lebanese factions sympathetic to Iraq.[150] Apparently, the discussions also focused on US support for the proposed construction of an Iraqi oil pipeline to the Jordanian port of Aqaba to compensate for Syria's closure of the IPC pipeline in April 1982.[151]

The Rumsfeld visit was an important historical milestone in the evolution of US–Iraqi relations, and it paved the way for the resumption of full diplomatic relations in 1984. In less than a month, Washington had taken decisive measures to strengthen ties with its longtime ally Israel and, to recoup its waning position in the region *vis-à-vis* the Syrian–Iranian axis, to forge closer links with its new Arab ally

Iraq. The US diplomatic offensive at the end of 1983 did not bring immediate gains, but it laid the ground for a new US-led strategic consensus in the Middle East that would eventually limit the power of the Tehran–Damascus partnership.

The final phase of the Syrian–Iranian struggle against the USA

While armed clashes continued in Beirut, in the latter half of December, the Shiite resistance in southern Lebanon stepped up its activities against the IDF. The Israeli response was to bomb the Sheikh Abdullah barracks in Ba'albek in the early hours of 21 December. On the same day, two violent explosions rocked the headquarters of the French MNF contingent and a bar frequented by US serviceman, resulting in 13 French casualties. An anonymous caller contacted the AFP bureau in Beirut claiming that Islamic Jihad had carried out the attacks and warned that unless the French and US forces were not evacuated within ten days, 'the earth would move under their feet'.[152] Despite this incident, the next day, the French government disclosed that it would send a large arms shipment to the Lebanese army, including 100 AMX-13 tanks, ten Gazelle helicopter gunships and Puma transport helicopters.[153] This was meant to show the Gemayel regime's opponents that incessant attacks on French forces in Lebanon would not sway Paris to alter its policy. The Mitterand government believed that France, with its historical involvement in Lebanon, was in a unique and advantageous position to bring about a national reconciliation with Gemayel still at the helm. The French were determined to frustrate Syrian aspirations to maintain their hegemony over Lebanon, and hoped that their activist role in the Levant would provide the Arabs with an alternative ally, instead of turning only to the USA or USSR.[154]

By the end of 1983, the USA had failed to bring the various parties involved in the Lebanese civil war to the negotiating table. Although secretary of state Shultz and national security adviser McFarlane insisted on maintaining their course of action, Assad's 'sword and shield' policy had paid handsomely. The momentum was now unquestionably with the Syrians. With the situation in Lebanon coming to a head and the date of an Islamic summit in Rabat drawing closer, Tehran sent deputy foreign minister Hussein Sheikholislam to Damascus on 3 January 1984 to deliver a message from President Khamene'i to Hafez Assad and discuss recent developments. In their deliberations, Sheikholislam informed the Syrian leadership of Iran's intention to boycott the Rabat conference because of the poor state of

Moroccan–Iranian relations and King Hassan's 'blatant' pro-Iraqi stance in the Gulf conflict. One outcome of the talks seems to have been a hardening of the Syrian–Iranian position in Lebanon and an upsurge of activities against their common foes. This was manifested in the assassination of the president of the American University of Beirut, Malcolm Kerr, and the kidnapping of the Saudi consul general, Hussein Farraj, by Islamic Jihad in mid-January.[155]

There is evidence that Islamic Jihad was initially a front that members of the Islamic Amal movement used to obscure their true identity and allow them to carry out operations against their enemies with impunity. By the end of 1983, Tehran had grown disenchanted with Hussein Musawi's failure to mobilize support among the Shiites in the Bekaa region, so it turned to a number of activist Shiite clerics to accomplish the task.[156] Islamic Amal eventually disbanded and joined Hezbollah.[157] However, Musawi continued to head the action wing of Hezbollah, which still used the name 'Islamic Jihad'.[158] The USA also braced itself for more attacks against its interests in the Middle East. In reference to the looming threat, US secretary of state Shultz posited, 'we see these things increasingly originating in Iran and taking place with the acquiescence of Syria'.[159] Alluding to earlier statements by his Syrian counterpart Khaddam that his country was succeeding in wearing down the USA, and collapse of the US position was imminent, Shultz was adamant that Washington would not bow to Syrian–Iranian sponsored terrorism by withdrawing the US Marines from Beirut.[160]

The Tehran–Damascus axis was dealt a limited blow in late January at the Islamic summit in Rabat. The final resolution invited Egypt to rejoin the OIC, despite Syrian efforts to rally support against such a move. In the end, the resolution was passed 31 to 10, with the Syrian delegation walking out after the vote. Although non-Arab members played an important part in passing the resolution, another big step had been made towards reintegrating Egypt into mainstream Arab politics. Against the backdrop of the rift between the PLO and Syria, the budding friendship between Cairo, Amman and Baghdad, and Mubarak's historic meeting with PLO chairman Arafat in December 1983, the OIC resolution underlined Egypt's gradual return to major Arab–Islamic political fora and its status as an essential actor.[161] Indeed, with the impending collapse of Washington and Tel Aviv's earlier dream of a Pax Americana–Hebraica in Lebanon, and the Egyptian–Jordanian–Iraqi axis still in its infancy, the early months of 1984 saw the triumph and zenith of Syrian–Iranian power, but also its limits. The subsequent decline, which became apparent only a year later, can be attributed first to the prolongation of the Gulf conflict and Iran's inability to achieve a decisive victory, thereby magnifying Arab demands for an activist Egyptian role, and second, to the emergence of a new Egyptian–Jordanian–Iraqi counter axis with the encouragement of Washington and Riyadh, in the light of Syrian–Iranian gains in the Levant.

On 25 January, a Syrian delegation led by deputy prime minister Abd al-Qadir Qaddurah arrived in Tehran with a message from Hafez Assad for Ali Khamene'i. During the two-day visit, the Syrian representatives also met Prime Minister Musavi and Speaker Rafsanjani to discuss the situation in Lebanon, Egypt's re-entry into the OIC, and the need for closer economic cooperation. Although omitted from their official statements, there is no doubt that the Syrians told the Iranians of their intention to deliver a decisive blow to the Gemayel government. Tehran, for its part, advised its Arab ally of its plan to launch in the coming weeks its first major offensive against the Iraqis in over a year. Before leaving for Damascus, Qaddurah declared: 'We are side by side with our brothers and our Muslim Iranian friends, more than ever before. Both Iran and Syria are the hope of all the free and honest people of the world and our enemies intend to extinguish the light of God, but they shall never succeed.'[162]

In early February, intense fighting broke out in Beirut between the Lebanese army and Shiite Amal militia. The hostilities spread rapidly throughout the capital and outlying areas. The Shiites called for the removal of Amin Gemayel and the resignation of all Muslim cabinet members, prompting Prime Minister Shafiq Wazzan and other Muslim ministers to resign. Without any remaining Muslim support and the US reluctant to be involved, Gemayel was left to fend for himself, hoping the army would be able to hold its ground. Rearmed and re-equipped with supplies provided by Syria and Iran, the Syrian-backed Amal and Druze militias, pro-Syrian Palestinian and pro-Iranian Shiite forces launched a coordinated offensive in the Shkhar area (between the Damour River and Beirut) and in the southern and western suburbs of the capital to wrest control from the Lebanese army. In Shkhar, the Druze fighters swiftly overran the fourth brigade's position, while Amal fighters seized control of the remaining Beirut suburbs under government control. Thousands of Muslim and Druze Lebanese army personnel heeded a call by the opposition to lay down their arms and, within a matter of days, these defections had reduced the strength of the 37,000-man Lebanese army by more than half.[163]

Two-thirds of Beirut and 80 per cent of the country (excluding the Israeli-occupied south) came under the control of anti-Gemayel forces.[164]

As the fighting raged on for six days, on 6 February, Reagan announced that the US Marines would be withdrawn from Lebanese soil before the end of the month and 'redeployed' offshore on ships.[165] With Damascus clearly on the ascendant, Syria reiterated that there would be no political settlement unless the 17 May agreement was abrogated and all 'foreign' troops withdrawn from Lebanon. It added that Amin Gemayel could stay in power if he took steps to reconcile differences with the Lebanese opposition. Weakened and isolated, Gemayel accepted an eight-point peace plan crafted by Saudi Arabia, which called for a full ceasefire, the replacement of the MNF by a UN force, the resumption of negotiations between the various factions in Geneva and agreement in principle to a simultaneous withdrawal of Syrian and Israeli troops. Gemayel's main concession, however, was to abandon the 17 May agreement. In exchange, according to the terms of the proposal, Gemayel could stay in office. The events of early February put the Shiite Amal militia centre stage as the most powerful political group in the country. With a decisive blow having been dealt to the Gemayel government, Amal leader Nabih Berri now demanded his removal. However, on 19 February, Berri went to Damascus to hold talks with Assad and other Lebanese opposition leaders (including Walid Jumblatt whose presence the Syrian leader had requested). Having gained the upper hand, Assad was determined to impose a Pax Syriana in Lebanon by creating a new consensus among his allies. Consequently, with events unfolding rapidly, it was deemed necessary to have a common position in response to the Saudi initiative.

Finally, on 29 February, Gemayel, desperate to preserve his remaining power, made a historic 'pilgrimage' to Damascus for deliberations with Assad. He agreed to abandon his pro-Western orientation, abrogate the Lebanese–Israeli treaty and appoint the pro-Syrian Sunni Muslim leader Rashid Karami as the new prime minister. Four days after ending his visit to Syria, Gemayel announced the annulment of the agreement with Israel. A jubilant Assad telephoned Gemayel to congratulate him for his bold move, which he described as 'a victory for the Lebanese and Syrian people, as well as the entire Arab nation'.[166]

Assad had gained much since the 1982 defeat. Thanks to Soviet support, neither the USA nor Israel dared risk a full-scale war with Syria, while effective use of proxies had enabled Damascus to deny

Tel Aviv the fruits of its earlier success in the Lebanon war. The achievements of the Syrian–Iranian counteroffensive of 1983/4 were impressive in several respects. For the first time, the limits of Israeli military power were revealed, the Reagan administration suffered its worst foreign policy setback ever, and an Arab state rescinded an agreement with Israel under US auspices, which set a precedent. Not surprisingly, by the spring of 1984 'in Damascus there [was] an intoxication of victory accompanied by much caution'.[167] The Syrians could be proud that they had turned the tables on their foes in Lebanon in the face of what seemed insurmountable odds. On the other hand, they were well aware that they had only achieved a defensive victory. They were unable to end the sectarian strife and affect the outcome of the Lebanese civil war, which raged on for another six years. The limits of Syrian influence in the seamless web of Lebanese politics and the continued Israeli occupation of the south meant that the alliance with Iran still had a great deal of utility for Damascus. Iranian assistance would be essential if they were to mobilize the Shiite population of the south (which had already become radicalized by the prolonged Israeli occupation) to wage guerrilla warfare against the IDF. Indeed, the day after the abrogation of the 17 May agreement, an editorial in the Syrian daily *Al-Ba'th* elucidated:

> Now that the US–Israeli shadow has been removed from Lebanon by the abrogation of the agreement, the battle has become very clear. All efforts must be pooled to saving Lebanon from Israeli occupation so that Lebanon can restore its independence, sovereignty and role in its Arab environment ... and stripping the Zionist entity of the gains it obtained through invasion and aggression.[168]

The way was open for the next phase of the struggle against Israel, the campaign to drive the IDF from its last foothold in Lebanon.

Syrian-Iranian relations and the Gulf War

As the war dragged on in the Gulf, Iran decided to resume the offensive in mid-summer 1983 by launching a series of limited attacks to wear down the Iraqi defenders. This was part of Tehran's overall strategy to prosecute the war of attrition. Less than a week before the beginning of the first attack (Operation Wal-Fajr 2 in Iraqi Kurdistan), the Syrian minister of state for foreign affairs Faruq al-Shara arrived in Tehran and held talks with President Khamene'i on regional developments and ways to improve bilateral cooperation. Exactly a week after the commencement of Wal-Fajr 2, a second offensive (codenamed Wal-Fajr 3) was begun in the south near the strategically positioned town of Mehran. Both operations proved to be limited successes for the Iranians.

Given Iraq's inability to affect the outcome of events in the ground war, Baghdad decided to improve the capability of its air force and threaten to disrupt the flow of Iranian oil out of the Gulf unless Iran sued for peace. The French had agreed to provide Iraq with five Super Etendard aircraft in January 1983, thus enhancing the Iraqi air force's ability to attack Iranian oil facilities and tankers. On 12 August, the Iraqis declared a specified area in the northern Persian Gulf (including Kharg Island) to be an exclusion zone, warning all foreign shipping to stay away. Despite the thinly veiled threats and much bravado, Iraq received the Super Etendards only in October and only began to use them in March 1984 when they had been properly integrated into the air force and were operational.

As tensions slowly increased at the prospect of Iraq unleashing its air power, a GCC attempt to mediate between Iraq and Syria greatly disturbed Iranian officials. On 10 October, when the French announced that the Super Etendards had left France, the UAE revealed that a delegation headed by UAE President Sheikh Zayid bin Sultan al-Nuhayan would visit Baghdad and Damascus 'within the framework of current Arab efforts to clear the Arab atmosphere'. Qatari Foreign Minister Suhaym bin Hamad al-Thani accompanied the UAE delegation. They met Saddam Hussein on 9 October and held talks the following day with Hafez Assad. Meanwhile, Tareq Aziz and Abd al-Halim Khaddam talked in New York during the UN General Assembly session. This was the first high-level exchange between Iraqi and Syrian officials since the two heads of state had met at the Fez II summit in September 1982. Besides trying to thaw Syrian–Iraqi relations, a primary objective of the mediation was to persuade Damascus to reopen the trans-Syrian (IPC) pipeline. Such a move would not only represent a major blow to Iran's economic warfare against Iraq, but would also substantially ease Baghdad's financial woes and enable the GCC states to cut back their monetary assistance to the Iraqi Ba'thist regime. In response to the flurry of Arab diplomatic activity, Tehran dispatched an emissary to Damascus on 18 October to win guarantees from the Syrians that they would not be swayed by pressure from the anti-Iranian camp. The Iranian deputy foreign minister discussed the situation at hand with Hafez Assad and subsequently travelled to Libya, Algeria and South Yemen to rally some Arab support for Iran's position. The GCC initiative proved to be in vain because no discernible change occurred in Syrian policy.[169]

Operation Kheiber, the tanker war and Syrian mediation

By early 1984, Khomeini and the hawks on the SDC (including Khomeini's personal representative Rafsanjani) had grown impatient with the lack of success in the war of attrition, hence they pushed to resume major military offensives against Iraq as soon as possible. Over 250,000 men were mobilized and, on 22 February, after a series of limited probes and diversionary attacks (Wal-Fajr 5 and 6), the Iranians launched their greatest offensive since 1982 – Operation Kheiber, north of Basra. To gain a substantial foothold on Iraqi territory and cut off the Baghdad–Basra highway, the main thrust was directed at the Hawizeh marshes. The hostilities, which were some of the bloodiest in the war, raged on for more than two weeks. Eventually, when the fighting died down, the Iraqis had successfully repulsed the Iranian onslaught and inflicted enormous losses on the invaders.[170] Although the failure of Operation Kheiber was a major strategic triumph for the Iraqis, Iran was able to claim a limited, but nonetheless important tactical victory when it seized (and resisted numerous Iraqi counterattacks to regain) the oil-rich Majnoon islands in the marshes during the offensive.[171] However, the overall failure of the offensive once again created dissension and led to squabbling within the ranks of the Iranian leadership. While the hawks led by Rafsanjani advocated resuming full-scale military operations, President Khamene'i, Prime Minister Musavi, and Foreign Minister Velayati urged caution, disapproving of such a course of action for the time being.[172]

Operation Kheiber prompted Baghdad to step up its air offensive (which it had initiated in January on a limited scale with occasional raids on Iranian oil facilities and shipping in the Gulf). As the fighting raged on in the Hawizeh marshes, on 27 February, the Iraqi air force bombed Kharg Island. Between 25 February and 1 March seven ships were hit in the Gulf.[173] Overall, the Iraqi high command's decision to initiate the 'tanker war' was based on four major considerations to:

❑ cripple the Iranian military machine by denying Tehran vital oil revenues needed to finance the war effort;
❑ internationalize the conflict to rally Gulf Arab and foreign support against Iran's recalcitrant stance in the conflict;

❏ force Syria to reconsider its relationship with Iran once Arab dip-
    lomatic pressure was brought to bear, and the flow of Iranian oil
    to its Arab ally was disrupted; and
❏ utilize the air force as an offensive instrument against the Irani-
    ans, due to their inability to conduct any effective land and naval
    operations. At the time it was the only viable military option.

In short, from Baghdad's perspective, it made political, economic and
military sense to expand the conflict into the waters of the Gulf.

With the escalation of the tanker war and in the wake of the battle
for the Majnoon islands, on 7 March, Iraq's foreign minister Tareq
Aziz requested the urgent convocation of Arab foreign ministers in
Baghdad 'to discuss the serious situation endangering the entire Arab
region in the light of the escalation of Iran's aggression'.[174] He insisted
that 'Iraq's sacrifices in defending the region's security, should be met
with an effective Arab stand'.[175] In response, a meeting was convened
on 14 March with 13 foreign ministers and one deputy foreign minister present. Syria and Libya refused to send any representatives, while
Algeria, Tunisia, Lebanon and South Yemen sent low-level delegations. The meeting reiterated the 1950 joint Arab defence agreement
and condemned Iran's intransigent policy of 'continuing aggressions'
against Iraq.[176] Iran's reaction can be summed up by the comments of
Prime Minister Musavi who warned that 'reactionary' states in the
region supporting Iraq would be dealt with in an 'appropriate'
manner.[177] In general, Iran's renewed offensives in early 1984 and the
eruption of the tanker war had the net effect of generating regional
and international pressure on Syria to reconsider its position in the
conflict, galvanizing GCC support for Iraq and highlighting the need
for Egypt's return to the Arab fold, due to its political weight and
military prowess.

It is worth noting that after Saudi Crown Prince Abdullah visited
Syria in late February, Rif'at Assad, who opposed many of his
brother's policies, mounted a direct challenge to his elder brother's
authority by demanding the dismissal of Prime Minister Raouf al-
Kasm and a number of other cabinet members, including the president's close aide and confidant, defence minister Tlas. The Syrian
leader responded immediately in a resolute fashion by calling loyal
army units into the capital and arresting one of the senior commanders of the defence companies, Colonel Selim Barakat, for insubor-
dination. The upper echelons of the officer corps were subsequently
reshuffled to weaken Rif'at's power base. Many observers were con-

vinced that Saudi Arabia had precipitated the showdown in Damascus because Rif'at, who enjoyed close ties with Riyadh, objected to Syrian policy towards Iran, the PLO and the USSR.[178]

From the early stages of the Gulf War, the Saudis had been Saddam Hussein's main financial backers. By 1984, they were bankrolling the Iraqis to the tune of $7–8 billion a year. Riyadh was clearly frustrated at Syria's consistent refusal to reopen the IPC pipeline, which would have greatly eased its financial burden. Despite their displeasure with Syria's posture, the Saudis continued to pay $750 million a year to Damascus, as arranged under the terms of the 1978 Arab summit agreements. The financial help was seen as providing some leverage and influence over Syrian policy, even if only in a limited sense.[179]

Ironically, in the aftermath of Rif'at's failed putsch, the Kremlin also tried hard to achieve a Syrian–Iraqi *rapprochement* and convince Syria to reopen the IPC pipeline. In a series of visits, the first deputy prime minister Geidar Aliyev and the Soviet Union's top Middle East expert, Karen Brutents, attempted to persuade Damascus to allow the Iraqi oil to flow through the pipeline as a first step towards a genuine reconciliation between the two rival wings of the Ba'th Party. The Syrians rebuffed Moscow's overtures, arguing that Syrian–Iraqi relations would have to be rebuilt on totally new foundations before they could contemplate such a move.

Moscow and Riyadh's successive failures to induce Damascus to realign with Iraq and the anti-Iranian camp augmented Syrian power and prestige both on the regional and international level. The inability of its superpower patron and of a main Arab aid donor to use their influence to bend its will boosted Syria's confidence and gave it more room for manoeuvre in the political arena. Officials in Tehran noted and appreciated Syria's steadfast position and unwavering support for its Iranian ally. At this juncture, when Iraqi raids during March and April caused a fall in Iranian oil exports by as much as 50 per cent for some days, and the regular shipment of oil from Kharg to the Syrian port of Banias became problematic, Syria resorted to buying Libyan oil to make up the shortfall.[180] Damascus remained stalwart in its backing of Iran, despite the pressure from many fronts. However, within a matter of weeks, it became apparent that the Iraqi air force was incapable of totally disrupting the flow of Iranian oil to the international market. At best, it could only achieve brief sporadic drops in Iranian exports. Tehran, for its part, acknowledged and rewarded the fealty of its Arab ally in late April when it renewed its previous arrangement (during the visit of a Syrian delegation led by oil minister Ghazi al-Durubi) to continue the delivery of 150,000–160,000 barrels a day of Iranian crude oil to the refineries at Homs and Banias. Under the deal, one million of the 7.6 million tons of oil exported to Syria would be free of charge, while the remainder would cost $25 a barrel – $3 below the official OPEC price.[181]

Tehran and Damascus made moves to reinforce their ties and cooperation at a time when each had come to recognize that gradual shifts and new political blocs had emerged in the region that were hostile to the Syrian–Iranian camp. In a significant move, the Egyptian foreign minister Kamal Hassan Ali visited Baghdad in late March to maintain the momentum of the Iraqi–Egyptian reconciliation that had been underway for some time. In Baghdad, he met his Iraqi counterpart, Tareq Aziz, to discuss ways to normalize and expand relations. At a press conference before his departure, he expressed complete support for Iraq in the Gulf War and stated that Egypt was ready to intervene militarily in the conflict if Iraq requested assistance. Shortly afterwards, Jordan's King Hussein flew to Baghdad to confer with Saddam Hussein on regional developments and coordinate policy particularly vis-à-vis Syria and Iran.[182]

With the final withdrawal of the US Sixth Fleet from Lebanon's territorial waters in early spring, the Syrian state-controlled media boasted of a triumph over the USA and Israel.[183] Indeed, while the Lebanese venture proved to be the biggest foreign policy debacle of Ronald Reagan's first term, the genesis of the Egyptian–Jordanian–Iraqi counter axis cushioned the blow and allayed fears in Washington.[184] Despite the collapse of the US–Israeli 'condominium' in Lebanon, Assad still needed Iran to inspire and mobilize the Shiites to expel the IDF from the south, and counterbalance the emergent Arab camp hostile to Syrian designs in the area.[185] Thus, in a television interview broadcast in Syria and the USA, Assad reasserted that:

> We consider the Islamic revolution in Iran a great victory for us, the Arabs ... there is no contradiction between Arab nationalism and Iranian nationalism. Furthermore, there is no contradiction between Arab nationalism and Islam. ... Iran is a neighbouring Muslim country where a revolution erupted against a previous situation that did not express the Iranian people's interests. This revolution stands at the Arabs' side in their struggle against the Israeli invasion and for regaining the Palestinians' rights.[186]

On 27 March, as the Iraqis intensified their air campaign in the

Persian Gulf, they eventually unleashed the much vaunted Super Etendards, which hit three tankers in the vicinity of Kharg. A series of raids and counter raids ensued, finally forcing the Iranians to take action in early May by attacking Saudi and Kuwaiti tankers. From Tehran's viewpoint, Saudi Arabia and Kuwait were not neutral states in the conflict, but close allies of Ba'thist Iraq. Saddam Hussein's admission in an interview with Kuwaiti journalists that Saudi AWACS had provided Iraq with valuable data and intelligence on Iranian troop movements during Operation Kheiber reinforced this perception.[187] Iranian leaders had for months been warning the Gulf Arab sheikhdoms to stop supporting Iraq or face the consequences. In a sermon on 18 May, Rafsanjani declared that the fact that Kuwait and Saudi Arabia sold oil on Iraq's behalf made them *de facto* co-belligerents in the war.[188]

Escalating tensions and a widening rift between Iran and the Gulf Arabs led to an Arab foreign ministers' conference in Tunis on 19 May to discuss Iranian attacks on Saudi and Kuwaiti shipping. After some deliberations, a resolution was passed condemning Iranian attacks on Gulf shipping and imploring the UN Security Council to take appropriate action to prevent the destabilization of the area. The resolution was passed despite Syrian and Libyan objections.[189] It is interesting to note that only Libya expressed a formal reservation; Syria was less vocal in its protestations. The Syrians feared that the Iranians were falling into a trap that the Iraqis had set for them, namely that by attacking ships from non-combatant states, Iran was further alienating Gulf states and the international community and thus providing the West with the pretext it needed to establish a naval presence in the region. Furthermore, within the context of inter-Arab politics, with the transformation of the Jordanian–Iraqi partnership in 1980 into what by mid-1984 looked like a pro-US Egyptian–Jordanian–Iraqi–Saudi bloc, Damascus wanted to avoid becoming sidelined and isolated in inter-Arab politics.[190] This did not signify a shift in Syrian policy towards Iran, but was rather an indication of Syria's displeasure at Iranian strikes on tankers belonging to the Gulf Arab littoral states, and the awkward position in which it placed the Syrian Arab Republic. Therefore, to prevent further polarization and US interference in the Gulf, the Syrians deemed it necessary to defuse the potentially explosive situation as soon as possible.

The opportunity came soon after the Tunis conference on 22 May, when Saudi King Fahd sent the deputy commander of the Saudi National Guard, Sheikh Abdul Aziz Tuwaijeri, to Damascus requesting Syrian intercession in the tanker war. Assad responded promptly the next day by sending the newly-appointed vice president Khaddam, and foreign minister Faruq al-Shara on a peace mission to Tehran. The Syrian emissaries went into session almost immediately with President Khamene'i, presidential assistant Mostafa Mirsalim, foreign minister Velayati, and minister of state for executive affairs Aghazadeh. Khaddam conveyed a message from Assad impressing on the Iranian government the need to ease tensions and prevent any further escalation in the Gulf War, since the 'grave situation' threatened the entire region and 'help[ed] imperialism and Zionism to achieve their ambitions in the region'.[191] On the day the Syrian envoys arrived, the Iranian parliament (*Majles*) passed a bill approving the continuation of oil deliveries to Syria and rescheduling Syria's oil debt, which now amounted to $993 million.[192] Recent shortfalls in Iranian oil production and the steady accumulation of a massive Syrian debt compelled the government to seek parliamentary approval before proceeding with more oil deliveries to its Arab ally. Velayati argued in favour of the bill, asserting that 'we have the responsibility to aid such a government in its path, especially at a time when the reactionary governments of the region, because of Syria's refusal to come to an agreement with the Iraqi regime, have cut off their aid to Syria.' He added, 'we must support Syria in its struggle against the United States, Israel, and Iraq, which is the correct path.'[193] On the second day of their visit, Khaddam and al-Shara met Khomeini's representative on the SDC and the speaker of parliament Rafsanjani. They once again reiterated their support for the Islamic Republic in the war, but cautioned that further escalation and expansion of the war must be avoided. Rafsanjani explained that if the Gulf became insecure for Iranian shipping, other regions would become unstable. At a *Majles* session later that same day, he repeated Iran's previous threat to close the Strait of Hormuz, if it was unable to use the Gulf.

Damascus was eager to use the mediation as justification for its close ties with Tehran. According to its logic, in the light of the crisis in the Gulf, the Arab world needed an effective channel of communication with the Islamic Republic to voice Arab concerns. Assad was hoping that, having been put in an extremely awkward position over the eruption of the tanker war, he could win political capital by defusing tensions and portraying himself as an Arab saviour.[194] However, Baghdad was determined to stop Syria exploiting the situation to achieve a diplomatic victory. As Khaddam and al-Shara left Tehran for Jeddah to brief King Fahd on the results of their negotiations, Iraqi warplanes struck two tankers near the Iranian coast. The Iranian riposte was swift, with an attack on a vessel in Saudi waters. Thus, initial hopes that tensions might decrease were quickly dashed after a week-long lull in the tanker war. Saddam Hussein also promised to continue attacks on Iranian shipping and render Kharg Island useless. Baghdad sought to discredit Syria and its alliance with Iran in the eyes of the Arabs, using every possible means.[195]

Iran's leaders felt that, with Operation Kheiber's failure to score a battlefield victory and at times the significant drop in oil exports because of Iraqi attacks on Kharg Island, the only way they could retaliate for the raids and deter Gulf Arab support for Iraq was to take part in the tanker war.[196] The Syrians consistently argued that Iranian officials had assured them that Iraq had initiated the tanker war, but that they had no wish to escalate the war and threaten the Gulf sheikhdoms. Moreover, they stated their commitment to extend military assistance to the GCC members in the event of Iranian aggression.[197] But, despite their assurances to Damascus and a wish not to extend the conflict, Iran still felt compelled to strike back at Gulf Arab shipping in retaliation for Iraqi raids. Tensions were heightened on 5 June when Saudi F-15 fighters, backed by US-manned AWACS, shot down an Iranian F-4 hunting for ships in Saudi territorial waters. Tehran decided against responding militarily in the Gulf for fear of drawing outside parties into the conflict. However, an Iranian riposte came two days later in Lebanon, where an explosive device went off outside the Saudi consulate in Beirut, and Islamic Jihad gunmen stormed and occupied the Saudi embassy for 30 minutes.[198]

Iran's international isolation and dependency on Syria

The continuation of the tanker war and the growing rift between Iran and many of its Arab neighbours prompted Tehran to launch a diplomatic offensive in the summer to mend fences with non-regional states. In early June, the Iranian foreign ministry sent Mohammad Sadr, director-general for European and American affairs, to Moscow in an attempt to thaw relations with the USSR. The visit of a high-level Soviet delegation to Tehran followed a few weeks later.

Tehran found it prudent to make an overture to Moscow at a time when Iraq was cultivating close ties with both the USA and USSR. Iranian officials were perturbed by Baghdad's ability to form close ties with both superpowers at a time when they were acutely aware of their own isolation and vulnerability; the US–Iraqi *rapprochement*, which was paving the way for the eventual restoration of full diplo-matic relations between the two countries, quite unsettled them. The Islamic Republic found US claims of neutrality in the Gulf War unconvincing. In late June, Dr Kamal Kharrazi, director of the SDC's war information headquarters, announced that Iran had reliable evidence that the USA had delivered several shipments of chemical weapons to Iraq in January before the start of Operation Kheiber.[199] Reports that Saudi Arabia had agreed to finance $2.5 billion worth of Iraqi arms purchases from the USSR and of UAE attempts to induce Syria to reopen the IPC pipeline, further compounded Iranian frustra-tions.[200] The overall success of Iraq's political and military strategy, and the ascendancy of the moderate Arab camp on the regional scene underlined the need for more cooperation between the main rejec-tionist states. Consequently, on 10 July, Iranian foreign minister Velayati, and the Libyan People's Bureau secretary for foreign liaison Dr Abd al-Salam al-Turayki, arrived in Damascus for talks with their Syrian counterpart, Faruq al-Shara. Velayati also delivered a message from President Khamene'i to Hafez Assad and had discussions with vice-president Khaddam and defence minister Tlas. The Syrians again stressed the need to contain hostilities so as to avert the deployment of US naval forces in the Gulf. Velayati assured the Syrian leadership that Iranian policy precluded the spread of 'turmoil' in the Gulf and the annexation of Iraqi territory.

In an interview on 23 July with the Lebanese magazine *Al-Kifah al-Arabi*, the Syrian foreign minister elaborated on the outcome of the meetings with Velayati by explaining that:

> we and Iran have developed a complete understanding on the need to avoid expanding the area of the Iran–Iraq war, on preventing the involvement of any Gulf state in this war, on rejecting US intervention in the region's affairs, and refraining from attacks on oil tankers in the Gulf if Iraq stops its attacks on tankers. ... The Iranians have emphasized to us more than once that they have no ambitions against any inch of Arab territory.

He went on to point out that Iraq had started the tanker war and had also attacked some Arab oil tankers in the Gulf; ultimate respon-sibility for the situation in the Gulf and the complications arising from it lay squarely with Baghdad. Throughout the summer, Syrian officials played down Iran's war strategy and objectives, blaming Iraqi recklessness for internationalizing a conflict it had begun and could no longer finish on its own terms. For example, in an interview in *Al-Majallah* of 4 August, defence minister Tlas explained Syria's wish for the termination of the war. He mentioned that Damascus had obtained personal assurances from Ayatollah Khomeini that Iran would 'not violate the sovereignty of any Arab country'.

Iran's policy at this point was to pursue a two-pronged attempt to strengthen relations with Arab allies and any non-regional actors it considered important, and at the same time, use various means to put more pressure on Iraq's primary backers. While the Islamic Republic adopted a less aggressive posture to avoid raising the stakes in the Gulf (for fear of alienating Syria and drawing in the USA), it tried to strike back at Iraq's allies and paymasters by mining the Red Sea. When Baghdad declared the naval exclusion zone in the northern Gulf in early spring, the Iraqi navy had mined the Iranian ports of Bushehr and Bandar Khomeini (formerly Bandar Shahpour). In fact, Iraq's mining campaign had damaged and sunk more ships than its air force's aerial attacks. On 1 August, Islamic Jihad claimed it had laid 192 mines in the Red Sea. In the next few days, mines damaged a Turkish ship and sank a Liberian vessel. On 7 August, Tehran radio praised Islamic Jihad for its actions in the Red Sea. Although some Iranian leaders subsequently issued statements denying any involvement or link with Islamic Jihad, the inconsistency in Tehran's position seemed to suggest an internal split in the regime over the conduct of the war and foreign affairs. This was then demonstrated on 11 August, when the newly-elected *Majles* sacked five cabinet members, including the minister of defence. However, there is clear evidence that Iran conducted the mining operation to create unease in the backyards of four of Iraq's main supporters – Saudi Arabia, Jordan, Egypt and the Sudan. Two Iranian ships had passed through the Suez Canal on 26 July, while Rafsanjani had earlier threatened to wage war against the pro-Iraqi camp in a new theatre of operations and attack oil installations in the Red Sea region. Egyptian defence minister Abu Ghazalah stated that Cairo was '70 per cent' certain that Iranian and Libyan ships had laid the mines. The Iranian state-controlled media denied any involvement in the affair and, along with Syria and Libya, pinned the blame on the USA, arguing that Western imperialism had precipitated the crisis in order to return to the region after its disastrous defeat and expulsion from Lebanon.

Amid the brewing crisis in the Red Sea, Kuwaiti foreign minister Sheikh Sabah al-Ahmad al-Jabir arrived on a mission in Damascus to solicit Syrian support to end the Gulf War. He met Khaddam and al-

Shara and later delivered a letter for the Kuwaiti emir to Hafez Assad. His visit coincided with the arrival of the Iranian minister of the Revolutionary Guards corps, Mohsen Rafiqdoust. Rafiqdoust first met defence minister Tlas and deputy chief of staff General Ali Aslan, and then delivered a message to and held further discussions with Hafez Assad. The deliberations centred on the tanker war and the situation in Lebanon. Rafiqdoust reaffirmed Iran's commitment to continue the Gulf War until Saddam Hussein was overthrown and to cooperate with Syria in the struggle against Israel. However, he assured the Syrians that the Islamic Republic would not aggravate the situation in the Gulf and had no ambitions towards Arab territory. After his deliberations in Damascus, Rafiqdoust left for Libya to harmonize positions and coordinate policy with the Qadhafi regime.

Iranian shuttle diplomacy in July and August was a result of the clerical leadership's disappointment at its failure to achieve a breakthrough in the Gulf War after two years, and the gradual drift towards regional and international isolation. Iran's overtures to the USSR, Germany and Japan had no immediate or direct impact on its ability to prosecute the war successfully with Iraq. But they helped Tehran strengthen its economic links enough to prevent a rapid deterioration in domestic conditions and to continue a war of attrition against its formidable Arab foe. Iran's obstinate stand on the war, particularly in the aftermath of Operation Kheiber and the outbreak of the tanker war, polarized the situation, thereby widening the gulf between it and many of its Arab neighbours. Conversely, Iran became more dependent ideologically on its relationships with Syria and Libya. While it could not remain passive to Iraqi attacks on its shipping in the Gulf, it nurtured its friendship with Damascus with a generous oil deal and tried to accommodate Syrian demands in Lebanon to the best of its ability.[201] The decision to pursue the war, punish Iraq's allies and maintain a defiant stance against an ever growing anti-Iranian coalition raised the value of the Syrian–Iranian alliance enormously in the eyes of the clerical regime. From 1984 onwards, with the expulsion of the MNF and the phased withdrawal of the IDF from Lebanon, the *raison d'être* and utility of close Syrian–Iranian cooperation in the Levant rapidly diminished, especially from the Syrian perspective. However, on the ideological level, the Tehran–Damascus axis provided Iran's revolutionary leaders with an avenue through which to continue their activities against the 'Zionist entity' and dismiss pro-Iraqi accusations that the Gulf War was a historical extension of Arab–Persian rivalries. By now, the conflict with Iraq and a continued presence in Lebanon had assumed huge ideological significance in the eyes of the Iranian leadership. Regardless of the financial, material and human costs, the government had decided to embark on a path to realize its revolutionary designs. The alliance with Syria had become a vital component – an adjunct to the pursuit and realization of those ideological objectives.

For instance, during the May parliamentary debate on rescheduling Syrian debts and renewing the oil agreement, foreign minister Velayati pleaded emphatically for the passage of the bill in ideological terms:

> [Syria has] deep difference with Iraq ... we must grab this opportunity to help keep it on the path of righteousness. ... I must stress that under the current circumstances the only way we can fight the Zionist regime is through our aid to Syria, to the Palestinians and to the Muslim groups in Lebanon who are determined to fight on. If we fail in this, we will be ridiculed all over the world as do-nothing phrase-mongers.[202]

Iranian efforts in August to perpetuate and bolster the Syrian–Iranian axis coincided with an Iraqi initiative to boost relations with Egypt and Jordan. On 12 August, Iraqi foreign minister Tareq Aziz arrived in Cairo for talks with Egyptian officials on how to broaden their cooperative activities, particularly in military matters. The first deputy prime minister Taha Yasin Ramadan was also sent to Jordan to promote the expansion of commercial and economic links between the two states. Despite its failure to launch offensive military operations in the land war, Baghdad's ability to put up a formidable defence against Iranian incursions and enlist sizeable support from the Arabs and both superpowers gave it a major psychological boost in the life-and-death struggle against its intractable Iranian foe.[203]

In the meantime, Iran continued its systematic campaign of terror and intimidation against Iraq's most generous financial backer, Saudi Arabia. The state-controlled media criticized the Saudis for financing French and Soviet arms sales to Iraq, condemned Riyadh's close ties with Washington, and blamed Saudi overproduction for the oil glut on the international market. Besides trying to target vessels bound for Saudi ports in the tanker war, and the Red Sea mining incident, Tehran enlisted the help of pro-Iranian groups on several occasions during summer 1984 to attack Saudi diplomatic outposts, most notably in Lebanon. On 24 August, pro-Iranian Shiite militants stormed the consular section of the Saudi embassy in Beirut and set

fire to the building. The demonstrators, some of them armed Hezbollah fighters, tore down the Saudi flag in the compound and raised
an Iranian flag in its place.[204] Saudi–Iranian relations remained tense
throughout this period. During the hadj, Tehran accused Saudi
security forces of harassing Sunni Iranian clergymen in Mecca, and
aiding and abetting a large group of Iraqis who assaulted some
Iranian pilgrims.[205]

As the rift between revolutionary Iran and many of its immediate
Arab neighbours widened, Syria and Iran took steps to attune their
policy objectives and collaborate more closely in different arenas.
This was highlighted by the visit of Iranian President Ali Khamene'i
to Damascus on 6 September. Khamene'i, who led a high-level delegation, was the most senior ranking Iranian official to visit Syria since
the 1979 revolution. Foreign minister Velayati, commander of the
army Colonel Shirazi, and the Revolutionary Guard corps minister
Rafiqdoust accompanied him. Discussions centred mainly on more
political and military cooperation in the Levant and Gulf. During the
three-day visit in Syria, Colonel Shirazi made an impromptu visit to
Ba'albek under heavy Syrian protection, where he advised Hezbollah
leaders to accept Syria's authority in the city and to concentrate on
expelling the IDF from the occupied south. In an earlier meeting with
Hezbollah leaders in the Syrian capital, Khamene'i also stressed the
need for 'positive cooperation' with the Syrians, and pledged to
support the Shiite resistance in its struggle against the Israelis. In his
discussions with Khamene'i, Assad expressed concern about the
possibility of the Gulf War spreading beyond its present confines and
drawing the superpowers into the conflict. In a joint statement issued
by both leaders before Khamene'i's departure from Syria, the two
sides reaffirmed their commitment to help the Lebanese resistance
against the Israeli invaders, denounced Baghdad's attempts to expand
the scope of the Gulf War, and reiterated their support for the struggle of the Iraqi people against Saddam Hussein. The Iranian delegation subsequently flew to Libya and Algeria to seek support for Iran's
position in the Gulf War and the Arab–Israeli conflict.

Khamene'i's state visit to Syria coincided with the USA vetoing a
draft resolution the Lebanese government had submitted to the UN
Security Council condemning Israel's heavy-handed tactics in the
occupied south. The Lebanese ambassador to the UN expressed 'profound regret' over Washington's decision. On 7 September, the
Iranian foreign ministry issued a statement condemning US support
for Israeli actions that had resulted in the deaths of 'thousands of

innocent Lebanese and Palestinian youths' since the Israeli invasion of June 1982.[206] The next day, anonymous callers informed two foreign news bureaux in Beirut that the Islamic Jihad would retaliate by striking 'an American installation in the Middle East soon'. It was thus no surprise when a suicide bomber drove a truck laden with explosives into the US embassy annex in northeast Beirut on 20 September. An hour after the incident, Islamic Jihad telephoned the AFP office to claim responsibility for the attack. Despite the US State Department's numerous security measures and US intelligence being aware of a recent shipment of explosives from Iran to Lebanon via Syria, Washington was unable to prevent the attack on its only remaining diplomatic outpost in Lebanon. At least 14 people, including two Americans were killed in the blast, while many more were injured. It later transpired that the Lebanese middleman Hassan Hamiz, who had been involved in financing the bombing of the US Marine barracks, was also involved in this operation. US intelligence was able to establish the identity of the suicide driver (who had two or three aliases) as a member of Hezbollah.[207]

There is little doubt from the available evidence that this particular bombing incident, like the previous ones, was carried out with the support of Tehran and the acquiescence of Damascus. Although US–Syrian tensions had decreased since the withdrawal of US forces in late February, the Assad regime was determined to make the Reagan administration pay for persistently backing Tel Aviv; and it would use any means short of a direct US–Syrian confrontation. In Iran's case, the clerical regime had an ideological axe to grind, for anti-Americanism was one of the cornerstones of Iran's Islamic universalist ideology. Also, on a practical level, harming US regional interests was seen as a way of showing Washington that its *rapprochement* with Baghdad and its stance on the Arab–Israeli conflict were not free of costs. Such attacks also enhanced the credibility of the Syrian and Iranian leaders who consistently tried to portray themselves as the vanguard of progressive revolutionaries bent on ousting US and Western imperialists from the Middle East. Anti-Americanism persisted as a common reference point in the ideological outlook and pragmatic calculations of policymakers in both Damascus and Tehran.

Although the USA suffered many setbacks in the region between 1983 and 1984 at the hands of the Syrians and Iranians, in the closing months of 1984, it gradually became apparent that the Reagan administration and its Arab allies were making a major comeback in the region. The first sign of the shifting balance of power came only days after the bombing of the US embassy annex when Jordan announced its decision to restore full diplomatic relations with Egypt after a five-year break. It was the first symbolic, but nonetheless important, step towards the formation of a new Arab alliance intended to serve as a counterweight to the Syrian–Iranian axis, which had been at its apex in the winter of 1983/4. With the Jordanian–PLO *rapprochement* well underway, Jordan's King Hussein believed that the only viable option to resuscitate the Arab–Israeli peace process and simultaneously isolate Syria was to mend fences with Cairo. Despite Egypt's isolation in the Arab world, King Hussein judged the resumption of relations to be a prudent move in several respects. Egypt still carried tremendous political clout in the eyes of the Americans, Arabs and Israelis, and was playing a vital role in sustaining the Iraqi war effort against the Iranians. Furthermore, neither Washington nor Tel Aviv could afford to ignore their most valuable Arab ally, particularly at a time when Egypt was beginning to assume an activist role in regional politics. Jordan's move was the first major milestone in Egypt's gradual reintegration into mainstream Arab politics, which eventually became formalized at the November 1987 Amman summit. Its more immediate impact was that it served as a major catalyst for the formation of the emergent Egyptian–Jordanian–Iraqi–PLO axis. Iraq needed Egyptian assistance to build a credible defence against its intransigent Iranian foe, while King Hussein and Yasser Arafat calculated that with Egypt's weight behind them, they could adopt a more assertive stance in the Levant and neutralize Syrian dominance in the area. Assad's success in gaining a high profile in Lebanon, the Arab–Israeli arena and the Persian Gulf had convinced Amman that radical measures had to be taken to reverse the current trend. The triumph of the Syrian–Iranian alliance had been viewed with much consternation in many Arab capitals. King Hussein and Yasser Arafat firmly believed that rehabilitating Egypt's position in the Middle East far outweighed the risk of incurring the wrath of Syria and Iran, at a time when they were at the zenith of their power.

Syria and its superpower patron the USSR interpreted the move as a US-backed initiative to push Syria off centre stage and limit the Kremlin's margin for manoeuvre at a time when the Soviets were also attempting to mend fences with Jordan and Egypt. Indeed, because the Reagan administration was fixated on looking at regional events through the lens of cold war politics, US policy aimed to sideline Moscow by thwarting its two-tier approach of capitalizing on Syria's gains and simultaneously cultivating links with the moderate Arab states. Furthermore, Washington intended to deny Damascus and Tehran the fruits of their earlier victory.

President Mubarak arrived in Jordan on a three-day state visit 15 days after Jordan announced its intention to re-establish diplomatic relations. After extensive talks on how to cooperate and extend relations, a joint communiqué was issue on 11 October in which the two parties justified the Jordanian–Egyptian entente as an effective means to 'restore the Palestinian people's legitimate rights ... and bolster cohesion that is essential in supporting fraternal Iraq in its just battle'.[208] It is worth mentioning that on a symbolic level, the Mubarak visit to Amman was an explicit gesture to other Arab states to follow in Jordan's footsteps by extending recognition to Cairo and creating a new and formidable Arab bloc.

Damascus and Tehran severely rebuked King Hussein's decision to normalize relations with Egypt and Mubarak's subsequent trip to Jordan. In a sermon delivered at Tehran University on 5 October, Rafsanjani delivered a scathing critique of the Jordanian move, he passionately argued that:

> we see the Islamic Republic dealing so decisively with the Israeli issue; Lebanon, with the hard work done by Syria and by the Hezbollahi people in Lebanon, slapping the USA and global arrogance in the mouth; when the struggles in southern Lebanon demonstrate that the people really can fight Israel ... instead of renewing their [Jordan] vigour and starting to move and follow behind this Hezbollahi line of Lebanon, [they] are moving in the opposite direction and in the name of bringing Egypt back to the Arab countries' fold are themselves falling into the embrace of Israel and the USA.[209]

Similarly, an editorial in the Syrian daily, *Al-Ba'th* on 9 October, analysed the emergence of 'the new Arab reactionary alliance' in a disparaging manner. The article explained:

> The concept of this alliance may have been inspired by the US Administration following the defeat sustained by Washington's policy in Lebanon at the hands of Syria and its allies. ... Washington realized that it was essential to establish a broad regional alliance aimed at confronting this sweeping national rise that is being led by Syria in the region against all the US administration's arrangements.

The rapid pace and direction of political developments in the region greatly alarmed Hafez Assad, who decided to visit Moscow on 15 October, accompanied by a high-level delegation to seek certain assurances from Premier Chernenko.

Soviet Middle East policy's impact on Syria

For many months, the new trend in Soviet Middle East policy under Chernenko's leadership dismayed the Syrians. Throughout this time, Damascus steadily became apprehensive about Soviet intentions in the region. On assuming power, Chernenko reformulated Soviet Middle East policy in an attempt to lessen dependence on Syria as the primary instrument of furthering Soviet objectives in the area, and broadening support beyond the traditionally pro-Soviet radical Arab camp. In the initial phase, the new strategy proved to be quite effective. His overtures towards Amman thawed Soviet–Jordanian relations, resulting in the Jordanian chief of staff's visit to the USSR in August 1984 to negotiate the purchase of Soviet arms and seek clarification on the Soviet peace plan of 29 July, which proposed creating a Jordanian–Palestinian confederation that included the occupied territories. The Syrians were also infuriated by the restoration of Soviet–Egyptian relations during that summer. To add insult to injury, Soviet foreign minister Andrei Gromyko met his Israeli counterpart during the UN General Assembly in New York in September 1984, and PLO chairman Yasser Arafat in East Berlin on 7 October. The unmistakable reorientation in Soviet Middle East policy, coupled with the consolidation of the Jordanian–Egyptian entente, persuaded Assad to visit Moscow to seek clarification on Soviet intentions in the region and acquire additional assistance from the Kremlin.

This was Assad's first trip since his historic visit in October 1980, which led to the bilateral treaty of friendship and cooperation. This time, however, the results were not what he expected. The Soviets tried to persuade him to adopt a more conciliatory approach to Jordan, Egypt and the PLO. They said that Syria should re-evaluate its stance on the Gulf War and stop supporting Iran. They also advocated reopening the IPC pipeline as a first step towards a Syrian–Iraqi reconciliation. To Assad's chagrin, Chernenko linked any increase in Soviet economic and military aid to a Syrian *rapprochement* with the moderate Arab bloc involved in the peace process. Despite the failure to reach an understanding, Damascus refrained from explicitly criticizing Moscow. While the Syrian media reported on the visit in very positive terms, Syria's leaders had no illusions about the decline of their importance from the Soviet perspective.

The tepid state of Soviet–Syrian relations prompted Assad to place more emphasis on cooperating with his regional allies while trying to ease tensions with France. On his return from Moscow, he sent vice-president Khaddam to Libya and Algeria to discuss King Hussein's recent moves and the need to maintain a steadfast position on the USA and Israel. In fact, Damascus and Tehran were very concerned about the growing momentum behind various initiatives to contain their combined power and influence. With US encouragement, Jordan's King Hussein was at the forefront of an overall effort to nullify the recent gains of the Tehran–Damascus axis. Within a week of Mubarak's historic visit, the Jordanian monarch visited Baghdad to discuss the Jordanian–Egyptian *rapprochement*, assistance for the Iraqi war effort, and US moves to bolster this nascent Arab counter axis to frustrate Syrian–Iranian intentions.[210] Much to the consternation of Iran, King Hussein's visit coincided with the delivery of eight new French Mirage F-1 EQ5s to Iraq. The F-1 EQ5 had a longer range than the Super Etendard and earlier versions of the Mirage F-1 received by the Iraq air force. With a combat radius of 700 nautical miles it was capable of hitting Iran's southernmost oil terminal in the Persian Gulf at Lavan Island. Iraq now possessed the ability to strike at any Iranian facility along the Gulf coastline.

In the closing months of 1984, Washington took enormous strides to recoup its losses and regain its previous stature in the Middle East. In the run-up to the US presidential elections in early November, the US and Egyptian military held joint air and naval exercises in the Mediterranean Sea. Moreover, the day after Ronald Reagan's election victory, US assistant secretary of state for Near Eastern and South Asian affairs Richard Murphy travelled to Baghdad to finalize arrangements for the restoration of US–Iraqi relations later that month.

Assad reacted to these developments by sending vice-president Khaddam and foreign minister al-Shara to Tehran. The purpose of the visit was multifold: with a gradual improvement in Franco–Syrian relations well underway, Assad sought to bridge the existing differences between Tehran and Paris; furthermore, with the commencement of bilateral negotiations between Israel and Lebanon on troop withdrawals, he intended to gain Tehran's assurance that it would not try to aggravate the situation in the south and consequently derail the talks.[211] Syrian concerns came at a time when the pro-Iranian Hezbollah movement was growing fast, attracting a large following and eclipsing the more moderate pro-Syrian Amal movement led by Nabih Berri. Furthermore, Assad wanted to moderate some of Iran's policies in the Gulf to prevent further polarization in the region, to the detriment of the Syrian–Iranian camp. Although some press reports at the time stated that the Syrians were hoping to persuade the clerical regime to end the Gulf War, this seems unlikely. During their one-day visit, the Syrian delegation met Rafsanjani, Velayati, and senior presidential adviser Mirsalim. In addition to discussing issues pertaining to the Gulf War, Lebanon and bilateral ties, Khaddam also briefed the Iranian leadership on the results of his deliberations in Libya and Algeria. At the end of the visit Khaddam declared: 'Syria gives special priority to the strengthening of relations with Iran and views the [recent] visit of the Islamic President of Iran, Mr Khamene'i, as an important turning point in bilateral relations and in the union of the progressive countries vis-à-vis conspiracies of imperialism, Zionism and reaction.'[212]

After the talks, al-Shara flew to Riyadh to inform his Saudi counterpart, Prince Saud al-Faisal, of the results of the negotiations in Tehran. Despite much speculation about a major diplomatic breakthrough of some sort leading to a thaw in Iran's relations with the Gulf states or France, no such changes occurred. In the period leading up to a state visit by French President François Mitterand to Syria, in the closing days of November, Assad held an interview with a group of French journalists in which he ardently defended Syria's position in the Gulf War. He vehemently denied that Syria supported Iran, but blamed Iraq for starting a conflict that clearly harmed Arab interests. He went on to posit:

> The [Iranian] Islamic revolution wants to support the Arabs ...
> [and considers] the Palestinian cause an Iranian cause. ... None
> of the Arabs can put Iran and Israel on an equal footing. We
> have a certain joint history and a number of ties with Iran. Iran
> did not and will not claim possession of Arab territories in Iraq
> or in any other Arab country.[213]

Several days later, the French president arrived in Damascus to establish what he described as 'more constructive relations' with the Syrians. It was the first time a French president had visited Syria since it gained independence. Given the historical significance of his arrival and the marked hostility between the two states in the early 1980s, Mitterand made some conciliatory remarks by highlighting that 'nothing can be achieved in the Middle East or in the Near East without Syria'.[214] Although the visit did not bring any major political breakthroughs, particularly with regard to the situation in Lebanon and the Persian Gulf, Franco–Syrian relations did improve to some degree as a consequence. In was clear that Assad's intention was to jolt the USSR into being more forthcoming with military and economic aid by partially feigning a major shift in its foreign policy orientation. To underline this point, Damascus announced its intention to acquire armaments from France and other Western countries.

During Mitterand's visit to Syria, Iraqi foreign minister Tareq Aziz flew to Washington to cement relations with the USA. Following a meeting with President Reagan on 26 November, a joint declaration was issued on the resumption of full diplomatic ties effective immediately. Tareq Aziz was then whisked to a series of meetings with vice president Bush, secretary of state Shultz, defence secretary Weinberger, and national security adviser Robert McFarlane. The move came as no surprise. By the end of 1984 the USA had provided $450 million in financial assistance to Iraq, and extended a $663 million line of credit for the purchase of American wheat. Washington had also consented to the delivery of 60 Bell military helicopters and several Lockheed military transport planes to Baghdad.[215] Predictably, Egypt, Jordan, and Saudi Arabia warmly welcomed the announcement, while Libya, Syria and Iran bitterly criticized it as an act of 'capitulation' and 'treachery'. The latter depicted the action as the final step in Iraq's total abandonment of the 'progressive anti-imperialist' cause in order to join the ranks of the reactionary camp composed of Egypt, Jordan, Israel and the USA.

The beginning of the decline of Syrian–Iranian power

A series of events between December 1984 and March 1985 set in motion the decline of Iran's power and ability to prosecute the Gulf War successfully. At the same time, the reversal of fortunes in the conflict and Israel's decision to begin a three-phased withdrawal from Lebanon had a profound effect on the balance of power in the Syrian–Iranian relationship. Tehran's failure to achieve any real gains against Baghdad, its growing isolation in the Arab world and its increasing uselessness at furthering Syria's agenda in Lebanon, helped turn the alliance into a highly asymmetrical relationship with Syria as the dominant partner. In fact, the growing power of radical pro-Iranian groups in Lebanon like Hezbollah became more of a liability than an asset, for they were growing at the expense of the more moderate Syrian-backed Amal militia. Iranian policy in Lebanon presented an obstacle to the implementation of Syrian designs, especially once it became clear that the IDF was on the retreat in the south.

To a degree, the alliance became a victim of its own success. Contrary to popular belief, from its genesis it had been a defensive alliance. Between 1980 and 1982 the Syrians gave vital assistance to their Iranian allies to stem the Iraqi invasion of Iran and turn the tide of the war. On the other hand, from 1982 to 1985 Tehran gave invaluable support to Syria and the Lebanese Shiites to frustrate US and Israeli ambitions in Lebanon, and eventually to expel them from that war-torn land. By early 1985, it had slowly become apparent that the Islamic Republic had missed a window of opportunity between 1982 and 1984 to bring the Gulf War to a successful conclusion. This can primarily be attributed to the ruling clerics' dismal failure to consider the new constellation of political forces arrayed against them and the changing balance of military power during these years. Against the senior military commanders' better judgement, political and military exigencies were ignored in futile attempts to overthrow the Iraqi Ba'thist regime. Indeed, Iran's revolutionary fervour and missionary zeal had proved to be a double-edged sword. Though vital for mobilizing the Iranian masses to drive the Iraqis out of their homeland, and useful for rallying support among the Lebanese Shiites to thwart US and Israeli policies in Lebanon, the clerics' determination to export their revolution clouded their ability to recognize the resilience of their opponent and the resurgent power of the pro-Iraqi bloc, which had become unmistakably evident by the winter of 1984/5.

By now, the restoration of US–Iraqi relations and the gradual crystallization of the Egyptian–Jordanian–Iraqi axis boosted Iraqi morale and self-confidence. These developments, coupled with the steady stream of French and Soviet armaments, enabled Baghdad to alleviate some of the country's economic woes and pursue a more aggressive military strategy. Starting in December, the Iraqi air force intensified its attacks on Iranian oil shipping in the Gulf. A new prolonged anti-tanker campaign, which proved to be quite effective, was commenced. Within a period of two months, the Iraqis struck 16 tankers in the Gulf, cutting Iranian exports by almost half. Mubarak's second visit to Jordan in early January magnified Iranian vulnerability in the diplomatic arena. Tehran reacted by dispatching emissaries to its various Arab allies and neighbours in an effort to improve its overall regional standing and reverse the slide into isolation. Events were unfolding quite rapidly on several fronts in the Middle East, thereby necessitating some degree of policy coordination.

In addition to the Iraqi air offensive and swift pace of Egyptian integration in regional politics, the Israeli cabinet's decision on 14 January to begin a phased withdrawal from Lebanon required some consideration by the rejectionist states.[216] Deputy foreign minister Hossein Sheikholislam went to Damascus for consultations with Syrian officials and to make arrangements for a meeting of foreign ministers from Iran, Syria, Libya, Algeria and South Yemen: a joint meeting of Syrian, Iranian and Libyan foreign ministers took place in Tehran on 26–27 January. The tripartite talks centred primarily on the current situation in the region and on how to expand cooperation. The Syrian foreign minister al-Shara and his Libyan counterpart al-Turayki also held a series of meetings with President Khamene'i, *Majles* speaker Rafsanjani and Prime Minister Musavi.

As tensions rose in the Gulf, Kuwait and Saudi Arabia led a GCC initiative to try to end the war. On 2 February, the Kuwaiti foreign minister Sheikh Sabah al-Ahmad al-Jabir arrived in Damascus to solicit Syrian support for a peace proposal. Parallel to this visit, Saudi foreign minister Saud al-Faisal went to Baghdad to talk to Iraqi officials. Following the departure of the Kuwaiti foreign minister, Khaddam was sent to Algiers to consult with President Benjedid, whom Iran and Iraq both perceived as an impartial mediator. The plan called for a ceasefire, frontier demarcation and the reopening of the Shatt al-Arab. Suggestions were put forth to have a four-nation committee composed of representatives from Saudi Arabia, Kuwait, Syria and Algeria to supervise and guarantee the implementation of the peace plan.[217] The initiative proved to be futile because of Iran's uncompromising position. The GCC proposal quickly faded into oblivion when Rafsanjani announced on 7 February that the Islamic Republic would not even accept mediation by Syria and, furthermore, intended to launch a major offensive against Iraq.

It seems that by early 1985, with the Israeli threat receding in Lebanon and Iranian obduracy facilitating Egypt's return to the Arab fold, Damascus was becoming more amenable to a negotiated settlement. Throughout 1984, when the Shiite resistance in southern Lebanon stepped up its activities, there were on average 50 attacks on the IDF a month, but by February 1985 the number had doubled.[218] Israeli losses mounted to more than 600 dead and the occupation was costing $1 million a day. Although the Israelis were on the retreat, the PLO–Jordanian agreement (in February 1985) to make a joint attempt to revive the Arab–Israeli peace process heightened Syrian fears of becoming increasingly marginalized in Arab politics.

Operation Badr and the Egyptian–Jordanian–Iraqi entente

On 11 March, Iran launched its first major offensive since the ill-fated Operation Kheiber the previous year. The offensive codenamed 'Badr' was a duplicate of the 1984 operation, although on a relatively smaller scale. Once again, the Iranians hoped to secure a bridgehead west of the Hawizeh marshes in order to push towards Basra and other towns in the southern part of the Tigris–Euphrates delta. Eight divisions composed of 55,000 men, primarily Revolutionary Guards and *baseej* (volunteers), participated in the assault. Against the better judgement of senior military commanders, hawkish clerics on the SDC led by Rafsanjani had once more prevailed in the internal debate. Initially, the Iranian forces made some impressive gains, cutting off the Basra–Baghdad highway, reaching the Tigris and inflicting heavy casualties on the Iraqi defenders. However, after absorbing the initial Iranian attack, the Iraqis swiftly regrouped and repulsed the invaders, driving them back into the marshes. By 17 March, after a week of heavy fighting, the battle was over. The remnants of the Iranian force were in full retreat and all the territory the Iraqis lost in the early stages had been recovered. In strategic terms, it was the worst defeat suffered by Iran in the war. Both combatants incurred heavy losses; the Iraqis lost between 2500 and 5000 men, while Iranian losses were between 8000 and 12,000. Although Iran had suffered worse losses in other battles, this time it had nothing to show for them. Operation Badr was a major fiasco for the Islamic Republic. The defeat sent tremors throughout the ruling establishment and eroded the credibility of the regime in the eyes of the Iranian masses.

Meanwhile, Iraq continued the tanker war in the Gulf while at the same time opening up a large-scale aerial campaign to target Iranian cities. The intensity of the air war was such that within a three-day period the Iraqi air force conducted 158 sorties. Tehran finally felt compelled to target Baghdad and other urban centres in Iraq with Scud-B missiles, which Libya and perhaps Syria had supplied. In the final analysis, Iraq had demonstrated its ability to choose and dictate the terms of engagement in the air and sea. Moreover, in the ground war it had displayed considerable skill in conducting an effective defence. However, in political and symbolic terms a major blow was delivered the day after the battle ended when, on 18 March, Egyptian

President Mubarak and Jordan's King Hussein flew to Baghdad for deliberations with Saddam Hussein and to congratulate him for the impressive victory. Much to the dismay of Iran and its Arab allies, the Mubarak–Hussein visit was a *coup de théâtre* in regional and inter-Arab politics. The sight of Saddam Hussein in military uniform greeting the two Arab leaders at Baghdad airport and walking shoulder to shoulder with them made a profound psychological impact not only on the Iraqis and their allies but also on their opponents. The pictures and television images of the event put beyond dispute Egypt's re-entry into the Arab fold, the consolidation of this new and formidable Arab counter axis and the growing perception that the Gulf War was indeed an Arab–Persian confrontation. After having reached their zenith in 1983/4, Syrian–Iranian power and influence were unquestionably on the decline in the spring of 1985.

Conclusion

The period between June 1982 and March 1985 was one of the most important in the modern history of the Middle East. The events during those three years drastically altered the politics of the region. They ushered in a new era that has left an indelible mark on the international relations of the Middle East.

The Israeli invasion of Lebanon strengthened the Syrian–Iranian axis, giving it a new theatre of cooperation against their mutual foes. Furthermore, the prolonged Israeli occupation radicalized the Shiites, who subsequently (with Syrian and Iranian help) waged an effective unconventional war against the IDF, ultimately forcing the Israelis to cut their losses and withdraw from the Lebanese quagmire. At the same time, Iran's decision to invade Iraq in July 1982 polarized the Arab world, facilitating the reintegration of Egypt and the creation of a new moderate Arab alliance against the rejectionist states led by Syria and Iran. Furthermore, the Islamic Republic's poor conduct in the war and its inability to maintain cordial relations with the super-powers resulted in the thawing of Baghdad's relations with both Washington and Moscow. From 1984 onwards, Iraq figured prominently in the USA's Middle East strategy and played a pivotal role in the Reagan administration's overall approach to safeguard Western interests against states such as Iran and Syria. It should be noted that Israel's failure to attain its objectives in Lebanon had a profound impact on its self-image, and provided the Lebanese Shiites with an enormous morale booster. However, the Syrians and Iranians only achieved a limited victory on the Arab–Israeli front. Syria was unable to gain full control over Lebanon. The civil strife continued for several years. The limits of Syrian power and influence in the Levant were magnified in the winter of 1984/5 by the emergence of a loose alliance between Egypt, Jordan and the PLO, while the Baghdad–Amman–Cairo axis, which had the blessing of Washington and Riyadh, gradually undermined the Syrian–Iranian axis.

During this crucial phase, the Islamic Republic of Iran cooperated with the Syrian Arab Republic for the following reasons:

❑   To maintain an economic stranglehold over Iraq.
❑   To receive military, political, and intelligence support.
❑   To create a constituency among the Shiites in Lebanon to fight the Israelis, Americans, and the French.
❑   To gain some leverage over Syria in its backyard due to the asymmetry in the alliance.
❑   To dispel Iraqi claims that the Gulf War was an Arab–Persian war.
❑   To counter the Baghdad–Amman–Cairo axis.

For the Syrian Arab Republic the liaison with the Islamic Republic of Iran had a variety of purposes:

❑   To check Iraqi power at a time when Syria was confronting Israel and its allies in Lebanon.
❑   To receive generous Iranian oil shipments to compensate for the shutdown of the IPC pipeline.
❑   To utilize Iranian influence to forge an alliance and control the Lebanese Shiites.
❑   To use the Shiites as an instrument to expel the Israelis, Americans and French from Lebanon.
❑   To counter the emergent Egyptian–Jordanian–Iraqi axis.
❑   To act as a mediator in the Gulf to extract concessions from Saudi Arabia and Gulf states, and increase its influence in the area.

However, by early 1985, new political conditions in the region had eliminated much of the *raison d'être* for the alliance, thereby leading to intra-alliance tensions and the decline of Syrian–Iranian power in the Middle East. The alliance went through a critical test of strength and durability between 1985 and 1988, but managed to survive.

Chapter 3

Intra-Alliance Tensions and the Consolidation of the Syrian–Iranian Axis, 1985–88

The period between spring 1985 and summer 1988 was the most tur-bulent and problematic in the history of the Syrian–Iranian alliance. Clashes of interest and disagreements arose in almost every area in which the two states had previously cooperated. The continuation of hostilities between Iran and Iraq in the Persian Gulf, and the gradual internationalization of the conflict, with Tehran continuing to attack shipping bound for the Gulf Arab states in reprisal for Iraqi raids, put Syria in an increasingly awkward position. Moreover, when Iran pulled off its most significant military breakthrough since expelling Iraqi forces from Iran in May 1982 by capturing the strategically-located Faw peninsula in February 1986, Syria was at pains to justify its continued support for a non-Arab state now occupying a sizeable amount of Arab territory. In the Levant, with the completion of the three-phased Israeli withdrawal from most of occupied Lebanon to the self-declared 'security zone' in June 1985, Tehran and Damascus developed con-flicting agendas in that war-torn country. With Hezbollah's rise as a political force among Lebanon's largest minority (the Shiites) at the expense of the pro-Syrian Amal movement, the two sides were increasingly at odds over Lebanon's political future, with the pro-Iranian Hezbollah movement wanting an Islamic republic in Syria's backyard and Amal a secular state within Syria's sphere of influence.

In addition, Iraq's intensive bombing of Iran's oil facilities from August 1985 and the oil price crash in March 1986 in which Tehran's oil revenues were cut by almost 70 per cent in a matter of a few months, added to its economic woes and further complicated bilateral relations with Syria. Iran's refusal to meet Syria's oil requirements and the latter's failure to pay off its oil debts, strained the already troubled relationship. The Iranian leadership was also greatly alarmed by the growing *rapprochement* between Syria and Jordan in early 1986, and King Hussein's subsequent efforts to resolve the differences between Hafez Assad and Saddam Hussein. Jordan's diplomacy received the blessing of other Arab states eager to separate Syria and Iran, mend fences between the two Ba'thist regimes and force Iran to accept a ceasefire. These moves were backed not only by Riyadh and Washington, but also by Syria's superpower patron, the USSR.

Throughout the period between 1985 and 1988, Arab states and the USSR were trying hard to entice Assad to abandon his friendship with Iran. Apart from Syrian–Iranian relations having reached a nadir in 1986/7, Assad had good reason at the time to abandon his alliance with Khomeini's Iran. For a start, it would improve his overall position because he was facing several important challenges simultaneously. These included:

❑ the need to secure Syria's eastern flank with Iraq because of the prospect of a conflict with Israel;
❑ Syria's marginalization in Arab politics with the consolidation of the Egyptian–Jordanian–Iraqi axis;
❑ the marked deterioration of relations with the West and international opprobrium over Syria's alleged involvement in the Hindawi affair;
❑ Iranian activism and interference in Lebanon;
❑ Hezbollah's rise at Amal's expense as a dominant force in Lebanon;
❑ growing Arab–Iranian polarization because of the Gulf War;
❑ Iran's refusal to continue oil deliveries to Syria;
❑ the dismal state of the Syrian economy; and
❑ the gradual cooling of Soviet–Syrian relations in the Gorbachev era, and subsequent abandonment of the quest for 'strategic parity' with Israel.

Why Assad refused to distance himself from Iran and join mainstream Arab politics to minimize the risk of conflict with Israel and the West baffled many observers, for he would have derived considerable benefits, including oil and financial rewards, from the pro-Iraqi camp. Indeed, the USSR, Saudi Arabia and Jordan put considerable pressure on Syria to sever its links with Iran and mend fences with Iraq. Such a move could have eased its security dilemma with Israel, improved its regional and international standing and ensured a flow of economic and financial aid to remedy its dire domestic economic situation.

An examination of how the bilateral ties between Syria and Iran evolved during this critical period reveals the flawed conclusions of those who argued that the alliance was a marriage of convenience, a short-term tactical link between two regimes with disparate ideologies and objectives. It also exposes the limits of the realist school of thought in explaining the behaviour of these two states. If immediate security concerns and material interest had been the driving forces in their foreign policies, particularly in Syria's case, the relationship would have collapsed. However, both parties had broader, long-term strategic concerns derived from their national security priorities and based on their respective ideologies and world views. They saw a unique role for themselves in the region and utility in preserving the alliance to pursue an independent foreign policy to shape events in the Middle East in a desirable manner in the long term, and to minimize foreign influence and penetration of the region.

In this chapter, within the broad context of a rapidly changing regional and international environment, I explain the sequence of events and analyse the conflicting policies Damascus and Tehran pursued in the Persian Gulf region and Levant between 1985 and 1987. To meet emerging challenges, address their most immediate security concerns and balance them with their respective long-term strategic interests and ideological aspirations, the two sides were forced to reassess their priorities. They had to delineate the extent of their influence and activities in the other's backyard and fine tune the workings of the alliance to determine properly the parameters of cooperation and unilateral action without impinging on their partner's primary interests. Consequently, the partners had to formulate a new rationale for their relationship and redefine their goals and functions. Furthermore, their ability to engage in constant dialogue and bilateral consultations, avoid losing sight of long-term strategic interests and modify their ideological principles helped them lay down new foundations for continued cooperation between the two parties and, moreover, the eventual consolidation and institutionalization of the Damascus–Tehran axis. Consequently, by 1987/8 the Syrian–Iranian alliance was maturing into a stable and durable working relationship despite growing Amal–Hezbollah rivalry in Lebanon, despite Mikhail Gorbachev radically changing Soviet Middle East policy by distancing himself from Hafez Assad, despite the USA intervening in the Persian Gulf War as a *de facto* co-belligerent on the side of Baghdad, and despite Iraq finally seizing the initiative and turning the tide of the war.

Syrian–Iranian response to 'pan-Arabization' of the Gulf War

After Iran's disastrous defeat in Operation Badr and the tripartite summit in Baghdad between Saddam Hussein, King Hussein and Mubarak, Syria and Iran quickly engaged in a damage-limitation exercise to bolster their respective positions. This became even more necessary when the GCC council of ministers met in Riyadh between 17 and 19 March and at the end of its deliberations issued a statement in support of Iraq's position in the conflict. Damascus and Tehran adopted a two-pronged strategy to shore up support among regional states and advance their own political agenda. For Syria, this entailed rallying the rejectionist states behind its position and trying to dispel the argument of the pro-Iraqi camp that the Gulf War had become an Arab–Persian conflict. Revolutionary Iran pursued a similar two-track policy of trying to maintain the sympathy and support of the Steadfastness Front and allay the fears of GCC states that Iran was bent on exporting its revolution and had designs on Arab land.

To counter the impact of the tripartite summit and demonstrate their displeasure at the Jordanian–PLO peace initiative, the Syrians held a meeting in Damascus of senior officials from the Steadfastness Front and Iran. Iranian foreign minister Velayati was first sent to Algiers and Tripoli to discuss latest developments with Algerian and Libyan leaders. He then proceeded to Damascus for the opening of the talks, but before this, he delivered a message from President Khamene'i to Hafez Assad. Over a two-day period, Velayati also met his Syrian, Algerian and South Yemeni counterparts, and Libya's Major Jallud. The consultations ended on 21 March with a quadripartite meeting of Syrian, Algerian, Libyan and South Yemeni representatives to coordinate policies and 'confront the deviationist and capitulationist line being peddled by imperialist and Zionist forces'.[1]

Overall, that the main rejectionist states gathered in Damascus for talks enabled Syria to uphold its pan-Arab credentials and partially offset the symbolic effect of the tripartite summit in Baghdad. However, the Steadfastness Front was in a sorry state and now served as nothing more than a talking shop. In sharp contrast to the active military support Jordan and Egypt provided to Iraq, the Syrians were aware that in the event of a conflict with Israel, there was very little that its Arab allies could do to help. Moreover, Damascus failed to get a consensus among the members to schedule a meeting of their respective heads of state to revive the Steadfastness Front formally. Revolutionary Iran, for its part, appreciated Syria's efforts to associate it with the Arab rejectionist bloc, and Syria and Libya's continued willingness to provide it with long-range surface-to-surface missiles for use against Iraq in the ongoing 'war of the cities'.[2]

In the last week of March, at the Arab League meeting in Tunis, Syrian foreign minister Faruq al-Shara reiterated his country's commitment to safeguarding pan-Arab interests, and justified the liaison with non-Arab Iran in terms of guaranteeing the security of the Arab East. He elucidated:

> Syria has at least tried to prevent an expansion of the war to include other Arab states, because we have seen and felt the real dangers of the war becoming an Arab–Persian war – a war that could threaten the national interests of all Arab states and constitute a threat to the security and stability of the region. ... Our continuous contacts with Iran have resulted in the Iranian government's commitment, despite what has happened, not to entertain any expansionist designs on any Arab territory, whether in Iraq or any of the Gulf states. All these efforts are a source of pride to us in Syria and should be a source of pride for the Arab nation. This is because they stem from pan-Arab stands that are aimed at safeguarding the nation's rights and interests.[3]

At the end of the meeting on 28 March, a mild statement was issued to reiterate the Arab League's solidarity with Iraq in defence of its sovereignty, independence and territorial integrity. It also called for an immediate end to the hostilities and a negotiated settlement to bring a just and honourable peace. There was no explicit condemnation of Iran's intractable stance.[4]

The Iranian leadership became increasingly aware that many Arabs saw its determination to carry on the war until Saddam Hussein's overthrow and its ideological imperative to unite Arabs and Iranians under the banner of revolutionary Islam as contradictory. The pro-Iraqi camp was able to exploit growing public disillusionment with Iran by portraying the Gulf War as a continuation of the age-old Arab–Persian rivalry, and depicting Iran's ayatollahs as 'turbaned shahs' bent on imposing Persian dominance on the Arabs under the guise of political Islam. For the Iranian regime, the conflicting currents in its conduct of the war and appeal for Arab popular support represented a major dilemma. On one hand, the general aim to ensure the country's future security by defeating the Iraqi military machine and toppling the Iraqi Ba'th had become inextricably linked with the broader revolutionary goal to set up an Islamic republic in Iraq and create a 'Shiite axis' stretching from the Persian Gulf to the Mediterranean. On the other hand, prolongation of the conflict was prompting an increasing number of Arab states to join the pro-Iraqi camp or, at the very least, tilt towards Baghdad, thereby resulting in Iran's growing isolation and putting its few remaining allies – Syria and Libya – in an awkward position.

From the vantage point of Tehran's revolutionaries, Iran's gradual marginalization in the Arab Islamic world changed the Arab–Israeli theatre, particularly Lebanon, into an arena in which to show their commitment to 'the pan-Islamic struggle against the Zionist entity' and prevent an Arab–Persian schism. They needed a bridgehead in the east Mediterranean to support Lebanese Shiite coreligionists, strive for unity among Lebanon's Shiites and Sunnis and defend Palestinian rights within the country. Tehran's determination to maintain its position as one of the key players in Assad's backyard, its growing reliance on Syria and Libya for certain weapons and its wish to preserve its links with the two main Arab rejectionist states to prove its pro-Arab stance made the Iranian–Syrian nexus asymmetrical, with Iran more dependent on Syrian goodwill.[5]

While Iran's opponents tried to depict the war as a struggle between the 'defender of the Arab East' and the traditional Persian foe, Iranian leaders tried to transcend the nationalist debate and elevate the conflict to a higher plane of progressive, revolutionary forces fighting reactionary nationalists who served foreign masters. In a telling speech to a group of visiting theologians from Islamic countries on 4 May, Rafsanjani declared:

> We consider the Arabic language as one of the noblest in the world and believe that Arabic literature is a divine blessing bestowed upon humanity by the Almighty. It is the language of the Quran, the Prophet, the imams, as well as our religion and history. Our glories in the libraries are all in Arabic. ... Our prayers and more than half of the vocabulary in our literature are in Arabic. So you see that there is no anti-Arab sentiment in the Islamic Republic. On the contrary, we hold a pro-Arab bias. ... Nevertheless, the enemies of Islam are raising the issue of the Arabs and non-Arabs. Fortunately, such Arab countries as Libya and Syria, which are alongside us, have thwarted this propaganda of the enemies. If this issue existed at all, Syria and Libya would not side with us. ... You and us in Iran must be

examples of cooperation between Arabs and non-Arabs, a model of Shiite–Sunni unity, and present a prominent example of Muslim unity. ... If we succeed in keeping ablaze this sacred flame lit by the Islamic revolution in Iran and spread it elsewhere, then there could be hopes for the salvation of the people and the oppressed.[6]

As Iran's loyal supporter, the Syrians were aware of Arab disenchantment with Tehran's conduct in the Gulf region, of the widening rift between Iran and the GCC states as the war against Iraq dragged on, and of the increased chances of hostilities spilling over to engulf the southern littoral states. In the weeks following Operation Badr, Syria engaged in quiet diplomacy in a bid to ease tensions between the GCC and Iran. Damascus focused on trying to thaw Saudi–Iranian relations and it soon became apparent that both Riyadh and Tehran were receptive to the Syrian initiative.

False dawn: Iran attempts reconciliation with GCC states

To improve Arab–Iranian relations and to dent the unity of the pro-Iraqi camp, Tehran went along with Syria's strategy and also embarked on its own 'charm offensive' to allay Gulf Arab fears and mend fences. While the Iranians had no wish to ease the pressure on Ba'thist Iraq, they hoped to persuade its financial backers to adopt a more balanced posture in the war. Syria's effort bore fruit, for both sides sent positive signals. The ensuing flurry of diplomatic activity led to a series of bilateral exchanges between Iran and the Gulf sheikhdoms.[7] The most notable achievement was Iranian foreign minister Velayati's invitation to his Saudi counterpart Prince Saud al-Faisal and his subsequent three-day visit to Tehran in mid-May. Besides two rounds of talks with Velayati, Prince Saud also met President Khamene'i, Prime Minister Musavi and Rafsanjani. Despite their conflicting positions on the Gulf War, both sides seem to have concurred on the need to prevent the expansion of the conflict and strengthen bilateral cooperation. On the issue of the hadj, Tehran promised to refrain from instigating provocative acts during the annual pilgrimage to Mecca, and in return, Riyadh agreed to provide regular shipments of refined petroleum products to Iran for domestic use. Following the successful outcome of the visit, Iran decided to build on the momentum that had been achieved in thawing Saudi–Iranian relations by bridging differences with other Gulf countries. A delegation headed by Velayati's adviser Ali Shams-Ardakani toured the UAE, Qatar, Bahrain, Kuwait and Saudi Arabia to reassure their governments of Iran's intentions in the war. Keenly aware of Iran's wish to reverse its unpopularity in the Arab world, the stalemate in the land war and Iraq's growing assertiveness in the air campaign, the GCC states concluded that the best way to modify Iran's war aims and to prevent the Gulf War spilling over was to engage it in intensive dialogue. Their long-term rationale was to prevent the alienation of Iran from its Arab neighbours, provide it with a stake in normalizing relations and, with a deadlock in the ground war, persuade it to accept a negotiated settlement.

With their wish to enter a constructive dialogue with the Islamic Republic, throughout 1985, the Arab sheikhdoms and other members of the pro-Iraqi camp sought to win over Iran's primary Arab backer, Syria, by trying as a first step to reconcile its differences with Jordan and Iraq. Although their efforts bore fruit as the year progressed, at first, it looked as if developments in the Gulf War and greater inter-Arab polarization would further complicate the overall equation.

The inter-Arab rift, Syrian policy and the Casablanca summit

During the summer of 1985, the rift grew wider between the moderate Arab states and the radical bloc as the two sides jockeyed for power and influence in the region and emerged with diametrically opposed positions on the Arab–Israeli question and Gulf War. Jordan and Egypt spearheaded a movement to resolve the Arab–Israeli conflict peacefully by reviving the dialogue and advocated pan-Arab support for Iraq, accusing the pro-Iranian Arab camp of betraying the greater interests of the Arab nation. Syria and Libya took every opportunity to block their moves and, like Iran, engaged in diplomatic manoeuvring to strengthen the rejectionist camp and minimize any signs of an Arab–Iranian cleavage. Besides political posturing, both camps intensified their propaganda wars against one another.

Syrian and Iranian prestige were enhanced in June by their involvement in the peaceful resolution of the TWA 847 hijacking in Beirut. Besides helping them to some degree shed their unpopular image in the West, their pivotal part in convincing the hijackers to release the remaining passengers led the USA to reassess its policy towards the two countries, particularly Iran (see section on hijacking, pp. 150–2).

Syria's growing power and influence in the Middle East

While Syria's role in resolving the TWA hijacking restored some of its credibility internationally, and boosted its prestige in the region, its Arab adversaries reacted sharply by intensifying their propaganda to portray the Assad regime as a sponsor of terrorism and betrayer of the Arab cause. Jordan, Egypt and Iraq escalated their war of words to diminish Syria's stature and influence in the region. The Jordanians in particular were convinced that Syria was behind the numerous attacks on their foreign representations, including diplomatic out-posts and airline offices abroad in the months following the joint Jordanian–PLO declaration of principles (February 1985). Jordan accused Syria of orchestrating a massive effort aimed at destabilizing the Hashemite kingdom.

In the aftermath of the completion of the third phase of the Israeli withdrawal from southern Lebanon and the peaceful resolution of the TWA hijacking, Syrian power and prestige seemed to be at its pin-nacle. Coupled with its unswerving support for the Iranian war effort and incessant efforts to derail the PLO–Jordanian peace initiative, Syria's notable gains alarmed the moderate Arab states. In view of these developments, an unscheduled meeting between King Hussein and President Mubarak took place in the Jordanian city of Aqaba on 4 July to discuss ways to counter Syria's growing power. Besides Syria's potential to fill the power vacuum left by Israel in Lebanon, the two Arab leaders were fearful that Assad may have exacted a price from the Reagan administration for Syria's role in ending the TWA inci-dent, possibly relating to the Arab–Israeli peace process. Egypt's position on Syria and its other regional rivals was clearly articulated in an interview with its prime minister Kamal Hassan Ali, published in *Al-Watan Al-Arabi* on 19 July, in which he openly accused Damas-cus and Tripoli of involvement in terrorist acts and described the Syrian–Libyan–Iranian camp as an obstacle to Arab solidarity and destructive to Arab interests. The Jordanian news media were also full of reports alleging Syrian involvement in terrorism in Jordan, Leba-non, Kuwait and the Gulf region, underlining Assad's treachery by aiding the aggressive Iranian war effort 'to kill the Iraqi people'.[8] Syria's growing assertiveness was also manifested in a number of incidents in mid-July, when its warplanes crossed into Iraqi airspace in a show of force to intimidate its Ba'thist rival.

Along with maintaining the Syrian–Iranian pincer against Iraq, Tehran continued its policy to forge new links with the Gulf Arabs and drive a wedge between them and Iraq. In late July, a high-level Iranian political-oil delegation arrived in Riyadh to coordinate policy on OPEC affairs with the Saudis to ensure price stability in the international oil market. The Iranian representatives held talks with Saudi foreign minister Saud al-Faisal, and also submitted a message from Ali Akbar Velayati.

As the Gulf War and Arafat–Hussein initiative increased divisions in the Arab world, on 27 July, King Hassan II of Morocco announced his intention to host an emergency Arab summit in Casablanca to clear the air and restore a semblance of unity among Arab ranks. The meeting, the first of its kind in three years and scheduled to start on 7 August, was intended to discuss all aspects of the Palestinian question, including giving King Hussein and Yasser Arafat an opportunity to explain how closely their blueprint conformed to the Fez peace plan of September 1982. While Iraq and the UAE immediately backed the move, Syria was vocal in its protestations, denouncing the scheduled summit as a 'shameful scheme' that threatened the future of the Arab nation.[9] Interpreting the event as a vehicle for advancing the Jordanian–PLO agenda, Damascus immediately signalled its intention to boycott the meeting. Syria's traditional allies, Libya, Algeria, Lebanon and South Yemen, also boycotted the event.

As it turned out, the Casablanca summit was a symbolic victory for the pro-Syrian camp with the 16 delegations present failing to endorse the Hussein–Arafat peace plan, despite the Jordanian monarch's appeal for Arab support. Instead, at the end of the two-day conference, a communiqué was issued to reaffirm the participants' support for the Fez peace plan. Irrespective of Syria's absence and Jordan's lobbying, most Arab states agreed with Assad's position that Arabs must negotiate from a position of strength. Through a combination of obstinacy, intimidation and his opponents' inaction, Assad had prevailed on this occasion.[10] However, decisions were taken at the Casablanca summit that would have a profound impact on Syrian–Iranian relations over the next two years. The participants agreed to form a committee composed of Saudi and Tunisian representatives to mediate between Syria and Jordan, and Iraq and Syria.

The failure of the summit no doubt pleased Damascus and Tehran. On 10 August, the Syrian daily *Al-Thawrah* denounced the whole affair as a meeting of 'capitulationists', while Iran's prime minister Mir Hossein Musavi posited that 'the failure of the so-called Arab summit in Casablanca' was to be expected given the absence of the progressive Arab states.[11] Also, to reaffirm their tripartite cooperation and as a partial riposte to the emergency Arab summit in Casablanca earlier that month, on 24–25 August, the foreign ministers of Syria, Iran and Libya met in Damascus to discuss their relations and developments in the region, and to harmonize their positions in view of the forthcoming meeting of NAM foreign ministers in Damascus. Following their deliberations, a joint statement was issued in which they condemned the PLO–Jordanian agreement and the 'capitulationist' Iraqi–Jordanian–Egyptian–PLO axis, described as detrimental to the Palestinian people, and Arab–Islamic interests respectively. To Tehran's contentment, they denounced 'Saddam Hussein's unjust war against the Islamic revolution in Iran', and criticized Iraq's bombardment of cities, attacks on oil tankers and the use of chemical warfare.[12] The Syrian and Libyan foreign ministers also declared their satisfaction with Iran's repeated guarantees that it had no designs on Iraqi territory and sought good, neighbourly relations and Islamic brotherhood with the Iraqi and Arab peoples. In conclusion, they announced their intention to hold the next tripartite meeting in Tripoli in December of that year.

In many respects, this was the one of the last trouble free meetings Syrian and Iranian officials were to have until 1988. By the autumn, new developments in the Gulf conflict and inter-Arab politics would threaten their alliance and trouble the relationship for almost two years. Tensions were emerging over the two partners' growing rivalry and disparate objectives in Lebanon. The rise of Hezbollah as a key player in the domestic Lebanese power game in the winter of 1984/5, coupled with Syria's and Iran's conflicting visions of Lebanon's political future, ushered in a competitive period of recurrent disputes between Damascus and Tehran. In spring 1985, cracks had already begun to appear in the alliance. Intra-alliance tensions and distrust were soon magnified because of unforeseen events in the Gulf conflict and attempts by pro-Iraqi states to persuade Syria to abandon its friendship with Iran. Before looking at events in the Persian Gulf, the changing dynamics of the Syrian–Iranian alliance need to be reviewed within the context of the evolving situation in Lebanon.

The beginnings of Syrian–Iranian rivalry in Lebanon

By spring 1985, with a power vacuum emerging from Israel's retreat, Syria and Iran wanted to enjoy the fruits of their common victory by playing a major role in Lebanon's political future. However, they had conflicting views of how the war-torn country fitted into the broader framework of their regional foreign policies. Syria, having thwarted the creation of an Israeli–US condominium in Lebanon in 1984/5, and having ousted hostile foreign forces from the country, now had a chance to stabilize the situation by bringing the entire country into its sphere of influence. Furthermore, with its new-found prestige and status, Syria was determined to pursue a more activist regional foreign policy to frustrate the moderate Arab states' attempts to reach an agreement with Israel (without addressing Syrian concerns) and to weaken the pro-Iraq camp by exploiting differences among its members to extract concessions from them whenever possible.

Iran's pivotal role in frustrating Israeli–Western designs in Lebanon by helping its Syrian ally and Lebanese Shiite coreligionists had been one of its crowning foreign policy achievements, particularly in ideological terms. By dealing a blow to the 'Zionist–Imperialist' camp, it had demonstrated that the struggle to liberate Palestine was not the exclusive domain of the Arabs. Although the Islamic Republic was at war with a 'reactionary' Arab regime in the Gulf, this in no way diminished its sense of solidarity with progressive Arab states in their struggle. With the Israeli threat now receding, Iran sought to replicate the establishment of a theocratic state in Lebanon as a means of spreading its revolution, and use it as a springboard to strike against Israel in the campaign to liberate Palestine.

Besides the stark contrast in their ideological objectives in Lebanon, Syria and Iran fell out over a number of important issues during the course of 1985. The three main areas of contention revolved around the growing rivalry between the Shiite Amal and Hezbollah militias, Amal's attempts to blockade the Palestinian refugee camps, and Syria's confrontation with the IUF (*Harakat al-Tawheed al-Islami*) in the northern port city of Tripoli.

The rise of the pro-Iranian Hezbollah movement

As stated earlier, after Israel started its phased withdrawal from most of southern Lebanon in December 1984, Amal and Hezbollah fighters stepped up their attacks on the IDF in the occupied areas and, by January 1985, the Israelis had lost more than 600 men and the occupation was costing them over $1 million a day.[13] While the Syrian, Iranian and Libyan foreign ministers were at a tripartite meeting in Tehran in January 1985, intelligence officials from the three countries held talks at the same venue to coordinate their efforts to help the Lebanese resistance roll back the Israelis. As a direct outcome of the deliberations, Iran was given easier access to Lebanon via land routes from Syria previously reserved for the Syrian army. Libya also agreed to finance Syria's purchase of a consignment of Soviet-made Grad and Sagger anti-tank missiles for use by Hezbollah in southern Lebanon.[14] As clashes between the combatants intensified in the following weeks, the Israelis withdrew from Sidon on 16 February.[15] By March, there had been 1145 reported attacks against the Israelis over two years.[16] Soon afterwards, Israeli prime minister Shimon Peres promised the Israeli public that the IDF would pull out of Lebanon within ten weeks. Furthermore, in an interview on 3 April, defence minister Yitzhak Rabin admitted that Tel Aviv had several times tried to reach an understanding with the Lebanese Shiite leaders, but that 'Syria had foiled most of those contacts'.[17] In a meeting on 25 April with Lebanese Muslim leaders in Damascus, Syrian president Hafez Assad called on the Lebanese resistance to redouble its efforts to expel the Israelis and their allies from Lebanon, declaring that 'the south has become Israel's Vietnam ... no effort should be spared to support the nationalist resistance until the Israeli enemy is driven out of all Lebanese territory.'[18] By the end of April, the IDF had pulled out of Tyre and strategic positions in southeastern Lebanon facing Syrian positions.

Eventually, on 6 June 1985, the third anniversary of the invasion of Lebanon, Major-General Ori Orr, commander of the IDF northern command, announced that his forces had completed their three-phased withdrawal to the self-declared 'security zone' in south Lebanon, where its surrogate force, the 3000-strong SLA and 1000 Israeli soldiers were deployed to prevent attacks on northern Israel. By then, the Israelis had lost 750 troops in Lebanon. Although they had succeeded in eliminating the PLO presence in Lebanon, they now faced an implacable fearsome foe that was home grown, Hezbollah.

The Israeli withdrawal in the first part of 1985 fundamentally transformed the Lebanese equation and general perceptions of the contending parties inside and outside Lebanon. Besides bringing Syria and Iran into conflict, other players also tried to pursue divergent agendas in the Lebanese arena. Domestic groupings like the Phalangists, the IUF (Tawheed) and Hezbollah tried to advance their own agendas, even if they ran counter to Syrian wishes, while Yasser Arafat saw the IDF retreat as a chance to re-establish a Palestinian foothold in Lebanon to strengthen his hand against the Israelis and his Arab rivals, particularly Syria. As it would turn out, while many of their actions were destructive to Syrian interests in Lebanon, Iran was to varying degrees sympathetic to the Shiites, Sunnis and, to Syria's chagrin, even the Palestinians. The rapidly unfolding events and conflicting goals of the various parties created an extremely complex situation, at times, pitting the Syrians against their Iranian and Libyan allies. Assad's initiative to establish a Pax Syriana in Lebanon and buttress the position of Nabih Berri's Amal militia encountered resistance in many corners of Lebanon. The first of a series of crises erupted in spring 1985 when Amal tried to assert itself in Beirut and its environs.

The dominance of Amal and Iranian activities

Despite Hezbollah's rise, the Amal militia was still the most dominant Shiite party in Lebanon in 1984/5. As Tel Aviv continued its phased withdrawal in April–May 1985 and Palestinian fighters began to trickle into Lebanon with the help of some Lebanese parties, Amal tried to assert itself in Beirut and the south. While Amal, with Syrian consent, gradually began to clamp down on pro-Arafat Palestinians and their Sunni allies, and tighten its control over the areas it occupied, Iran embarked on a campaign to bolster the position of its Shiite allies, consolidate relations with the Sunni fundamentalists it had been cultivating for some time and, to boost Islamic solidarity in the war-torn country, forge close cooperative links between the Shiite and Sunni communities. Tehran seems to have sensed that the opportune moment had arrived to lay the ground for the eventual creation of an Islamic state in Lebanon by rallying Lebanese Shiites and Sunnis around the banner of revolutionary Islam.[19] In fact, Hezbollah already had steadfast support from Sunni fundamentalists. At least six prominent Sunni clerics in West Beirut were sympathetic to Hezbollah, while in Sidon, a Shiite cleric with Iranian ties, Sheikh Maher Hammoud, set up the 'Islamic Front', an umbrella organization for Shiite and Sunni clerics who espoused Hezbollah's cause. Moreover, in the Sunni-dominated city of Tripoli in northern Lebanon, Tehran and Hezbollah forged close ties with Sheikh Said Shaban, leader of the IUF (Tawheed). While receptive to overtures from Iran and its Lebanese allies, Shaban, who governed the city as an Islamic fiefdom, was anti-Syrian and opposed pro-Syrian forces in the region.

To promote their grand design in Lebanon, Hojjatolislam Mehdi Karrubi, Khomeini's representative and head of the powerful Martyrs' Foundation, led an Iranian delegation to Syria and Lebanon in early May 1985 to review developments with their Arab allies and coordinate their efforts. While in Lebanon, Karrubi consulted Sheikh Fadlallah, Hezbollah's spiritual leader, and Hassan Khaled, the mufti of Lebanon's Sunni community. He described his visit as a congratulatory tour in view of the triumph of the Muslim resistance against the 'Zionist occupiers in southern Lebanon' to lend additional support to the strugglers against the 'Zionist state'.[20]

Iran's revolutionary clerics clearly intended to profit from the situation in Lebanon. With the IDF in retreat and a weak Lebanese government, Tehran sought to fill the political void by creating a Shiite–Sunni bloc to dominate Lebanese politics and tow the Iranian line. Having since 1982 put enormous resources into establishing a bridgehead in Lebanon, Iran's clerical regime was now determined to export its revolution to an Arab state bordering Israel and to maintain its new springboard for future endeavours in the eastern Mediterranean. Its failure to topple Saddam Hussein and establish an Islamic state in Iraq after three years of trying, clearly reinforced its determination to implement the project in Lebanon. Only in Lebanon had the Iranians gradually been able to win over the hearts and minds of many Shiites and Sunnis, and sow seeds in its fertile ground for the growth of revolutionary Islam. Given the stalemate in the Gulf conflict, Lebanon offered the only promising channel for Tehran's missionary zeal. Conversely, Syria's intention to stabilize the situation by creating a secular government composed of all the various sects and maintaining the country firmly within its sphere of influence, put Tehran and Damascus on a collision course. Interestingly, Palestinian attempts to make inroads in Lebanon precipitated the first major crisis between the two allies in the spring of 1985.

The beginning of the 'war of the camps' in Lebanon

With PLO fighters continuing to return to Lebanon in early 1985, infiltrating the three main Palestinian refugee camps of Sabra, Shatila and Bourj al-Barajneh in West Beirut, the situation came to a head in late May when Amal, in a bid to destroy Palestinian armed strength and assert its control, laid siege to the camps. By the time the fighting erupted on 20 May 1985, it is estimated that 5000 PLO guerrillas had made their way back to Beirut.[21] By the end of May, Amal, with the help of the Lebanese army's predominantly Shiite sixth brigade, had routed Arafat loyalists in Sabra and brought the camp under its control. However, to their surprise and to that of their Syrian patrons in Shatila and Bourj al-Barajneh, PLO and anti-Arafat elements joined forces to resist the Amal onslaught. The assault on the camps galvanized the rival Palestinian groups. To Assad's dismay, the anti-Arafat Damascus-based PNSF performed a volte-face. George Habash, head of the Popular Front for the Liberation of Palestine, left Damascus in protest and the DFLP's relations with Syria became strained. The siege dragged on and by early June, Amal and the sixth brigade also occupied much of Shatila. They insisted the Palestinians give up their weapons and allow the sixth brigade to oversee security in the refugee districts. PLO loyalists and even the PNSF, which claimed to speak on behalf of camp residents, rejected their terms outright.

Syria had only recently dealt decisive blows to the Israelis and Americans in Lebanon, but the 'war of the camps' now threatened to undermine its new power and prestige as champion of the Arab–Palestinian cause. It also jeopardized its relations with the radical states in the region, including Libya, Iran and South Yemen, all of which were now critical of its conduct. Revolutionary Iran was in an awkward position *vis-à-vis* its closest Arab ally. Tehran reacted cautiously when fighting broke out, with its foreign ministry issuing a vague statement about the clashes being 'a product of a dangerous conspiracy intended to divert the struggle of Muslim forces from the real enemy'.[22] For Iran's alliance with Syria and its interests in the region, the conflict between Amal and the Palestinians came at an inopportune moment and was detrimental in several respects. As previously mentioned, with the impasse in the Gulf and growing Arab disenchantment with Iran's conduct in the war, Tehran needed to confirm its revolutionary credentials by maintaining harmonious relations with Syria, strengthening its foothold in Lebanon, encouraging Shiite–Sunni unity and keeping up the momentum in the struggle against the Israelis in order to liberate Palestine and discredit proponents of the PLO–Jordanian initiative. Not only was the fighting straining its relations with Damascus, but it was also creating undesired effects, including dividing the Shiite community, exacerbating cleavages between the Shiites and Sunnis, diverting attention from the Israeli presence in the south and undermining the position of opponents of the Arafat–Hussein peace plan.

As the hostilities continued, top Iranian clerics voiced displeasure at the events unfolding in Beirut. At a meeting of Lebanese clerics and theological students in the holy city of Qom on 28 May, Khomeini's chosen successor, Grand Ayatollah Montazeri, denounced those who exploited Lebanese Shiites for their own political ends and caused bloodshed between Muslim Palestinian refugees and groups of struggling Lebanese Shiite Muslims. Montazeri lashed out, arguing 'these people must repent and change their ways, and end the bloodshed and killing of Muslims which is unfortunately done in the name of Shiism in Lebanon. They must not provide so much propaganda material for the media of the enemies of Islam.'[23]

Within ten days of the fighting erupting, Iran had launched a concerted diplomatic effort to end the hostilities and exercise damage control. A foreign ministry team led by director-general for political

affairs Hossein Lavasani was sent to Damascus in late May for meetings with Syrian foreign minister Faruq al-Shara and anti-Arafat
Palestinian leaders. On 30 May, it proceeded to Beirut to see Sheikh
Hassan Khaled, the Sunni mufti, and Sheikh Hussein Fadlallah of
Hezbollah. The next day IRGC minister Mohsen Rafiqdoust arrived in
Syria bearing a message from Ali Khamene'i for Hafez Assad. Prior to
his arrival, Rafiqdoust had been in Libya holding talks on recent
developments with Qadhafi. Although the ostensible purpose of his
mission was to negotiate an end to the crisis in Lebanon, his main
priority seems to have been to obtain surface-to-air and surface-to-
surface missiles from Tripoli and Damascus to counter the Iraqi air
offensive and retaliate against Iraqi targets.[24] By all accounts, on his
arrival in Damascus, Hafez Assad received Mohsen Rafiqdoust reluctantly. Assad expressed deep displeasure at the caustic remarks of
some Iranian leaders and asserted that Syrian interests took primacy
in Lebanon. Rafiqdoust, for his part, while trying to allay concerns
and request assistance from the Syrian leader, stressed that Iran had a
privileged position in Lebanon and that the other parties could not
ignore its power and influence.[25]

Meanwhile, in a bid to defuse the crisis, Mehdi Karrubi travelled to
Syria and Lebanon again at the head of a delegation. On 1 June, he
met Syrian vice-president Khaddam in Damascus, then proceeded the
next day to Beirut to contact, in his words, 'revolutionary and
concerned forces ... to quell the fire of dissension and war, and rally
all the forces against the real enemies ... the Zionists and the USA'.[26]
Aware of the delicacy of the situation and Syrian sensitivities, in an
interview in Beirut on 4 June Karrubi tried to portray Syrian–Iranian
relations in a positive light. He stated: 'we agree with Syria that these
clashes are the results of plots against the Lebanese and Palestinian
people.' Treading even more cautiously when asked if Iran wanted to
see an Islamic republic created in Lebanon, he explained that Lebanon's government was a domestic issue for the Lebanese people to
decide. He added: 'we respect the right of nations to decide their
destiny; we will accept any system which has been approved by the
majority of the Lebanese people.'[27]

With the continuation of the siege, Iranian–Amal relations plunged
to new depths when Amal militiamen detained Karrubi's entourage
while he was touring southern Lebanon and forcibly took them back
to Beirut. Angered by what was seen as Amal's intransigence with
Syrian acquiescence, Iran's prime minister Musavi castigated Syria for
what he called its implicit 'cooperation' with Tel Aviv and Washing-

ton. He postulated that 'the disarming of Palestinians in Lebanon is serving Israeli interests and strengthens the hand of America the warmonger'.[28] Montazeri also reacted sharply to the Karrubi incident, contending that 'the fighting between the Palestinians and Shiites will create deep wounds and hatred between Muslims. It is the aim of America and Israel to destroy Islam's unity. All those who encourage such a scheme are traitors to Islam.'[29]

By early June, the situation was spiralling out of control on several fronts, with Syria losing its grip in Lebanon. In the northern city of Tripoli, Tawheed fighters, angered by Syria's policies, engaged the mainly Alawite pro-Syrian ADP militia in armed conflict, while in Beirut, the pro-Nasserite Murabitoun mounted hit-and-run attacks against Amal and the sixth brigade, apparently with Libya's blessing. But the worst was yet to come. Walid Jumblatt's PSP, having all along been sympathetic to the Palestinians' plight, became increasingly alarmed by Amal's actions. In the early stages of the Amal–Palestinian clashes, Druzes passively supported the Palestinians by giving protection to those fleeing the carnage and passing on Libyan arms and supplies to Palestinian fighters in the camps. However, the situation finally came to a head on 11 June, when large-scale fighting broke out between PSP and Amal fighters in West Beirut.

The TWA 847 hijacking and Syrian–Iranian intervention

To gain the upper hand in their struggle for the soul of Lebanon's Shiite community, Shiite radicals decided to voice their grievances against Israeli policies in the south on the world stage. On 14 June, as the internecine fighting intensified, Shiite militants hijacked TWA flight 847 carrying 145 passengers from Athens to Rome. As a consequence, international attention suddenly focused on Lebanon and tensions rose to new heights. The hijackers demanded the release of 753 Lebanese Shiites whom the Israelis had apprehended and transported back to Israel, and 17 Shiites imprisoned in Kuwait implicated for bombing US and French installations in the emirate two years earlier. The aircraft initially shuttled back and forth between Beirut and Algiers. As negotiations between the hijackers and the authorities got underway, the hijackers gradually agreed to release different groups of passengers, including women, children and non-Americans. Eventually, only 39 male Americans remained captive.

The hijacking was part of a broader power struggle between Hezbollah and Amal, which Shiites associated with Hezbollah had orchestrated to secure the release of their coreligionists detained by Israel, to win the support of the Lebanese Shiites and to undermine Amal's position. Sensing that the hijacking might be a potential embarrassment, Nabih Berri quickly offered to mediate in the crisis. He persuaded the hijackers to take the remaining hostages off the plane in Beirut. The hijackers kept some and Amal militiamen took others into custody. After 17 days, largely due to Syrian and Iranian intervention, the crisis was finally resolved on 30 June with the 39 passengers being freed and Israel buckling under pressure to allow an 'unrelated' release of 300 Shiite detainees. In the immediate aftermath, Berri's standing rose considerably in the eyes of both the West and Lebanese Shiites, for he was able to portray himself as politically astute and reasonable, with the hostages being freed unharmed and some of the Shiite prisoners being released by the Israelis. Berri had snatched victory out of the jaws of defeat, ostensibly by cutting a deal with both Hezbollah and the USA. It should be stressed that both Syria and Iran had played a crucial role in ending the affair through intensive deliberations and behind the scenes bargaining.

A solution to the crisis was found immediately after the Iranian speaker Rafsanjani had visited Damascus after a trip to Libya. He came at the head of a delegation that included foreign minister Velayati and Revolutionary Guards minister Rafiqdoust. During their meetings with Hafez Assad, the Syrian leader urged them to intervene and persuade Hezbollah to free the hostages.[30] The Syrians were eager to resolve the crisis as soon as possible and so avert a potential showdown with the USA. The hijacking and ensuing crisis had come at an inopportune time, further complicating an already extremely complex situation for the Syrians in Lebanon. The composition of the Iranian delegation and the fact that its previous stop had been Tripoli suggested that its objectives were multifold. Tehran was keen to secure more Soviet-made missiles from its Arab allies both for use against Iraq and to force Amal to lift the siege on the Palestinian camps, which it saw as detrimental to Muslim unity and its revolutionary aspirations in Lebanon.[31] During the visit, Rafsanjani publicly denounced Amal for not being a genuine representative of Lebanon's Shiites, for it was helping 'imperialist-Zionist' aspirations to annihilate the Palestinians.[32]

Following the deliberations between Syrian and Iranian officials, a group of prominent Shiite and Sunni clerics, including Sheikh Shamseddin, Sheikh Fadlallah, Sheikh Shaban of Tawheed and the Bekaa council of ulema arrived in Damascus to meet Rafsanjani to discuss conditions in Lebanon and find a solution to the TWA affair.[33] During consultations with Syrian and Lebanese Muslim leaders, Rafsanjani expressed his willingness to intercede. According to some sources, Syria and Iran agreed to an arrangement whereby Tehran would help Damascus secure the hostages' freedom in exchange for assistance in procuring desperately-needed Soviet weaponry for the war effort against Iraq.[34]

Syrian and Iranian moves in Lebanon during the summer of 1985

From the outset of the TWA affair, the Syrians also stepped up efforts to resolve the Amal–Palestinian conflict in an attempt to avoid the erosion of their position in Lebanon. Although the Syrians had a major stake in Lebanon's political future, they were loath to intervene militarily in Beirut for fear of being pulled into the fray and sustaining heavy casualties. Syria did not want to be seen as an ally of any group, taking sides against another. The protracted siege had not only embarrassed Syria, and called into question its position as champion of the Palestinians, but had also jeopardized its relations with Iran, Libya and even to some extent, the USSR.

The five-week 'war of the camps' finally ended when the Syrians brokered a ceasefire concluded in Damascus on 18 June. The accord, which Vice-President Khaddam put together and Amal and the PNSF signed, stipulated that the Palestinians could keep their light weapons and entrusted Lebanese gendarmes with security in the refugee camps. The agreement won the approval of the other Palestinian factions and of the Druze PSP. In reality, it was a setback for Amal and the Syrians, for the Palestinian guerrillas were entitled to retain their light arms and, to Amal's dismay, the PNSF was given an official political role in Lebanese affairs. Amal had had to give up its declared objective of putting the camps under the control of the predominantly Shiite sixth brigade. Despite gaining ground in the fighting, Amal had suffered extremely high casualties and could not have sustained its campaign without incurring the wrath of the Murabitoun, Hezbollah, the Druze PSP and various Palestinian factions.[35] At the same time, the ceasefire could not have come sooner for the Palestinians, since they had almost run out of ammunition, and suffered enormously. More than 600 refugees were killed and 2500 wounded during the blockade.[36] Within days the siege was lifted.

Though Assad eased tensions and restored a semblance of peace in Beirut, despite constant efforts throughout the summer of 1985, he failed to get Lebanon's leading political leaders to accept a reconciliation plan that entailed reforming the country's archaic political system. In early autumn, Assad then focused his energies on forging a consensus among the three main militia leaders, Berri, Jumblatt and Hobeika. He decided to bypass the traditional political leaders, who were being obstinate and uncooperative, and seek a solution by getting the three most powerful militias in the country, Amal, PSP and the Lebanese Forces, to reach an agreement. In September, he arranged reconciliation talks between them in Damascus.

Throughout this period, Syria and Iran jockeyed to strengthen their hand and consolidate their position in Lebanon. Iran, for its part, continued to cultivate relations with fundamentalist Lebanese and radical Palestinian groups to preserve its revolutionary credentials, expand its base of support in Lebanon and inspire its followers to wage war on 'the Zionists and agents of Western imperialism'. In August, during the Arab summit in Casablanca, a PNSF delegation led by Abu Musa and Ahmed Jibril visited Tehran and met Prime Minister Musavi and Foreign Minister Velayati. Prior to their departure from Tehran, at the end of their eight-day visit, in a press conference, Abu Musa described the Casablanca summit as a failure and declared that Iran was the first non-Arab country to recognize the PNSF as the representative of the Palestinians. In fact, the Palestinian mission in Tehran, previously run by PLO personnel, was handed over to Abu Musa, giving the PNSF its only major representation outside Syria.[37]

Immediately following the PNSF delegation's visit, Hussein Musawi and Sheikh Subhi al-Tufayli of Hezbollah arrived in Tehran where they held talks with Revolutionary Guards minister Rafiqdoust and foreign minister Velayati about the situation in Lebanon and the fate of seven Americans and four Frenchmen held hostage by Hezbollah. Damascus was pressing Tehran at the time to use its clout to secure their release.[38] The two sides also explored ways to cement their relations. Musawi and al-Tufayli were subsequently granted an audience with Ayatollah Montazeri, who was a strong advocate for the establishment of an Islamic republic in Lebanon.[39]

The taming of Tripoli and Iran's intercession

While Syria and its Lebanese allies made good progress in stabilizing the situation in Beirut and southern Lebanon, the longstanding dead-lock in the northern city of Tripoli persisted. With tensions between Tawheed and the pro-Syrian ADP, and Tawheed's close links with the PLO and its attempts to prevent Syria controlling the city and its

environs, Damascus tried to assert itself by insisting that Tawheed
acquiesce to the deployment of Syrian troops in Tripoli and disarm its
fighters, in effect relinquishing control of the city to the Syrian army.
Sheikh Shaban agreed to Syrian forces being positioned in certain
sections of Tripoli to back up Lebanese army units and gendarmes
maintaining security in the city, but steadfastly refused to accept that
his militiamen surrender their weapons and give up control of the
city – a privilege Tawheed had enjoyed for two years.

Once again, events in another part of Lebanon put Syria and Iran at
loggerheads, this time in the north. Besides Iran nurturing the growth
of Hezbollah at Amal's expense in the south and supporting the Palestinians in Beirut, the two allies now found themselves on opposite
sides of the fence in Tripoli. This was the third major area of contention in Lebanon between the two in 1985. Apart from the ongoing
rivalry between Tawheed and the ADP, unconfirmed reports of the
PLO channelling funds and resources back into the Tripoli area and
of its fighters beginning to trickle back in under Tawheed's protection
exacerbated the situation and, on 15 September, fighting broke out
again between Tawheed and ADP militiamen. The Syrians subsequently sent a military delegation to arrange a ceasefire and impose
their conditions, but to no avail. So intense was the fighting during
the first ten days that 250,000 of the city's 700,000 inhabitants fled
their homes, 150 to 200 people were killed and 600 were wounded.[40]
Iran sent its deputy foreign minister Hossein Sheikholislam to Damascus to meet Syrian officials, express Iranian concern about the conflict in Tripoli and try to find a peaceful solution to it. With Shaban
refusing to yield to a Syrian diktat, Damascus abandoned its efforts to
persuade him to agree to its terms on 27 September, and opted to
break the impasse through the use of force. Assad was determined to
demonstrate his unbending resolve to impose control and hegemony
over Lebanon.

The Syrians assembled a coalition of militias from the SSNP, LCP
and Lebanese Ba'th Party in Syrian-held areas on the outskirts of Tripoli to attack the city and dislodge the Tawheed fighters. Although
pro-Syrian, these parties had a score to settle with Shaban: they had
been driven out of Tripoli in 1983 when Sunni fundamentalists seized
control. Determined to roll back Tawheed and re-establish a presence
in Tripoli, the pro-Syrian forces launched a coordinated assault on
Tawheed positions and advanced under cover of a Syrian artillery and
rocket barrage. They attacked on three fronts while ADP militia
engaged Tawheed forces in the city.

Meanwhile, Sheikholislam continued his deliberations with members of the Syrian leadership, including Assad, Khaddam and al-Shara. Tehran was anxious to stop the bloodshed, particularly in view of Syria's heavy and indiscriminate bombardment of the city. As a direct result of these talks, the Syrians reluctantly accepted Sheikholislam's proposal to send a delegation of Iranian diplomats from the Damascus and Beirut embassies to Tripoli to initiate talks with Shaban and to bring him back to Damascus for direct negotiations with Syrian leaders.[41] Although the Iranian team made it to Tripoli, increased fighting on 28 September prevented them from bringing Shaban out. Subsequently, efforts were made to impose a temporary ceasefire to allow Shaban to travel to Syria. On 1 October, Khamene'i called Assad and discussed the crisis with him at length. As a direct consequence, an Iranian team was sent once again to Tripoli, returning successfully this time with Shaban and one of his associates. Negotiations between Shaban and the Syrians took place in the presence of Iranian officials and Hezbollah leaders. Finally, on 3 October, Assad presided over the signing of an accord ending the hostilities. The agreement signified a Syrian victory, leaving no doubt that Syria would be the dominant actor in Tripoli from now on. While Shaban's movement had avoided total defeat and annihilation, and Tripoli was spared a fate similar to Hama, Tawheed was militarily defanged. Under the terms, which Shaban accepted, all medium and heavy weapons were to be turned over to the Syrian forces and small arms stored in specified depots subject to Syrian inspection. All secular parties banished from the city were allowed to re-establish a presence. Syrian troops, supplemented by Lebanese army and gendarme units, were stationed in Tripoli to maintain law and order, while the responsibility for overall security of the city was given to the commander of Syrian forces in northern Lebanon.[42]

On 6 October, four battalions of Syrian soldiers and tanks entered Tripoli and dispersed throughout the city. Tawheed fighters and their opponents handed over their weapons as stipulated in the agreement.[43] The 'taming of Tripoli' had been a bloody affair. By the time the ceasefire was imposed after three weeks of fighting, 500 people had lost their lives, more than 1000 had been wounded and extensive collateral damage had occurred.[44] While Syrian troops had not been directly involved in the fighting, the showdown demonstrated the extent to which Assad was willing to go to impose a Pax Syriana in Lebanon. Moreover, at a time when he was going through painstaking efforts to persuade the leaders of the Phalange, Druze PSP and Amal to agree on political reforms and a new order in Lebanon, Assad had deemed it necessary to pound the defiant Sunni enclave mercilessly, and to set an example for potentially recalcitrant parties.[45]

Syrian–Iranian rivalry and the tripartite agreement

Syria's fight with Tawheed caused a great deal of umbrage in Tehran. Iran's clerics saw Syrian moves to prop up Amal at Hezbollah's expense and crush the Palestinian resistance movement in Lebanon as detrimental to their grand plan to unite Lebanon's Shiites and Sunnis, along with the Palestinians, under the banner of revolutionary Islam and liberate Palestine. During the crisis, editorials in Iran's state-controlled media lambasted Syrian conduct, accusing Damascus of waging a 'war against Islam'.[46]

Given the Syrian regime's sensitivity to being called anti-Muslim or anti-Sunni, the vitriolic rhetoric from Tehran caused disenchantment in official circles in Damascus. Iran's criticism of the ongoing tripartite talks in Damascus between Berri, Jumblatt and Hobeika put Syrian–Iranian relations on a shakier footing. The participation of Hobeika, who had been responsible for the Sabra and Shatila massacres in 1982, gnawed at the Iranians. They were also infuriated that the Palestinians, Sunni fundamentalists and Hezbollah were excluded from the process. The Iranian press characterized Syria's approach to reaching a settlement in Lebanon as 'smacking of compromise, hypocrisy and peaceful coexistence with Zionists'.[47] On 21 October, the chairman of the Iranian *Majles*'s foreign affairs committee decried the presence of the Phalangists at the Damascus peace talks, asserting that the oppressed masses of Lebanon would settle for nothing less than Muslim majority rule.[48]

In late October, Ayatollah Jannati, a prominent member of Iran's Guardian Council, travelled to Syria and Lebanon to iron out differences with Syria over Lebanon's fate and to promote Muslim unity. He conferred with Hafez Assad in Damascus and then toured southern Lebanon to meet Muslim clerics. Jannati visited Sheikh Mohammed Salim Jalaleddin, the Sunni mufti of Sidon, and a number of other Sunni and Shiite clergymen and political activists. During these discussions, he stressed the importance of Muslim solidarity and of the need to prevent rifts among their ranks.

While Iran was busy preserving a foothold in Lebanon and actively promoting Muslim unity with a view eventually to create an Islamic state in its own image, Syria continued to negotiate an agreement among the top three militia leaders in the country, while trying to prevent them falling out with one another.[49] From September to December, Syrian vice-president Khaddam tried to coax them into adopting and implementing a reconciliation plan. The Syrian reform package proposed to restructure the executive branch, with Maronite Christians retaining the presidency but, as in the past, transferring executive powers to the prime minister, a Sunni Muslim. In the legislative branch, a Shiite would continue to serve as speaker of parliament, but the number of members in the legislature would be raised from 99 to 142, divided equally among Christians and Muslims. It also proposed abolishing the government's sectarian structure at the end of a three-year transition period. On security arrangements, the plan contained eight points for the imposition of a comprehensive ceasefire throughout Lebanon, to be maintained by the Syrian army and Lebanese police. Furthermore, it proposed reorganizing the Lebanese army, repatriating the refugees and disbanding the militias.

Although the Damascus peace plan was ready to sign in October, mistrust and rivalry held up the conclusion of the agreement. The signing ceremony was repeatedly postponed and, as a result, the elements of speed and secrecy were lost. As details of the plan became public, Lebanon's traditional politicians (particularly Amin Gemayel and Camille Chamoun), who had been left out of the negotiations, vehemently objected to it. Samir Geagea, Hobeika's predecessor cum rival in the Lebanese Forces, also criticized the Syrian-sponsored initiative. In late October, armed clashes occurred between Hobeika's and Geagea's respective supporters.

However, the setbacks did not deter the Syrians who tried tirelessly to persuade the three militia leaders to endorse the plan. Finally, on 28 December, after revisions to the period of transition and number of deputies in parliament, Berri, Jumblatt and Hobeika signed the document, known as the tripartite agreement, intended to end officially the decade-long Lebanese civil war.[50] It would prove to be an extremely short-lived victory for Assad. While the US–Israeli–Maronite compact had been soundly defeated by 1985, the victors, the members of the Syrian–Iranian–Muslim coalition were now falling out over Lebanon's political future and proving incapable of successfully bringing the civil war to an end.

The Kharg raids, Saudi policy and their regional implications

In mid-1985, Iraq received the latest French Mirage F-1 EQ5 warplane capable of launching Exocet missiles and advanced French and Soviet-made laser-guided bombs, which enabled its air force to hit targets with pinpoint accuracy. With its enhanced capabilities, Baghdad resolved to sever Iran's economic lifeline by intensifying its aerial campaign against the main oil export facilities on Kharg Island. In fact, Kharg housed the world's largest oil terminal, where 90 per cent of Iran's oil exports originated. On 15 August, the Iraqi air force escalated its operations by launching daring raids against the oil facilities at Kharg, and continued this effort for the remainder of the year.

Although the damage was quickly repaired each time, the initial raids caught the Iranians, who were surprised by the tenacity of the Iraqi attacks, off guard. In late August and early September, exports from Kharg were reduced from their normal 1.5 million barrels a day, but repairs rapidly restored the operational capacity to its previous level. Tehran responded by increasing its naval prohibitions and searching ships bound for Gulf Arab ports. Despite Iranian threats to resume attacks on ships heading to GCC states, Iraq continued its aerial offensive against Kharg. By mid-September, the Iraqi air force had launched nine major attacks on Kharg, causing temporary disruption or reduction of Iran's oil exports. On 19 September, Baghdad carried out a highly effective raid that destroyed one of the jetties and severely damaged the pumping station on the island, thereby cutting Kharg's export capacity from 1.5 million to approximately 0.75 to one million barrels a day.[51] Determined to cripple revolutionary Iran's capacity to prosecute the war and bring it to its knees, the Iraqis carried out their eleventh raid in the six-week bombing campaign against Kharg on 24 September. On this occasion, the terminal's operational capacity was gravely affected when several direct hits were scored. As a result, loading operations could not be continued and, for the first time since the outbreak of the Gulf War, the flow of oil from Kharg stopped.[52]

The efficacy of the early raids had profound implications for the clerical regime, which relied heavily on oil revenues to finance its war effort. In 1985, a third of the Iranian government's annual budget was assigned to military expenditures. At this point, oil revenues made up 80 per cent of the budget. Iran's only other oil export facility, on Lavan Island in the southern Persian Gulf near the Straits of Hormuz, exported only 200,000 barrels a day. The crisis Tehran faced was so great that President Khamene'i threatened to 'close the Straits of Hormuz to all oil exporting countries in the region' if Iran could not continue to export oil.[53] However, by now such statements were seen as empty threats, for Iran did not have the capability to maintain a blow-for-blow doctrine, or the intention to sever its own economic lifeline. Iraq, with the blessing of Saudi Arabia and the other Gulf sheikhdoms, continued its aerial attacks unabated.

The Saudis, for their part, tried to take advantage of the confluence of a number of events to put pressure on Iran to accept a peaceful settlement. Several factors, among them growing anti-war sentiment inside Iran, the Saudi–Iranian *rapprochement*, the kingdom's greater capability to defend itself, its ability to export oil through the Red Sea, Iraq's improved ability to hit Kharg and the reconciliation committee's nascent initiative headed by Saudi Arabia to bring Syria into the Arab fold (thereby isolating Iran diplomatically in the region) led the Saudis to conclude that the opportune moment had come to try to force the clerical regime to the negotiating table. The overall rationale was to thaw Saudi–Iranian relations enough to have some leverage and then to apply sufficient political, military and economic pressure to force Iran eventually to sue for peace.

Ironically, after the havoc wreaked by the attacks in late September, the Iranians reorganized and bolstered their anti-aircraft defence network on the island and its environs, making it harder for the Iraqis to repeat their earlier successes. Subsequent Iraqi raids during the last three months of 1985 had little impact on export operations and Iraqi casualties started to rise with an increasing number of Mirage F-1s being shot down. Through improvisation and the resourcefulness of their engineers, the Iranians were not only quickly able to restore export operations but also boosted export production to almost two million barrels a day by late October to compensate for their earlier shortfall.[54] In fact, on average, between 1984 and 1985 Iranian oil production rose from 1.36 to 1.8 million barrels a day, and annual revenues from $10.9 billion to $12.95 billion.[55]

In early autumn, while the Iraqi air campaign was gaining momentum, Riyadh started its initiative to bring Syria back into the moderate Arab camp and to exert indirect diplomatic pressure on Iran. In mid-September, the committee set up at the Casablanca summit to mend the rift in Syrian–Jordanian and Syrian–Iraqi relations (which Saudi Prince Abdullah led) visited the three capitals where it met Hafez Assad, King Hussein and Saddam Hussein. On 14 September, after the tour of the three capitals, it was announced that the mediation effort had borne fruit and that Syrian prime minister Abd al-Raouf al-Kasm and his Jordanian counterpart Zayd al-Rifai had agreed to meet in Jeddah the following week in the presence of the Saudi heir apparent. Abdullah stressed that he would use his good offices to bring Syria and Iraq together at the negotiating table to achieve Arab unity and solidarity. On 16–17 September, the Syrian and Jordanian prime ministers arrived in Jeddah and held two closed working sessions with the reconciliation committee chaired by Prince Abdullah. At the end of their negotiations, the Saudi crown prince issued a statement declaring that 'the two sides agreed on a number of steps to create a propitious atmosphere' in which to cultivate closer relations and cooperate in forging an 'Arab consensus' on important issues. The two parties had also agreed to continue their dialogue under Saudi auspices in October.[56]

During the Syrian–Jordanian talks in Jeddah, Assad had sent vice-president Khaddam to Tehran to discuss developments in Lebanon and the Gulf with Iranian officials and reassure them that Syria was not about to soften its position on the Arab–Israeli conflict. On his arrival, President Khamene'i received Khaddam, who handed him a message from Hafez Assad. Later, in a statement stressing the importance of Syria's political stance and invaluable support for the Islamic Republic, Khamene'i said: 'The credibility and political prestige of Syria are backed by that country's clear-cut stand *vis-a-vis* the Zionist regime. Today, the whole world considers Syria the only country in the forefront of the Steadfastness Front, countering Israel. ... We attach great value to our friendship with Syria.'[57]

Before leaving Tehran, Khaddam also met the speaker Rafsanjani, the prime minister Musavi, and foreign minister Velayati.[58] The main topics of discussion were the Syrian–Jordanian dialogue, the evolving situation in Lebanon, especially the siege of Tripoli, and Iranian oil deliveries to Syria, which had been stopped since September. Besides voicing concern about Syria's intentions in accepting the Saudi mediation, and its suppression of emergent Islamist movements in Lebanon, the Iranian leadership was wary of Syria's inability to make timely payments for oil deliveries and running up a huge debt, which by September 1985 stood at approximately $1–1.3 billion. While no solution was reached on future oil shipments, Khaddam reassured Iranian officials that Syria would not modify its position on Israel. He in fact pointed out that Syria had asked Jordan to reconsider its stance by abandoning the PLO–Jordanian initiative, and made it a precondition for further negotiations between Damascus and Amman.[59] While seeing Khaddam off at Tehran's Mehrabad airport, Velayati explained to the press: 'Our Syrian brothers have given a negative reply to an important part of the requests of the delegation. They have accepted a meeting between the prime ministers of Jordan and Syria, provided Jordan give up its compromising positions.'[60]

Overall, Assad calculated that being receptive to the reconciliation committee's overtures could help stave off complete isolation by repairing ties with some of the moderate Arab states and extracting financial or material concessions from them. At the same time, by engaging them in dialogue, he stood a better chance of modifying their positions on important issues, particularly Jordan's with regard to peace talks with Israel. A number of emerging trends and new realities on the ground also influenced and reinforced Syria's desire to diversify its relations and mend fences with the moderate Arab bloc. These were related to the evolution of its ties with Iran and the USSR, and the shifting Arab balance of power. They included:

❑ Syria and Iran's conflicting visions of Lebanon's political future and of the role of Islamist parties;
❑ Iran's inability to prosecute the war successfully in 1985;
❑ its failure and unwillingness to meet Syria's oil requirements;
❑ the gradual cooling of Syria's relations with its superpower patron following Mikhail Gorbachev's ascension to power in March 1985;
❑ the prominence of the Egyptian–Jordanian–Iraqi–Saudi axis in regional politics; and
❑ concern about the potential success of the PLO–Jordanian initiative in reaching an understanding with Israel that would completely sideline Syria in the Arab–Israel arena.

Along with Iraqi moves to curb Iranian oil exports, and Saudi attempts to wean Syria away from its non-Arab ally, in late September, Riyadh's oil minister Sheikh Zaki Yamani threatened to unleash the oil weapon and bring oil prices crashing down unless OPEC members desisted from violating their allotted quotas and selling below market prices. He posited that the kingdom, in an unprecedented move, intended to sell its oil outside the OPEC pricing structure. Yamani also threatened to flood the market with Saudi oil, thereby depressing prices to around $15–18 per barrel in early 1986, if other OPEC members failed to maintain discipline in the coming months. By flooding the oil market, the Saudis could punish countries that had violated previous OPEC agreements, instil discipline and prevent their own oil revenues from shrinking. This would also cripple the Iranian war effort and push Tehran's revolutionaries to the negotiating table by reducing Iran's income to finance military expenditures – and all at a single stroke. Against the backdrop of the ongoing Iraqi aerial bombardment of Kharg and their own efforts to pull Syria away from Iran, the Saudis decided to adopt a gradualist approach by giving matters more time.

The Saudi bid to reconcile differences between Damascus and Amman seemed to pay off in late October when the Syrian and Jordanian prime ministers met again in Riyadh, this time in Prince Abdullah's presence. On this occasion, substantial progress was made as the two sides agreed to adhere to the Arab peace plan, adopted at the 1982 Fez summit, rejecting 'partial and unilateral settlements with Israel', and supporting a UN-sponsored international peace conference to resolve the Arab–Israeli problem. Since sufficient common ground had been created during the two meetings in September and October, both prime ministers agreed to hold more meetings in Damascus and Amman to explore avenues of cooperation. There were hints that Hafez Assad and King Hussein could possibly meet in the coming weeks, while Syria, under considerable pressure from Saudi Arabia, also agreed to attend the next Arab summit scheduled to take place in the kingdom in early 1986. To Tehran's consternation, it was also announced that as a first step towards healing the Syrian–Iraqi rift, security officials from the two countries would meet on their common border to discuss matters of mutual concern. News of high-level contacts between the Ba'thist rivals against a backdrop of deteriorating Syrian–Iranian relations caused by the discontinuation of Iranian oil exports to its Arab ally, and unease among the revolutionary clerics over Assad's handling of the Tripoli crisis earlier in the month, raised questions in Iranian political circles about whether Syria might abandon its alliance with Iran.[61] To allay Iranian fears, Assad sent a message to Musavi reassuring him of continued Syrian support in the war against Iraq, while the Syrian ambassador to Iran, Ibrahim Yunis, delivered a letter from Faruq al-Shara to Ali Akbar Velayati, reiterating that the prospects for reconciliation between Damascus and Baghdad were non-existent because of the 'fascist' nature of the Iraqi regime, and the 'criminal war' it was waging against the Islamic Republic. The Syrians had informed the reconciliation committee that there was no basis for further negotiations to thaw Syrian–Iraqi relations.[62]

Velayati reacted to al-Shara's letter by trying to dismiss reports of strains in the Syrian–Iranian alliance and a shift in Syria's position in the Gulf War. He expressed his appreciation of Syria's stance and played down the significance of the ongoing dialogue with Jordan, elucidating:

Our close relations with the regional progressive countries stem from their revolutionary, anti-imperialist, anti-Zionist and anti-reactionary stands. We are convinced that the ties and the solidarity between our three countries – Syria, Iran and Libya – are a strategic bond. Our enemies cannot touch it by such methods. Our confidence in our Syrian brothers is too deep to be affected by such propaganda.[63]

Several days later, while visiting Kuwait, Iraq's Tareq Aziz admitted that, despite talks between the Iraqi and Syrian representatives sponsored by the Arab reconciliation committee, tangible results had yet to be achieved in bringing the two sides closer together. At the same time, Iran's deputy foreign minister Sheikholislam travelled to Damascus for talks with the Syrian vice-president Khaddam.

In early November, while Iraq announced its 33rd raid on Kharg Island since 15 August, the leaders of the six GCC countries met in the Omani capital, Muscat, to discuss how to bring the Gulf War to an end and review their relations with Iran. After four days of deliberations, they issued a joint communiqué expressing deep concern about the recent escalation of hostilities that threatened to destabilize the Gulf region. Interestingly, they announced that they would try to persuade the Iranian leadership to abandon its stated objective of toppling the Iraqi Ba'thist regime and to terminate the conflict. This represented a discreet change in tactics by the Saudi-led GCC countries to prod Iran into accepting a ceasefire. It could best be described as a subtle carrot and stick policy, both bringing pressure to bear on Iran on various fronts and sending a clear message to Tehran that the GCC was open to forming closer cooperative links and mediating in the conflict. The Saudi-crafted strategy was clear – tighten the noose around Iran's neck by uncoupling Syria and Iran, increase Iran's economic woes and encourage Iraq to inflict losses on Iran, thereby leaving Tehran with no alternative but to accept GCC mediation to end the war.

The Saudis were pleased that the Syrian–Jordanian dialogue, initially started under their auspices, had gained enough momentum for the two countries to continue the reconciliation on their own. To Riyadh's satisfaction, to further the reconciliation process, Jordanian prime minister al-Rifai arrived in Damascus on 12 November at the head of a high-level political and economic delegation and first met his Syrian counterpart. During two days of talks, al-Rifai, accompanied by foreign minister Tahir al-Masri and ministers holding the portfolios for industry, trade and finance, also held discussions with various Syrian officials to establish economic cooperation between the two sides. Al-Rifai later met Assad and submitted an invitation from King Hussein to the Syrian leader to visit the Hashemite kingdom. The two sides agreed to harmonize their positions on the Arab–Israeli peace process and forge economic links.

Since a tripartite meeting of foreign ministers of Syria, Iran and Libya was scheduled to take place in December 1985 (to coordinate their regional policies), and Iran was starting to prepare a major offensive against Iraq in the winter of 1985/6, Tehran sent Velayati on a tour of several Arab capitals to revive support for Iran's position in the Gulf War. He left for Damascus on 16 November and the next day discussed 'the situation in the region and issues of mutual interest' and the agenda of the upcoming tripartite meeting with Assad, Khaddam and al-Shara. He then departed for Libya and Algeria.[64]

Syria and Iran were both wary that their strategic alliance was beginning to unravel. Disappointed at its policies in Lebanon and annoyed at its Arab ally's repeated failure to service its oil debt, Tehran continued to deny Syria oil shipments. Furthermore, Iranian concerns about the Syrian–Jordanian *rapprochement* and its broader implications were mounting. Although some at the time argued that Iran stopped the shipments because the Iraqi raids were effective, that was not the case. As mentioned previously, Iran was able to restore its production capacity and even increase it to compensate for the sporadic shortfalls in the autumn of 1985. In truth, Tehran was holding back to gain more leverage over Damascus to get it to modify its behaviour in the region, particularly in the Arab–Israeli arena *vis-à-vis* the Palestinians and Lebanese Islamist movements.

To prop up relations with his Iranian ally, on 1 December, Syrian prime minister al-Kasm travelled to Tehran with a high-level political and economic delegation and, immediately on arrival, met his Iranian counterpart, Mir Hossein Musavi. The two countries' ministers for foreign affairs, commerce, industry and economic affairs also attended the first session. A second meeting of the two prime ministers, the Syrian and Iranian foreign ministers and the Iranian deputy prime minister was held the same day to review the two sides' regional political cooperation.[65] At the end of the three-day visit a joint communiqué was issued to announce that a protocol on commercial and economic relations and a letter of understanding on political cooperation had been signed. As in previous Syrian–Iranian communiqués, Iraq was criticized for starting a 'cruel war' against revolutionary Iran and castigated for attempting to escalate and expand the war by bombarding cities, attacking oil tankers in the Gulf and using chemical weapons. Both called for an end to the foreign military presence in the Gulf, while Iran again reiterated that it had no designs on Iraqi territory. With regard to Lebanon, they demanded the 'immediate, unconditional and complete withdrawal' of Israeli forces from the country. Syria was also praised for its 'sincere efforts to ensure the unity of Lebanon'.[66]

The communiqué and two allies' recent moves showed they were both trying to come to terms and accept the primacy of their partner's interest in its own backyard. Syria was loath to criticize Iran for continuing the Gulf War and attacking shipping bound for Arab ports, while Iran was slowly trying to come to terms with Syria's clout in Lebanon. Iran was determined to continue supporting Hezbollah and other Lebanese Islamist movements and aimed to protect the Palestinians from Syria's proxies, particularly Amal. However, if Damascus was adamant or even willing to commit forces to protect something of paramount importance, Tehran was beginning to realize that it would have to bow to it and accept the primacy of Syrian interests. On the other hand, the two parties were apparently unable to agree on two critical issues: the resumption of Iranian oil shipments to Syria and the Damascus–Amman dialogue. Iranian officials were adamant that Syria would have to start paying before any resumption of oil deliveries. Syria, meanwhile, could begin paying off its debt by exporting industrial and agricultural products to Iran. Also, the mere fact that the Syrian–Jordanian dialogue was never mentioned showed that Tehran was highly critical and suspicious of Syrian motives.[67]

On 7 December, Iranian foreign minister Velayati was sent to Riyadh to cultivate closer ties with the GCC states, which seemed keen to improve relations following the Muscat summit. For the first time since the Iranian monarchy's overthrow six years earlier, King Fahd received a minister of the revolutionary regime. Velayati remained in the kingdom for three days and held several rounds of talks with Saudi officials. However, the gulf between the two sides was too great for the deliberations to yield any substantive results. The Saudis had hoped to persuade Iran to let the GCC mediate to help end the war. Even before leaving for Saudi Arabia, Velayati said that the Islamic Republic would reject a GCC initiative unless Saddam Hussein was 'officially recognized and condemned as the aggressor'.[68] The disparity in their respective positions was no doubt a disappointment to both sides, particularly the Saudis, who had tried since May 1985 to thaw relations with Iran and persuade it to accept a ceasefire. After three days of negotiations, Velayati tried to put on a brave face, describing the outcome of his visit as 'satisfactory'.[69] In sharp contrast, his Saudi counterpart, Saud al-Faisal praised Iraq's willingness to accept a peaceful resolution to the conflict and posited, 'we sensed no development in the Iranian stance that would allow positive action towards ending this devastating war'.[70]

On 10 December, the day after Velayati ended his visit to Saudi Arabia, Syrian prime minister al-Kasm arrived in Amman accompanied by foreign minister Faruq al-Shara and interior minister Mohammed Ghabbash. The Syrian delegation held discussions with Jordanian prime minister al-Rifai on expanding their cooperative links and was later received by King Hussein. By the end of the second day, both sides had agreed to adopt a common approach to the Arab–Israeli peace process and, for the first time since January 1979, King Hussein accepted an invitation from President Assad to visit Damascus before the end of the month. In some observers' eyes, the reconciliation talks and al-Kasm's announcement that the Jordanian monarch would visit Syria seemed to presage a new alignment in the Middle East. At the end of the negotiations, a joint communiqué was released highlighting the need for a comprehensive peace settlement by holding an international peace conference, with both Amman and Damascus reaffirming 'their rejection of partial and separate solutions as well as direct negotiations with Israel'.[71] By now, it was clear that the Saudis' astute diplomacy had borne fruit within a period of three months. They had also facilitated the *rapprochement* by providing material incentives to the Syrians. With Iran refusing to provide Syria with much needed oil, since October, Jordan had been serving as the transit point for Saudi and Kuwait oil shipments to Syria to make up for the shortfall.[72]

After the announcement in Amman of the impending meeting between Syrian and Jordanian leaders, the Arab reconciliation committee said it would step up efforts to reconcile differences between Syria and Iraq by visiting Damascus and Baghdad in the near future. News of the ongoing *rapprochement* between Damascus and Amman and the reconciliation committee's plan to arbitrate in the dispute between the two rival wings of the Ba'th Party in Syria and Iraq were, however, little consolation to the Iraqi regime in the closing weeks of 1985 as it braced itself for a major Iranian push into Iraq. Frustration also mounted as its air campaign to stifle Iranian preparations and obstruct Tehran's oil exports proved to be in vain.

With Iran preparing for a major operation on the southern front, and massing half a million troops east of the Iraqi port of Basra, on 16 December, Saddam Hussein made an unscheduled trip to the USSR, his main supplier of military hardware. His visit to Moscow was his first since 1978. Saddam hoped to win assurances from Mikhail Gorbachev that the gradual thaw in Soviet–Iranian relations since 1984 would in no way be to the detriment of Soviet–Iraqi relations, and press him to use his clout to prise Syria and Iran apart and persuade Iran to terminate the hostilities.[73]

Alongside preparations to welcome the Jordanian monarch in Damascus, on 21 December, the foreign ministers of Syria, Iran and Libya gathered in Tripoli for their scheduled consultations. At the end of the two-days of talks, a tripartite communiqué was issued with the Syrians and Libyans reaffirming their support for Iran in the Gulf War. Iran again stressed that it had no intention of annexing Iraqi territory and that it aimed to achieve good neighbourly relations and Islamic solidarity with the Iraqi people and other Arab states. The communiqué also highlighted the need for Arab–Iranian cooperation in effectively confronting Israel. Afterwards, commenting on the third round of the tripartite foreign ministers' meeting, Syrian foreign minister al-Shara asserted that 'these three countries are in one trench and the results of this session indicate the depth of our mutual solidarity. ... It is imperative that we remain firm in our stance and continue our solidarity against our common enemies in order to wrest our rights from them.'[74] Despite a façade of harmony and solidarity, Syria and Iran were unable to resolve some of their outstanding differences revolving around issues such as Iranian oil deliveries, the Syrian–Jordanian reconciliation process and Hobeika's involvement in the Lebanese peace negotiations.

The Assad–Hussein summit and Syrian–Jordanian *rapprochement*

In the weeks leading up to the Assad–Hussein summit, steps were taken to thaw relations between Syria and Jordan. In an extraordinary move, King Hussein publicly expressed regret at having given sanctuary to the Syrian Muslim Brethren in the past and allowed them to use Jordan as a base for their activities against the Assad regime.[75] He vowed that it would not happen again.[76] Furthermore, the Jordanian media stopped criticizing Syrian policy in Lebanon and instead lauded Damascus for its constructive role in the war-torn country. Amman removed restrictions on Jordanians travelling to Syria, and telecommunication links between the two countries improved. In addition, Jordanian power stations began to supply areas of southern Syria, including four cities, with electricity.

Both leaders had strong reasons to mend fences. The collapse of the PLO–Jordanian peace initiative through mutual distrust and divergent goals, Jordan's disillusionment with US policy in the region and its vulnerability to any hostile moves by Israel, all provided King Hussein with good reasons to secure his northern flank and try to negotiate with Israel from a position of strength. Syria, for its part, wanted to break out of its relative isolation in the Arab world, bolster its political and military position vis-à-vis Israel, mitigate the challenge the Iraqi–Jordanian–Egyptian axis posed, diversify its ties in view of cooling Soviet–Syrian relations, prod Iran into being more flexible on oil deliveries and cooperative in Lebanon and, as rewards for its liaison with Jordan, continue to receive shipments of oil and financial aid from Saudi Arabia.

Eventually, on 30 December, King Hussein arrived in Damascus for a two-day visit with Hafez Assad to discuss normalizing bilateral relations, developments in the region and the need for Arab unity. Both sides agreed to exchange ambassadors, for their relations had been downgraded in 1980 when they almost went to war. But, despite the warmer relations, the meeting produced neither a radical shift in Syria's political alignment nor a defection from the radical camp. More significantly, the two-day visit did not result in a joint communiqué being issued prior to King Hussein's departure. There was a complete news blackout in Syria's state-controlled media on the Jordanian monarch's visit and its aftermath. While Jordanian officials subsequently claimed that the absence of a joint communiqué did not indicate failure, they must have been disheartened by Assad's refusal during the talks to start a dialogue with Baghdad.[77] In fact, an official Syrian statement issued after the summit reaffirmed Syria's support for Iran in its struggle until the removal of the Iraqi 'aggressor'.[78]

Assad's decision to mend fences with King Hussein was a tactical move to alleviate his security concerns in the Levant and increase his room for manoeuvre between the rapidly emerging pro-Iraqi bloc in the region and his Iranian allies. The Syrian leader had no wish to sever links with revolutionary Iran or throw his weight behind his bête noire, Saddam Hussein. Although disagreements over oil and Lebanon had strained Syrian–Iranian relations in 1985, two events in early 1986 made it necessary, from Assad's standpoint, to preserve the relationship with Iran – the collapse of the Damascus agreement and Iran's seizure of the strategically-located Faw peninsula.

Iran's seizure of the Faw peninsula and its consequences

On 9 February 1986, Iran launched its first big offensive against Iraq since the disastrous defeat in Operation Badr the previous year. The bitter lessons learnt from the military setbacks and resultant losses of 1984/5 had led the clerical regime to reassess its conduct of the war and reappraise the relationship between the country's political and military leaders. Consequently, in 1985/6, the revolutionary regime gave its military commanders more say in planning and conducting offensive operations against the Iraqis. The prime objective of the operation, codenamed 'Wal-Fajr 8' (Dawn 8), was to seize the strategically-situated Faw peninsula, Iraq's primary outlet to the Persian Gulf, by crossing the Shatt al-Arab, overwhelming the Iraqi defenders and deploying sufficient forces to prevent the Iraqis from regaining it. From the Iranian standpoint, success in this endeavour offered three important advantages: it would deny Iraq access to the Gulf; enable Iran to threaten the city of Basra from the south; and position Iran to cut off Iraq's lines of communication with Kuwait.[79]

On the night of 10–11 February, under cover of darkness in a thunderstorm, Iranian troops crossed the Shatt al-Arab and quickly established bridgeheads at six points. They then ferried additional men, supplies and vehicles across the river. Over the next days the Iranians routed the Iraqi forces on the Faw peninsula and fortified their position by building ten supply bridges across the Shatt al-Arab for ferrying equipment and more than 25,000 men. By 16 February, they had occupied 300 square miles of Iraqi territory. They also reached the outskirts of Umm Qasr and captured Iraq's main air control and warning centre for the Persian Gulf area.

The Iraqi high command was slow to react to the Iranian advances on the Faw peninsula. As a result, Iran was able to achieve a strategic surprise and deploy enough men and *matériel* to consolidate most of its initial gains and repulse Iraqi attacks. Once the Iraqi counter-offensive got underway, it was impeded by lack of air cover due to poor weather conditions. The battle for Faw raged on for almost a month until mid-March. By then the frontlines had stabilized, with both the Iranian offensive and Iraqi counterattacks sputtering out. Iran was able to hold onto most of its gains, and maintained an active force of 20,000–25,000 men on the peninsula.

Wal-Fajr 8 was the Iranian military's best planned and executed operation since the expulsion of the Iraqi army from Iranian territory in spring 1982. The offensive required extensive preparations and a high degree of coordination between the various services, including the army, Revolutionary Guards and volunteers. Meticulous planning and proper preparation and execution ensured success. The victory on Faw won the professional military a greater voice in the future conduct of the war.

The occupation of the Faw peninsula sent tremors through the Gulf Arab states, particularly Kuwait and Saudi Arabia, which now had to consider a long-term Iranian military presence near their borders and the prospect of an Iraqi military defeat in the war. On 16 February, during the first week of fighting, Saudi foreign minister Saud al-Faisal, and his Kuwaiti counterpart Sheikh Sabah al-Ahmad al-Sabah, flew to Damascus to discuss the Gulf conflict with Hafez Assad and Faruq al-Shara. The ostensible purpose of their visit was to persuade the Syrians to moderate Iran's behaviour and to withdraw their support if Tehran proved unreceptive to their entreaties. Prince Saud also delivered a message from King Fahd to Hafez Assad. Given the proximity of the fighting and their vulnerability to Iranian attacks, the events in Faw particularly alarmed the Kuwaitis.

Close on the heels of the one-day visit of the two Arab foreign ministers, Iranian deputy foreign minister Mohammad Besharati travelled to Damascus and Tripoli to brief Syrian and Libyan leaders about the situation on the war front and consult them on other regional issues. In Damascus, Besharati conferred with Hafez Assad and delivered a message from President Khamene'i. After their deliberations, Besharati told a press conference that Iran would continue the war until the Iraqi Ba'thist regime had been overthrown. While underlining that Iran's decision to pursue its effort vigorously to topple and punish the aggressor was 'final and irrevocable', he attempted to allay the fears of the Gulf states by positing that Tehran extended 'a hand of friendship to all its Arab neighbours'.[80]

As the fighting in the Gulf raged on, having visited Libya, Besharati stopped off in Damascus again on the return leg of his trip to discuss the latest developments with the Syrians. After a meeting with Besharati on 22 February, Hafez Assad publicly expressed his satisfaction with Tehran's assurances that it did not covet any Iraqi territory. Besharati also told journalists that 'Iran was determined to regain its legitimate rights violated by the Iraqi regime, through punishment of the aggressor'. He added that once its goals were achieved, it was up to the Iraqi people to 'take their destiny into their own hands', and decide on their future.[81]

Overall, Syria seemed ambivalent about the success of Wal-Fajr 8. On one hand, to Syria's delight, the Iranian victory increased the chances and even held out the prospect of an Iraqi defeat in the 65 month-old war. On the other hand, the seizure of Faw made Syrian statements that Damascus could moderate Iranian behaviour seem dubious. The Syrians continued to defend Iran's military campaign, but qualified their support by declaring that if the Iranians showed any expansionist tendencies or coveted Arab land they would sever their links with Iran. On the whole, Syria's ideological stance and justifications for its alliance with non-Arab Iran seemed increasingly untenable and left it exposed to charges of betraying Arab interests. Iran's breakthrough at Faw, and subsequent intimidation of the lower Gulf states, gave more ammunition to its opponents who portrayed the Gulf War as an Arab–Persian conflict.[82]

Iran's military success alarmed neighbouring Arab states and prompted Arab League foreign ministers to convene an emergency meeting on 24 March in Tunis. The decision to hold an extraordinary meeting reflected the level of unease in the Arab world over Iran's seizure of Faw and the possibility of a total Iraqi collapse. The success of Wal Fajr-8 sent shockwaves through the Arab world and polarized it more than ever before. Both camps, particularly the pro-Iraqi bloc, now resolved to bring pressure to bear on Tehran to avert an Iraqi defeat in the war. During March 1986, Saudi Arabia, which for some time had been threatening a price war in the oil markets, unleashed the oil weapon by flooding the international market with Saudi crude. Overnight, oil prices plummeted from around $30 a barrel to just under $10. At a stroke, Iran's oil revenues, vital for financing its war effort, were cut by almost 70 per cent. Apart from economic considerations (like the desire to restore discipline in OPEC and recoup its lost influence in the cartel), the Saudi move was also clearly motivated by a desire to cripple Iran's war machine and force the clerical regime to the negotiating table to settle the conflict peacefully. The simultaneous oil price collapse and opprobrium brought by the seizure of the Faw peninsula in March 1986 reinforced Tehran's sense of embattlement and political isolation in the region, thus increasing its dependence on the goodwill of its remaining Arab allies, particularly Syria.[83]

On 20 March, Syrian foreign minister al-Shara visited Tehran, with a message from President Assad to his Iranian counterpart and conferred with Iranian officials about recent developments. In a drastic move, revealing the extent of Iraq's fury at Iran's success at Faw and at al-Shara's trip to Iran, a few days before the Arab League meeting in Tunis, Iraqi foreign minister Tareq Aziz sent a memorandum to

Arab League secretary-general Chedli Klibi severely reproaching Syria's stalwart support for Iran, calling it treasonous behaviour. In the memorandum, Tareq Aziz stated that Syria was flagrantly violating the Arab League charter and the Arab defence pact through its continued support for Iran. He characterized al-Shara's visit to Iran as a provocative act, contrary to 'all Arab values and principles'. He also depicted Syria's conduct *vis-à-vis* the Palestinians and its policies in Lebanon as gross violations of the Arab League charter.[84]

During the stormy session in Tunis, despite the vehement objections of the Syrian and Libyan delegations, the Arab League issued a strongly-worded communiqué condemning Iran's occupation of Iraq and supporting Baghdad in its rightful and legitimate defence of Iraq's 'national sovereignty, security and territorial integrity'.[85] At this point, the occupation of the Faw peninsula and Iranian officials' repeated threats to prosecute the war until the overthrow of the Iraqi Ba'thist regime and punish Iraq's Arab backers made Syria's justifications for supporting Iran look highly implausible, if not completely absurd, from the perspective of many Arab League members.

Riding high on the victory at Faw, Iran seemed unshaken by the Arab League's condemnation and more determined than ever to continue the war until it had overthrown Iraq's Ba'th regime: a negotiated settlement was the last thing on its mind. An interview with foreign minister Velayati, which appeared in the Persian-language daily *Ettela'at* on Friday 31 March, reflected the mindset of Iran's leaders at the time. He expressed the futility of mediation attempts to end the war and, after the recent setbacks suffered by the Iraqi army on the battlefront, urged the Gulf states to distance themselves from Saddam Hussein. He brushed off Saudi attempts to heal the Syrian–Iraqi rift and decouple Syria and Iran. Velayati emphasized that Tehran and Damascus had a common stand on the issue of the Gulf War and the fate of the Baghdad regime, adding 'we are confident about the firmness of the political position of our friendly and brotherly country'.

While the mood in Tehran was buoyant after Wal Fajr-8, it was tempered by concern that the Arab world was increasingly ostracizing Iran. The clerical regime's policies in the Gulf and Lebanon were also causing sharp differences with Syria. Moreover, the oil price collapse in early 1986, coupled with Iran's growing isolation and war weariness at home, brought a gradual realization that the war effort could not be sustained indefinitely.[86] If Iran were to achieve its objective to topple Saddam Hussein, it would have to be done within a limited time frame. So, for the next few months, Iranian leaders began to talk about a 'final offensive' to deliver the *coup de grâce* against Baghdad. After the success of Wal Fajr-8, Iranian military planners set to work carefully drawing up a strategic plan for their next major operation.

The collapse of the tripartite agreement: Syria's predicament

After the tumultuous events of 1982–85, the Syrians invested much effort in hammering out the tripartite agreement signed by Hobeika, Berri and Jumblatt. But from the outset, the accord lacked legitimacy, particularly in the Maronite camp. It was Samir Geagea, with the support of the influential Maronite monastic orders led by Abbot Bulos Naaman and prominent political figures like Amin Gemayel and Camille Chamoun, who resolved to torpedo the agreement.

On 8 January, elements in the Lebanese Forces loyal to Samir Geagea engaged pro-Hobeika forces in combat, culminating in intense intra-Maronite fighting. After seven days of fierce clashes, Geagea's men stormed Hobeika's headquarters and slaughtered 200–300 pro-Hobeika militiamen. However, Hobeika and some of his key aides were spared and, after intense Syrian pressure, allowed to leave the country. His departure on 15 January signified the collapse of the tripartite agreement.[87] Hobeika's overthrow was a double coup: one for Geagea against Hobeika's faction in the Lebanese Forces; the other for Amin Gemayel against Assad to show contempt for the Syrian-sponsored agreement. No doubt Geagea's action came as a profound shock to Hobeika and Assad, who had been unaware of the conspiracy brewing against them.[88] The failure of the 28 December accord was a major disappointment for Damascus, for there could be no durable solution to Lebanon without Maronite participation. On 18 January, three days after the rout of Hobeika's forces, the National Unity Front, comprised of pro-Syrian Lebanese political parties, declared a boycott of Amin Gemayel, with Nabi Berri and Walid Jumblatt subsequently demanding his removal from office.

Besides eroding its position in Lebanon, the collapse of the tripartite agreement was a major blow to Syria's regional and international prestige, which must have pleased its opponents. Although we cannot determine whether the anti-Hobeika camp received any direct foreign support, Tel Aviv and Washington viewed the outcome in a positive light, for they had scores to settle with Damascus. The collapse of what seemed to be an emerging Pax Syriana in Lebanon meant that Damascus needed to cultivate as many allies as possible in Lebanon in its efforts to forge a new consensus and stabilize the situation. Indeed, had the tripartite agreement succeeded, Syria could have afforded to assume a more confrontational stance towards groups like Hezbollah. However, the failure of the accord called for an adjustment to avoid alienating the rapidly growing pro-Iranian militia and unnecessarily straining relations with Tehran. Regionally, and on the domestic front in Lebanon, Assad needed to carry out a careful balancing act, trying to advance Syrian interests but not venturing so far as to antagonize the revolutionary clerics in Tehran and the radical elements in Lebanon, a point that was reinforced by the outbreak of fighting in the winter between various factions throughout the country. While Syria and Iran tried on a number of occasions to restore order by forging a consensus among Amal, Hezbollah, the PSP, the Murabitoun and the Palestinians, conditions had become so fluid and strife-ridden that they could no longer contain the political crisis.

The crisis worsened as PLO fighters continued to infiltrate Lebanon, bringing a new round of Amal–Palestinian clashes and an escalating spiral of tensions as Syria backed Amal, and Iran and Hezbollah threw their weight behind the Palestinians. Despite his differences with his Iranian allies, Assad was loath to jeopardize his strategic partnership with Iran. He was also reluctant to commit troops to crush his Lebanese opponents. He had to tread cautiously in attempting to assert Syrian control in Lebanon.

As the year progressed, the tensions between the two camps increased. There was fighting between Amal and joint Hezbollah–communist forces in Beirut in early February and clashes the next month between Hezbollah and Syrian forces in the Bekaa Valley. Despite the growing friction between the Syrian army and Hezbollah, which had its regional headquarters in Ba'albek, Assad was reluctant to move against them for fear of jeopardizing his alliance with Iran and of Hezbollah destabilizing the situation in Lebanon. The same month, when leaders of various Muslim militias including Amal, the Murabitoun and PSP, agreed to form a 1500-man joint strike force under Syrian auspices in West Beirut to impose order, Hezbollah declined to take part.[89]

With Syria already embattled on several fronts, a series of events in late 1985 and early 1986 put it and Israel on a seemingly irreversible collision course. When Israeli warplanes shot down two Syrian MiG-23 aircraft over Syrian airspace on 19 November 1985, Damascus moved SAM missile batteries across the border into the Bekaa region, thus precipitating another missile crisis, much like that of 1981, which was eventually resolved through US mediation. Another crisis flared up on 4 February 1986 when the Israeli air force brought down a Libyan executive jet bound for Damascus with a high-ranking Syrian delegation on board, including the assistant secretary-general of the Syrian Ba'th Party, Abdullah al-Ahmar. Damascus was outraged when Washington vetoed a resolution introduced in the UN Security Council condemning the Israeli action. In March and April, a number of bombings in Syria killed at least 140 civilians and wounded many others. The authorities blamed either Iraqi or Israeli agents for these events. These violent incidents, along with the discovery of a bomb intended to blow up an El Al aircraft at London's Heathrow airport, which Syrian air force intelligence had allegedly planted, exacerbated the situation and exposed Syria to international opprobrium. Although the perpetrator, Nizar Hindawi, a Jordanian national, later came forward and confessed to being a Syrian operative, there is reason to believe that he may have been a double agent and that the plot had been set up to incriminate the Syrian government. In fact, Western intelligence operators later commented on the amateurism of the plot and surmised that Israel may have orchestrated it as a convenient *casus belli* during the spring of 1986 should it opt to precipitate a military confrontation with Syria.[90]

As Tel Aviv and Damascus edged closer to war by conducting large-scale manoeuvres on the Golan front, Washington and Moscow were unnerved by the prospect of another Arab–Israeli conflagration and took measures to contain the situation by urging both sides to exercise restraint. In May, Mikhail Gorbachev and Ronald Reagan took steps to avert a military confrontation, at the same time, reaffirming their commitment to safeguarding the security of their regional partners. The superpowers thereby succeeded in moving their respective allies away from the brink of war.

In the aftermath of the Hindawi affair, the prospects of international condemnation and isolation, along with the West imposing potentially-damaging economic sanctions on Syria, were quite unsettling to the Syrian leadership at a time when the threat of a major military confrontation with Israel was looming on the horizon. As Damascus felt ever more embattled and insecure in the region and internationally, in spring 1986, it threatened to withdraw its support in the Gulf War unless its Iranian ally was more forthcoming in using its influence in Lebanon to free the nine French and five US hostages.[91] Visiting Iranian emissaries to Damascus were reportedly told bluntly that if Tehran failed to secure their release, Syria would both reassess its policy towards Iraq and use brute force to suppress Iran's Shiite fundamentalist allies in Lebanon.[92] At this point, Syria could ill afford Iranian and Hezbollah obstinacy if it were to stave off British-led efforts to punish it for its involvement in the Hindawi affair and strengthen its hand in inter-Arab politics.

In Lebanon, tensions rose to new heights on 1 May, when Syrian army units in Ba'albek reportedly tried to secure the release of foreign hostages held in the Sheikh Abdullah barracks. The incident occurred at the start of the G-7 summit in Tokyo to discuss, among other things, Syria's role in sponsoring international terrorism. During a one-hour gun battle, three Hezbollah militiamen were wounded, one Syrian soldier was killed and three others injured.[93] Immediately after the incident, Hezbollah kidnapped two Syrian officers. The Syrians then promptly detained a number of Hezbollah members while demanding the immediate release of the officers. The militiamen complied that same evening and the Syrians released the Hezbollah fighters the following morning. The Syrians cordoned off Ba'albek by establishing roadblocks in and around the town and, as a security measure, forbade anyone to enter or leave it. More fighting the next day resulting in ten men on both sides being wounded.[94]

On 1 May, during the fighting in Ba'albek, Velayati arrived in Damascus for talks with Assad and other Syrian officials on developments in the region. Then, 11 days later, his Syrian counterpart, Faruq al-Shara, flew to the Iranian capital to demand the immediate release of the Western hostages from Iranian officials and threatening to withdraw support in the Gulf conflict. According to the Kuwaiti daily Al-Qabas of 16 May, the Iranians apparently refused to use their influence with Hezbollah to gain the freedom of the hostages without concessions from the West. That the release could ease tensions between Syria and the West in the aftermath of the Hindawi affair and prevent the EC and USA taking measures against Damascus was not enough to sway the Iranians.[95]

As tensions with Israel continued to rise, Damascus made efforts on every front to avoid sliding into further isolation and inviting the Israelis to carry out a first strike. With Assad still mending fences with Jordan's King Hussein, in May 1986, Syria bolstered its defences and put them on heightened alert to deter an Israeli attack.[96] To relieve pressure from Washington and Paris an all-out effort was made to secure the release of the hostages. To back up al-Shara's moves in Tehran, Assad called Ali Khamene'i to ask him to intervene in the Lebanese hostage affair. On 28 May, Syrian defence minister Mustafa Tlas confirmed that the Syrian army had been negotiating with the captors to secure the release of the French hostages.

The war of the camps and Syrian–Iranian mediation

The situation in Lebanon became more complex in May and June 1986 as PLO fighters trickled back into Lebanon and made their way to the refugee camps, thus precipitating another Amal siege of the Palestinian refugee camps and putting Syrian–Iranian relations to the test. In late May, heavy fighting erupted between Amal militiamen and Palestinian fighters in southern Beirut, costing the lives of more than 80 people in the first two weeks. Tehran sent deputy foreign minister Besharati to the Levant to stop the bloodshed and hammer out an agreement. Talks held at the Iranian and Algerian embassies in Beirut were initially fruitless. Besides meeting Amal and PNSF leaders, Besharati also had talks with Lebanese prime minister Karami. Prior to his arrival in Beirut, Besharati had discussed the Amal–Palestinian conflict in Damascus with Assad. The Iranian envoy eventually managed to negotiate a temporary ceasefire to allow six Iranian doctors on a two-hour mercy mission to take eight ambulances into the besieged Bourj al-Barajneh camp to evacuate wounded Palestinians. Meanwhile, Nabih Berri travelled to Damascus to persuade Syrian leaders to send troops to Beirut to restore peace and order. As Syrian and Iranian negotiating teams headed by Khaddam and Besharati continued their deliberations to find a solution, Karami and other Lebanese Muslim leaders subsequently arrived in Damascus, pleading for Syrian military intervention to end the war of the camps. Finally, in mid-June, Amal and the PNSF announced a truce. The two agreed to form a 1500-man special force under Syrian auspices to maintain the ceasefire.[97] Although the siege was not lifted, the three weeks of hostilities ended, having taken the lives of 140 people and leaving 800 injured.[98]

As fighting died down temporarily in Beirut, in early July, elements of the special force to monitor the ceasefire took up positions in the capital. This included deploying 200–300 Syrian special force commandos in West Beirut, thus marking the return of a Syrian military presence in the city after four years. A security committee composed of representatives from West and East Beirut met to coordinate efforts to restore peace and order, and reopen crossings along the green line. Many Christian leaders, though not Gemayel, welcomed Syria's moves. By the latter part of the month, senior Syrian military intelligence officers had started negotiating with Hezbollah leaders to extend the security plan to their strongholds in the suburbs of southern Beirut, where the French and US hostages were believed to be held.[99] Despite the pro-Iranian movement's initial opposition, after almost four weeks of sensitive negotiations, Hezbollah bowed to pressure from the Syrians, and its Iranian benefactors, consenting to the deployment of Syrian and Lebanese security forces in southern Beirut on the understanding that the Shiite fundamentalists would retain their positions and continue to operate freely.[100] So, on 4 August, 750 Lebanese soldiers and gendarmes and 200 Syrian troops entered the Shiite suburbs of south Beirut to curb the violence and prevent more Palestinian guerrillas from entering the refugee camps.[101]

Under pressure from Iran, Hezbollah grudgingly accepted the Syrian-sponsored security plan in Beirut. Tehran clearly did not want to antagonize its main Arab ally, even if it meant partially curbing Hezbollah's freedom of action. The situation in Lebanon settled down for a few months until fighting between Amal and the Palestinians flared up once more in the closing weeks of the year.

The Syrian–Jordanian *rapprochement* and Iran's response

By mid-1986, conflicts of interest over Lebanon's political future, the Amal–Hezbollah rivalry, the fate of the Western hostages and Syria's failure to service its oil debt had strained relations between Syria and Iran. Tehran's ruling elite had split into two opposing camps on how to handle its relationship with Damascus. Velayati, at the head of the 'pro-Syrian lobby', strongly advocated continuing the seven-year alliance. He cited Syria's support in the early stages of the Iraqi invasion and occupation between 1980 and 1982, allowing Iran to establish an important presence in Lebanon and its incessant lobbying on behalf of Iran in the Arab League over the years.

Other prominent political figures in the Iranian leadership led by chairman of the Majles's Foreign Affairs Committee Ahmad Azizi, however, opposed perpetuating an alliance that at this stage yielded few, if any, tangible benefits to Iran's revolutionary cause. They argued that preserving links with Damascus was to their detriment, because Syria was more than $1–2 billion in arrears on payments for Iranian oil shipments since 1982, the Syrian army had consistently hampered the activities of the Islamic Revolutionary Guards in Lebanon, and Syria's current contribution to the Iranian war effort by selling Soviet-made light weapons to Iran was negligible at best.[102] Dominant elements in the Iranian regime were worried about Syria's threat to withdraw its diplomatic and military support in the Gulf conflict, its insistence on freeing the Western hostages in Lebanon without Iran deriving any tangible benefits, its efforts to circumscribe the activities of Hezbollah and the Palestinian resistance in Lebanon, and its inability to service its outstanding debt to Iran. Iranian concerns were heightened in May when Assad accelerated his policy of thawing relations with Jordan.

From Syria's standpoint, the combination of the precarious situation in Lebanon, the spectre of a military confrontation with Israel in the aftermath of the Hindawi affair and its troubled partnership with Iran made it very vulnerable. Assad felt exposed on several fronts. He needed to adopt a proactive policy to alleviate Syria's precarious security situation and strengthen his bargaining position *vis-à-vis* Tehran to obtain its compliance on resuming oil shipments and restoring order in Lebanon. Syria decided to continue on the path towards normalizing relations with Jordan for a number of reasons: to secure its southern flank, to have an Arab ally also bordering Israel in case of a military showdown with Tel Aviv, to extract concessions from Iran (and perhaps Saudi Arabia) by feigning a *rapprochement* with Iraq and, if the opportunity arose, to exploit renewed links with Baghdad without giving up too much in return.

Assad travelled to Amman on 5 May for a two-day visit, his first since 1977. While nothing concrete came from the talks, the fact that both sides expressed optimism about their future bilateral relations and that Mubarak made an unscheduled visit to Aqaba five days later for talks with the Jordanian monarch, raised hopes. Speculation increased when Assad declared on 9 May, while addressing a group of Syrian lawyers, that the time had come to end the Gulf War.[103] In the days that followed, Syrian vice-president Khaddam revealed that the meeting between Assad and King Hussein had cleared the path towards normalizing relations and rebuilding trust and confidence. He stated that Damascus and Amman had agreed to harmonize their positions on Israel and to refrain from entering into bilateral negotiations with Tel Aviv to secure separate peace agreements. Khaddam asserted that Syria would pursue the path of reconciliation with Jordan to further its regional interests.[104]

Prior to Assad's visit to Jordan, Iranian foreign minister Velayati and Revolutionary Guards commander Rafiqdoust visited Tripoli and Damascus to confer with their Arab allies, but there were no indications that anything substantial came out of the Syrian–Iranian talks. Despite Hezbollah clashes with Syrian forces in the Bekaa, Syrian pressure on Iran to obtain the Western hostages' release (to deflect criticism from the West) and Tehran's adamant refusal to resume oil shipments to Syria, the Iranian media dismissed reports of a possible Syrian–Jordanian reconciliation. By mid-May, the Syrians felt plagued on a number of fronts. Britain's decision to expel three Syrian diplomats produced a similar riposte on the part of Syria, while President Reagan's threats of punishment should Syria pursue policies similar to those of Libya, unnerved Assad. Mixed signals from Israel compounded the sense of siege in Damascus. Some Israeli officials tried to play down reports of an imminent military confrontation with Syria, but on 13 May, Shimon Peres bluntly declared that Israel could not reach an understanding with Syria so long as Assad remained in power.[105] These events coincided with Faruq al-Shara's visit to Tehran, where he met Khamene'i, Musavi and Velayati for a review of the situation in the region, particularly the prospects of Israeli military action against Syria and Iranian cooperation in convincing Hezbollah to release the Western hostages.[106]

At this critical stage, Damascus believed that Israel and the USA had strong motives to opt for a military confrontation. Since 1982, the Syrian armed forces had grown by more than 60 per cent and, equipped with the latest Soviet-made hardware, could achieve 'strategic parity' with Israeli in both quantitative and qualitative terms. The Syrians believed that Peres would want a military victory to cut the Syrian military down to size. He could then call for general elections and win decisively at the polls before having to hand over power to his Likud coalition partners in October 1986. There was also little doubt that, having been humbled by Damascus and its allies in Lebanon in 1983/4, the Reagan administration would look favourably on an ignominious defeat for Syria. Vanquishing Assad would in effect derail the nascent Syrian–Jordanian *rapprochement* that threatened to build a unified position against Tel Aviv and isolate Jordan. It would leave King Hussein with little choice but to enter into direct negotiations with Israel to secure his western frontier. While treading carefully, and considering his options, Assad decided to bolster his defences by deploying troops along the Golan Heights in a bid to deter an Israeli first strike.[107]

Although Syria had for many months had no oil deliveries, on 15 May, its former oil agreement with Iran officially expired and no steps were taken to negotiate a new deal. The Syrian leadership felt frustrated during this crucial period by Iran withholding oil shipments and by refusing to secure the release of the Western hostages. Sensing an opportunity to accelerate the reconciliation process with Syria and exploit the Syrian–Iranian rift to lay foundations for a Syrian–Iraqi *rapprochement*, King Hussein intensified his efforts in late May and early June to achieve a major breakthrough.

By spring 1986, Syria was in dire straits economically. Unable to pay the $1–2 billion it owed Iran, Damascus continued to seek Saudi and Kuwaiti assistance to meet the shortfall in its domestic oil requirements and, since March, had also begun to buy 48,000 barrels of crude oil every 15 days on the Mediterranean market.[108] Plagued by shortages of various goods, by the end of May, the country's foreign exchange reserves had been reduced to a meagre $100 million, equivalent to two weeks worth of imports. Its total foreign debt stood at approximately $18 billion, with the lion's share of $15 billion being owed to Moscow for the procurement of Soviet arms. The only significant foreign financial aid Syria was receiving was an annual sum of $500–700 million from Saudi Arabia and Kuwait under the terms of the 1978 Baghdad summit resolution of the Arab League.[109]

The pro-Iraqi camp now had high hopes of separating Syria and Iran, thus ending their alliance and paving the way to an Arab summit in the summer.[110] King Hussein sought to bring Syria and Iraq together not only to restore unity among Arab ranks and bolster Jordanian security, but also to isolate Khomeini's Iran and force it to seek a negotiated settlement to the six-year Gulf war. So, on 24 May, with Prime Minister Zayd al-Rifai and Foreign Minister Taher al-Masri in tow, the Jordanian monarch made an unscheduled seven-hour visit to Damascus and held two rounds of talks with Assad. The main items on the agenda were bilateral relations and the prospects of thawing Syrian–Iraqi relations.[111] Less than 24 hours after returning to Amman, on 26 May, King Hussein travelled to Baghdad to discuss his deliberations with Saddam Hussein. The negotiations in both Arab capitals had been so encouraging for the Jordanians that on 27 May, the king sent Prime Minister al-Rifai to Athens on a four-hour visit to meet Assad, who had arrived in the Greek capital the previous day on a three-day state visit. Al-Rifai reportedly delivered a message from King Hussein to the Syrian leader, and briefed him on the progress of the reconciliation effort subsequent to the bilateral meetings in Damascus.[112]

After al-Rifai's consultations with Assad, expectations for a break-through ran high. On 27 May, *Al-Siyasah* reported that Amman had got both sides to agree to a summit between the Syrian and Iraqi presidents. However, Tareq Aziz subsequently revealed that the foreign ministers were to have a preliminary meeting and that it was premature to predict its prospects and outcome. Meanwhile, Baghdad continued to broadcast anti-Syrian propaganda advocating the overthrow of Assad and describing him as 'the intimate ally of the enemies of Arabism and the Arab nation'.[113] By the end of the month there were clear indications that the purpose of the meeting between Faruq al-Shara and Tareq Aziz would be to set the stage for an Assad–Saddam summit. King Hussein, confident that his efforts would bear fruit in the coming weeks, left for Paris, London and Washington to discuss the deadlocked Middle East peace process and the emergent Syrian–Iraqi *rapprochement*.

In early June, Arab League secretary-general Chedli Klibi announced that if the Jordanian initiative healed the rift between Damascus and Baghdad, an Arab summit would be held in Casablanca in July. Meanwhile, an Iraqi delegation had arrived in Syria to discuss reopening the trans-Syrian IPC oil pipeline, shut down since April 1982 when the Syrian–Iranian alliance was formalized.[114] Over the next few days, Tareq Aziz and King Hussein each announced that the foreign ministers of Iraq and Syria would meet on 13 June on their common border to pave the way for a summit between Saddam and Assad aimed at ending the Gulf War and resuscitating the Arab–Israeli peace process. The Jordanian monarch was confident by this stage that his mediation efforts were going to pay off, ending the state of paralysis and disunity in Arab politics. In view of Iran's seizure of the Faw peninsula earlier in the year and Syria's stance in this regard, he confidently asserted that: 'Syria's leadership and people believe, as we do, that Arab land is sacred and must be safeguarded ... that is part of the Arab interest and the Arab identity.'[115]

Iran's riposte and the failure of Jordanian diplomacy

Despite Syria's assurances that it was not about to abandon its alliance with Iran, Tehran's political leadership was ill at ease: it was acutely aware of Syrian displeasure at its refusal to resume oil shipments and its lack of cooperation on a number of key issues in Lebanon like the Amal–Hezbollah rivalry, the war of the camps and the Western hostages. Iran was in a dilemma: while determined to prosecute the 'imposed war' against Ba'thist Iraq until final victory and to expand its foothold in Lebanon, it could ill afford to alienate its key Arab ally, for Syria played a key role in maintaining the 'pincer' against Iraq and allowing Iran access to the Lebanese theatre. While Assad's state visit to Jordan in early May worried the Iranians, when they witnessed Jordan's intense shuttle diplomacy as the month progressed, with growing signs of a potential Syrian–Iraqi reconciliation, they became distinctly alarmed. Tehran showed its displeasure at the Syrian–Jordanian *rapprochement* by inviting the leader of Syria's outlawed

Muslim Brotherhood to visit.[116] However, the need to keep its most valuable Arab partner, partly to prevent the formation of a united anti-Iranian coalition (vital both in practical and ideological terms) became more imperative when, on 17 May, Iraq launched its first major attack across the border since the outbreak of the Gulf War in 1980 and captured the strategically-located town of Mehran. Baghdad's success and subsequent reports that numerous Egyptian and Jordanian troops were fighting alongside the Iraqis in the front lines accentuated Iran's sense of regional isolation.[117]

Despite their differences, it is doubtful that Syria ever meant to make a clean break with its Iranian ally. The situation in the Levant necessitated mending fences with Jordan, but realignment with Iraq would do little to mitigate Syria's security concerns or further its regional interests. Iraqi oil deliveries and more financial support from the Gulf Arabs could ease the economic situation in Syria in the absence of Iranian oil shipments, but would not help Syria stabilize the situation in Lebanon or further its quest to be the leader of the Arab world. From Assad's viewpoint, reconciliation with Saddam Hussein, whom he deeply distrusted, would have a marginal impact on Syria's ability to bolster its position in the Middle East peace process and regain the Golan Heights. In strategic terms, the Syrian leadership calculated that a breach with Iran in favour of Iraq would do little to further its long-term interests. A limited *rapprochement* with Iraq to gain material benefits from it and its allies would cure Syria's economic woes and persuade Iran to modify its position and cooperate with Damascus.[118]

Even as plans were underway for the al-Shara–Aziz meeting on 13 June at the Tanaf security point along the Iraqi–Syrian border, in sharp contrast to King Hussein's assertions that the Iranian conquest of the Faw peninsula had prompted Syria to reassess its position in the Gulf War, Assad declared in early June:

> We are against the occupation of any Arab land. In the Gulf War, we are against the occupation of Iraqi territory. Iran will withdraw its troops from Iraqi territory once it has attained its objectives – the overthrow of the regime in Baghdad. I am certain that Iran has no designs on any Arab territory. If the case is the contrary, we will reconsider our position. Syria discusses with Iran all dangers and difficulties ... facing the Arab conscience. This lies in the interest of the Arabs, Syria, and Iran.[119]

To pre-empt a possible Syrian–Iraqi reconciliation, an Iranian delegation headed by deputy foreign minister Besharati arrived in
Damascus a week before the scheduled meeting between the two
Ba'thist rivals for talks with Syrian and Lebanese Shiite leaders to
patch up differences with Syria and mediate in the Amal–Palestinian
conflict in Lebanon. After the discussions, Assad said that Syria had
always wanted to form 'a united entity with Iraq against the Zionist
entity, but the policy of the Baghdad regime, including the imposition
of war on Iran, disrupted this plan'.[120] Ties between Syria and Iran
were described as 'firm and strategic'. Khaddam thanked Iran for
providing its good offices in Lebanon and elucidated that 'Syria views
the Islamic revolution of Iran as a gain not only for the Iranian
nation, but for Arab nations and the Islamic liberation movement'.[121]
Having delivered a message from Ali Khamene'i to Hafez Assad,
Besharati dismissed reports about strains in the alliance and the
discontinuation of oil deliveries to Syria. He stressed that Iran would
continue to supply Syria with oil and give it more time to pay off its
$1.5 billion debt to Iran.[122] In fact, Besharati's week-long visit to Syria
and Lebanon coincided with the arrival of an Iranian oil tanker
carrying at least half a million barrels of oil, believed to have been the
first Iranian oil delivery since at least the end of 1985.[123]

In the days leading up to the meeting between Tareq Aziz and
Faruq al-Shara, Baghdad was still denouncing Damascus. In a statement broadcast on Iraqi radio and published in the Egyptian daily *Al-
Akhbar* on 11 June, for example, Iraqi information minister Latif
Nassif Jasim rebuked Syria and Libya for what he described as their
'betrayal of the Arab nation and their support for Iran against Iraq'.
Eventually, only hours before the two foreign ministers were due to
meet, Jordanian sources in Amman announced that the talks had
been 'postponed to allow for further consultations'.[124] There were conflicting accounts of what actually happened. Some Arab sources
claimed that negotiations between the two had taken place but had
been so disastrous that the two parties and their Jordanian mediators
agreed to deny their existence.[125] Irrespective of the verity of these
reports, the Syrian–Iraqi dialogue foundered because Syria refused to
abandon its strategic partnership with Iran. Damascus insisted the
talks either be limited to economic cooperation or focus on a fully-
fledged political union between the two countries. Baghdad, by contrast, demanded that the war in the Persian Gulf and Syria's relations
with Iran be including in the agenda and dealt with accordingly.[126]

Despite reports in the Western and Arab press that Syria backed down because of Iranian pressure and threats to foment unrest in Lebanon,[127] it is improbable that Syria ever seriously considered severing links with Iran. Instead, it saw a limited opening towards Iraq as a way of coaxing Iran into cooperating on a number of vital issues, while at the same time encouraging the Gulf Arabs to be more forthcoming with financial contributions. Overall, Assad was determined both to preserve his partnership with Iran and to exploit opportunities to obtain concessions from both sides. Several days after the scheduled meeting failed to take place, Petra, the official Jordanian news agency, reported that the talks between the Syrian and Iraqi foreign ministers had been postponed indefinitely.

While the resumption of Iranian oil deliveries no doubt gave Damascus good reason to cancel the 13 June meeting, the Syrians intimated that it was not enough to stop the gradual *rapprochement* with Iraq. If anything, Assad was now better placed to exploit the regional situation by demanding more concessions from Saudi Arabia and the other Gulf states in return for improved relations with Iraq. Assad's risky gambit had paid off. Not only had he succeeded in bolstering his regional influence and prestige by prevailing on the Iranians to resume the flow of desperately needed oil and placed himself in a stronger position to demand more advantageous terms from the pro-Iraq camp but, with Iranian cooperation, he had also secured the freedom of two French hostages in Beirut on 20 June, thereby ingratiating himself with Paris and, against the backdrop of the Hindawi affair, driving a wedge between the Western allies.

Damascus maintained its leverage with Jordan and the Gulf states by officially keeping the door open to any third-party mediation. Despite the setback in thawing Syrian–Iraqi relations, Jordan continued its *rapprochement* with Syria, with King Hussein starting a new round of quiet diplomacy to bridge the gap between the Syrian and Iraqi positions. When the Syrian–Iraqi meeting was cancelled, Iraq intensified its attacks on the Assad regime. Tareq Aziz accused the Syrians of opportunism in trying to benefit from both Iran and the pro-Iraqi bloc.[128] He also depicted the Syrian–Iranian strategy towards the Gulf Arabs as deceptive, with Tehran threatening the Arab littoral states and Syria blackmailing them by creating an illusion of being their guarantor of security and shielding them from 'Iranian expansionism'. He condemned Syria and Libya as the source of all problems in the Arab world.[129] The Iraqi Ba'th Party daily *Al-Thawrah* also advocated isolating Syria as the only viable solution.[130]

Iran's assertive role on the regional and international level

As summer 1986 progressed, Iran not only renewed its links with Syria, but also scored some major political and military gains. Interestingly, its relations with France and the USSR (Iraq's two main arms suppliers) warmed up. While the gradual thaw in relations with Moscow (due partly to Mikhail Gorbachev's ascent to power and partly to Iran's political expediency in not sliding into isolation) led to more economic cooperation between the two countries, the changes in relation to France were more complex. The spree of abductions in Lebanon and a bombing campaign Iranian agents had orchestrated in France in 1985/6 forced the Mitterand government to modify its stance on the Gulf War: it now agreed to repay a billion-dollar Eurodif loan to Iran (from the Shah's era) in several tranches, expel the Iranian Mojahedin from France and extend a billion-dollar line of credit to Tehran to buy unsophisticated French armaments.[131] Iran's ability to get France to agree to its demands, along with Syrian pressure, led to the release of a number of French hostages in 1986.

Following the cancellation of the Syrian–Iraqi reconciliation talks and French capitulation, Iran won a small but significant military victory on 2 July, when it launched a counteroffensive resulting in the recapture of Mehran after a week of heavy fighting. Iraq's seizure of Mehran thus proved to have been short-lived, and Baghdad's earlier claims that the war had entered a new phase with Iraq assuming offensive operations as part of its 'active defence' strategy to force Iran to the negotiating table did not seem credible. Furthermore, within 72 hours of the Iraqi defeat in Mehran, a 35-man Syrian delegation led by economics minister Mohammed al-Imadi arrived in the Iranian capital for a week-long visit to renegotiate a series of economic and commercial agreements that had been concluded in 1982.[132] Among the items on the agenda was a comprehensive review of the previous bilateral oil agreement. Al-Imadi met Musavi, and both agreed to cooperate more in confronting their main enemies – Israel, Iraq and the USA. During their deliberations, Musavi emphasized that 'cooperation between Syria and Iran is imperative and more urgent than ever to counter the conspiracies of the two countries' common enemies'.[133]

After lengthy negotiations lasting more than four days, on 9 July, it was announced that under the terms of a new arrangement approved by both parties, Iran would sell 2.5 million tons of oil to Syria over a six-month period from 1 October 1986 to the end of March 1987.[134] The agreement, which Ghazi al-Durubi and his Iranian counterpart

Gholamreza Aghazadeh signed, was another sign that the alliance was being restored to its former status. The day after the conclusion of the accords, al-Imadi met Iranian President Khamene'i, expressed satisfaction at the outcome of the bilateral negotiations and reaffirmed Syria's unswerving support for Iran's cause.

In mid-July reports (confirmed by Baghdad) of purges in the Iraqi Ba'th Party and army following a coup attempt heartened Tehran and Damascus. They claimed that economic malaise and military setbacks had produced a severe political crisis in Iraq where Saddam Hussein was more vulnerable than ever. Iraq was feeling the pinch economically. It was fighting to survive and needed to take firm action to avert disaster and force Iran to accept a negotiated settlement.[135] But Iran's revolutionary leadership was in no mood to compromise. While economic conditions in Iran were visibly deteriorating, with victories at Faw and Mehran and meticulous preparations for the 'final offensive' underway, Tehran calculated that a decisive engagement in the coming months producing a major military victory would ultimately cause the overthrow of Saddam Hussein and the Iraqi Ba'th Party. Syria's refusal to abandon its alliance with Iran and a thaw in relations with Iraq's main backers, the USSR and France, boosted Iran's confidence and fortified its conviction that victory could be at hand. In July, Khomeini's special representative on the SDC and *Majles* speaker Rafsanjani repeated Iran's conditions for ending the war in the Gulf: 'punishment of the aggressor or the downfall of Saddam Hussein', and $200–300 billion in war reparations.[136] He also warned Saudi Arabia, Kuwait and other regional states against continuing to finance the Iraqi war effort. Rafsanjani went further by calling them 'reactionary' for supporting 'Iraq's acts of wickedness', and stated that they would be held responsible and 'pay for such aggressions'.[137] The threats and vitriolic rhetoric coming from Tehran were partly responses to reports in the Arab press that the Gulf Arabs had pledged Iraq four billion dollars for military expenditure.[138]

While the GCC states were trying to buttress Iraq financially and economically, Jordan's King Hussein again tried to resuscitate the Syrian–Iraqi reconciliation by flying to Damascus on 26 July to attempt to persuade Hafez Assad to resume a dialogue with Iraq. The talks between the two leaders lasted 13 hours over a two-day period, but Assad, convinced that the rift with Ba'thist Iraq was irreparable, refused to yield. As a result, the Jordanian monarch left Syria empty handed on 27 July. In an unprecedented move a few days later, in an open letter, Saddam Hussein called on Iran's leaders to desist from further hostilities and to end the six-year war. Needless to say, the clerical regime rebuffed his offer. Unable to turn the tide in the ground war, financially strapped and politically on the defensive on several fronts, Baghdad escalated the air war by intensifying the bombing campaign against Iran's oil facilities.

On 12 August, Iraq conducted its first air attack on Iran's new oil loading terminal at Sirri Island (600 kilometres east of Kharg Island). The raid was so effective that operations on Sirri had to be discontinued and moved to Larak Island, 200 kilometres further east near the Straits of Hormuz. Sirri was beyond the normal range of Iraqi aircraft. That the Iraqi air force managed to conduct the attack meant that its aircraft had either refuelled in the air or landed in one of the lower Gulf states during the course of the mission. Iran claimed that, from the radio communications and radar signals it had picked up, the warplanes had flown via one of the GCC states.[139] Rafsanjani even claimed that Iran had transcribed the Iraqi pilots' conversations and recorded the radar readings, proving that they had refuelled in one of the neighbouring Arab countries.[140]

The air campaign that followed cut Iran's oil exports by about a third from 1.6 to 1.8 million barrels a day to between 0.8 and 1.2 million.[141] In the aftermath of the Saudi-instigated price crash earlier in the year, the escalation of the Iraqi air campaign against the oil installations eroded Iran's already precarious economic situation even further, prompting Tehran to lash out at the Gulf states, threatening retaliation if they continued to provide aid to Baghdad. Such was the intensity of Iran's war of words against the GCC states that, at the Saudis' behest, Syrian foreign minister al-Shara arrived in Tehran on 19 August to mediate and defuse tensions between Iran and its southern neighbours. Al-Shara, who was carrying a message from Assad to his Iranian counterpart, met Khamene'i, Musavi and Besharati during his one-day visit. Al-Shara's departure coincided with heightened Iraqi aerial activity, prompting Khamene'i on 22 August to accuse the Gulf states directly of assisting Iraq's air campaign to disrupt Iran's oil exports and threatening to respond in kind if they did not desist from such actions. At the same time, he stressed: 'We don't want to expand the war. If we had wanted to, it would have expanded already to the GCC countries.'[142] He also posited that Iran wanted good relations with its southern neighbours 'in spite of all we know about the help they give Iraq'.[143] In the days that followed, Tehran again pointed a finger directly at Saudi Arabia and Kuwait for supporting Iraq. Alarmed by the Iranian accusations, Syrian officials continued their role as intermediaries at Riyadh's request to ensure that Iran did not widen the scope of the hostilities. Subsequently, Assad sent vice-president Khaddam and foreign minister al-Shara on 22 and 23 August respectively to seek clarification, and prevent the expansion of the conflict. In their meetings with Khamene'i and Musavi, they were assured that Iran had no intention of escalating the war to engulf the lower littoral states.[144]

On the eve of an NAM summit in Zimbabwe, Iran's foreign minister Velayati flew to Damascus with al-Shara on 24 August to take part in the previously scheduled fifth tripartite meeting of the foreign ministers of Syria, Iran and Libya to review regional developments and coordinate their positions before attending the summit in Harare. The talks centred on the Gulf War, the Arab–Israeli conflict, the Libyan–US confrontation and the NAM summit's agenda, with the Syrians and Iranians denouncing Washington's attempts to intimidate and cow Tripoli into submission.[145]

Despite a relative improvement in Syrian–Iranian relations in summer 1986, as the year progressed, renewed tensions surfaced as disagreements arose over a range of issues. Their conflicting agendas in Lebanon for the Amal–Hezbollah rivalry, the resumption of the 'war of the camps' and the continued captivity of the Western hostages combined to plunge Syrian–Iranian relations to new lows. As a result, the period between autumn 1986 and summer 1987 was one of the most troubled phases in the Syrian–Iranian alliance, with the two sides holding frequent consultations to articulate their concerns and interests, iron out their differences through mutual accommodation and compromise in an attempt to prevent an irreparable rift and restore their relations to a normal footing.

Iran's diplomacy and impact of the Iran–Contra revelations

By late 1986, it was clear that the Iranian leadership knew that the war could not last indefinitely. War weariness at home and low oil prices internationally meant that the conflict could only be sustained for a limited period. With the price of a barrel of oil hovering around $11–12, and export capacity fluctuating through Iraqi raids on oil refineries and loading terminals, in 1986 Iran was only generating $6–8 billion in revenue.[146] Iran continued to mobilize its forces for a 'final offensive', massing 600,000 troops in the southern front by the end of the summer. In early October, during the UN General Assembly's annual session in New York, Iran's foreign minister Velayati stated that, with the defeat of the 'Iraqi aggressors', the Gulf conflict was coming to an end. With a statement in mind that Hafez Assad made earlier that week that while Syria sided with Iran in the conflict it would not condone the seizure of Arab territory, Velayati explained that Iran might have to overrun a large area of Iraq to achieve its ultimate objectives. However, he elucidated, 'we are not going to occupy the lands of Iraq forever'.[147] Drawing an analogy with the Allied effort to defeat Nazi Germany, he asserted that Iran would not stop the struggle until the Iraqi Ba'th Party had been swept away.[148]

While Iran's revolutionary leadership was becoming more confident that it could deal a devastating blow to Ba'thist Iraq in its next major offensive, it was also acutely aware that it could not pursue the conflict with Baghdad indefinitely. The window of opportunity to determine the outcome of the war on the battlefield would remain open for only a limited period because of domestic political and economic considerations, as well as Iran's growing isolation in the Arab world. Tehran firmly believed that Riyadh and the sheikhdoms were aiding and abetting Iraq's aerial attacks in the southern Persian Gulf, just as their desire to deny Iran the financial resources to prosecute the war had partially motivated the Saudi-engineered oil price collapse in early 1986. The Islamic Republic assumed an increasingly confrontational stance in the August OPEC meeting and in the annual hadj attended by 150,000 Iranian pilgrims that same month. The Iranian pilgrims' demonstrations and rallies in Mecca and Medina led to clashes with Saudi security forces and over 100 arrests.[149] Baghdad stepped up its aerial campaign against Iran's oil industry in autumn 1986. The Iraqi raids were so intense that, by October, petrol rationing had to be reintroduced in Iran for the first time since the September 1980 Iraqi invasion.

At this point, it was vital for Iran to preserve its alliance with Syria to prevent Iraq from reaping any political, economic or strategic gains from a fissure in Syrian–Iranian relations. For the clerical regime, attaining victory over Iraq took precedence above all else. As a result, even in Lebanon, in the remaining months of 1986 while Iran tried to reconcile differences between the various Islamic and revolutionary groupings, it ultimately deferred to the Syrians whenever a conflict of interest arose. Ensuring Syrian fealty was of paramount importance and, whenever their bilateral ties appeared to be in danger, Tehran would take appropriate action to prevent any rifts from occurring.

On 8 October, a week after Hafez Assad's statements about Iran's occupation of Arab territory and call for 'total and immediate unity' between Syria and Iraq as a way to end the war, the minister of the

Islamic Revolutionary Guard corps, Mohsen Rafiqdoust, was sent to Damascus to seek clarification on Syria's position and to coordinate policy. The Syrians described the official purpose of the visit as 'an exchange of important information'.[150] The fate of US and French hostages in Lebanon was also apparently on the agenda for Rafiqdoust's talks with Syrian officials.[151] During his week-long stay in Damascus he met foreign minister Faruq al-Shara and head of the Syrian NSO (National Security Organisation) Ahmed Diyab; President Assad received him on 12 October. Rafiqdoust subsequently stated that he had discussed the most recent developments in the Gulf with the Syrian president and, in an illuminating remark, underlined that the special relationship between Iran and Syria 'has been effective in dispelling the misconception perpetuated by imperialism which attempts to depict the war as an Arab–Persian conflict and not a war against oppression. Such misconceptions seek to denigrate our just defence'.[152] The Syrian leader also declared in an interview that he had received assurances from his Iranian allies making 'it clear that they have no ambitions on Iraqi territory, will not seek to annex any Iraqi land, or try to impose hegemony ... we are not worried about this'.[153]

In the latter half of November, once the Reagan and Shamir administrations had owned up to their role in selling arms to Iran, Baghdad and its allies intensified their attacks on Iran.[154] In another blow to the pro-Iranian bloc, after renewed fighting in the refugee camps in Lebanon and a three-day meeting of the PLO executive committee in early December to discuss regional issues, PLO chairman Arafat delivered a statement condemning Iran's dealings with the USA and Israel, and Syria's anti-Palestinian policies in Lebanon, and advocating Arab solidarity with Iraq.[155] The political firestorm created regionally and internationally by the Iran–Contra scandal, and the start of a new round of clashes in Lebanon between Palestinian fighters and the Amal militia, prompted Tehran to resume efforts to mediate in the Lebanese quagmire in a bid to stop the cycle of violence. Iran was walking a tightrope in trying to discard its tarnished image by hammering out a deal between the Palestinians and their pro-Syrian opponents to show it could play a constructive role in the Arab world and at the same time further its revolutionary interests in the Levant without overstepping its bounds in the eyes of the Syrians. This was imperative at a time when it both wanted to recoup its position because of the Iran–Contra scandal and was making final preparations to launch its biggest offensive in five years against Arab Iraq.[156]

Syria tries to block Palestinian power and Iran mediates

Although Syria's troop deployment in West Beirut in summer 1986 partly stabilized the situation there, the political impasse remained unresolved and intermittent interfactional fighting continued. Despite Hezbollah's initial objection to Syria's military presence, and refusal to participate in the joint security plan, Iran went along with Syrian actions as long as they did not impede Hezbollah's activities. The Iranians also tried to persuade their protégé not to thwart Syrian moves in the Lebanese capital, where the streets were cleared of gunmen and militia offices were closed down.

The steady influx of Palestinian guerrillas into the country, however, and Hezbollah's ability gradually to win over the hearts and minds of the Shiite poor in West Beirut and in the outlying southern and eastern parts of the city continued to trouble Syria and Amal. By late 1986, between 6000 and 9000 Palestinian guerrillas had returned to Lebanon by various means.[157] For Amal, the challenge was twofold: the large Palestinian camps in Beirut housed an increasing number of Palestinian fighters, while the camps themselves separated Amal strongholds in West Beirut from the Shiite ghettos to the east and south where Hezbollah was attracting a large following at the expense of the secular, pro-Syrian movement.[158]

To stem the flow of fighters and weapons to the Palestinian strongholds and turn the tide in its favour, the Amal militia attacked the Palestinian refugee camps in Beirut and the south on 21 November. The fighting that ensued lasted for almost three months and marked some of the worst violence since the 1982 Israeli invasion. In Beirut, Berri's men and the predominantly Shiite sixth brigade of the Lebanese army attacked Bourj al-Barajneh and fighting quickly spread to Sabra and Shatila. In the south, the Rashidiyyah camp near Tyre and the Ain El Helweh and Mieh Mieh camps on the outskirts of Sidon were also besieged. The Palestinians put up surprisingly stiff resistance and in some instances pushed back the attackers. In southern Lebanon, Palestinian fighters captured the strategically-located town of Maghdousheh on a hilltop overlooking Sidon (including Ain El Helweh, Mieh Mieh and the coast highway to Beirut) from Amal.

Unable to overrun the camps, Amal and its allies resorted to shelling them: they inflicted many civilian casualties and caused outrage in much of the Arab-Islamic world. Mainstream Arab states and Syria's closest allies Iran and Libya alike condemned Amal's actions. Amal's failure to knock out the Palestinians and regain Maghdousheh prompted it and its Syrian patrons to seek a face-saving way out of the conundrum. With consultations between Syrian, Amal and PNSF officials underway in Damascus, an Iranian delegation that had been touring Syria and Lebanon since mid-November travelled to Tyre and Sidon to try to broker a ceasefire agreement. Meanwhile, Nabih Berri met Iranian ambassador Mohammad Hassan Akhtari in Damascus. Libya's Colonel Qadhafi sent his right-hand man, Major Jallud, to try to mediate, but Amal vehemently objected to any Libyan role, arguing that only Syria and Iran could sponsor a settlement.[159] As tensions mounted, Iranian foreign minister Velayati and Revolutionary Guards minister Rafiqdoust also arrived in Damascus on 28 November to confer with Assad and other Syrian officials.

By the end of November, 500 people, many of them refugees, had been killed in the Amal–Palestinian clashes. The combatants refused to accept a joint nine-point ceasefire proposal drafted by Iranian, Syrian and Libyan officials, but on 5 December, after much effort, Iran's deputy foreign minister Sheikholislam got Amal and the PNSF to consent to a ceasefire pending a comprehensive agreement.[160] The fighting then decreased, but PLO loyalists rejected the Iranian-sponsored plan and continued to engage in sporadic clashes with Amal militiamen. Meanwhile, to Syria's consternation, PLO chairman Arafat called from his headquarters in Baghdad for an emergency meeting of Arab League foreign ministers in early December to obtain a pan-Arab commitment to protect the camps, with the Jordanians and Iraqis immediately signalling their readiness to participate.[161] Despite a brief pause, renewed hostilities broke out after a few days, again prompting Iranian negotiators to redouble their efforts to find a durable solution.[162] As the fighting raged on, two committees headed by prominent Lebanese clergymen (Sheikh Maher Hammoud, a Sunni cleric from Sidon, Sheikh Said Shaban of Tawheed and Sheikh Hussein Fadlallah) were formed under Iranian supervision to facilitate negotiating and implementing an agreement.

While the death toll had risen to 700 by mid-December, the fighting eased as Iranian mediators brought the rival parties closer together.[163] Syria and the PLO agreed to underwrite an Iranian plan for an immediate ceasefire, lifting Amal's siege of all refugee camps and a phased withdrawal from Maghdousheh of all Palestinian guerrillas to be replaced gradually by Hezbollah and leftist militiamen. But with the arrival of Hezbollah gunmen and the evacuation of PNSF fighters from Maghdousheh, Amal insisted that it ought to regain control of the town. This led to the outbreak of violence in Beirut and the south, with PLO loyalists rapidly moving into Maghdousheh to block an Amal takeover. Despite this setback, the Iranians were undaunted and carried on trying to disengage the combatants and relieve the camp inhabitants. By this stage, it had become evident that Iran's standing had risen considerably in Lebanon, for it was the only outside party with communication channels open to all the warring factions. It had failed to end the Amal–Palestinian conflagration, but compared with Syria and Libya it had more room in which to manoeuvre and negotiate with the different parties.

The protracted fighting damaged Syria's image and drove it to desperate measures, begging Iran and Libya to mediate. By the end of 1986, it was evident that Syria could not impose its will in Lebanon and had to enlist the support of Iran and its Lebanese allies to restore a semblance of order and stability in the country. Assad and Berri had clearly overplayed their hand. Although opposed to the main thrust of Iranian and Hezbollah policies in Lebanon since 1985, they clearly preferred to enlist their support and use their good offices to resolve the situation rather than have the Arab League or pro-Iraqi states meddle and intervene in what from the Syrian perspective was considered an 'internal affair'.[164]

The 'war of the camps' in the winter of 1986/7 accentuated the rise of pro-Iranian sympathies among Lebanese Shiites and Palestinians, with Tehran's power and influence momentarily eclipsing that of Damascus. Amal's failure to accomplish its objectives swiftly, Syria's inability to manage the crisis effectively and constant Iranian pressure prompted Nabih Berri to order a ceasefire as a goodwill gesture just before New Year's Eve 1987 'because of the sisterly stand of Syria and the wish of the Iranian President'. Iranian emissaries also announced that Amal had agreed to lift the siege of Rashidiyyah for humanitarian reasons.[165] However, a series of events in the early weeks of 1987 exacerbated the situation in Lebanon, once again putting Iran and its Lebanese protégé on a collision course with Syria and its surrogates.

Karbala 5, the battle for Basra and regional consequences

From Tehran's ideological perspective, the need to play an active role in Lebanon to stop the Amal–Palestinian clashes and restore a semblance of Muslim unity by protecting the rights of Palestinian refugees and re-establishing Shiite–Sunni harmony had a direct bearing on its ongoing efforts to dispel anti-Iranian rhetoric depicting the Gulf War as an Arab–Persian conflict. By proving to be a major power broker in Arab politics it could dispel pro-Iraqi racist propaganda and partially restore its tarnished image in the aftermath of the Iran–

Contra revelations. Alongside its activities in Lebanon in the winter of 1986/7, Iran finalized careful preparations that had been underway now for almost two years to launch its greatest offensive since Operation Fatah al-Mobin in March 1982 in a bid to capture the port of Basra, Iraq's second largest city.

Damascus was clearly concerned about the possible ramifications of Iran's impending assault on a major Arab city and its impact on Syria's reputation and stature in the Arab world. The humbling of Saddam Hussein and the Iraqi Ba'th Party undoubtedly would have pleased the Syrians, but the mere fact that a non-Arab country closely aligned with them would potentially fulfil this role produced a great deal of ambivalence among Syrian leaders who were keen to uphold their pan-Arab credentials.[166] Another point of contention was the upcoming OIC summit scheduled to take place in Kuwait in late January 1987. While Iran had indicated its steadfast refusal to attend such a gathering hosted by one of Iraq's main financial benefactors, Syria had adopted a different position by signalling its readiness to attend the summit. Despite their differences, as a way of trying to ensure Syrian loyalty, on 11 December, the Iranian parliament approved a bill to provide a million tons of oil to Syria free of charge during the last quarter of the Persian year ending on 20 March.[167]

Iran's 'final offensive' and its outcome

Iran spent December 1986 and early January 1987 finalizing preparations for its greatest offensive in five years, Karbala 5, intended to draw the Iraqis into a decisive engagement and lead to the seizure of Basra. The Iranians opted to launch the attack in winter during bad weather to minimize the impact of Iraq's air superiority and restrict its advantage in armour – wet and marshy terrain made movement difficult. There were also political considerations. With the OIC summit scheduled to take place in Kuwait in late January, Tehran calculated that threats and a large-scale offensive close to the host country could force the Kuwaitis to call off the meeting. As the Kuwaitis were the most vocal of the GCC states in supporting Iraq, and played a vital role in the transhipment of war *matériel* to Iraq, Iran regarded them as *de facto* co-belligerents. President Mubarak's unprecedented participation (since 1979 when Cairo concluded the Camp David accords) reinforced Tehran's decision to boycott the summit.

In the days preceding the start of Karbala 5, deputy foreign minister Besharati was sent to Damascus to talk to Assad and other Syrian officials about regional developments and the Kuwait summit. Syrian leaders must have been briefed about the imminent Iranian offensive, for they were concerned about the regional repercussions of the fall of a major Arab city to a non-Arab adversary and its impact on Syria's pan-Arab credentials.

Finally, on 9 January 1987, the 'battle for Basra' began in earnest as Iran launched a full-scale offensive to break the five Iraqi defensive arcs east of the city. It committed a total of 200,000 troops to the operation: four Iraqi divisions and five Republican Guard brigades faced them.[168] A four-pronged offensive was launched with the Iranians starting 30 to 40 miles away from their main objective. The next six to seven weeks saw some of the most brutal and bloody fighting in the history of the first Persian Gulf war. By 22 February, when the Iranians launched their last major frontal attack, they occupied 100 square kilometres, had overrun four of Iraq's defensive arcs and advanced to within six miles of Basra. But these limited gains were won at a huge cost. At least 40,000 Iranians were killed or wounded, while Iraqi losses stood at around 10,000–15,000.[169] By this stage the Iranian drive had been blunted. Having lost some of their finest infantry units and most seasoned veterans in the attack, the Iranians were bled dry.[170] On 26 February, Tehran issued a communiqué announcing the end of Operation Karbala 5.[171] The seven-week battle was a strategic victory for Iraq, for Iran not only failed to take Basra but also suffered critical losses, including many of its best troops.

While the clerical regime put on a brave face, saying that Karbala 5 had been a success and more offensives would follow until final victory, it had in fact come to the painful realization that it was unable to defeat the Iraqis in a major engagement and humble its Ba'thist opponent. The 'battle for Basra' marked a turning point and the beginning of the end of the war.[172] Iran now limited its actions against Iraq to small operations with modest objectives. As a result, Iran began to lose the initiative in the conflict and Iraq, with more room for manoeuvre, gradually regrouped and turned the tide of the ground war the following year.

Besides the setback on the military front, to Tehran's chagrin, the Islamic summit went ahead as scheduled in Kuwait City. Despite some misgivings and initial hesitation, Assad decided to attend the OIC meeting to avoid the risk of further isolation in the Arab-Islamic world. This vexed his Iranian allies who criticized Syria's participation in their state-controlled media.[173] Meanwhile, the Syrian leader reaffirmed his support for Iran in the Gulf conflict. Prior to his departure for Kuwait, in an interview with the Kuwaiti daily *Al-*

Qabas, he clarified that Iran had no designs on Iraqi territory and criticized Baghdad for sowing the seeds of regional discord by sabotaging the Syrian–Iraqi unity talks at the beginning of the 1980s and then going on to invade Iran. He blasted his Ba'thist rival by saying, 'Saddam Hussein wants us to alienate a nation of 45 million that rediscovered itself in Islam and wanted to confront Israel under its banner. That was a golden opportunity. The Iran of Khomeini is anti-Israel. Iran was the only country to send forces when Israel invaded Lebanon in 1982.'[174]

By this stage, Assad was treading a fine line. While determined to stick to his previous policies in Lebanon and the Persian Gulf, to avoid becoming a complete outcast in Arab politics, he also thought it necessary to make conciliatory gestures towards the Gulf states and the moderate pro-Iraqi camp. With Arafat, King Hussein, Mubarak and King Hassan attending the conference, prudence dictated that he take part to forestall the formation of a formidable Arab-Islamic bloc opposed to Syria and its regional policies. Also, if he adopted the middle ground, he calculated that Iran might show more flexibility in its policies in the Levant and in the Gulf in an attempt to appease its most valuable Arab ally.[175]

At the outset of the Kuwait conference, Syria expressed its reservations about a draft resolution (which the majority of the member states supported) highlighting Iraq's willingness to accept a negotiated settlement and calling for the withdrawal of the combatants to their internationally-recognized borders. However, Assad eventually relented and approved the final resolution, which also called for an immediate ceasefire. During the summit, Assad held talks with Mubarak; it was the first time he had met an Egyptian head of state since the Camp David accords. Although the Syrians subsequently described the meeting between the two leaders as devoid of 'political significance', it must have come as a severe psychological blow to the Iranian clerics to have to witness the political discussions in Kuwait City unfold in their absence while they were preoccupied with the greatest battle they had ever waged inside Iraq.[176]

Overall, the Kuwait summit marked the beginning of Egypt's formal re-entry into the Arab-Islamic fold and exposed the short-comings of Syria's foreign policy, leaving the self-declared standard-bearer of Arab nationalism open to charges of betrayal. As a firm supporter of Iraq in the Gulf War, a backer of the PLO and a proponent of the Jordanian–Palestinian *rapprochement*, Mubarak was well on the road to restoring Egypt's pan-Arab credentials. Conversely, Assad was paying dearly for his continuing alliance with non-Arab Iran and for supporting Amal in the struggle against the Palestinians in Lebanon. The Syrian leader was the only person to condemn Egypt's peace treaty with Israel in his speech at the Kuwait summit. With heavy fighting in Basra and no end in sight to the 76-month war, the Gulf Arabs were convinced more than ever that drastic steps were needed to reverse the current situation. Mubarak's presence reinforced their conviction that they needed Egypt to restore unity to the Arab ranks, maintain security in the region and tip the balance of power in their favour.[177]

Iranian retaliatory raids on oil tankers in the Gulf, particularly those owned or chartered by Kuwait, compounded the GCC states' sense of vulnerability. Between December and March, 15 of the 20 Arab tankers destroyed or sunk were Kuwaiti. These events helped Egypt's return to the Arab fold and prompted Kuwait to ask Moscow and Washington to reflag its tankers in subsequent months.[178] These developments put Iran's remaining Arab allies in an awkward position, with both Damascus and Tripoli trying to distance themselves from Tehran. Some Syrian officials stated on the record that they had stopped arms shipments and facilitating weapons procurement for Iran.[179] Besides the Iran–Iraq inferno, a series of events in early 1987 relating to Lebanon, Iranian oil deliveries to Syria and Iraq's renewed dialogue with Damascus, put the Syrian–Iranian alliance to the test. A severe clash of interests in Lebanon precipitated the first crisis.

End of 'war of the camps' and Syria re-enters Beirut

The 'war of the camps' continued in Beirut and southern Lebanon in the early weeks of 1987 and, by the end of January, Amal's resumed bombardment of the Palestinian refugee camps had destroyed much of Shatila and Bourj al-Barajneh. The situation was so critical that, according to several reports, some refugees in Bourj al-Barajneh had turned to cannibalism.[180] The dire conditions finally led PLO guerrillas in Maghdousheh to pull out as a concession to Amal and turn the village over to pro-Iranian Hezbollah and Sunni militiamen to ensure, at the very least, that Amal would not use the strategic heights to shell the Ein el-Helweh camp near Sidon.

Throughout this period, Iranian mediators tried to negotiate a ceasefire and persuade Amal to lift the siege. Despite a pledge by Nabih Berri to allow humanitarian supplies into the camps after the Palestinians had left Maghdousheh, the stalemate continued. The situation was further aggravated on 13 February when a convoy of UNRWA trucks (carrying 16 tons of food for the inhabitants of Bourj al-Barajneh) and Iranian ambulances came under gunfire from Amal fighters as they tried to enter the camp in the presence of Iranian diplomats and Amal officials. This led to a violent exchange in which a Lebanese employee of the Iranian embassy was killed and two others injured.[181] To defuse a potentially explosive situation, Amal relented and allowed food and medical supplies to be delivered over the next two days under the supervision of Iranian and Syrian officials.[182] In the south, Berri agreed to lift the siege of Rashidiyyah for 48 hours to allow the delivery of food and medical supplies for the first time in 17 weeks. This brief respite enabled 10,000 Palestinian refugees to leave the camp.[183]

But Amal had gone too far. Its heavy-handed tactics against the Palestinians and efforts to wrest control of West Beirut from other militias was greatly resented, especially by Jumblatt's Druze PSP. The growing rivalry finally prompted Jumblatt and other left-wing groups to take decisive action. On 15 February, the combined militias of the PSP, LCP, SSNP and Murabitoun attacked positions held by Amal and the sixth brigade, leading to five days of heavy fighting. Amal and its allies suffered major losses and were pushed out of most areas they had controlled in West Beirut. Syria frantically tried to salvage Amal's position by attempting to broker a ceasefire agreement on 18 February, which was ultimately ignored.

As the violence continued, Sunni leaders like prime minister Rashid Karami and Selim Hoss, and the Shiite speaker of parliament Hussein al-Husseini, appealed for Syrian intervention to restore peace. Meanwhile, Berri and Jumblatt travelled to Damascus and, after painstaking negotiations, agreed to hand over security matters in West Beirut to Syrian forces. In addition, Berri announced at a press conference in Damascus that he would lift the siege of the Palestinian camps due to the positive attitude of the anti-Arafat PNSF towards Iranian and Syrian peace initiatives. Eventually, on 22 February, the Syrian 85th brigade reinforced by armour and other units entered West Beirut to impose order. The move brought a welcome sigh of relief from the population. The Syrians deployed 7000 troops, which 2500 Lebanese soldiers transferred from the Bekaa and northern Lebanon supported.[184]

It is worth noting that Syria had many reasons to re-enter Beirut with a sizeable force after a five-year absence. First, Assad could ill afford to stand by while his main Lebanese proxy was routed; the Syrian intervention in fact saved Amal from certain defeat. Furthermore, the Syrian leader knew that if the moderate secular Amal movement collapsed, there would definitely be a resurgence of PLO power in Lebanon and enable Hezbollah to fill the void left in the Shiite community and radicalize it. This, in turn, would also allow Iran to play an even greater role in Lebanon by expanding its power and influence.[185] By this point, he had come to realize that it was useless to employ traditional divide-and-rule tactics to achieve minimum control without cost to Syria. It was no longer enough to rule indirectly through proxies and the token force of 200 elite Syrian troops deployed in Beirut the previous July. Decisive steps had to be taken to stop the situation spiralling out of control and to restore a semblance of law and order.

Brigadier Ghazi Kan'an was charged with implementing the nine-point Syrian plan the Muslim Lebanese leaders had accepted to enforce the ceasefire and disarm the militias. Within days of entering the Lebanese capital, the Syrians took firm measures to control the streets, close down 75 militia offices and disarm gunmen.[186] Those who defied them were arrested or shot on the spot. Amal's foes, in particular, were treated harshly. On 24 February, the Syrians escorted about 1500 Druze PSP and communist fighters out of the city.[187] However, on the same day, a grave incident occurred that could have plunged Syrian–Iranian relations into a major crisis, but nonetheless put the alliance to one of its greatest tests in the Levant.

Massacre of Hezbollah and its impact on Syrian–Iranian relations

By early 1987, Hezbollah's growing power and increasingly bold acts – at times apparently without its Iranian patrons' knowledge or support – greatly perturbed Syria. In addition, a deepening factionalism in Iranian political circles (as the Iran–Contra affair and its subsequent exposure illustrated) indicated that Tehran was not pursuing a uniform, consistent strategy in Lebanon and this complicated Syrian attempts to coordinate policy on Lebanon with its Iranian partner and come to grips with the difficult situation in the war-torn country.

Even before deciding to re-enter West Beirut, several demonstrations of Hezbollah intransigence and independence alarmed Syria and jeopardized its regional and international standing. There were violent clashes between Amal and Hezbollah supporters in the Lebanese capital in September 1986, and a number of subsequent confrontations pitting Syrian forces against Hezbollah in the Bekaa and Beirut between October 1986 and February 1987 aroused serious concern.[188] Meanwhile, with Syria trying to reassert control in Lebanon and restore its image after the damaging Hindawi affair, the kidnapping in

Beirut of three Americans between 9 September and 21 October (after a 15-month pause) enraged Damascus. Although Hezbollah was clearly responsible for these abductions, it is unclear how much Iranian complicity there was, but some radical elements in the regime probably supported them.[189] In early 1987, however, when Hezbollah kidnapped eight more Westerners (four Americans, two Germans, one Frenchman and the Archbishop of Canterbury's special envoy Terry Waite) the situation reached a critical point. Syria was incensed by Hezbollah's reckless actions, and grew more determined to take drastic measures even if it meant direct military intervention to restore order and curb Hezbollah's power and influence. The final straw was the disappearance of Anglican Church envoy Terry Waite on 20 January when he set out to negotiate with Hezbollah members (using the cover name 'Islamic Jihad') to secure the release of two American hostages. The incident prompted Syrian, Iranian and Druze emissaries to shuttle back and forth between Damascus and Beirut amid a flurry of behind-the-scenes activity to determine the fate and whereabouts of the Briton.[190]

By and large, these factors combined to harden Syria's resolve to check Hezbollah's power and deeds, or at least those that were detrimental to its interests in Lebanon and countered its efforts to cast off the stigma of the Hindawi affair and improve relations with the West. An important sign of Assad's determination to assert his authority and curb the power of religious extremists was that he reassigned three colonels from the Syrian special forces, Hisham al-Mouallaq, Ali Deeb and Abdul-Hamid Sultan (who had played a key role in crushing the Hama insurrection in March 1982) and their units to the Lebanese capital. The presence of the three men, noted for their brutal efficiency and loyalty to the Syrian Ba'th Party, was a clear sign of Syria's determination to achieve political and military control. Stern warnings were also issued to the Shiite community through local clerics that 'the severest possible punishment' would be meted out if the captors killed any of the Western hostages.[191]

Consequently, within 48 hours of the Syrian entry into West Beirut, an incident occurred that initially threatened to pit the Syrians in an open confrontation against Hezbollah and plunge Syrian–Iranian relations into a major crisis. On 24 February, when Syrian troops entered the Basta district of West Beirut, a Hezbollah stronghold, they reacted in a heavy-handed manner once they encountered resistance during their deployment in the neighbourhood. After a gunman opened fire, and wounded a soldier in the leg, Syrian troops stormed a three-

storey building that housed the local Hezbollah headquarters, known
as the Fathallah barracks. Initial reports indicated that in the ensuing
mêlée 20 Hezbollah militiamen were killed, but as the dust settled, a
different picture of the incident emerged.

It was subsequently revealed that Hezbollah personnel gave themselves up and peacefully handed over the Fathallah barracks to the
Syrians, though 23 Hezbollah militiamen and five women were
rounded up, had their hands tied, were lined up against a wall and
shot. Those who remained alive were knifed to death, which wit-
nesses and medical staff who later examined the bodies at a Beirut
hospital confirmed.[192] While the Syrians justified their action as legitimate self-defence, Hezbollah described it as 'an act of liquidation'.[193]
The movement issued a communiqué that accused Damascus of
'deliberately massacring' its members and some militants vowed
revenge. The next day, as a sign of solidarity and outrage in the Shiite
community, the funeral procession for the dead in the southern suburbs of Beirut drew more than 10,000 mourners and some chanted
'Death to Syria'.[194] Hezbollah fighters were also placed on high alert in
case the Syrians tried to enter the southern neighbourhoods and
clamp down on them. Prominent Shiite clerics spoke in unison
against the Syrian action, with Sheikh Fadlallah condemning what he
called the 'massacre' perpetrated by the Syrians, and Sheikh Subhi al-
Tufayli accusing Damascus of conspiring with Israel and demanding
an apology.[195]

The Syrian army, for its part, expressed no regret about the
incident, and signalled its determination to stay its course. In fact,
following the killings, at midnight on 24 February, Ghazi Kan'an
issued a statement to the effect that every gunman was 'an enemy of
the city' and his forces would 'not discriminate' between members of
any organization carrying weapons.[196] The next day, Damascus stated
that those who resisted the efforts of its forces to halt the violence
and chaos would pay dearly, urging the Lebanese to turn their guns
away from each other since the violence was only 'serving the
interests of Israel'. Through their robust presence in West Beirut, the
Syrians put an end to the looting and disorder. As a way of showing
who the masters were in West Beirut, Syrian soldiers proceeded to
take down portraits of Ayatollah Khomeini that had been placed in
the streets and replace them with those of Hafez Assad.[197]

Iran's reaction to the Basta incident

Tehran's reaction to the Basta affair was cautious and restrained.

Syria's decision to enter West Beirut, and the killing of Hezbollah personnel two days later, no doubt caught the Iranian government off guard. Deputy foreign minister Sheikholislam only returned to Tehran on 20 February after spending three months in Lebanon trying to end the siege of the camps. The day after Syrian forces entered West Beirut, foreign minister Velayati and Revolutionary Guards minister Rafiqdoust hastily left for Damascus to seek clarification on Syria's motives; they were subsequently assured that Hezbollah would not be suppressed.[198] Their one-day visit, which included a meeting with Assad, was cloaked in secrecy and they left without any formal statements. During their deliberations its seems that Assad made it quite clear to his Iranian allies that they would have to defer to him in determining the course of events in Lebanon and understand that, in the Levant, Syrian interests were paramount.[199] On arriving in Tehran, Velayati publicly warned the Syrians to be careful about their moves in Lebanon, and on a defiant note declared, 'no other country in the world has as much influence in Lebanon as Iran'.[200] In reality, Iran's leaders were acutely aware that if Assad deemed it necessary, there was very little the Islamic Republic could do to stop him crushing its Lebanese followers. In any case, with Operation Karbala 5 in full swing, now more than ever before, Iran's revolutionaries knew that their main concern was the successful prosecution of the Gulf War. Lebanon was a sideshow and did not constitute their primary interest, especially at this critical stage.

Iran's reaction to the Basta affair – reflected in the statements of government officials and in the state-controlled news media – was to express disapproval but refrain from holding the Syrian regime responsible for it. Prime Minister Musavi went so far as to denounce the killings as an act that only benefited the 'cause of imperialism'.[201] Rafsanjani advised both the Syrians and Hezbollah to avoid confrontation because it would serve Israel. He described the Basta massacre as 'bitter' and emphasized that the 'friendship' between Damascus and Hezbollah 'should be preserved'.[202] The day after the clash, the Persian-language daily *Kayhan* described the incident as an unfortunate mistake caused by ill-disciplined Syrian soldiers, adding that Syria knew perfectly well that Hezbollah was a force to be reckoned with and that Iran would not accept it being weakened or sidelined. A few days later, another major daily *Ettela'at* exonerated the Syrian regime by explaining, 'without doubt, this action was not consistent with the political and military command instructions of Damascus, and it smacks of a plot hatched by an errant group in the military'.[203] Overall, Tehran refrained from pinning the blame on the Assad regime and conveniently attributed the killings to renegades within the Syrian army. It demanded that those responsible be identified and brought swiftly to justice to prevent a similar recurrence in the future.

Iran's hardline politico–religious figures like Ayatollah Montazeri and the interior minister Mohtashami were more outspoken in condemning the Basta killings, but again fell short of holding Damascus responsible. Montazeri appealed for reconciliation and unity among all Lebanese, Palestinians, Syrians, Sunnis and Shiites.[204] In general, most Iranian leaders were sceptical about Syria's military presence in West Beirut, with some fearing that the imposition of a Pax Syriana at the expense of Iranian influence had the implicit backing of Washington and Tel Aviv. Over the next few days, Tehran thus took steps to ensure that there would be no further moves against Hezbollah and tried to convince Syria that any hostile action targeting its Lebanese acolytes would be interpreted as an attack on Iran.

Meanwhile, after some lashing out at Syria, Hezbollah's leaders took stern measures (perhaps in consultation with the Iranian government) to ease tensions and contain the situation. They issued a fatwa ordering their followers to avoid confrontation with the Syrians.[205] Furthermore, in the days that followed, many Hezbollah members left West Beirut for the southern suburbs, while those who remained or entered the city kept a low profile. Fadlallah also went out of his way to dismiss reports of a pending showdown with the Syrian forces.

While exercising restraint to prevent more friction with its Arab ally, Iran tried to bolster its negotiating position *vis-à-vis* Syria and to boost Hezbollah morale and confidence in its Iranian patron by stressing the strong bond between Tehran and its Lebanese protégé. To emphasize that the two were inseparable and that any move against Hezbollah would be seen as an assault on Iran's interests, the clerical regime sent a new ambassador, Ahmad Dastmalchian, to Lebanon in early March. Moreover, a high-ranking delegation of two ayatollahs and two hojjatolislams representing Khomeini and his designated successor accompanied him. After a rapturous welcome from thousands of Hezbollah supporters and Shiites from southern Beirut, one of the Iranian delegation's first moves was to visit the cemetery where the Basta victims were buried and pay tribute to them. Dastmalchian called the killings a 'hideous and inexcusable crime'.[206] Later, they visited the Basta district to meet the families of the fallen. One Iranian delegate, Ayatollah Jannati, tried to show that Iran and Hezbollah were inextricably linked by saying that the Islamic Republic valued all its combatants equally, be it 'on the battlefields of the Iraqi-imposed war, or in the war front against the Zionists'.[207] Though showering praise on Hezbollah for its valiant efforts against Israel, France and the USA, by urging patience and prudence, the Iranians also tried to discourage their Lebanese followers from taking retaliatory action against Syria. Jannati articulated this by declaring: 'Revenge belongs to Allah. Your patience in this phase will merit Allah's best reward ... victory is the ally of patience.'[208]

Along with the Iranian initiative in Lebanon, the Tehran leadership decided to send an envoy to Damascus to ascertain Syrian intentions in both the Levant and the Gulf, and try to reach some sort of *modus vivendi* on both fronts with its Arab ally. In view of the Syrian deployment in West Beirut and the Basta incident, Tehran was concerned that Assad was taking an independent path in Lebanon and seemed to be reconsidering his position on the Iran–Iraq conflict. Only two days after the Syrian–Hezbollah clash, he delivered a speech warning his Iranian allies that if Basra were overrun, the Arab world would unite against them.[209]

Thus, with Dastmalchian's arrival in Lebanon, on 6 March, interior minister Mohtashami was sent to Syria on an unscheduled three-day visit.[210] Mohtashami met his Syrian counterpart Mohammed Ghabbash the next day to discuss their 'bilateral relations and matters of mutual concern', and reaffirmed Iran's support for Syria's goals and aspirations. On 8 March, Mohtashami was finally granted an audience with Assad; he delivered a message from Ali Khamene'i and they spoke for three hours on developments in Lebanon. The Syrian leader apparently assured him that he had no intention of disarming Hezbollah, for he was aware of its crucial role in the past in thwarting Western and Israeli designs. In addition, he emphasized that the killing of Hezbollah members had not been premeditated. Assad apparently said that Hezbollah would be allowed to operate against the Israelis in the south, and that Syrian troops would not move into Beirut's southern suburbs. But he also told Mohtashami that no activity that ran contrary to Syrian interests would be tolerated and that he expected both Tehran and Hezbollah to cooperate in this respect.[211] In effect, if Iranian–Hezbollah interests diverged from those of Syria, the latter would take precedence in Syria's Lebanese backyard. Hafez Assad drove home this point on the day Mohtashami returned to Tehran when, in an address at Damascus University commemorating the 24th anniversary of the 1963 Ba'thist revolution, he reiterated the primacy of Syrian interests in Lebanon, elucidating:

'A solution will not come from overseas, or from anywhere outside the borders of Lebanon and Syria … those who are against imperialism and Zionism must go along with Syria, appreciate Syria's direction in Lebanon and respect and support that direction'.[212] He also expressed his wish for the Lebanese to put aside their differences and reach national accord to restore peace in their country. Assad signalled his readiness 'to extend all possible help' towards that end.[213]

In an interview on his return to Iran, Mohtashami expressed satisfaction at the outcome of his talks because he had ascertained Syria's position and reached an understanding on strengthening bilateral relations and Hezbollah's future role.[214] Mohtashami stressed that forging closer links with Syria was 'a must'.[215] Initial Iranian fears that Syria wanted to break with its non-Arab ally had proved unfounded. From Iran's perspective, maintaining Hezbollah as an armed resistance movement, directing its attention to the struggle against the Israeli occupation in the south and continuing the alliance against Iraq, by far, outweighed entertaining notions of establishing an Islamic republic in Lebanon and jeopardizing the strategic partnership with Syria. It thus came as no surprise when, on 13 March, during the Friday sermon at Tehran University, speaker of parliament Rafsanjani declared that Damascus had no intention of standing in Hezbollah's way. He depicted Syria as the 'strongest bastion of resistance against Israel' that had succeeded in the vital task of establishing relative peace in Lebanon through its military presence.[216] The Syrian–Iranian alliance had survived the crisis caused by the Basta affair. Assad had succeeded in dictating the rules of the game in Lebanon and the parameters of Iranian–Hezbollah activities. The partnership had survived an important test. However, it was to face further challenges in the months that followed.

Areas of contention and the Syrian–Iraqi rift

For the time being at least, Syria and Iran had reached a *modus vivendi* on Lebanon. Though Assad had persuaded his Iranian ally that Syrian interests took precedence in his bailiwick, this did not mean that he could dispense with their support, or indeed Hezbollah's, in Lebanon's fractious political landscape. As a major movement, rallying a growing number of supporters in the Shiite community, Hezbollah was a force Syria intended to co-opt and accommodate, and imperative given the opposition Damascus faced to its policies in the Christian and Palestinian camps. Furthermore, Syria's dilemma was exacerbated because its own ally, Amal, was experiencing an internal crisis and beginning to disintegrate. Several of its key members who had become disenchanted with Berri's policies were either dismissed or defected. Amal had been badly mauled in the latest round of fighting in Beirut, and in the south many of its fighters were joining Hezbollah. Corruption within the Amal ranks and its brutal tactics alienated many young Shiites who turned to its pro-Iranian rival for inspiration.[217]

Apart from the precarious situation in Lebanon, Damascus faced formidable challenges requiring it to diversify its relations and be flexible in its dealings with the moderate Arab camp. The acute economic crisis that had plagued it since 1985 continued to take a severe toll on the country, forcing Assad again to rethink strategy and become more amenable to Arab and Soviet entreaties to mend fences with Iraq and the PLO. (See next section on the impact of Gorbachev's new thinking on Syrian foreign policy in the Middle East.) A steadily declining GDP, shrinking foreign currency reserves and an inability to finance its current accounts deficit meant that from late 1986 onwards, Syria was forced to cut its defence expenditures, disband military units and mothball heavy equipment.[218] Assad's cherished goal of achieving 'strategic parity' with Israel was looking ever more elusive and Syria continued to have problems paying for the Iranian oil shipments. In fact, due to financial constraints, under the previous arrangement, Syria had taken a million tons of free Iranian oil and purchased at most only one-fifth of the amount it was entitled to buy at a 25 per cent discount. By March 1987, a month before the agreement expired, it had accumulated a debt of between $1.7 and $2.3 billion.[219] Kuwait, meanwhile, had stepped in and made up for the shortfall. Other reports indicated at the time that Syria was also receiving Libyan oil and purchasing additional supplies on the Black Sea spot market.[220]

To ease its economic hardship and reduce its political isolation in the Arab–Islamic world, in early 1987, Syria tried to accommodate the moderate pro-Iraqi bloc – hence Assad's decision to attend the OIC summit in Kuwait and condemn Iranian moves to occupy Basra. King Hussein of Jordan tried to exploit this new window of opportunity to bring Syria back into the Arab mainstream and heal the Syrian–Iraqi rift. The Jordanian monarch had already met Hafez Assad at the Kuwait meeting on 28 January. A week after the OIC conference ended, King Hussein spent two days in Damascus discussing regional issues and bilateral ties with Assad. This initiative coincided with renewed Soviet efforts to bridge the gap between Syria and Iraq. Moscow welcomed

the Syrian–Jordanian reconciliation and their support for an international peace conference on the Middle East to restore order in the
Arab world, diminish the chances of a US proposal like the Reagan plan
being implemented, and enhance Soviet influence and standing in the
region. In addition, the Soviets were strong advocates of a Syrian–
PLO *rapprochement* to create a unified Arab position in the Middle
East peace process. Along with its efforts to resuscitate the Arab–
Israeli negotiations, Moscow also aimed to end the Gulf War, for it
considered the conflict detrimental to the prospects of resolving the
Arab–Israeli problem. Besides, it saw the Iran–Iraq hostilities as
giving the USA a pretext to increase its presence and influence in the
Gulf region.[221] Overall, there was a significant convergence of interests
and similarities between Jordanian and Soviet moves in this period to
effect a Syrian–Iraqi reconciliation to restore Arab unity, isolate Iran
and force the clerical regime to sue for peace. Interestingly, in mid-
February, as fighting raged on the outskirts of Basra, Saddam Hussein
sent his foreign minister Tareq Aziz to Moscow and Amman for talks
with Andrei Gromyko and King Hussein on the war and bilateral
affairs. King Hussein then paid a one-day visit to Baghdad on 8 March
for consultations with the Iraqi leader.

Assad, for his part, had no intention of abandoning his strategic
partnership with Iran: he was still receiving shipments of Iranian oil
and needed Tehran's good offices to control Hezbollah and steer
events in Lebanon. Also, his nemesis, Saddam Hussein, was still tied
down in a desperate struggle for survival against the Iranians. However, he calculated that, to contain the economic crisis at home, he
needed to take tactical steps to mitigate his regional isolation and
security dilemma while extracting financial and material benefits
from both sides. The confluence of several events provided this
opportunity in April 1987. With the previous oil agreement due to
expire in April, Iran delivered its last major load of crude oil (260,000
tons) to Syria in early March, and stated that renewing the agreement
would be contingent on Syria's ability to settle its outstanding debt.[222]
Jordan and Saudi Arabia tried harder to persuade Syria to abandon
Iran by offering to resume Iraqi oil shipments as part of a Syrian–Iraqi
reconciliation, and for Saudi oil and financial support to compensate
it for the termination of Iranian oil deliveries and repayment of its
foreign debts. So, on 3 April, King Hussein arrived in Damascus on an
unscheduled visit and held a seven-hour meeting with Hafez Assad
on regional developments, including inter-Arab politics and the
Arab–Israeli conflict. Then, in late April, the Syrian leader was

scheduled to make his first state visit to Moscow since June 1985 to meet Mikhail Gorbachev and boost bilateral cooperation. With Syrian–Iranian relations seemingly on shaky ground, and Syria facing a myriad of political and economic problems at home and abroad, Moscow, Amman and Riyadh believed they could now induce Damascus to abandon its alliance with Iran in favour of Iraq, thereby restoring Arab unity and dealing a major symbolic and practical blow to Iran, which would be left isolated in the region, ideologically bankrupt and without any supporters in the Arab East.

Gorbachev, Syrian–Soviet relations and their impact on the alliance

The Syrians had been concerned about new trends in Soviet foreign policy since Mikhail Gorbachev came to power in March 1985. Like Chernenko, his predecessor, he seemed less sympathetic to Syrian concerns and, to make fresh inroads in the region and lessen Moscow's dependency on traditional allies like Syria, took the Kremlin's Middle East policy in a new direction. Furthermore, from Syria's perspective, Gorbachev's overtures to Israel were an extremely worrisome aspect of his new approach.

Predictably, Assad's first meeting with Gorbachev on a visit to Moscow in June 1985 went badly. The two disagreed on almost every issue. The Soviet premier had reservations about supporting Syria's doctrine of 'strategic parity' with Israel, emphasizing the need for diplomatic solutions. Also, he disapproved of Assad's hostile stand on Arafat and Saddam Hussein, underlining the need for Arab unity and a coordinated approach to the Gulf War and Arab–Israeli problem. Although Hafez Assad had a rude awakening and came away from the talks empty-handed, he kept to his previous course, which, however, did not lead to a rupture in Soviet–Syrian relations.[223]

By spring 1987, given the plethora of domestic and external problems he faced, Assad knew that he would have to show flexibility and comply with some Soviet demands when he embarked on his second state visit to the USSR to meet Gorbachev. From Assad's standpoint, his negotiations in Moscow (23–25 April) went quite well – in fact better than expected considering the dire straits Syria was in at this stage. He was able to secure desperately needed assistance in return for a few concessions. A number of economic and industrial agreements were concluded, entailing Soviet assistance in developing Syria's oil and phosphate industries and building a hydroelectric dam on the Euphrates River. Gorbachev agreed to reschedule Syria's $15 billion debt and to deliver weaponry that had been promised, including MiG-29s.[224] Assad agreed to Gorbachev's request to hold a secret meeting with Saddam Hussein in Jordan to iron out their differences upon his return to the Middle East, and publicly reaffirmed his support for an international conference, with Soviet participation, to resolve the Arab–Israeli dispute in a comprehensive manner.[225]

It should be noted that, despite his political and economic woes, Assad took an unusually hard line on certain issues. The Syrian leader brushed off Soviet criticism of his quest to attain 'strategic parity' with Israel, and Gorbachev's insistence on pursuing a diplomatic option only. Assad, a firm believer in negotiating from a position of strength, pointed out that the increasing levels of US aid to Israel made Tel Aviv more intransigent and less amenable to compromise in peace talks, particularly when the USSR was showing reluctance to aid its Arab allies.[226]

Overall, cooling Soviet–Syrian relations produced a gradual reformulation of Syrian foreign policy, including its means and objectives. The diminished likelihood of matching Israel in terms of conventional weapons meant that, to attain its objectives, Syria would have to rely less on its superpower patron and instead enlist the support of regional states like Iran and local actors like radical Lebanese and Palestinian groups. Herein lay another good reason not to alienate the emergent Hezbollah movement in Lebanon. As long as the radical Shiites did not prove to be an obstacle to Syrian policy, the Western hostage issue and the guerrilla warfare in the south targeting the Israelis and SLA could further Syrian objectives. This, in turn, meant maintaining cordial relations with Iran to keep Hezbollah in line, and also exploring further avenues of cooperation with Iran in the Gulf.

The Syrian-Iraqi dialogue and Iran's riposte

The day after leaving Moscow on 25 April, Assad travelled to Jordan to hold secret talks with Saddam Hussein.[227] Given the acute economic crisis at home and volatile situation in the region, along with intense lobbying and pressure from Moscow, Amman and Riyadh, the Syrian leader decided he had nothing to lose by meeting his Iraqi Ba'thist rival. To the contrary, the occasion gave Syria a convenient opportunity possibly to extract concessions from the pro-Iraqi camp, while gaining greater leverage over Iran through some delicate diplomatic manoeuvring and posturing.

The Syrian and Iraqi presidents negotiated for two days (26–27 April) in Jafra (a town near an air base) in the northeast corner of the Jordanian panhandle close to the Syrian–Iraqi border.[228] King

Hussein and Saudi Crown Prince Abdullah attended the opening round.[229] Deliberations on the second day only involved the two Ba'thist leaders and their personal aides, and lasted five hours. A major sticking point was Saddam Hussein's insistence that a reconciliation between the two would require at minimum Syrian neutrality in the Gulf War.[230] Although no major breakthrough occurred, the two sides agreed gradually to scale down hostilities and explore avenues of cooperation in a number of areas as a way of building confidence and thawing relations. Both agreed to curtail the activities of exiled opposition groups based in their countries and the propaganda wars directed against one another.[231] They also agreed to call a halt to activities designed to destabilize each other, and to free political prisoners loyal to the other side. In addition, both parties agreed to convene a meeting of their oil ministers to discuss the possibility of reopening the IPC oil pipeline closed in 1982, and form joint committees to discuss various issues, including the use of Euphrates water and harmonization of their positions vis-à-vis Turkey in this regard.

In general, the Syrian–Iraqi summit (the first of its kind between the two leaders since the collapse of the 1979 unity talks) was a significant achievement for King Hussein and underlined the efficacy of Saudi and Soviet lobbying. The outcome of the bilateral talks at the time seemed to have laid the foundations of a genuine *rapprochement*, and heralded a new phase in Damascus–Baghdad ties. Confident that they had finally succeeded in weaning Syria away from Iran, the Saudis leaked details about the outcome of the meeting to the Arab press that were subsequently picked up and publicized in the Western news media.[232] Besides Jordan and Saudi Arabia serving as intermediaries, it was evident that the Soviets had played an instrumental role in persuading Assad to meet his rival.

In fact, Assad's gambit paid off. The meeting and subsequent disclosures about it raised hopes of a Syrian–Iraqi *rapprochement*, with the moderate Arab camp offering Damascus incentives to ease the process and a flurry of activity by Iran to ensure that its most important Arab ally did not abandon it. For the next few months, the Syrians proved quite adept at exploiting the new conditions that had emerged as a result of the Jafra summit.[233]

While Iran must have known that Syria was under pressure from the USSR and key Arab states to end their alliance and realign with the moderate pro-Iraqi bloc, the Syrian–Iraqi talks still surprised it. Only days before Assad left for Moscow, deputy foreign minister

Sheikholislam had been in Damascus to discuss regional developments and the Gulf War with Faruq al-Shara, who reaffirmed Syrian support for Iran.[234] During Assad's visit to Moscow, Syrian oil minister Ghazi al-Durubi arrived in Tehran to negotiate a new oil agreement with Iran. Due to Syria's economic plight and political considerations, Iran seems to have back-peddled on its previous position and agreed to supply oil, despite Syria's outstanding debt. As it turned out, on 25 April a new 12-month agreement was concluded between al-Durubi and his Iranian counterpart Gholamreza Aghazadeh, whereby Iran would continue to deliver a million tons of crude free of charge and sell 1.5 to 2.5 million tons at a 25 per cent discount.[235]

Within a week of details of the Jafra summit being leaked to the press, Faruq al-Shara was sent to Tehran to brief Iranian leaders on the outcome of the Syrian–Iraqi talks and reassure them that Damascus was not contemplating a major policy shift on the Iran–Iraq issue. Al-Shara arrived on 12 May for a one-day visit. He first met President Khamene'i to deliver a message from Assad. He asserted that 'despite all efforts undertaken in Baghdad ... Syria will stand by the Islamic revolution of Iran'. Khamene'i, for his part, stressed the need for continued expansion of bilateral relations.[236] He then had meetings with Musavi and Rafsanjani before departing for Syria later that day. One topic of discussion during his deliberations with Rafsanjani was the Syrian–Soviet summit. Rafsanjani expressed frustration at Moscow's Middle East policy, highlighting that the most important impediment to improved Soviet–Iranian relations was the Kremlin's continued support for Iraq. When a reporter asked him about Syrian–Iraqi negotiations at Tehran's Mehrabad airport, where foreign minister Velayati saw him off, al-Shara gave an elusive response, stating: 'If you mean how Iran–Syria relations are, I should say that these relations are firm and steadfast. In relation with international issues, our stand is quite obvious.'[237]

By now, Tehran and Damascus both realized that developments were not moving in their favour at a local, regional or international level. For Syria, mounting domestic problems, the fluid situation in Lebanon and the gradual cooling of relations with the USSR meant that it would have to engage in a careful balancing act on the regional stage to safeguard its interests. There was no question of severing links with Iran. However, Syria's growing marginalization in inter-Arab politics and Egypt's gradual return to the Arab fold, called for more flexibility in its regional diplomacy.

As the year progressed and Tehran became increasingly isolated in the Arab–Islamic world, it became more vital to preserve its alliance with Syria.[238] However, the Iran–Contra affair, the failure of Karbala 5 and the two superpowers' reflagging operations radicalized Iranian politics and allowed extremists to gain the upper hand. With US and west European attitudes to Iran hardening in the first half of 1987, the more pragmatic Iranian leaders had to abandon their previous policies and adopt a hardline posture to safeguard their position and prove their revolutionary credentials.[239] Incidents that led to a marked deterioration of relations with Britain and France also highlighted Iran's growing isolation.

These developments led to a downward spiral in Iran's fortunes. In fact, over the next year, Tehran gradually resorted to desperate and reckless acts in the Gulf and beyond, eliciting decisive responses from regional and extra-regional actors, especially the two superpowers, which paradoxically guaranteed Saddam Hussein's survival. By mid-1987, Iran had begun to embark on a self-destructive path that would condemn it to regional and international isolation and give the USA a convenient excuse to become a *de facto* co-belligerent in the Gulf conflict on the side of Iraq. Tehran's ill-conceived strategies, mis-judged conduct and maladroit diplomacy sealed its fate. They ensured that it failed to attain its war objectives and became the target of Arab and Western opprobrium.

In sharp contrast to its Syrian partner, where prudence, careful calculation and setting realistic objectives were a hallmark of its foreign policy, revolutionary Iran again tried to use an evolving crisis to gain short-term benefits without regard to long-term interests or attainable goals. As in the past, style and form took priority over substance and solid accomplishments. Within a few months of spring 1987 Iran ventured down a perilous path, alienating key Western and Arab states with its reckless conduct and brinkmanship in the process. Whether intentional or not, Tehran made a critical mistake in the summer by trying to take on the USA (and USSR initially) in its backyard (albeit indirectly) by planting mines in Gulf shipping lanes. The stalemate in the ground war had reinforced its determination to take action and challenge foreign navies in the Persian Gulf.[240]

Superpower diplomacy and foreign presence in the Gulf

In spring 1987, the USA and USSR engaged in a flurry of diplomatic activity in the Gulf to pave the way towards implementing the reflag-ging agreements. As part of this initiative, Soviet deputy foreign minister Vladimir Petrovsky would tour the region to hold talks in

Iraq, Kuwait, Oman and the UAE. Petrovsky's visit to the region in late April, where he also met Saddam Hussein and Tareq Aziz in Baghdad, coincided with the Gorbachev–Assad summit. It was no coincidence that the two Ba'thist rivals met Soviet officials just prior to the surreptitious meeting in Jafra. Gorbachev was determined to bring about a Syrian–Iraqi *rapprochement* to restore Arab unity and force Iran to accept a negotiated settlement.[241]

Syria avoided criticizing Soviet moves in the Gulf, but joined the chorus of Iranian condemnation of US policy. Both the Syrian and Iranian media denounced the US assistant secretary of state Richard Murphy's visit to Gulf just a week after Petrovsky's trip. A scathing editorial in the Syrian daily *Al-Thawrah* on 8 May, entitled 'A Tour of Deception and Dupery', described Murphy's tour of Iraq and the six GCC states as a Washington ploy to exploit the tense situation that had arisen from Iraq's aggressive moves to increase US military forces in the Gulf and act provocatively against the littoral states. Furthermore, an editorial in the Iranian daily *Jomhuri Eslami* on 11 May called Murphy's mission a sign of 'desperate' US action in the aftermath of the Iran–Contra revelations. Another article in the same newspaper the following day scoffed at Murphy's assertions that a Kuwaiti ship flying the US flag would not be considered Kuwaiti. As it put it: 'No matter what flag it shows, a Kuwaiti ship will be considered a Kuwaiti ship and cannot serve the Baghdad regime and the war criminals ruling over Iraq. It cannot be allowed to be actively involved in strengthening the enemy's military might.'[242]

Despite the polemical nature of Syrian and Iranian statements on the purpose of Murphy's tour, they were close to the truth. The US assistant secretary of state visited Baghdad on 10–11 May where he first met foreign minister Tareq Aziz to discuss US–Iraqi relations, the regional situation and the Gulf War. The next day, he held talks with Saddam Hussein and gave him a written note from Ronald Reagan. His visit came at a critical time in view of the US decision to reflag the Kuwaiti tankers and him being the most senior US official to visit Iraq since the Iran–Contra scandal. To restore Iraqi confidence in the USA and prove its commitment to end the war on terms favourable to Iraq, he informed Iraqi leaders that the USA would soon introduce a resolution in the UN Security Council favouring Iraq. The resolution, which would disadvantage Iran, urged the two parties in the conflict to cease hostilities and withdraw to their internationally-recognized borders – meaning Iran would have to give up all the territorial gains it had made in Iraq since 1982. To give the resolution teeth, any party that refused to abide by it would be subject to an international weapons embargo. Naturally, Baghdad was expected to accept the resolution, while Iran would reject it. The reflagging and UN resolution were part of an overall package of US plans and assistance to prove that Iran–Contra had been an aberration in US policy and that Washington was now going to use all the tools at its disposal to cow Iran.[243] At a press conference before departing from Baghdad, Murphy posited that 'understanding had prevailed in his talks without exception'.[244] The growing momentum of US activity in the Gulf to prop up Iraq and rally the Gulf Arabs was such that even the inadvertent Iraqi attack on the USS *Stark* – just six days after Murphy's meeting with Saddam Hussein – had minimal impact, if any, on Washington's relations with Baghdad.

As the Reagan administration assumed more of a war footing against Tehran, Moscow tried to defuse tensions and curry favour with its southern neighbour. Two factors facilitated this endeavour. First, both Soviet and Iranian policymakers wanted to prevent a US military build-up in the Gulf, fearing it might be a prelude to a permanent deployment in the area. Second, Gorbachev was concerned that the Reagan administration's new initiative in the Gulf was aimed at patching up US–Arab relations in the aftermath of the Iran–Contra scandal and impeding Soviet efforts to cultivate ties with the Gulf states. Numerous statements US officials made at the time clearly indicated that the purpose of a high-profile presence of US forces in the Persian Gulf was to thwart Iranian and Soviet power and influence. Assistant secretary of state Richard Murphy candidly pointed out that the purpose of the US presence was to prevent the encroachment of Iran and the USSR in a region vital to the West, while Ronald Reagan pledged publicly on 30 May that 'the use of the vital sea lanes of the Persian Gulf will not be dictated by the Iranians. These lanes will not be allowed to come under the control of the Soviet Union.'[245]

The Soviet–Iranian *rapprochement* gained further momentum with the passage of UN Security Council Resolution 598 on 20 July 1987. Although the unanimously approved resolution called for an immediate ceasefire and the release of POWs, several important articles in it reflected the success of Soviet diplomacy in avoiding the passage of a resolution with a distinctly anti-Iranian slant, as the US–Arab bloc had wished. The resolution asked the secretary-general to mediate between the two belligerents, and called on other countries to 'refrain from any act which may lead to further escalation and widening of the conflict'. As a result, Moscow subsequently accused Washington of aggravating conditions in the Gulf by sending in a large armada. Moreover, to show Iran their willingness to take a more even-handed approach to the war, in the Security Council debate, the Soviets asked for the addition of an article calling for the creation of an impartial body under the auspices of the UN secretary-general to determine responsibility for the outbreak of the conflict.[246]

Since the resolution partially accommodated some Iranian demands, Tehran's response was not an outright rejection, but it made its acceptance contingent on certain changes, especially that the formal ceasefire and identification of the aggressor occur simultaneously. In contrast to the Iraqi position that the resolution be accepted as an 'integral and indivisible whole', Iran's reservations concerned the sequence of its implementation. The US–Arab bloc saw the Iranian riposte as stonewalling, and urged the Security Council to impose a worldwide arms embargo on Iran. Iraq and other states, including the USA, introduced a draft resolution to this effect, but the USSR stifled its efforts by arguing that the secretary-general should be given time to resolve outstanding issues with Iran. While the Kremlin was no doubt taking full advantage of emerging US–Iranian tensions in the Gulf to thaw relations with the clerical regime, it was trying to adopt a more balanced position on the Gulf War because, unlike Washington, it had open channels of communication with both belligerents. Just as Syria maintained links with Iran and pro-Iraqi Arab states to enhance its regional power and status and obtain benefits from both sides, so the USSR found it useful to engage both camps diplomatically to bolster its influence and status in the Middle East.

After the subtle shift in Soviet policy on the Iran–Iraq conflagration in summer 1987, Moscow's stance remained consistent for the next year until the war ended in August 1988. It attempted to improve relations with Iran in a bid to persuade it to accept a negotiated settlement and deny Washington further grounds to boost its military presence and political influence in the Persian Gulf. But Soviet efforts came to naught. Tehran's insistence on fighting to victory or a negotiated settlement on its own terms reduced the prospects of a Soviet–Iranian *rapprochement* as Gorbachev continued the flow of arms to Saddam Hussein to forestall an Iraqi collapse. Ultimately, the US attempt to punish Iran by drafting a resolution unacceptable to it weakened the pragmatists in Tehran (who wanted a negotiated settlement that would identify the aggressor in the conflict) and strengthened the radicals who were bent on pursuing the military option. Ironically, Washington's determination to give Iran no quarter and to close off all avenues to a political settlement bolstered the hardliners in Tehran and prolonged the conflict.[247] The continuation of the hostilities for another year gave the USA an opportunity to appear indispensable to the security of the Gulf Arabs and, as Moscow had feared, to expand its foothold in the region.

In the final analysis, Iran's futile efforts to crush Iraq held up the normalizing of relations with the Kremlin and enabled the USA to intervene effectively in the Gulf arena to deny it any hope of victory. Tehran then gave the Reagan administration a convenient pretext for a military confrontation by laying mines in the Gulf, naively thinking that the USA would not respond decisively to its actions. The Iranians not only committed grave miscalculations in their strategy to prosecute the war but also made a number of other serious mistakes that brought greater opprobrium, severely straining its relations with the Arab world. By July 1987, Iran's long slide towards isolation and eventual defeat was becoming distinctly recognizable – epitomized by the *Bridgetown* and Mecca incidents.

Arab diplomatic efforts to separate Syria and Iran

With Iran increasingly isolated yet determined to meet the challenge in the Persian Gulf, moderate Arab states and the West tried for the rest of the spring and summer of 1987 to persuade Syria to distance itself from its Iranian ally. On 12 May, the day al-Shara visited Tehran to brief Iranian leaders about the Syrian–Iraqi summit and reaffirm Syria's commitment to their longstanding alliance, King Hussein began a new diplomatic initiative to revive the Syrian–Iraqi reconciliation process and restore Arab unity in a bid to bolster prospects for an international peace conference. He travelled first to Egypt for consultations with Mubarak, proceeding the next day to Baghdad and later to Damascus to meet the leaders of both states in order to mend the rift between the two Ba'thist rivals.

Despite al-Shara's assurances, the Iranians were apprehensive and suspicious of Syrian motives because of their growing isolation and Arab and Western governments' persistent efforts to wean Damascus away from them. A later meeting between al-Shara and his Iraqi counterpart Tareq Aziz fuelled their concerns about the imminent demise of their partnership with Syria.[248] Against a backdrop of superpower intervention in the Gulf and a marked deterioration in relations with Britain, France and much of the Arab world, between May and July, Iran embarked on an intensive campaign to salvage its remaining links with key Arab and Western states.[249] Tehran adopted a three-track approach to stave off isolation and mend fences. It sent envoys to Syria, the Gulf and Western Europe to contain the damage already done and head off any further moves to isolate it. In late May, Iranian ambassador to Syria, Mohammad Hassan Akhtari met Faruq al-Shara, handed him a message for Hafez Assad from Ali Khamene'i and reiterated Iran's support for Syria's struggle in the Levant. This was followed up within a week by the visit of an Iranian delegation headed by deputy foreign minister Sheikholislam, which met Assad and prime minister al-Kasm. Both sides agreed that US deployment in the Gulf threatened regional stability and Sheikholislam condemned the assasination of Rashid Karami, Lebanon's pro-Syrian prime minister, which had occurred just before he arrived on 1 June. Later, at a press conference, Sheikholislam expressed regret that some Gulf states were pursuing policies that inextricably linked their own security to the advancement of US and Iraqi interests in the region, stressing that 'there will be security in the Persian Gulf for all littoral states, or for none'.[250] Sheikholislam's talks in Damascus coincided with the visit of another Iranian delegation to West Germany and Italy led by deputy foreign minister for international and economic affairs Mohammad Javad Larijani, and that of a third team touring the Gulf sheikhdoms to reassure them of Iranian intentions as the escalating spiral of tensions continued in the area.

Frequent contacts between high-level Syrian and Iranian officials in summer 1987 produced a number of agreements and the expansion of bilateral relations. Iran clearly worried about the ongoing Syrian–Iraqi dialogue that led to meetings between Khaddam and Tareq Aziz in May and al-Shara and his Iraqi counterpart in June.[251] The Arab press hinted that these talks were to prepare for another summit between Assad and Saddam Hussein.[252] A high-level Iranian delegation headed by Mohsen Rafiqdoust visited Damascus in late June. The ostensible purpose of this trip was to seek clarification on the recent Syrian–Iraqi talks and fortify bilateral ties with Damascus. At a press conference in Damascus after his initial consultations, he claimed that reports of a Syrian–Iraqi reconciliation were 'baseless speculation and lies'.[253] He emphasized that the strategic alliance between Tehran and Damascus remained intact, and that Syria was not about to abandon it for one with 'a weak and dying regime'.[254] The negotiations involved their respective ministers of finance and economics and led to the conclusion of a bilateral agreement to further develop cooperation in commercial, industrial, banking and technological affairs.[255]

The diplomatic tug-of-war to win over Syria continued as King

Hussein started a new round of shuttle diplomacy to affect a Syrian–Iraqi *rapprochement*. On the heels of Rafiqdoust's departure, the Jordanian monarch arrived in Damascus on 24 June (for the seventh time since 1985) and Assad met him at the airport. His visit coincided with a mission by Kuwait's minister of state for foreign affairs, Saud Mohammed al-Usaymi, to Syria and Jordan to seek support for Kuwait's position in the Gulf War. Al-Usaymi held talks with both Assad and King Hussein. The Jordanian monarch subsequently affirmed that Jordan and Kuwait would coordinate their policies to restore Arab unity.[256] Alarmed by King Hussein's renewed attempts to bridge the gap between Damascus and Baghdad, and by Kuwait's initiative to win Syrian support for its stance on the Gulf conflict, Tehran announced that it was preparing to send Prime Minister Musavi to Damascus at the head of a 40-member delegation to expand and consolidate bilateral relations. King Hussein followed up his discussions with Assad by flying to Baghdad on 30 June for talks with Saddam Hussien, which the Jordanian media characterized as part of 'persistent efforts to achieve Arab solidarity' and in preparation for a Syrian–Iraqi summit.[257]

Rumours and numerous reports in the Arab and Western press of an imminent meeting between Assad and Saddam Hussein persisted throughout this period.[258] The postponement of Musavi's visit to Syria fuelled the speculation.[259] To dissipate Iranian concerns and dispel rumours of a Syrian–Iraqi reconciliation, Faruq al-Shara arrived in Tehran unexpectedly on 12 July to brief Iranian leaders on Syrian moves and coordinate their policies. To his Iranian counterpart, he pledged Syria's continued support for Iran in prosecuting the Gulf War.[260] At the same time, hoping to enlist Iranian support, al-Shara expressed disappointment at the turn of events in Lebanon (including Hezbollah's kidnapping of US journalist Charles Glass) and stressed that the need to secure the release of Western hostages was of vital importance to Syria.[261] Also, during a two-and-a-half-hour meeting with Velayati, al-Shara condemned the US and foreign naval presence in the Persian Gulf, for 'this would only electrify the atmosphere and spread the war'.[262] The next day, he spent more than two hours clarifying Syria's stance on various regional issues with President Khamene'i. Besides downplaying the prospects of reconciliation with Iraq as a direct result of Jordanian mediation, al-Shara also allayed Iranian fears about the Kuwaiti initiative, cautioning, 'It will be better for Kuwait to remain neutral in the war, otherwise it might be crushed by the tension created by itself.'[263] After their deliberations, Khamene'i confidently declared: 'Fortunately, our Syrian brothers have always proved that they are strongly committed to the expansion and deepening of relations with the Islamic Republic of Iran. This is something resented by colonialism and world imperialism.'[264]

Besides al-Shara's visit, once US reflagging started in earnest on 22 July, the Syrian media stepped up its criticism of US policy in the Gulf, stating that it reflected Washington's 'dreams of domination'. The move was explained as part of long-held aspirations 'to dominate the entire Gulf region' that were reinforced by the loss of their main pillar in the area, the Shah of Iran. Damascus claimed that Washington was using freedom of navigation as an excuse to justify intervening on Iraq's behalf.

At the time of Syria's renewed pledge to back Iran, Syrian–Iraqi tensions rose considerably when Iraqi air-defence units shot down a Syrian MiG-21 fighter on 28 July over Iraqi airspace.[265] Despite Syrian denials, Baghdad claimed that the warplane had been on a 'combat mission'.[266] The MiG pilot was captured alive, but *Al-Qadisiyah* claimed that Saddam Hussein would not allow him to be referred to as a prisoner, perhaps to salvage the prospect of a reconciliation with Damascus. Nonetheless, the incident caused mutual recriminations.[267]

As Iran's foes in the West and Arab world multiplied, Tehran's revolutionary clerics aggravated conditions by trying to raise the stakes during the hadj. Enraged at Kuwaiti and Saudi moves to bring foreign powers into the fray and help their activities in the Persian Gulf, on 31 July, Iran committed a colossal blunder in the holy city of Mecca that affirmed its pariah status in the eyes of many in the Middle East and beyond, and was a godsend to the pro-Iraqi camp. Then, Syria played its most crucial role ever – probably since the early months of the Gulf War – in standing up for its Iranian ally in various regional fora and preventing its total isolation.

The Mecca incident and the efficacy of Syrian diplomacy

As stated before, the Iran–Contra affair not only prompted the Reagan government to take a harder line on Iran to restore its credibility in the eyes of Iraq and the Gulf states, but it also let the radical elements in the Iranian regime regain the initiative, with the pragmatists forced to follow their lead to ensure their own political survival. A new phase in Iranian foreign policy followed the radicalization of politics in 1987. This, combined with the frustration of being unable to score a victory in the land war and outrage at Iraq's Gulf Arab supporters inviting US and Soviet navies into what Iran considered *mare nostrum*, led Tehran to adopt aggressive and militant policies to confront the ever more formidable coalition of Western and Arab forces arrayed against it. With a growing sense of embattlement, desperation and paranoia, and at the height of the hadj in the holy city of Mecca, Iran took a desperate gamble.

By organizing massive pro-Iranian demonstrations in Mecca among the 150,000 Iranian pilgrims performing the hadj, Tehran hoped to take advantage of Saudi sensitivities about their relations with the West and their potential vulnerability as the 'guardian of the holy places' to conduct a political *tour de force* to unnerve Riyadh and force it to stop cooperating with the USA and pro-Iraqi camp. On 31 July, as on other occasions in previous years, Iranian cadres organized a large demonstration of pilgrims chanting anti-US and pro-Iranian slogans. This time, however, Saudi police and National Guards stopped them entering the Grand Mosque as they began to advance on the complex. Clashes erupted as the Iranians tried to break through, with some using knives and other instruments, including handguns. After initial attempts to disperse the mob with tear gas and other non-lethal means, some Saudi forces used firearms on the Iranians. In the ensuing mêlée, more than 400 people were killed and 650 others injured. Among the dead were 275 Iranians and 85 Saudi security personnel. Both sides then made false claims. Tehran said Riyadh provoked the incident, while the Saudis flatly denied that their forces had fired any shots.[268]

Iran's gambit failed miserably. Rather than forcing the Saudis to perform a *volte-face*, it backfired by plunging relations between the two countries to unprecedented lows. More worrying for the clerical regime in practical and ideological terms was that the events in Mecca produced a new Arab–Iranian schism and created the impression in the Arab world that Iran's brand of Islamic fundamentalism was heretical and knew no bounds.

With tensions in the Gulf already at an all time high, the Mecca incident sent shockwaves through the region, threatening further instability. Both sides engaged in intense diplomatic activity to buttress their respective positions and keep the other side on the defensive. Iran continued to accuse Saudi Arabia of instigating the clashes and tried to rally its few Arab allies (particularly Syria) behind it. The pro-Saudi bloc redoubled its efforts to isolate Iran and persuade Syria to change allegiance. Damascus, which was in an awkward and sensitive position, still tried to mediate between the two sides to defuse tensions and mend the damage done to Arab–Iranian relations. Until an Arab League summit was convened in Amman in early November, both camps tried to advance their respective agendas.

Within 24 hours of the Mecca incident, Iran's deputy foreign minister Sheikholislam came to Damascus and directly on arrival met Hafez Assad to discuss the crisis and submit a message from Ali Khamene'i.[269] He stayed in the Syrian capital for several days for talks with high-ranking officials like vice-president Khaddam and foreign minister al-Shara, and to devise a strategy to deal with the severe crisis in Arab–Iranian relations.[270] Their deliberations seemed to result in the Syrians and Iranians agreeing to separate but complementary strategies for dealing with the fallout. Once reassured of Syria's solid support, Tehran took steps to win the backing of neighbouring Arab and Muslim states, while the Syrians chose to mediate between the two sides and discourage Arab countries from shunning Iran. On 2 August, the day after the Assad–Sheikholislam meeting, Assad called King Fahd to express his deep regrets and, according to Saudi sources, described the Iranian pilgrims' conduct as 'unacceptable from any quarter'.[271] Alongside his attempt to mollify the Saudis, he sent a message to his Iranian counterpart, Ali Khamene'i, asking Tehran to tone down its anti-Saudi rhetoric and ease tensions with Riyadh.[272] It is noteworthy that Syrian officials refrained from making public statements about the Mecca incident, and the media avoided criticizing Iran's role in the affair.[273]

As the only party to communicate openly with both Tehran and Riyadh, the Syrians were in a delicate position, for the two antagonists now demanded Syria's support against the other. But, since it enjoyed important political links and was the recipient of economic and financial benefits from both countries, it was loath to alienate either one completely. While maintaining its alliance with Iran, Syria tried to assuage the concerns of the Gulf states about further Iranian subversion and adventurism. Syria could not afford to jump ship to join forces with mainstream Arab states like Egypt and Iraq (its two main rivals in the Arab world) who were trying to take advantage of the Mecca incident for their own purposes. Iraq tried to portray it as proof of Iranian hypocrisy and expansionism in the Arab world. Saddam Hussein stated that it showed that 'even when the Iranian rulers say they have a religion, it is not the Islamic religion'.[274] The Egyptians also tried to get full mileage by condemning Iran's actions as 'an ugly crime against Islam'. Mubarak appealed for an emergency OIC meeting to discuss the issue. The Syrians were thus conscious that Iraq's position in the Gulf War and Egypt's reintegration into the

Arab world would be boosted if they sided with Riyadh. The most logical option was to use diplomacy to try to defuse the crisis, thereby impeding Iraqi and Egyptian moves to exploit the crisis, without abandoning the alliance with Iran.

As part of a joint Syrian–Iranian diplomatic offensive, to allay the fears of Arab states and to prevent the formation of a solid Arab bloc against it, Tehran tried to boost relations with Arab states that were fairly sympathetic to Iran or not blatantly pro-Iraqi. On 5 August, Sheikholislam arrived in Abu Dhabi to discuss the crisis in Saudi–Iranian relations with UAE President Sheikh Zayid bin Sultan Al-Nuhayan, and to deliver a message from Ali Khamene'i. Another Iranian envoy, Ali Shams-Ardakani, went to Muscat on a similar mission, where he was received by Sultan Qaboos.[275]

On 5 August, Faruq al-Shara visited Tehran to reaffirm Syrian support for its ally and coordinate policy. During his one-day visit, he held talks with his Iranian counterpart, the prime minister, and delivered a note from Hafez Assad to Ali Khamene'i. Although al-Shara denied press reports that his presence in the Iranian capital was part of a Syrian initiative to mediate between Riyadh and Tehran, he was careful not to criticize Saudi Arabia.[276] Instead, he expressed regret about the tragic events in Mecca, and accused Washington of having been involved in the affair to exacerbate the Gulf Arab–Iranian rift, and legitimize its high-profile naval presence in the area.[277] Besides stressing Syrian solidarity with Iran, he stated:

> I am confident that the Islamic Republic of Iran is capable of preventing the aggressors from achieving their aims, and just as US plans have been faced with defeat in the past, they will face defeat in the future too ... US and Arab reaction wish to spread the war and turn it into an Arab–Persian war, but the Islamic Republic of Iran has managed to defeat that conspiracy.[278]

After al-Shara's visit, the two sides kept in close touch as the pro-Saudi camp hastened its efforts to mobilize support to isolate Iran for its intransigence. To show support for Iran, and exert indirect pressure on the Gulf Arabs to prevent them from throwing their weight behind the USA, the Syrian media stepped up its propaganda against the US naval presence in the Gulf. Washington was depicted as trying to acquire direct control of the 'Arab oil lake' by using the need to protect tankers and ensure freedom of navigation as a pretext.

It accused the Reagan administration of 'reckless, aggressive behaviour' to impose its hegemony.[279]

As expected, the Arab diplomatic offensive to isolate Iran rapidly got underway in the days after the tragic events in Mecca, with Tunisia leading the call for an emergency meeting of the Arab League council. Initially, Kuwait was designated to host the meeting on 15 August, but the need for additional preparatory consultations and scheduling problems led to the postponement of the gathering until the 23rd, with the venue being shifted from the Gulf to Tunisia. UAE president Sheikh Zayid engineered the delay in a last-ditch effort to buy time and, with the Syrians and Algerians, to mediate between Saudi Arabia and Iran. He also agreed to follow up on Jordan's earlier initiative to bridge the gap between Damascus and Baghdad. The UAE president arrived in Damascus on 16 August and prolonged his stay to negotiate with Hafez Assad, thus heightening expectations for a possible solution. During his discussions in Damascus, Sheikh Zayid sent an envoy to Baghdad to see Saddam Hussein, but hopes of a breakthrough were dashed when no real progress was achieved and Iraq rejected the UAE mediation effort.[280] As a result, the stage was set for a major confrontation in the three-day Arab League meeting that started on 23 August with Saudi Arabia and Kuwait spearheading a drive to ostracize Iran, and Syria at the forefront of efforts to thwart them.

Syria's role in the Arab League meeting and its implications

The Arab League foreign ministers' meeting in Tunis was a major milestone in Arab–Iranian relations in the 1980s, for it had the most profound impact on the evolution of inter-Arab politics since Egypt's expulsion from the Arab fold in 1979. The meeting showed Syria to be a spoiler when it refused to countenance a pan-Arab consensus on a riposte to the Mecca affair. With Egypt's continued absence from the Arab League and Iraq still locked in a desperate struggle for survival against Iran, Syria was by default the key player in Arab affairs and held enormous sway. Its ability to prevent the passage of a harsh anti-Iranian resolution, despite overwhelming support from the majority of the members, underlined the urgent need for a major policy shift by the League on Egypt to tip the scales and dilute Syrian power and influence in Arab and regional politics. In many respects, the Tunis conference and Iran's continued refusal to accept UN Resolution 598 unconditionally paved the way for the Amman summit three months later, which set the stage for Egypt's formal re-entry into the Arab fold, and Iran's unanimous condemnation.

Against the backdrop of the seven-year Gulf War and the potential threat of hostilities engulfing neighbouring states, the events in Mecca increased general Arab disillusionment with Iran and underlined the need to signal intense displeasure at its conduct. On the eve of the Tunis meeting, the Syrians knew they would have to be at the vanguard to prevent a pan-Arab consensus against Iran. Already there were suggestions that Saudi Arabia wanted to revive the 1950 Arab Defence Pact (stipulating that aggression against any Arab League member was a threat to all members), thus enabling the Gulf states and others overtly to back Iraq. In addition, with the recent passage of UN Security Council Resolution 598, it was apparent that the anti-Iranian camp would try to build on the momentum it had generated by threatening punitive measures against Tehran unless it complied with the resolution. Prior to the opening session, the Syrians led by Faruq al-Shara convened a meeting in Tunis with Libyan, Algerian and South Yemeni representatives to harmonize their positions.[281]

On arriving in Tunis on 22 August, Saudi foreign minister Saud al-Faisal, who was to chair the emergency session, stated that in view of its 'anti-Arab actions' he would press to sever relations with Iran.[282] It was quite apparent that Saudi Arabia would assume a maximalist position to rally the other members, put any potential dissenters on the defensive and leave the meeting with tangible gains. In a ferocious attack on Iran, in his opening speech Saud al-Faisal denounced its 'terrorist and destructive actions against the Arab and Islamic worlds, particularly its neighbours in the Gulf'.[283] He went on to advocate a united Arab front, for Iran was bent on continuing the war at all costs, even by destabilizing the region. He also blamed Iran for laying mines in the Gulf, intervening unnecessarily in Lebanon and maintaining ties with Israel while 'hiding behind the slogans of Islam'.[284] Arab League secretary-general Chedli Klibi echoed his words when he condemned Iran for attempting to expand the war and destabilize its Arab neighbours, urging it instead to reconsider its policies and accept UN Resolution 598.

The opening speeches set the tone for subsequent statements by other participants, for the overwhelming majority, including Libya, Algeria and South Yemen, expressed solidarity with Saudi Arabia and Kuwait and displeasure at Iran's conduct in Mecca. Only Syria continued to support Iran and criticized the pro-Iraqi camp for depicting the Gulf conflict as an Arab–Iranian war.[285] Al-Shara fought off intense pressure from the Saudis and their allies to abandon the alliance; he argued against isolating Iran and for keeping open channels of communication with Tehran to modify its behaviour.[286] In fact, the Syrian foreign minister outspokenly criticized Iraq for starting the hostilities and condemned the foreign naval presence in the Gulf.[287] His words elicited a harsh response from his Iraqi counterpart, Tareq Aziz, who caustically retorted that the Syrian voice being heard in the session was 'a Persian voice rather than an Arab one'.[288]

While most delegates voiced outrage at Iran's behaviour, not all favoured taking an overtly anti-Iranian position. Of the 21 delegations present, 15 backed a draft resolution calling for the severance of diplomatic ties with Iran.[289] Libya, Algeria, Oman and the UAE supported Syrian arguments that ostracizing Iran would exacerbate the situation and in the long run prove counterproductive.[290] Saudi Arabia, Kuwait, Iraq and Tunisia led the effort to push through the draft resolution, but al-Shara would have none of it. The Syrians mustered the necessary support and thwarted this initiative. The delegates worked late into the night on the second day, modifying and watering down the text, until the Syrians grudgingly gave their consent.[291] The final resolution was unanimously passed the last day of the emergency meeting, 25 August, with some minor reservations.

Overall, it was the strongest stand the Arab League had ever taken on the Gulf War, reflecting its concern about the continuation of the conflict, possible expansion of the fighting and Iranian efforts to destabilize neighbouring Arab states. Although the final draft did not exclude a possible rupture in Arab–Iranian relations, it gave Iran until 20 September to reconsider its position and accept UN Resolution 598. Thereafter, the Arab League council would reconvene to formulate an appropriate response. The resolution restated Arab solidarity 'with Iraq in its legitimate defence of its sovereignty and territorial integrity' and condemned Iranian 'acts of sabotage and anarchy' in Mecca. It also appealed to the UN Security Council to adopt measures to ensure Iran complied with Resolution 598.[292]

Despite the harsh wording of this essentially anti-Iranian resolution, the Syrians had in fact succeeded in removing the teeth from the conference resolution. The issue of a rupture in Arab–Iranian relations was momentarily shelved and another proposal calling on the UN Security Council to impose an international arms embargo on Iran was also dropped from the final text. So, the resolution lacked punch, with Jordanian foreign minister al-Masri forthrightly describing it as 'incomplete'. The Saudis tried to put on a brave face by declaring the meeting a success and describing the final resolution as 'balanced'.[293] The Iranian media welcomed the outcome of the Arab

League deliberations, praising the 'realism and independence' of the pro-Iranian bloc led by Syria for thwarting this US-backed 'conspiracy' against Iran.[294] At a press conference on 26 August, Prime Minister Musavi pointed to the closeness of relations between Syria and Iran and mentioned that Syria had prevented the Gulf War being misrepresented as a conflict between Arabs and non-Arabs.[295]

The mainstream Arab states' failure to achieve their aims at Tunis induced them to mobilize more effectively to prevent the Syrians outmanoeuvring them once again, to intensify their efforts to separate Syria from Iran and to punish Iranian intransigence. Although Damascus had pulled off a diplomatic coup that it savoured and was greatly appreciated in Tehran, it would prove to be a short-term gain only. Furthermore, in the remaining months of 1987, the continuation of the Gulf War, clashes between US and Iranian forces and periodic Iranian attacks on Kuwait hardened the Arab position against Iran and brought Egypt back into the Arab fold, in effect eclipsing Syrian power and influence in the Arab world.

Arab strategy against the Syrian–Iranian alliance after Tunis

In the weeks prior to the 20 September deadline set by the Arab League, the mainstream Arab bloc led by Saudi Arabia and Jordan adopted a two-track approach to bringing about the demise of the Tehran–Damascus axis by trying to pull Syria into their camp and depicting the Gulf War as a continuation of the historical struggle between Arabs and Persians. Amman and Riyadh hoped that, as more and more Arab states drew away from Iran and the Arab propaganda war against the Iranians reached unprecedented levels, Assad would eventually yield and stop backing Tehran.

On 22 August, before the Tunis conference started, King Hussein sent prime minister al-Rifai to Damascus to ask the Syrian leader to reconsider his position in the light of recent events. Also, a week after the deliberations in Tunis ended, the Jordanian monarch paid a visit to Damascus (his second in four months) to try to persuade Assad to reconcile differences with Saddam Hussein. As in the past, the Syrians would not be swayed, but agreed on the need to prevent the Gulf War spreading to the southern littoral states.[296] King Hussein's two-day visit was immediately followed by the arrival of Syrian prime minister al-Kasm in Amman to discuss cementing bilateral relations. In general, Damascus continued its two-pronged approach to the Gulf conflict. On one hand it stood by Iran and even intensified its anti-Iraqi rhetoric when many Arab states, particularly Saudi Arabia, were escalating their propaganda war against Iran (see below). On the other hand, Syria continued to mend fences with Jordan and offered to mediate between Iran and the Gulf Arabs to ease tensions and prevent more hostilities. Despite much speculation and reports to the contrary in the Arab and Western media at the time, Damascus was still intent on preserving its links with Tehran, while as far as possible avoiding total isolation in the Arab world.[297]

Besides Jordan's initiative to wean Syria away from its non-Arab partner, the moderate Arab camp unleashed enormous invective against Iran and its remaining Arab allies, prompting some members of the former Steadfastness Front to draw closer to the Arab mainstream.[298] After the talks in Tunis, Saudi interior minister Prince Nayef defended his government's decision to publicize the Mecca incident widely, calling it a 'premediated' Iranian plot and signalling Saudi readiness to participate in an Islamic summit solely devoted to the Iranian threat.[299] The harsh statements emanating from Riyadh in subsequent weeks were notable for their viciousness and racism. To maintain the momentum of their anti-Iranian diplomacy in the region, and drive a wedge between Iran and as many Arab states as possible, the Saudi media continued their unrelenting campaign against Tehran. They rebuked Iran for occupying the three disputed islands in the Gulf, which the UAE also claimed, and for illegitimately controlling 'Arabestan', the southwestern part of Iran. Riyadh insisted that neither of these Arab homelands should be conceded to the 'Persian race' and drew parallels between Iran's policies towards GCC states and Sassanid Persian attempts to control the Arabian Peninsula in the pre-Islamic era.[300] By now, there were unmistakable similarities between Iraqi and Saudi propaganda. In essence, the Gulf War was depicted as an ethnic conflict between all Arabs and Persians, and not just between two regional states.

Syrian moves to defuse Arab–Iranian tensions in the Gulf

In late August, after a brief hiatus, Iraq resumed aerial attacks on Iranian oil facilities and shipping in the Gulf. Besides hitting more than 20 targets in the first half of September, the Iraqi air force intensified its bombardment of Iranian urban and economic centres, carrying out almost 50 raids between 16 August and 15 September.[301] Iran retaliated by attacking Gulf Arab shipping. In an unprecedented move, in early September, it fired a number of Chinese-made Silkworm missiles at Kuwait from the occupied Faw peninsula.[302] An emergency session of GCC foreign ministers was convened on 12

September in Jeddah to discuss this new dimension to the Iranian threat. The escalation of hostilities in the Gulf and heightened Arab–Iranian tensions coincided with a mission by UN Secretary-General Perez de Cuellar to Tehran and Baghdad to try to find some common ground between the two sides and persuade Iran to accept a ceasefire. Not surprisingly, Perez de Cuellar returned empty-handed to New York on 16 September, informing the Security Council that Iran's acceptance of Resolution 598 was contingent on an impartial international commission identifying the aggressor.[303] Due to the confluence of events, the Syrians moved in to fill the void by holding talks with Gulf Arabs and Iranians with a view to mediating effectively and easing tensions. Damascus realized it could not act as an intermediary between Iran and Iraq, but it could enhance its credibility as a mediator and prevent Iran from sliding into greater isolation by trying to defuse tensions between Iran and the GCC.

In the week before the second Arab foreign ministers' meeting in Tunis to consider the future of Arab–Iranian relations, Assad sent Vice-President Khaddam to Jeddah to hold talks with GCC foreign ministers, and Faruq al-Shara to Tehran to confer with Iranian leaders. Khaddam arrived in Jeddah on 13 September, the day after the emergency session of the GCC was convened. The GCC foreign ministers issued a communiqué demanding Tehran's full acceptance of Resolution 598, and exchanged views with Khaddam on the situation.[304] Three days later, al-Shara visited the Iranian capital where he submitted a message from Assad to Khamene'i and met his Iranian counterpart. The primary purpose of their talks was to discuss how to contain the situation and mend Gulf Arab–Iranian ties. Al-Shara's visit was immediately followed by the arrival of Syrian minister of economy and finance al-Imadi in Tehran to explore the expansion of bilateral economic and commercial links between the two allies. It is noteworthy that in the run-up to the two Syrian envoys' visits, Iran renewed its previous commitment to continue deliveries of a million tons of crude oil to Syria each year free of charge.[305] As the date for the Tunis meeting approached, it was apparent that Syria would not depart from its previous positions and would continue to maintain its strategic partnership with Iran, and oppose a rupture in Arab–Iranian relations. Moreover, in an interview on the eve of the Arab League meeting in Tunis, Hafez Assad cautioned 'it would not be possible to reach any results through the use of power or pressures' on Iran. Instead, he stated 'it is possible to reach results with Iran through friendly dialogue'.[306] On emerging Arab attitudes to

Iran, he reiterated his opposition to banishing Iran, positing, 'after Mecca, some Arabs wanted to change relations with Iran. ... It is against the interests of the Arabs to break relations with Iran.'[307] The Syrian leader restated that he had no wish to withhold support from Iran, and credited Syrian diplomacy for playing 'a major role in preventing the expansion of the war'.[308]

The reversal of Iran's fortunes (September–November 1987)

The Arab League meeting in Tunis and its consequences

When the Arab League council reconvened for an extraordinary session on 20 September in Tunisia, two crucial factors favoured the pro-Iranian camp. The UN Security Council had already opted for a diplomatic solution by giving Perez de Cuellar more time to bridge the gap between the two sides before considering the imposition of sanctions on Iran. Second, it was obvious that a consensus could not be reached on an Arab diplomatic boycott of Iran, for the Syrian-led camp in the Arab League (Libya, Algeria, South Yemen, Oman and the UAE) was vehemently opposed to such a move, and instead advocated further dialogue with Tehran.

On arrival in Tunis, the chairman of the meeting, Saudi foreign minister Saud al-Faisal, stated that the main goal would be to agree to hold an Arab summit to decide the future of Arab–Iranian relations. From the outset, the pro-Iraq camp realized it would be unfeasible to get a consensus at this stage on a common Arab stand towards Tehran, with at least seven Arab states, led by Syria and Algeria, advocating dialogue with Iran. Besides, so as not to be seen as out of step with the UN Security Council, the members decided to postpone any crucial decision, thus giving Iran more time to reconsider its position.[309] Also, a drastic move like severing ties with Iran had to be decided at the highest level by heads of state. Overall, the second meeting in Tunis was viewed as a stepping-stone towards gradually achieving a consensus and setting the stage for collective action if and when it was eventually deemed necessary.

In his opening speech to the delegates, the Saudi foreign minister again lambasted Iran for 'excessive intransigence and persistent rejection' of peace efforts, calling for collective Arab action to thwart its 'terrible scheme'.[310] By the end of the meeting, the members could only agree to hold an Arab summit in seven weeks' time on 8 November in Amman, Jordan. Though the resolution passed specified that the purpose of the summit would be 'to examine the developments in the Iran–Iraq war from all angles', as the conflict was 'now at the core of the Arab nation's concerns in view of the great dangers which its continuation and likely expansion constitute for the Arab nation', no agreement was reached on whether the Gulf War should be the only item on the agenda.[311]

At the proceedings, Faruq al-Shara voiced strong reservations about a gathering of Arab leaders discussing a single item, the Gulf War, while ignoring the Arab–Israeli conflict and other important issues, including the Palestinian question and Lebanese crisis.[312] On returning to Syria the day after the Tunis meeting, al-Shara immediately said that unless the Amman summit discussed major challenges facing the Arab nation, 'starting with basic and essential issues such as the Arab–Israeli conflict', Syria would not attend.[313] The Syrians were adamant that the summit agenda should reflect the primary importance of the Arab–Israeli struggle rather than hostilities in the Gulf. Several other Arab states including Libya and South Yemen agreed, thus raising the prospect of a number of Arab governments boycotting the summit.[314] Syria's objective in expressing reservations about giving the Iran–Iraq war priority over the Arab–Israeli issue, was threefold: to prevent its own concerns about unresolved issues with Israel being ignored; to avoid, as Iran's primary Arab supporter, criticism at the meeting for its stand on the Gulf War; and to prop up its Iranian ally by downplaying the Gulf conflict.

To dissuade Assad from boycotting the Amman summit, and fearing that several other Arab leaders might follow suit, on 24 September, King Hussein and Prime Minister al-Rifai arrived in Latakia where the Syrian leader was staying. But, despite their efforts, Assad would not be swayed[315] and insisted they formally broaden the summit agenda. The Syrian position was reaffirmed two days later during the visit of Vice-President Khaddam to Libya, where both sides stressed they would not attend the conference unless 'all issues of interest to the Arab nation' were discussed.[316] The Syrian media towed the official line by describing the Gulf conflict as a 'secondary issue'. For example, an article in the daily *Tishrin* on 4 October criticized the Iraqi attempt to divert Arab attention from the Palestinian front to focus on 'marginal, fabricated issues' since it only served Saddam Hussein's 'personal purposes', and the 'enemies of the nation'.

As conference host, King Hussein prudently decided to remove the bone of contention, the summit agenda, by declaring that there would be no specific agenda and all issues, including the Arab–Israeli problem, could be discussed.[317] Consequently, during a working visit to

Damascus by Prime Minister al-Rifai on 12 October to promote bilateral cooperation, Assad told the Jordanian envoy that he would accept the invitation to attend the Amman conference.[318] Although Jordan had made a concession to ensure the participation of Syria and a number of other states, one cannot be certain that Syria would not have altered its position at the last minute had it not been for Amman's gesture. With escalating tensions in the Gulf putting Iran on a collision course with the Kuwaitis and Saudis (also providers of financial and material assistance to Damascus) and Syria's own economic woes, as the date for the Amman summit approached, Assad may eventually have decided to attend. As at the OIC summit in Kuwait earlier that year, the Syrian leader may have reversed his previous position. In the final analysis, Damascus could hardly afford to alienate its few remaining Arab aid donors and become sidelined in Arab politics. Even if Amman had not given in to Syrian demands, Assad may eventually have concluded it was more to his advantage to defend his own precarious position, and that of his Iranian ally within Arab political fora, rather than avoid them.

Shrewd diplomacy and maintaining open channels of communication with both parties helped Syria preserve its room for manoeuvre and won vital breathing space for Iran in the three months between the events in Mecca and the Amman summit. However, in the weeks that followed, Iranian actions and the efficacy of US–Iraqi responses nullified some of the Syrian gains. The exposure of Iran's mining operations in the Persian Gulf, its willingness to be drawn into a *de facto* war with the USA, and its continued attacks on Kuwaiti oil installations and tankers, strengthened anti-Iranian sentiment in the region and beyond, increasing the resolve of the pro-Iraq camp to punish Iranian excesses and bring Egypt back into the Arab fold to help neutralize the Iranian threat and tip the Arab balance of power against Tehran's Arab allies. In effect, Iran's clumsy moves to challenge the USA and its Arab allies in the Gulf greatly weakened its hand and, in the process, worked to the detriment of Syrian interests.

The Iran Ajr *incident, the start of US–Iranian clashes and Arab reactions*

Iran was pleased with the outcome of events in Tunis. Having won a brief respite on the regional level through Syrian diplomacy, it now focused on appealing its case and winning international support at the annual session of the UN General Assembly in New York, where President Khamene'i was due to address the UN on 22 September. But, on the night of 21 September, within 24 hours of Khamene'i's speech, US naval forces in the Gulf attacked and captured an Iranian naval vessel, the *Iran Ajr*, laying mines 50 miles northeast of Bahrain; they killed six crewmen and detained the remaining 25. News of the *Iran Ajr* incident overshadowed Khamenei's address the following day, putting him in an extremely awkward position. He was left to fend off questions from reporters and deny the verity of reports, claming instead that the vessel had been an unarmed supply ship.

The USA no doubt deliberately timed the assault on the *Iran Ajr* (the first direct military clash between US and Iranian forces since the 1979 revolution) to discredit Khamene'i and derail the Iranian initiative at the UN.[319] Iran had been caught red-handed laying mines in international waters, which justified Washington's claim that it had to keep a high-level military presence in the region to protect the sea lanes and Gulf Arab shipping. Any remaining international support for Iran quickly vanished.

Iran's image, especially in the Arab–Islamic world, was further tarnished the day after the *Iran Ajr* affair when the PLO central committee publicly claimed it had documents proving secret Israeli–Iranian negotiations on Jewish Iranian emigration to 'occupied Palestine'.[320] Despite the multiple blows dealt to it on 21/2 September, Iran remained defiant and vowed revenge against the USA. Syria stood by its ally, supporting Iranian claims that the *Iran Ajr* had been a supply vessel and condemning 'US piracy' and Washington's application of the 'law of the jungle' in the Gulf.[321]

As hostilities intensified in Gulf waters and Iraq continued the tanker war, Iran pursued its 'blow for blow' doctrine undaunted by the prominent foreign naval presence. In a second US–Iranian clash on 8 October, three US helicopters attacked a number of Iranian speedboats, sinking one craft and killing eight crewmen.[322] In response, Tehran vowed revenge and fired a number of Silkworm missiles at Kuwaiti targets. On 16 October, one such missile struck the US-flagged Kuwaiti tanker, *Sea Isle City*, blinding its US captain and injuring 18 other crewmen. Washington subsequently declared that it would retaliate for the attack on the US-flagged ship.[323]

During these developments in the Gulf, Iran decided to send a high-level delegation headed by Prime Minister Musavi and Revolutionary Guards minister Rafiqdoust to Damascus to confer with the Syrians on regional issues and seek assistance. A few days before their scheduled visit, deputy prime minister for political affairs Ali Reza Moayyeri arrived in the Syrian capital to update the Syrians and highlight Iranian concerns. Moayyeri met Prime Minister al-Kasm and Foreign Minister al-Shara to discuss the Gulf War and the fate of Western hostages in Lebanon.[324] On 18 October, Musavi and Rafiq-doust, accompanied by deputy foreign ministers Besharati and Lava-sani, arrived in Damascus and immediately went into conference with al-Kasm and, later that day, with al-Shara. The following day, Hafez Assad received Musavi while al-Shara spoke to Besharati and Lavasani. The two allies discussed a number of important issues for three days. The main item on the agenda was the Arab League summit in Amman, only three weeks away, for the Iranians were worried that the pro-Iraqi bloc, now enjoying Riyadh's full support, would be able to muster enough support against Iran and succeed in finally outmanoeuvring the Syrians. Tehran feared that the growing momentum of pro-Iraqi diplomatic efforts would precipitate a total Arab breach with Iran.[325]

During the talks in Damascus, the Iranians apparently sought more Scud missiles from the Syrians to replenish their dwindling inventory.[326] The Syrians, for their part, asked Iran to adopt a less confrontational stance towards the USA and to coordinate future moves on the Western hostages with them.[327] Musavi reportedly agreed to defer the issue of Syria's $3 billion debt for another 18 months because of its economic woes.[328]

At this critical point, not only were the Syrians trying to serve as intermediaries between their Iranian ally on one side and the Arab and Western blocs on the other, but they were also trying to iron out differences between Iran and the USSR. It was rumoured that Musavi held secret talks with Soviet deputy foreign minister Yuli Vorontsov in Damascus.[329] Indeed, Musavi's three-day stay (18–20 October) in Damascus conveniently overlapped that of Vorontsov (17–19 October). Vorontsov had already met al-Shara on his first day, and held consultations with Assad the next day on the Middle East peace process and the situation in the Gulf, including the implementation of UN Resolution 598. Given the situation at that crucial stage, it would have been surprising if Vorontsov and Musavi had not met under such convenient circumstances. Vorontsov apparently insisted that Iran should stop provoking US forces in the Gulf if it wanted Soviet support in the UN Security Council and elsewhere.[330]

On 19 October, during the Syrian–Iranian negotiations in Damascus, the USA avenged the attack on the *Sea Isle City* by sending warships to destroy the Iranian Rostam and Reshadat oil platforms 120 miles east of Bahrain. Having fired more than a thousand rounds at the targets, US Navy SEAL teams moved in and blew up what remained of the two structures.[331] The move drew a rapid response from Tehran, where the SDC held an emergency session chaired by Khamene'i. The Iranian government subsequently pledged swift retribution through 'an appropriate and decisive' riposte.[332] It characterized the attack as 'blatant aggression', accusing the USA of waging a 'full-fledged war with the Islamic Republic'.[333] In Damascus, Musavi vowed that Iran would not remain silent, stressing that the US presence in the Middle East was a foreign one and, 'with the assistance of the people of Syria and Lebanon', revolutionary Iran would destroy its foothold in the region.[334] The Syrian media also tried to drum up support for Iran and justify Syria's policies by arguing that the US attack exposed 'its participation in the Iraqi regime's unjust war', and drew analogies between US policy in the Gulf and its earlier involvement in Lebanon. It went on to castigate Iraq for allegedly forging a covert relationship with the USA after the breakdown of the 1979 Syrian–Iraqi unity talks.[335] At a press conference prior to his return to Tehran on 20 October, Musavi stated that during his talks with Assad and al-Kasm, the Syrian leaders had reaffirmed their commitment to stand by Iran, and that the hostilities in the Gulf would be halted once Saddam Hussein had been punished.[336] He also mentioned that Washington had passed a message through Syria urging Iranian restraint to break the cycle of US–Iranian clashes in the Gulf, and considered the matter closed. Musavi posited, 'we will not let any blow go unanswered ... we will retaliate for this attack.'[337] Iran struck back on 22 October, this time by firing a Silkworm missile at Kuwait's Sea Island oil terminal, its main loading facility for supertankers. The terminal, which handled a third of Kuwaiti oil exports at the time, was put out of commission for a month.[338] After three tragic encounters with US forces, Iran was now careful to avoid attacks on US assets for fear of further retaliatory strikes. Instead, it concentrated on testing the parameters and degree of Washington's commitment by targeting its Gulf Arab allies in the weeks that followed.

With the flurry of diplomatic activity in late October as the date of the Arab summit drew nearer, it became evident that Syria would oppose the Saudi-led initiative to create an Arab consensus to pass an anti-Iranian resolution in Amman and to readmit Egypt into the Arab League. However, it was unclear what Assad could do to stem the tide of anti-Iranianism sweeping much of the Arab world, and the growing calls for Egypt's rehabilitation. The gradual marginalization of Syria's position, the cooling of Syrian–Soviet relations, active US military intervention in the Persian Gulf, and Iran's failure to adopt realistic goals in its struggle against Baghdad (and now Washington) together, made it difficult for Syria to defend its interests and shield its main regional ally from further blows.

Many observers wondered if Assad would buckle under pressure from the majority of the members, especially if, in view of the abysmal state of the Syrian economy, his two main aid donors (Saudi Arabia and Kuwait) threatened to withdraw assistance. That Syria's faltering economy finally prompted Assad to carry out a major shake-up of his government at the end of October fuelled the speculation. On 28 October, the ministers for industry and supplies were sacked for mismanagement and corruption.[339] A similar fate had befallen the ministers for agriculture and construction in previous weeks.[340] Two days later, on 30 October, Assad instigated the resignation of Prime Minister al-Kasm (after serving in his post for seven years), and replaced him with Mahmud al-Zubi, who had previously been president of the Syrian parliament. In all, 19 members of Syria's 35-member cabinet lost their posts, though Tlas and al-Shara retained the portfolios for defence and foreign affairs respectively.[341]

Six days before the summit, Kuwait's foreign minister had said that, unless certain demands were met, his government would discontinue its $50 million annual aid to Syria. There were indications that Riyadh was also reconsidering its position on $500 million in annual grants to the Syrians unless they changed their position on the Gulf War.[342] With emotions running high over controversial and potentially explosive issues that had to be addressed in Amman such as ostracizing Iran and re-embracing Egypt, King Fahd decided to stay out of the fray and send Crown Prince Abdullah (who enjoyed good relations with both Syria and Iraq) in his stead.[343] The battle lines had already been drawn in the days preceding the Amman meeting. While Saudi Arabia, Iraq and Jordan were now at the forefront of efforts to banish Iran and formally reintegrate Egypt into the Arab community, Syria was spearheading the move to block a complete Arab break with Iran and prevent Egypt's readmission to the Arab League. Although in a minority, Damascus was not without support, for Algeria, Libya, Oman and the UAE favoured keeping diplomatic channels with Tehran open.[344] Despite doubts about their ability to orchestrate an effective boycott of Iran, it was clear that the pro-Iraq camp was determined to formalize its rapidly expanding ties with Egypt.[345] With the expansion of the conflict, the Gulf Arabs wanted openly to seek Egyptian assistance in neutralizing the threat posed by Iranian revanchism.

Syrian participation in the Amman summit and its consequences

From the outset, Hafez Assad knew he faced a tall order in Amman. Apart from being in a minority on the various issues that were to be discussed, he realized that he could only score limited gains through shrewd diplomacy that would entail some degree of obduracy, compromise and deception. Assad knew that he could not prevail on all fronts, but he was determined to attain as much as he could in five areas that were of key interest to Syria. Essentially, these were to ensure that:

❑ the Arab world kept the door open to more diplomacy in the Gulf, thus giving Syria a chance to mediate between Arab sheikhdoms and Iran, and to use its influence in a constructive way;
❑ Syrian interests in the Arab–Israeli conflict were not ignored;
❑ Egypt remain excluded from the Arab League;
❑ Gulf Arab financial aid to Syria would be maintained; and
❑ any move by the pro-Iraqi bloc to condemn or excommunicate Syria would be thwarted.[346]

It was clear that the Syrians would have to take the lead and fight an uphill battle on several fronts. Libya's Colonel Qadhafi, who saw eye-to-eye with Assad on Egypt's continued exclusion and further Arab–Iranian dialogue, had announced on 2 November that he would not attend the conference, calling it a US-inspired event directed against Iran. Besides trying to raise the Gulf conflict to the level of an Arab–Persian war to drive a wedge between Iran and the Arab world, it was evident that the pro-Iraqi camp would try to censure Damascus for its support of Tehran and push it into a corner by demanding the suspension of aid to Syria. Many in the Arab world were already calling Assad a traitor and a pseudo-Arab,[347] but the Syrian leader was determined to confound his opponents and derail any initiative to excommunicate him or his political allies.

As the extraordinary summit got underway on the evening of 8 November, King Hussein warned in his opening address that the Gulf War was 'no longer confined to Iraq alone, but was now engulfing brotherly Kuwait and Saudi Arabia', and 'threatening the security of the whole region and world peace'.[348] He argued that disunity and weakness in the Arab world were exacerbating conditions in the Gulf and Arab–Israeli arenas. Drawing parallels between Iranian and Israeli behaviour, he accused Tehran and Tel Aviv of coveting Arab territory and using religion for political ends.[349] To frustrate their ambitions and bolster Arab power, he called for the formal readmission of Egypt into the Arab League, since its prolonged absence had contributed to 'weakening the underpinnings of the Arab order'.[350]

In the proceedings the next morning, both Syria and Iraq took a hard line. In his address, Saddam Hussein depicted the 'Iranian menace' as the greatest challenge the Arab nation had faced since the creation of the Arab League, demanding specific censure of Iran and, in a thinly-veiled attack on Syria, suspension of Arab aid to its Arab supporters.[351] He stated that, due to the 'changing and dynamic political situation' in the region, Egypt should be allowed to rejoin the Arab fold.[352] Assad, for his part, in a two-hour speech during the morning session, defiantly opposed Cairo's re-entry into the Arab League and advocated further dialogue with Tehran.[353] He questioned Egypt's ability, given the restrictions the Camp David accords imposed, to uphold the Arab League charter and 1950 joint defence pact.[354] Furthermore, the Syrian president opposed Egypt's return on the grounds that it implied the Arab League's tacit acceptance of the peace treaty with Israel.[355] In view of the huge gap between their positions, the Iraqi leader at one point became livid and threatened to walk out at indications that the participants might stop short of condemning his Iranian foe – 'the vile foreign aggressor' – as he called it.[356] King Hussein subsequently interceded and directed his efforts at reconciling differences between the two Ba'thist rivals over the next two days.

That afternoon, the Jordanian monarch persuaded Assad and Saddam Hussein to attend a four-hour mini summit in his hotel suite with five other Arab leaders: Saudi Crown Prince Abdullah, Algeria's President Benjedid, the Emir of Kuwait and the UAE and North Yemeni presidents. While the meeting went relatively smoothly with both Ba'thists articulating their positions and showing varying degrees of flexibility, Assad stressed that he would veto Egypt's readmission. The Jordanians tried to capitalize on the meeting by prematurely raising expectations of a breakthrough. Summit spokesman Akram Barakat called the encounter 'a promising start to a new era of brotherly relations between Syria and Iraq'.[357]

That evening, Assad and Saddam Hussein attended a banquet hosted by King Hussein. Although the Syrians denied it, there were reports that the two leaders held a bilateral meeting later that evening. The next morning, 10 November, Faruq al-Shara and Tareq Aziz met for several hours in the presence of Arab League secretary-general Klibi. This was followed up by another round of negotiations between Assad and Saddam Hussein under the auspices of the Jordanian king later that evening.[358] Once again, the Jordanians widely publicized these negotiations and portrayed them in a very positive light. However, the Iraqis were more circumspect in their statements, while the Syrians maintained total silence.[359]

By now, a picture was gradually emerging of how much ground Syria was willing to concede on the Gulf conflict and Egypt's status. Despite its posturing and tough stand, it became clear that Assad was going to make some concessions (a tactical retreat on both fronts) to achieve important gains in the overall equation and prevent alienating the other Arab states completely. Reluctant to swim against the powerful tide of pro-Iraqi sentiment in Amman, Assad indicated that he would go along with a statement condemning Iran's continuation of the war and attacks on the Gulf Arab states, but was unwilling to approve the formal readmission of Cairo into the Arab fold. After the Syrian–Iraqi talks, Iraq's deputy prime minister Ramadan expressed optimism about the prospects of Syrian backing for a final resolution supporting Iraq's position in the seven-year war. He described the shift in Syria's position as 'positive'.[360] He also said that the talks between the Syrian and Iraqi leaders generally had been constructive. Short of a split in Arab–Iranian relations, Ramadan emphasized that the 'minimum' Baghdad would accept was unanimous endorsement of Iraq's stand in the conflict, and unqualified support for UN Resolution 598 in the final summit resolution. He noted that any future Syrian–Iraqi reconciliation would depend on the degree of Syria's cooperation. Moreover, Ramadan astutely observed that such a breakthrough would severely undermine Tehran's ideological stand and 'internal propaganda campaign', for the clerical regime had justified its war effort in part because of the support it received from some key Arab states and its ideological appeal elsewhere in the region.[361]

On the same day, a special panel of Arab foreign ministers entrusted with drafting the final summit resolution began deliberations. Here, the Syrian strategy was twofold: ruling out any compromise on Egyptian membership of the Arab League and, at the same time, showing some flexibility on Gulf affairs. The Syrian delegation's official spokesman, Gibran Kourieh, issued a statement reiterating Syria's opposition to Egypt's readmission, and threatening to block any initiatives the Arab League undertook in other areas.[362] In other words, the price of Syrian acquiescence to the passage of an anti-Iranian resolution was the continued suspension of Egyptian membership. On the latter, Syria was not without support. To differing degrees, Libya, South Yemen, Algeria and even Tunisia questioned the hasty reinstatement of Egypt at this stage.[363] Even on the Gulf War, the Syrian and Iraqi delegations debated at length well into the night to devise a compromise resolution. Although the Syrians were fighting on several fronts and, despite Saudi and Kuwaiti statements that from March 1988 they would technically no longer be obliged to continue the ten-year subventions agreed at the 1978 Baghdad summit, the Syrians were still determined to extract as many concessions as possible, even on the issue of the Gulf conflict. In trying to score some gains on behalf of their Iranian partner and cushion the blow to Tehran, Faruq al-Shara demanded the inclusion of a statement condemning the US naval presence in the Gulf and, more significantly, opposed an Arab endorsement of Resolution 598 in its existing form.[364]

The modifications he wanted on the chronological sequence of the UN resolution, namely the appointment of an impartial international commission to determine the aggressor prior to (rather than after) a formal ceasefire, mirrored Iran's position. Significantly, the Syrians tried to downplay the importance of the UN resolution by proposing that a delegation of Arab heads of state, perhaps led by Assad, travel to Tehran to persuade Iranian leaders to sue for peace. However, the Iraqis turned down this proposal, insisting that Resolution 598 should be fully implemented without any modifications.[365]

Once the deliberations paving the way for the passage of the final resolution on 11 November had ended, it was quite apparent that the results were mixed. The Syrians had averted a rupture in Arab–Iranian relations in exchange for a strongly-worded resolution condemning Iran's conduct in the Gulf. Furthermore, the Syrians had to back down on their demands to condemn the US naval presence in the area and alter Resolution 598. On Egypt's rehabilitation, there was a certain amount of give and take, with both sides making concessions. The pro-Syrian camp won the debate about Egypt's status by thwarting its return to the Arab League. On the other hand, a major concession was given through the adoption of a specific clause in the final resolution recognizing that the decision to resume bilateral diplomatic relations with Cairo fell within the provenance of each individual member of the Arab League. Only Libya lobbied against this clause, with Syria and its other supporters expressing no reservations.[366]

The final statement and resolutions the participants approved on the last day of the summit, 11 November, condemned Iran's occupation of Iraqi territory, its continued aggression against Iraq and its refusal to accept a ceasefire.[367] The Arab League reaffirmed its support for Kuwait and Saudi Arabia in the wake of hostile Iranian moves against them. Specifically denounced were Iran's 'repeated attacks' on Kuwait and the 'acts of sabotage and rioting' by Iranians in Mecca.[368] The members expressed solidarity with Iraq, and urged Iran and the UN Security Council to implement Resolution 598 fully 'in accordance with the sequence of its clauses'.[369] Moreover, they indicated readiness to uphold their obligations towards Iraq as stipulated in the Arab League charter and 1950 joint defence pact. They also affirmed willingness to carry out similar obligations towards the GCC states in the event of further Iranian attacks against them.[370]

At a press conference immediately after the end of the proceedings, King Hussein proudly declared that it had been a 'summit of harmony and accord'.[371] With Syria, the 'beating heart of Arabism' and Iran's most important Arab ally, having grudgingly consented to the final communiqué and relevant resolutions, the Jordanian host could now claim some credit for breaking the political impasse that had paralysed the Arab League. With Assad now 'falling into line', an illusion of Arab solidarity against Iran had been created, albeit temporarily. More importantly though, the path was now clear for the *de facto* reintegration of Egypt into the Arab fold after a nine-year absence. By feigning solidarity with the mainstream Arab states, Syria had on this occasion escaped accusations of impeding joint Arab action to restore some semblance of unity among the Arab ranks.[372]

The relative success of the conference clearly enhanced Jordanian prestige. On the other hand, even before leaving Amman, the Syrian delegation took steps to dispel the illusion of Syrian solidarity with the pro-Iraq camp. Assad's spokesman, Gibran Kourieh, flatly denied Jordan's claims that King Hussein had reconciled the Syrian and Iraqi presidents. Indeed, when asked to shake hands in front of reporters at the end of the summit in the Royal Cultural Centre, Assad and Saddam Hussein pointedly declined to do so.[373] One Syrian official also said that the outcome of the Amman summit would have no real impact on the Damascus–Tehran axis.[374]

Some press reports at the time claimed that Assad had received pledges of $2 billion in financial aid and oil from GCC states in exchange for his political support. However, the evidence shows these claims were baseless, mere speculation.[375] Later, Iraqi foreign minister Tareq Aziz posited that some Gulf states promised to support Damascus on condition it pursued a constructive policy in the Gulf.[376] Syrian conduct in Amman reflected a shrewd calculation of profit and loss to carry out an effective damage limitation exercise and yield few substantial concessions. As in many past instances,

Assad had shown himself to be a master of manoeuvre, escaping Arab opprobrium without terminating his alliance with Iran. Damascus remained well positioned to coax the Gulf states to provide desperately needed aid without the loss of Iranian oil shipments.[377]

Predictably, Iran denounced the outcome of the Amman summit as 'a shameful, humiliating defeat for the Arab masses'.[378] On the condemnation of Iranian conduct in the Gulf region, Tehran reiterated that 'despite all the enemies' plots and propaganda', it was 'determined to continue its defensive war until the aggressor Baghdad regime' had been punished and 'Iran's rightful demands were met'.[379] The Arab League's decision on Egypt's informal re-entry into the Arab fold was depicted as an 'implicit acceptance of the Camp David Accords – an act of treason'.[380] The restoration of ties with Cairo was described as the legitimization of the 'Zionist entity', and abandonment of the Palestinian cause.[381] Overall, the outcome of the summit must been an immense disappointment to Iran's Islamist regime. Although Tehran greatly appreciated Syrian efforts in successfully blocking a rupture in Arab–Iranian relations, Iran nonetheless turned out to be the biggest loser in Amman, therefore highlighting the general failure of its Arab policy since the 1979 revolution.

The Amman summit was a major watershed and marked an important turning point in Syrian–Iranian fortunes in the 1980s. While the conference could be considered a tactical victory of sorts for the two states, particularly Syria, it showed that Iran's mismanagement of the general conduct of the war had rallied the majority of the Arab world against it and galvanized support for Saddam Hussein. Broadly, the clerical regime's ideological zeal, along with its inability to assess realistically the evolving political and strategic conditions in the Gulf and beyond, had led to its gradual isolation in the Middle East, had diminished Syrian–Iranian power and prestige in the region, had marginalized Syria's position in inter-Arab politics, and had increased Tehran's dependence on Syrian goodwill and cooperation. Iran's failure to harmonize its war aims and capabilities in the Gulf conflict, or integrate military and manpower needs with available domestic resources, led to the squandering of valuable assets and horrendous losses. Despite growing Arab and international support for Iraq since 1984, Iran's futile attempts to bring Iraq to its knees and intimidate its Gulf Arab allies internationalized the conflict and alienated most of the Arab–Islamic world. It gave Washington a pretext to deploy military forces in the Persian Gulf and to intervene as a *de facto* co-belligerent siding with Baghdad.

In many respects, the Amman summit sounded the death knell of revolutionary Iran's hopes and aspirations to export its Islamist ideology to other areas of the Middle East, just as the failure of Operation Karbala 5 earlier in the year finally drove home to some Iranian leaders that Iraq could not be defeated on the battlefield. From the standpoint of many Arab governments, the direct challenge posed by a neighbouring Islamic country to the *status quo* in the Arab East, both in terms of security and ideology (particularly a political ideology with an organic familiarity, legitimacy and appeal to some among the Arab masses) impelled the anti-Iranian camp to elevate Iran to enemy number one, thereby replacing Israel as a more serious and present danger. The Amman resolution portrayed Iraq, Saudi Arabia and Kuwait as 'confrontation states', much to the disappointment of Syria and Lebanon. With the Arab commitment to the Arab–Israeli struggle waning, in an unprecedented move, the Arab League relegated the Palestinian struggle to a secondary position.[382]

In general, the Amman summit was a symbolic and ideological blow to Iran. On one level, the strongly-worded resolution (which the overwhelming majority of the Arab League approved), harshly rebuking Iranian policies for the first time, gave the impression that the Iraqi–Iranian conflict had now been elevated to the level of a war pitting Arabs against Iranians. Also, the sharp denunciation of 'the bloody and criminal acts perpetrated by the Iranians' in Mecca (according to the text of the resolution) directly challenged the religious and ideological legitimacy of Khomeini's theocratic state. By putting the events in Mecca into an Islamic context, described in the resolution as 'erroneous practices which are contrary to the teachings of the true Islamic faith', a severe blow had been dealt to Iran's Islamic credentials. The message was clear: supporters of Arab nationalism and Islam throughout the Arab–Islamic world were obligated to confront the Iranian threat.[383]

Although Syria had headed off an Arab–Iranian break by the Arab League, in effect securing a tactical and symbolic victory for itself and its non-Arab partner, in reality, by the end of 1987, this was a moot point. Arab–Iranian relations had reached a nadir, with key states such as Iraq, Jordan, Saudi Arabia, Egypt, Tunisia, Morocco and several others no longer having diplomatic relations with Iran. A *de facto* Arab–Iranian rift had occurred, leaving the clerical regime politically isolated and ideologically discredited.

Syria's predicament was in many respects comparable with Iran's, though less grave. Assad had succeeded in orchestrating a careful balancing act in Amman by swimming with the tide of Arab unity to condemn Iranian policies and maintain open diplomatic channels with the pro-Iraqi camp, while extracting noteworthy concessions and preserving the alliance with Iran. Damascus achieved tactical victories by prevailing on others to defer the question of Egypt's membership in the Arab League, and to refrain from severing links with Iran. To a limited extent, Syria had shown its ability once more to be a spoiler and score certain gains. In reality though, they were only of short-term benefit, amounting to very little in substance.

With regard to Egypt's readmission to the Arab League, here again it had been a hollow victory. Given the clear consensus that Cairo needed to be reintegrated at some level (implicitly to diminish Syria's political clout and explicitly to neutralize the military threat Iran posed in the Gulf), Assad could not legitimately argue that other Arab governments did not have the sovereign right to re-establish bilateral relations with Egypt.[384] Already, on the last day of the Arab summit, Iraq and five GCC states officially declared their intention to restore diplomatic ties with Cairo after the end of the conference.[385] Within days of the resumption of full Iraqi–Egyptian ties, the UAE, Kuwait, Morocco, North Yemen, Bahrain, Saudi Arabia, Mauritania and Qatar (in that order) followed Baghdad's lead and rushed to restore normal relations with Mubarak's Egypt. In rapid succession, all these states re-established links with Cairo within a two-week period, much to the chagrin of Syria and its allies. In fact, by December 1987, only six states, Syria, Libya, Algeria, Lebanon, South Yemen and Tunisia had not followed the majority of Arab League members.[386]

Egypt's informal re-entry into the Arab fold was an indisputable sign that Syria's political fortunes had taken a turn for the worse, and it was being sidelined in Arab affairs. The decision to draw Egypt into the Saudi–Iraqi–Jordanian orbit when Syria was bogged down in Lebanon, and Iran, proving unable to affect the outcome of the war, was becoming entangled with the USA, meant that the pendulum had finally swung against the Syrian–Iranian axis. Events in the closing months of 1987 clearly demonstrated that the Damascus–Tehran nexus was gradually being overshadowed by a more formidable alliance that had Washington's full support.

Syria's response in the aftermath of the Arab League summit

When the Amman conference ended, Damascus took decisive steps to shore up its regional position. To prevent the continued decline of its political influence, it adopted a two-pronged approach by initiating a diplomatic campaign to reassure Iran of its continued commitment to the alliance, and offer its good offices to the GCC to defuse Arab–Iranian tensions in the Gulf. Syria's overall objectives in the immediate post-summit period were threefold: to support Iran as far as possible in the war against Iraq, to prove itself indispensable to the GCC states by serving as an effective mediator between them and Iran, and to dissipate Arab–Iranian tensions in the Gulf so as to render Egyptian proposals for military and political support of the Arab sheikhdoms superfluous, thereby impeding Cairo's attempts to reintegrate itself into the Arab fold.

Immediately after the summit, Syrian foreign minister al-Shara dampened expectations of a possible Syrian–Iranian split by saying that Syria disagreed with the Arab League's condemnation of Iran. He criticized Secretary-General Klibi for omitting certain Syrian reservations about Iran when reading the final statement. He also cautioned against exaggerating the significance of the talks between Assad and Saddam Hussein.[387] At the same time, the Syrian media denounced some other Arab states' attempts to 'distort' Syria's stance on Iran, and emphasized the continued importance of Syrian–Iranian cooperation.[388] An editorial in *Tishrin* on 14 November criticized the Arab League's attempt to isolate Iran by misrepresenting the Gulf War as an Arab–Persian conflict. It concluded that, 'in the final analysis, Iran is the natural ally of the Arabs in their battle against Israel and the United States'.[389] On the same day, al-Shara declared that 'Syria remains firmly on the side of the Iranians, and will never depart from its solidarity with the Islamic Republic'.[390] Two days later, on 16 November, al-Shara sent a message to Velayati stressing the continued need for Syrian–Iranian solidarity and indicating his intention to visit Tehran soon to brief his Iranian counterpart on what had transpired in Amman.

Apart from sending promising signals to Iran, Syria undertook to reduce the GCC's need for Egyptian military assistance, which took on greater urgency in the light of Iran's reaction to the Arab summit. (See next section.) Soon after the Amman meeting, Egyptian military officials were sent to several Gulf states, most notably Kuwait, to examine how to improve security. Among the issues discussed were bolstering air defence capabilities against possible Iranian aerial attacks, and beefing up internal security to counter subversive activities by local pro-Iranian groups.[391] Consequently, on 21 November, as a two-day meeting of GCC heads of state got underway in Abu Dhabi to discuss joint security and defence measures, Assad sent messages to GCC leaders assuring them that, in the event of Iranian aggression, Syrian troops would be sent to protect them.[392]

The Syrian president tried to increase his room for diplomatic manoeuvre between the antagonists by sending a trade delegation to Iraq on 21 November. It was to explore opportunities for renewed commerce between the two sides, restore telephone links between them and agree to refrain from propaganda campaigns against one another. However, since Syria was still unwilling to meet even Iraq's minimum demand to move towards neutrality in the Gulf War, the talks came to naught. Impatient with the lack of progress in the Syrian–Iraqi dialogue, King Hussein shuttled between Damascus and Baghdad from 25 to 30 November in an effort to persuade the Ba'thist rivals, as a first step in the normalization process, to re-establish diplomatic relations. Again he failed to break the deadlock.[393] During King Hussein's deliberations in the two capitals, on 29 November, Iran's ambassador to Damascus, Mohammad Hassan Akhtari, met Syrian information minister Mohammad Salman, who reassured him that Syria's stance toward Iran and the Gulf War remained 'unchanged'.[394]

Iran's response to the Amman summit and diplomatic moves in the Gulf

The outcome of the Amman summit was a major disappointment for Iran's revolutionaries, a symbolic and psychological blow to their struggle to transcend ethnic–sectarian cleavages by uniting Persians and Arabs under the banner of revolutionary Islam.[395] In view of the US resolve to use force in the Persian Gulf and continued Iraqi aerial attacks, Iran tried to muster the necessary strength to initiate new ground offensives to keep Baghdad under pressure and show the pro-Iraqi camp that the Islamic Republic remained undeterred, despite the political setback experienced in Amman. Iran had already begun another military mobilization. It claimed to have built up 200 battalions of volunteers (baseej) composed of 200,000 to 500,000 men. In reality, though, it was facing severe difficulties in this regard, with only 60,000 to 100,000 men reporting for duty.[396] On 13 November, two days after the Amman summit ended, Iran's SDC announced a new mobilization campaign, fuelling speculation that Tehran was planning a major winter offensive.[397] However, that Khomeini on this occasion had to issue a religious decree calling on all able-bodied men to enlist and all other citizens to donate money to pay for the cost of one soldier each at the front, underlined the magnitude of the brewing crisis within Iran.[398]

Meanwhile, the tanker war in the Gulf continued unabated with both sides escalating their attacks. As tensions rose once more, Crown Prince Abdullah of Saudi Arabia followed up on King Hussein's earlier initiative to mediate between Syria and Iraq by going to Baghdad on 19 December for talks with Saddam Hussein. The next day, he left for Damascus to see Hafez Assad. While little headway seems to have been made in healing the Syrian–Iraqi rift, a direct upshot of the Saudi–Syrian dialogue was that Damascus increased its mediation efforts between Iran and the GCC states. Faruq al-Shara embarked on a new round of shuttle diplomacy between Tehran and Riyadh from 22 to 29 December, achieving some real results.

Strong Syrian pressure stopped Iran attacking Gulf Arab shipping, which had peaked just before Christmas.[399] Between two visits to the Iranian capital, the Syrian foreign minister spent several days in Riyadh where GCC heads of state had gathered for the GCC summit. Again, al-Shara seems to have persuaded them to adopt a more moderate position on Tehran. Indeed, the final communiqué issued at the end of the GCC conference on 29 December was notable for its conciliatory tone, which contrasted sharply with that of the Arab League summit in Amman. While the participants expressed regret for the 'destructive' war between Iran and Iraq, and Iran's 'procrastination' in accepting UN Resolution 598, they omitted any reference to the Mecca incident and refrained from directly condemning Iranian conduct in the Gulf War.[400] Afterwards, in a surprising move, Saudi foreign minister Saud al-Faisal asserted that the GCC's 'dialogue with Iran has never ceased, it is continuing, and will continue'.[401]

Overall, the efficacy of Syrian diplomacy and the support it received from states like Oman and the UAE that wanted to maintain links with Iran, prompted both sides to take a step back and decrease hostilities in the Gulf, if only temporarily.[402]

The Gulf War and Syrian mediation (January–March 1988)

In early 1988, the Syrians followed up on their earlier success in easing Arab–Iranian tensions in the Persian Gulf by intensifying their mediation efforts. With the lull in the tanker war and the conciliatory position the GCC adopted towards Iran at the Riyadh summit, Damascus was determined to press on to defuse the potentially explosive situation and gain precious political capital by laying the ground for a GCC–Iran dialogue, and convince Tehran to desist from provocative acts in the Gulf. Moreover, the newly-appointed US defence secretary Frank Carlucci's tour of the Gulf sheikhdoms in early January, and a ground-breaking visit to the region by Mubarak scheduled for mid-January to consolidate the budding friendship between Egypt and the GCC, lent greater urgency to the Syrian initiative. Damascus was particularly concerned that Cairo would exacerbate the situation by playing up the Iranian threat in order to strengthen its emerging military ties with the Gulf states and, in so doing, diminish the efficacy of Syrian diplomacy to bridge the gap between the two sides.

Throughout the winter of 1987/8, as Iran tried to mobilize enough men and *matériel* for another possible offensive in the Basra area, the Syrians, in consultation with Gulf Arabs, anxiously tried to head off such a move, fearing that an operation like Karbala 5 would accelerate Egyptian moves to cement defence links with the GCC, galvanize support for Iraq and, in the process, push Syria to the sidelines of Arab and regional politics. Subsequent to al-Shara's successful shuttle diplomacy between Tehran and Riyadh in late December, Assad tried to build on the earlier gains by sending vice-president Khaddam and al-Shara to the Gulf states to offer their good offices once again. Khaddam's involvement underlined the seriousness of the Syrian effort to bring about an accommodation between Iran and the GCC. The Gulf states were also willing to give Syrian mediation a chance given that UN efforts had proved ineffective.

As Khaddam and al-Shara prepared to go to the Gulf, Carlucci toured the GCC states, meeting political leaders in Kuwait, Saudi Arabia, Bahrain and Oman. At the same time, Iranian foreign minister Velayati said that in view of the promising signals from the GCC and Syrian entreaties, Tehran was prepared to start talking with Gulf states.[403] Once Khaddam and al-Shara had begun their consultations in the GCC states, it became clear that their mission had more than one purpose. They were trying both to build diplomatic bridges across the Gulf to improve GCC–Iranian ties and contain the hostilities and to put forth a series of proposals to achieve a comprehensive peace in the region.[404] Damascus hoped to persuade Tehran not to carry out any major offensives against Iraq and to convince Baghdad, through Gulf Arab intermediaries, to continue its halt on attacks targeting Iranian shipping in Gulf waters. By preserving calm in the area, the Syrians hoped to prod the GCC into adopting a neutral position in the war (and pay Iran the reparations it demanded from Iraq) in exchange for an Iranian commitment to cease hostilities and withdraw from occupied Iraqi territory.[405] The Syrians were genuinely worried that a full-scale offensive by Iran would give Washington and Cairo the perfect pretext under which to intervene on the side of the pro-Iraqi camp, torpedo Syrian attempts to reach a diplomatic solution and bring about the passage of a UN Security Council resolution imposing an international arms embargo on Iran.

As Carlucci continued his talks with Gulf Arab officials, the Khaddam-headed Syrian delegation began to tour the GCC states, offering to arrange and even host a meeting between Iranian and GCC representatives.[406] In talks with Gulf Arab leaders, Khaddam and al-Shara suggested the GCC encourage Baghdad to continue its cease-fire in the Gulf. In exchange, Syria would do its best to discourage any possible Iranian land offensive. Under such circumstances, the GCC and Iran could start a dialogue under Syrian auspices to improve relations and explore possibilities of ending the war.[407]

Unfortunately for the Syrians, their strategy had three major weaknesses. First, the GCC countries were divided on this issue. While Oman, Qatar and the UAE were amenable to Syrian mediation and keen to thaw relations with Iran, the other three members, Kuwait, Saudi Arabia and Bahrain, were reluctant to support the Syrian plan wholeheartedly. Second, Iraq was deeply suspicious of Syria's motives and saw this initiative as part of an effort to break the unity the Arab ranks had achieved in Amman. Baghdad believed that Syria was trying to separate the GCC from Iraq by facilitating a GCC–Iranian *rapprochement*, thus assisting Iran by isolating Iraq. Third, Iran did not see eye-to-eye with its Arab ally on Syria's overall agenda. On one hand, the clerical regime appreciated Syrian moves to curb attacks on Iranian shipping and ease Arab–Iranian tensions. It interpreted the Syrian effort as a way of gaining room for diplomatic manoeuvre, buying time to weigh its options and reverse its slide into further regional isolation. On the other hand, the hardliners in the Iranian government who had Khomeini's full support were intent on continuing the war until the Iraqi Ba'thists were overthrown. The more pragmatic elements in the ruling elite hoped to cut Iran's losses by finding a face-saving way of getting out of the conflict. In general, it is extremely difficult to assess what was happening within the black box of Iranian decision-making at the time. Although some members must have welcomed the proposals their Arab ally put forth to end the war, it is clear that the hawks led by Ayatollah Khomeini were still in the dominant position and refusing to contemplate a negotiated settlement.

On 10 January, the head of the UAE foreign ministry's GCC department, Saif Said, arrived in Tehran with a message for Velayati. The UAE indicated that the purpose of Said's mission was to hold talks with Iranian officials aimed at 'defusing tensions in the Gulf and ending the Iran–Iraq War'. After these deliberations, Iranian deputy foreign minister Sheikholislam stated that the conflict would only end when Saddam Hussein was toppled, and called on the GCC to withdraw its support for Iraq. Predictably, Baghdad now seized the opportunity to end the tacit truce between the two sides brokered by Syria since late December. With Mubarak's visit to the Gulf only a few days away, Iraq launched new aerial attacks on Iranian targets, bombing the Tabriz oil refinery and hitting four tankers near Kharg Island between 10 and 12 January.[408] To avoid contributing to the collapse of the Syrian mediation effort and playing into Iraqi hands, Iran refrained from attacking Gulf Arab shipping and restated its readiness for a political dialogue with the GCC. On 12 January, Syrian minister of information Salman rather prematurely declared: 'We have succeeded in achieving an agreement by Iran and the Arab Gulf states to achieve a direct dialogue.'[409]

As Mubarak's visit got underway, Iran denounced what it depicted as Egyptian meddling in the Persian Gulf, and accused Cairo of stoking the fires in the region. The Egyptian leader toured the Gulf in mid-January to cement ties by bolstering military and economic cooperation with the GCC. He intended to wrap up a number of military cooperation agreements in exchange for more financial aid from the Gulf sheikhdoms.[410] To highlight Cairo's commitment to Gulf security, while in Saudi Arabia, Mubarak declared that 'Egypt is an Arab country and the security of this area is part of Egyptian security'.[411] At a press conference in Kuwait only a day later, he also implicitly rejected the Syrian mediation effort.[412]

Iran, for its part, was trying to perform a delicate balancing act. It wanted to avoid casting a pall over the Syrian initiative to defuse GCC–Iranian tensions, and thwart Egyptian attempts to make further inroads in the Gulf, yet felt compelled to respond to Iraqi attacks. Rafsanjani warned that Iran was poised to launch a new ground offensive and might have to abandon the restraint it had exercised out of respect for Syrian efforts. He urged the Gulf states to distance themselves from Saddam Hussein and 'come to the side of justice before it is too late'.[413] Only days later, on 15 January, Iran undertook a limited operation codenamed Bayt al-Moqaddas-2 on the northern front in Iraqi Kurdistan.[414] During the renewed fighting in the north, Tehran announced its wish to follow up the dialogue with the GCC, and sent the foreign ministry's director-general for Arab–African affairs, Mohammad Hossein Lavasani, to Abu Dhabi for further talks with UAE officials.[415] His deliberations with the UAE foreign minister resulted in an Iranian pledge to refrain from attacking vessels flying flags of GCC states.[416]

By late January, several issues were becoming clearer. Syria's feat in facilitating a constructive dialogue between the GCC and Iran had been limited at best. The GCC was still divided over the wisdom of pursuing such an approach. Indeed, Tehran's assurance that it would desist from hitting GCC ships was only a limited concession, for most of the vessels destined for the Gulf states were not flying those countries' flags. Moreover, Iran was clearly having severe difficulty mobilizing the numbers necessary to sustain a land campaign and another assault on Basra. Speculation now emerged that a slowdown in the land war was inevitable. These were all unmistakable signs that the Islamic Republic was running out of options and had pinned itself into a corner, despite Syrian attempts to heal the rift between Iran and the Gulf Arabs and find an acceptable way of ending the war. To maintain pressure on Baghdad and its allies, in mid-January, Iran decided to respond in kind to Iraqi attacks in the Gulf by once again targeting third country ships bound for Gulf Arab ports. Overall, Iran's riposte was ineffectual, for it perpetuated tensions in the Persian Gulf without yielding any substantive results in strategic terms. On land, it was now only capable of conducting limited offensives.

Iraq's reaction to Syrian–Iranian moves in the Gulf

After a brief pause from late December to mid-January, Iraq adopted an aggressive two-track plan to deal decisive blows to Iran to force it to the negotiating table and to discredit Syrian moves to bridge the gap between the GCC and Iran. Baghdad resumed the tanker war and, throughout January and February, carried out deep penetration raids against Iranian targets, highlighted by attacks on Kharg on 7 February and the Rey oil refinery on the outskirts of Tehran on 27 February.[417] Besides trying to bring Iran to its knees, the aerial campaign was also intended to impede Syria's effort to stabilize the situation in the Gulf and ease GCC–Iran tensions. Baghdad hoped that an intensive assault on Iran's strategic assets would fuel the fires and prompt Iran overtly to threaten the Gulf Arabs. Such a development would derail Syria's initiative and reveal the limits of Assad's influence. Meanwhile, Iraq finally broke its silence and renewed its propaganda against Syria for the first time since the Amman summit. The state-controlled media denounced Syria's attempt to revive a GCC–Iran dialogue because it violated the spirit of the Amman summit resolutions to create a united Arab front against Iran. Damascus was accused both of 'whitewashing Iran' and trying to isolate Iraq.[418] The Iraqi Ba'th Party unleashed an unrelenting barrage of criticism against its Syrian rival. Iraqi minister of information Jasim claimed that none of the Arab states trusted the Syrians because they had been 'Iran's constant allies'.[419] A few days later, on 26 January, foreign minister Tareq Aziz dismissed Syria's interference, reiterating that UN Security Council Resolution 598 was the only formula for ending the hostilities. He was pessimistic about the prospects of a Syrian–Iraqi *rapprochement*, because of Syria's insistence on breaking the pan-Arab consensus achieved in Amman.[420] Saddam Hussein publicly accused Syria of endangering Arab security by serving as Iran's strategic ally, urging it to remain neutral at the very least.[421] He blamed Syria for the return to the 'pre-summit atmosphere' by reneging on the anti-Iranian consensus reached at the Amman conference.[422] The anti-Syrian polemic from Baghdad increased during late January and early February. In an article published in *Al-Thawrah* on 31 January, deputy prime minister Ramadan called Syrian policy in the Gulf 'a dirty attempt to divide brothers', warning that Arab fragmentation would only encourage Khomeini to continue the war. Furthermore, he stated that Iran's strategy was to create a new Persian empire under the guise of exporting revolutionary Islam.

Syria's reaction to Baghdad's war of words was restrained. It is notable that the Syrians tried to exploit the recent unrest in the occupied territories to justify their stand in the Gulf War and deflect criticism. With the Palestinian *intifada* bringing a renewed focus in the region and beyond on the Arab–Israeli struggle, Syrian officials stressed that, from the outset, they had believed that Iraq's ill-conceived effort to wage war on Iran and attempt to depict the hostilities as an Arab–Iranian war were harmful to the combatants and diverted Arab attention away from the Palestinian issue. They rejected Iraqi accusations that their mediation in the Gulf was detrimental to pan-Arab interests, arguing that preventing an escalation of hostilities that could potentially drag the GCC states into the war, and establishing 'channels for dialogue and understanding between the Gulf states and Iran' would be beneficial to the Arabs.[423] Interestingly, Damascus countered that Iraq's condemnation of its initiative in the Gulf and deliberate policy to intensify its air campaign in the waterway could only be seen as an attempt to destabilize the region, and divert Arab and international attention away from the uprising in the occupied territories.[424]

As Iraq continued to criticize the Syrian–Iranian partnership, any lingering residue of Arab unity since Amman quickly dissipated. The marked deterioration in Syrian–Iraqi relations and the deadlock in the Gulf led to a flurry of diplomatic activity, with the various parties exercising damage control and jockeying for support to further their interests. King Hussein tried to cool Syrian–Iraqi tensions in late January by going to Baghdad and sending Prime Minister al-Rifai to Damascus. After talks with Saddam Hussein, he went to Damascus to meet Hafez Assad. Despite his efforts to contain the situation, neither Baghdad nor Damascus seemed willing to reconsider their policies. During the Jordanian initiative, Faruq al-Shara arrived in Tehran on 30 January for consultations with Iranian officials. Al-Shara conveyed a message from Hafez Assad to Ali Khamene'i and met his Iranian counterpart. They talked about how to contain the volatile situation in the Persian Gulf and strengthen GCC–Iranian ties.[425]

In the aftermath of al-Shara's visit, throughout much of February, Syria continued to encourage the GCC–Iranian dialogue, while Iran refrained from attacking vessels flying GCC flags. In fact, a period of relative calm prevailed in the Gulf between 12 February and 6 March as Iraq ceased the tanker war so Iran had no need to retaliate. The lull could partially be attributed to an incident on 12 February, reminiscent of the USS *Stark* attack, when an Iraqi TU-16 bomber hunting for targets in the Gulf mistakenly fired missiles at a US destroyer, USS *Chandler*, barely missing the warship and later mistakenly attacked and damaged a Danish tanker carrying Saudi crude.[426] One can only speculate that, as a consequence, Washington and Riyadh put pressure on Baghdad to suspend its raids, particularly given the absence of any Iranian offensive in the Basra region and the relative restraint shown by Tehran in the Gulf. (Indeed, the fighting was confined to the north in Kurdistan and was limited in scale.) More importantly in the broader picture, to give diplomacy a chance, Iraq seems to have acquiesced in the hope that a new US initiative in the UN Security Council would push Iran to the negotiating table. As president of the Security Council, and its term due to end on 29 February, that month, the USA announced its intention to push through a resolution threatening to impose sanctions on Iran after a 30-day period if the UN secretary-general failed to persuade Tehran to accept a negotiated settlement.[427]

While opting to give diplomacy a chance, Iraq took advantage of the lull in the tanker war and absence of a major Iranian land operation to finalize preparations for its own campaign to turn the tables on Iran and bring the conflict to a favourable conclusion, should US moves in the Security Council fail. Baghdad gradually felt confident it could seize the military initiative and turn the tide of the war. As the USA relinquished its presidency of the UN Security Council on 29 February, Iranian President Khamene'i reiterated that acceptance of Resolution 598 would be contingent on prior identification of Iraq as the aggressor by the UN body. That evening, Iraq fired 11 modified Scud-B missiles (named Al-Hussein) at Tehran in the most intensive missile attack ever on the Iranian capital.[428] For the next 52 days, almost 190 missiles were fired at Tehran and other major Iranian cities in a bid to force the clerical regime to the negotiating table. These were supplemented by hundreds of sorties by the Iraqi air force bombing civilian and economic targets in and around 37 Iranian cities and towns.[429]

Iranian foreign minister Velayati appealed in vain to the UN to intervene to stop the Iraqi attacks. Tehran also failed to achieve a 'balance of terror' with Baghdad during March and April. With only a limited number of Scud missiles in its inventory (supplied by Libya, Syria and North Korea) and fewer than 50 of its US-made warplanes still operational, it responded by firing about 70 missiles at Baghdad and other Iraqi urban centres, while the Iranian air force conducted only a handful of aerial assaults.[430] In March and April, it is estimated that the Iraqi bombardment killed 2000 Iranians and wounded 8000. The attacks had a devastating psychological impact on the regime and the people. As the leaders bickered, hundreds of thousands of civilians fled to the countryside and the east amid rumours that Iraq would launch missiles armed with chemical weapons against the cities.[431]

As the war of the cities escalated in early March, Iraq and Iran raised the stakes by adopting their old strategies of putting pressure on each other. On 8 March, Iraq ended its moratorium in the tanker war and recommenced attacks on Gulf shipping. In Damascus, the Syrian government criticized Iraqi actions and the renewed escalation of hostilities in the Gulf. Information minister Mohammed Salman restated that Syria had earlier won assurances from Iran that it would not attack Gulf Arab ships, putting the blame for the unstable situation squarely on Iraq's shoulders. He also brushed off Iraqi criticism of Syrian diplomacy aimed at reducing tension in the region. Meanwhile, his Iraqi counterpart, Latif Nassif Jasim, again dismissed the prospect of reconciliation with Syria, accusing it of 'stabbing Iraq in the back with its deception and lying'.[432] As so often in the past, with the sudden escalation of hostilities in the Gulf, and the intensification of the war of words between Iraqi and Syrian Ba'thist regimes, King Hussein tried to mediate between the two Arab rivals by visiting Baghdad and Damascus on subsequent days to hold talks with Saddam Hussein and Hafez Assad. However, his intercession produced no concrete results.

Iran, for its part, decided to retaliate against the Iraqi attacks on its urban centres and shipping in the Persian Gulf by launching an offensive, codenamed Wal-Fajr 10, into Suleimaniyiah province (150 miles northeast of Baghdad) on 13 March. The Iranian forces, with help from Iraqi exiles and local Kurds, scored significant gains by overrunning several border towns, including Halabjah, and then pushed towards the Darbandikhan reservoir and dam, one of the largest in the country, which provided hydroelectric power to much of northeast Iraq and Baghdad. To terrorize and punish the local Kurdish population for siding with Iran, on the night of 16 March, Iraqi warplanes dropped bombs containing poison gas on the town of Halabjah, killing between 2000 and 4000 Kurdish civilians.[433] This then reinforced Iranian claims that Iraq had been using chemical weapons extensively in the war since 1984. However, this was the first time that non-combatants were intentionally targeted. The incident, which provided undeniable proof of Iraqi chemical warfare, received extensive media coverage throughout the world and focused international attention on the issue more than ever before. Besides attempting to win sympathy for its position, Tehran tried to use the tragedy to stir up passions at home and drum up support for the war effort. However, with the Iraqi missile campaign in full-swing, the state-controlled media's focus on Halabjah may have backfired and unnerved the Iranian public, heightening concerns that Iraq might also fire missiles armed with chemical warheads at Iranian cities.[434]

Despite the Halabjah massacre, heavy fighting raged through late March and early April, with the Iraqis eventually recovering some lost ground and the Iranians again failing to achieve a major breakthrough. The Iranian war machine was running out of steam and popular support for the war was waning. It was now only a question time before Iraq would try to take advantage of the propitious circumstances and take the offensive. Indeed, the period from April to July 1988 would be fateful, with Iran suddenly suffering major reverses and Syria, being a mere spectator, unable to affect the outcome of events in favour of its ally.

Amal–Hezbollah rivalry as a factor in the alliance

In early 1987, following Iran's failure to seize Basra, Iran's revolution-

ary regime attached more ideological, symbolic and practical significance to Lebanon. As hopes of toppling the Iraqi Ba'thists and
exporting the revolution to their closest Arab neighbour began to
recede in the aftermath of Karbala 5, Iran's clerical leaders became
more determined to maintain and expand their foothold in Lebanon.
The carnage and misery the ongoing civil war and Israeli occupation
produced, made Lebanon a fertile ground in which Iran's ideologues
could win over adherents for their religious and political cause among
the Lebanese Shiites. Consequently, Tehran paid more attention to
the Lebanese arena in 1987/8, channelled more resources there and
showed sensitivity to other actors' attempts to undermine its influence. Although the Iranians were more resolute in their conviction to
expand their constituency in Lebanon, this was not supposed to be at
the expense of their strategic partnership with the Syrians.

For Syria, the need to restore order in Lebanon became more
urgent in 1988 because of the impending expiry of Amin Gemayel's
term in office and the expected election of a new Lebanese president
in September that year. Damascus hoped to strengthen its grip in the
fractious land to ensure a smooth transition and the selection of a
president to its own liking by the Lebanese parliament. As in the past,
Syria continued to view Iranian policy in its backyard, especially Hezbollah's activities, with ambivalence. On one hand, the guerrilla war
against the Israelis and SLA in the south had Syria's blessing – it was a
means of bleeding the Israelis and enhancing Syria's confrontation-
alist credentials. Moreover, supporting the resistance in southern
Lebanon became more important with the unexpected outbreak of
the Palestinian *intifada*, which again focused Arab and international
attention on the need to find a just and durable Arab–Israeli peace.
The uprising in the occupied territories and Syrian-backed Hezbollah
operations in southern Lebanon to some extent facilitated Assad's bid
to garner Arab support and tip the balance of power against the
Egyptian–Jordanian–Iraqi axis. Syria could emphasize once more that
it was the only true confrontation state and that giving it support was
a pan-Arab duty.

On the other hand, Hezbollah's stated long-term objective of establishing a religious order in Lebanon, and waging an incessant struggle
against Israel and its backers did not fit into Assad's plan to re-
establish a secular, multi-sectarian order in the country. In early
1988, as Iran continued to make inroads into the Shiite community at
Amal's expense and orchestrated a series of kidnappings (much to the
embarrassment of Nabih Berri and Hafez Assad), both Amal and Syria

became determined to take firm action to rein in Hezbollah. However, what could not be foreseen was that Iran and its Lebanese cohorts would respond in a forceful manner. While Tehran's ideologues believed they could ill-afford to give up their only bridgehead in the Arab–Islamic world, Hezbollah, with justification, interpreted events as a fight for survival. As a result, the contradictions in Syria's Lebanon policy came to the fore in spring 1988 and sparked off the worst confrontation ever between Amal and Hezbollah, which put the Syrian–Iranian alliance to the ultimate test.

With Iranian guidance and support, Hezbollah was turning into a real fighting force able to combine guerrilla tactics with conventional warfare to strike effectively at the IDF and SLA in the self-declared security zone. Damascus endorsed Hezbollah's military strategy in the south as long as it did not go too far; it feared that a major escalation could unwittingly drag Syria into a serious confrontation and perhaps even full-scale war with Israel. Besides direct contacts and their channels through the Iranians to ensure that Hezbollah did not go beyond certain bounds, the Syrians also expected Amal to keep the Shiite fundamentalists in check.[435] However, there was growing unease within the Amal leadership that Hezbollah was becoming too powerful and a major force to be reckoned with in Lebanon. Indeed, Amal resented Hezbollah's ability to win over the hearts and minds of many Shiites with a combination of ideological indoctrination, financial inducements and social benefits. The ability of the pro-Iranians to expand their base in the Shiite community at the expense of Amal and to outstrip their secular rival led Amal officials to accuse Hezbollah of being no more than Iranian 'robots', lacking genuine grassroots support.[436] Hezbollah inroads into Amal's traditional geographical base of southern Lebanon led to armed clashes between the two militias in September 1987, and vocal criticism by Nabih Berri of Ayatollah Khomeini and Tehran's policies in Lebanon.[437]

As Hezbollah grew more confident and assertive, it began to criticize aspects of Syrian policy. Its daily newspaper, *Al-Sabi*, and the weekly, *Al-Ahd*, occasionally took an anti-Syrian line, particularly over the prospect of a thaw in US–Syrian relations when US assistant secretary of state Richard Murphy visited Damascus in October 1987.[438] Another sign of mounting friction between Syria and the pro-Iranian movement was the temporary detention of 120 Hezbollah members by Syrian forces in northern Lebanon during November 1987.[439]

In the winter of 1987/8, the Reagan administration grew concerned about instability in the Middle East. Besides ongoing hostilities in the

Persian Gulf, the sudden eruption of the Palestinian uprising, the escalation of Hezbollah operations in southern Lebanon (with the blessing of Syrian military intelligence) and prospects of another political crisis in Lebanon when Amin Gemayel's presidency ended later in the year, convinced Washington that concrete steps were needed to mend US–Syrian relations and reach some sort of *modus vivendi*.[440] With Syria being the most influential player in Lebanon and Iran's only major ally, the US now considered its cooperation to be vital. Syria's participation was essential for restoring peace in the Levant and the Gulf, and securing the release of US hostages. So Richard Murphy travelled to Syria once more in early February to meet Hafez Assad and find some common ground on these issues. Although not all the details of their talks were divulged, it is clear that Assad asked Murphy to intervene to bridge the gap between Syrian and Maronite views on political reform in Lebanon and Gemayel's succession.[441]

After Murphy's visit, on 17 February, Hezbollah abducted Lieutenant-Colonel William Higgins, an American serving as head of the UN Truce and Supervision Organization's observer group (affiliated with UNIFIL) near Tyre in southern Lebanon.[442] Hezbollah demanded the release of Lebanese and Palestinian captives held by Israel in exchange for Higgins's freedom. Higgins's abduction was undoubtedly a major embarrassment to Amal and the Syrians since he had been kidnapped in an area nominally under Amal control, and his captors also intended to signal their displeasure at a possible US–Syrian *rapprochement*. With UNIFIL's collaboration, Amal cordoned off the area around Tyre and mounted an extensive search. Amal detained dozens of Hezbollah activists for questioning, but to no avail. Amal's clampdown also sparked minor skirmishes with Hezbollah fighters in the Bekaa and the south.[443]

It was suspected that some Iranian politicians were aware of, or indirectly involved in, Higgins's abduction, for the Iranian media accused Higgins of being a CIA operative. After the incident, Ayatollah Montazeri received Sheikhs Fadlallah and al-Tufayli in Qom to review the situation and later summoned Iran's ambassadors to Syria and Lebanon, and other Hezbollah officials to discuss Syrian demands for Higgins's immediate release. The kidnapping served Hezbollah and Iranian interests, for it dealt a blow to Amal and UNIFIL and provided some leverage in affecting the outcome of the US–Syrian *rapprochement*. Both were keen to carry on the struggle in southern Lebanon, and prevent being sacrificed as part of a deal between Damascus and Washington. Indeed, by mid-March, as Amal's frustration with its inability to locate Higgins grew, Nabih Berri condemned Iranian 'interference' in Lebanese affairs, emphasizing his concern about the security situation in the south. In addition, he tried to play the secular, Arab nationalist card by underlining that while Amal sought 'privileged and strategic ties with Iran', relations with Syria took precedence since it was 'an Arab country like Lebanon'.[444]

As Amal–Hezbollah relations approached breaking point, Assad continued his dialogue with the USA and resolved to take decisive action. Hezbollah's growing power and boldness, and the need to restore Syrian credibility in Washington's eyes prompted Damascus to mobilize Amal to curb Islamic extremism in Lebanon. Ironically, Iran's earlier mediation in the winter between the Palestinians and Amal, and the consequent cessation of hostilities around the refugee camps in Beirut and the south had freed up large numbers of Amal militiamen to take part in the impending showdown with Iran's clients. Eventually, on 4 April, Amal forces attacked Hezbollah strongholds in and around Nabatiya and Jezzine, near the Israeli-held security zone.[445] After three days of heavy fighting that left more than 50 people dead and 130 injured, Amal forces captured the village of Siddiqin, Hezbollah's last bastion in the south.[446] Hezbollah clerics and activists in the area were rounded up and expelled and detachments of Iranian Revolutionary Guards stationed in the villages of Sharqiyah and Jibshit were forced to leave the south. By 9 April, Amal boasted that its rival was 'finished militarily' in the south, and subsequently released a statement denouncing Hezbollah for carrying out 'evil deeds', including terrorism, kidnapping and hijacking. Hezbollah's Sheikh al-Tufayli countered these charges by accusing Amal of being 'an ally of Israel', and helping the USA implement its designs in the region.[447]

It is noteworthy that Assad and Berri underestimated both Hezbollah and Iranian resolve to perpetuate their presence in Lebanon. The scenario that they had envisaged would not materialize. By spring 1988, a number of factors had contributed to the complexity of the political equation involving Syria, Iran, Amal and Hezbollah. First, the gradual institutionalization of Hezbollah as a political actor in Lebanon meant that it was no longer simply an Iranian proxy, but was beginning to assert its independence by formulating and pursuing its own agenda. Second, growing cleavages in the Iranian leadership further confused the situation. While the pragmatists in the Tehran regime wanted stable, strategic ties with Damascus and to cooperate with it to ease tensions and gain the release of Western hostages, as long as some Iranian influence was tolerated in Lebanon, the more radical elements distrusted Syria and Amal, suspecting that Iranian and Hezbollah interests in Lebanon would eventually be compromised as part of an overall agreement between Syria and the USA on Lebanon's political future.[448] Third, major setbacks in the Gulf War in mid-April reinforced Tehran's determination to reverse the situation in Lebanon, as US and Iraqi forces dealt decisive blows on land and sea. Major gains by the anti-Iranian coalition in the Persian Gulf dimmed Iranian hopes of any success and an honourable peace, thereby strengthening Tehran's drive to maintain its precarious foothold in Lebanon.

The beginning of the end for Iran

As the war of the cities raged on throughout March and early April, the pro-Iraqi camp and the USA dealt Iran a series of devastating blows to cow it into submission. The period between April and June marked the turning of the tide in the Gulf conflict as Iraq seized the initiative in the ground war by launching a series of offensives that dislodged Iranian forces from prized possessions, including the Faw peninsula, the Shalamcheh region east of Basra and the oil-rich Majnoon islands. Meanwhile, the USA took steps to neutralize the threat Iran's naval forces posed in the Persian Gulf. By the end of spring 1988, the Islamic Republic was more vulnerable and isolated, both regionally and internationally, than ever before. Indeed, its military reverses on land and sea, coupled with the tragic shooting down of an Iranian passenger plane by the US navy in early July (highlighting the lack of sympathy and support from the international community) left it with no recourse and finally led to Tehran's unconditional acceptance of UN Resolution 598 in mid-July, thus ending the longest and bloodiest war in modern Middle East history.

On 18 April, Iraq began its first major offensive in seven years in the marshes south of Basra, aimed at recapturing the Faw peninsula. Part of the 7th army supported by Republican Guard units stormed the Iranian defensive lines. Enjoying the element of tactical surprise and outnumbering the defenders six to one, the Iraqis overran the Peninsula within a 35-hour period, inflicting heavy losses on the Iranians.[449] Within four hours of the Iraqi offensive in Faw getting underway, the US navy attacked two offshore platforms used by IRGC naval units in the southern Gulf in retaliation for damage to a US naval vessel four days earlier by a mine suspectedly planted by Iran. With large forces on both sides, the hostilities rapidly escalated.

When the fighting finally receded, the USA had inflicted huge losses on the Iranians. Apart from destroying two platforms, it sank an Iranian naval frigate, a gunboat and several speedboats, and damaged a second frigate. The USA only lost a marine helicopter.[450] Iraq's victory at Faw, the first major one in the land war since 1981, and the US navy's impressive success in the Gulf were important milestones in the progress of the Gulf War and huge setbacks for the Iranians. Iraq had clearly demonstrated that it could once again take the initiative in the ground war, while the USA had shown that it would not allow Iran to gain the upper hand in the Gulf theatre, putting out of action two of Iran's four major surface vessels in the process.

Though Washington and Baghdad never admitted collusion in their operations against Iranian land and naval forces, and denied any links between the two events, Iran was convinced that they had coordinated their moves to maximize the chances of success. It is highly improbable that the timing of the first major Iraqi land offensive in over seven years and largest US–Iranian military clash since the 1979 revolution, only hours apart on the same day, could have been a mere coincidence. Given the extent of US–Iraqi cooperation all through 1987 and 1988, at the very least, the two sides must have informed one another of their impending actions.

Predictably, international reaction to the events of 18 April was for the most part favourable towards the USA. Syria was the only country in the Arab East to criticize US actions.[451] A few days after the victory at Faw, on 21 April, Baghdad declared a unilateral moratorium in the war of the cities, while Washington announced that its forces in the Gulf would now come to the rescue of any ship Iran attacked, not just Kuwaiti tankers escorted by the US navy. With Iran still reeling from the double blows inflicted on land and sea, the USA expanded its protective umbrella in the Persian Gulf, and Iraq continued aerial raids against Iranian assets in the waterway.

In the light of its major military reverses and growing political isolation, Tehran sent Velayati to Damascus on 23 April to brief the Syrian leadership on developments in the Gulf and perhaps request further Syrian mediation to ease tensions between Iran and the Gulf states. On arrival, Velayati held talks with Faruq al-Shara and, the next day, Hafez Assad received him. Besides conveying a message from Khamene'i to Assad, the primary focus of the two-hour meeting between Velayati and Assad was the situation in the Gulf, and regional and international mediation efforts.[452]

Even if Syrian intervention to contain the damage to Arab–Iranian relations in the Gulf were seriously considered, by this stage, it would in all probability have been ineffective. Baghdad continued its air campaign in the Gulf (with US and Saudi help) and finalized preparations for its second big offensive scheduled for late May, aimed at driving Iranian forces east of Basra back across the international border. Throughout this period, as events in the Gulf continued to unfold rapidly, there was very little Syria could do to aid its Iranian ally. As Iran received a drubbing in the Gulf at the hands of the pro-Iraqi coalition, and Syria's patience with Hezbollah was stretched to the limit in mid-May (see next section), sensing that a propitious moment had arrived, Washington sent its UN ambassador, Vernon Walters, to Damascus and Baghdad to build a consensus on important regional issues and explore avenues of cooperation in the Arab–Israeli and Gulf arenas. With Iranian reverses in the Gulf and Syrian–Iranian tensions in Lebanon, at this critical juncture, Walters may have wanted to exploit the opportunity to decouple Syria from Iran and pave the way for some form of Syrian–Iraqi understanding. In any event, no radical shift occurred in the partnership between Damascus and Tehran.

Meanwhile, on 25 May, Iraq launched a major offensive to dislodge the Iranians from positions east of Basra (near the border town of Shalamcheh). After ten hours of intense fighting, the third army corps with the support of Republican Guards had completely routed the Iranian forces and pushed them back across the border. Despite these defeats, Ayatollah Khomeini remained defiant and maintained his unwavering conviction that a military solution would still have to be pursued against the Iraqi Ba'thist regime. In a message delivered on 28 May to the opening session of the third *Majles* (which had been elected the previous month), he urged the people to continue to support the war effort, reaffirming that 'the destiny of the war is written at the fronts, not at the negotiating table'.[453]

In mid-June, the Iraqi army retook key positions east of Suleiman-iyiah in the north, and further south, overran the strategically-situated Iranian border town of Mehran on 18 June. The Iraqi air force bombed targets throughout Iran, peaking on 23 June, with attacks on ten oil installations in the southwest – the heaviest raids since the end of the war of the cities in April.[454] On 25 June, Iraq started a full-scale offensive in the Hawizeh marshes, aimed at retaking the oil-rich Majnoon islands. Specially trained Republican Guard and amphibious units took part in this eight-hour operation. As in previous offensives, the Iraqis had overwhelming numerical superiority and were extremely well equipped, outnumbering their foe in terms of tanks and artillery 20:1. They enveloped the Iranian positions in the marshes and pushed into Iran itself after annihilating enemy units.[455] Once again, the victory was total. The Iraqis had attained their objective at minimal cost, while thousands of Iranian soldiers were either killed or captured during the fighting. Iran conceded more ground in Iraqi Kurdistan in late June and lost some warplanes in a desperate bid to expel Iraqi forces from Iranian territory east of the Majnoon islands.[456]

By now the Iraqi steamroller seemed unstoppable. In fact, many regional observers, including Iraqis, were surprised by the relative ease (compared with earlier campaigns) with which they defeated the Iranians. The string of Iraqi victories between April and June can be attributed to several factors. Overall, proper and meticulous planning by the Iraqis, low Iranian morale in the last phase of the war (when the initiative was lost after Operation Karbala 5), the Iraqi army's numerical superiority in men and *matériel*, extensive use of chemical weapons and adequate US satellite intelligence on Iranian troop dispositions together, helped turn the tables on revolutionary Iran in such a dramatic manner. By the end of June, it was apparent that an Iranian victory was beyond grasp, while Iraq had weathered the worst part of the conflict and was now indisputably on the ascendant.

Iran was now clearly on the defensive and could do little to decide the course of events on the war front. Momentous events in subsequent days strengthened the hand of those advocating a negotiated settlement and persuaded the hardliners, including Khomeini, to sue for peace. Both Iran and Syria played a largely passive role in the Gulf between April and July 1988. However, during the same period, they demonstrated their ability to serve as key actors in Lebanon and, in May, survived one of the most crucial tests the Syrian–Iranian alliance had ever faced.

The impact of the Amal–Hezbollah confrontation

After Amal routed Hezbollah forces in southern Lebanon between 4 and 7 April, Iran sent a high-level delegation headed by Ayatollah Jannati to mediate between the two Shiite organizations and resolve their differences. While Tehran sought to find common ground between the two rivals, it was also keen to restore Hezbollah's military presence in the south. At a press conference at the Iranian embassy in Beirut on 22 April, Jannati announced that his talks with the various parties had led to a joint decision to form a five-member commission composed of Fadlallah, Shamseddin, representatives from Amal and Hezbollah and himself to review the situation and seek a solution.[457] As the deliberations proceeded, it became clear that Berri was adamant in his refusal to allow a Hezbollah presence in the south.[458] Jannati was unable to bridge the gap in their positions on issues such as the UN presence in the south, and confrontation with Israel and its proxies in the area. The lingering tensions and frustration over the impasse again flared up as Amal and Hezbollah forces clashed in the Bekaa Valley on 26–27 April. To make matters worse, Berri accused Iran's ambassador to Lebanon, Ahmad Dastmal-chian, of provoking these incidents.[459] Nonetheless, the commission continued its efforts throughout late April and early May. However, a daring Israeli ground attack ordered by defence minister Yitzhak Rabin against a Hezbollah-held citadel in the village of Maydoun (well beyond the self-declared security zone in the southwestern part of the Bekaa) on 2 May reinforced Hezbollah's sense of siege and belief that its enemies in Lebanon and beyond wanted to eradicate it. Over two days of fighting, the Hezbollah stronghold was completely destroyed and 40 of its guerrillas were slain.[460]

Alongside Iran's mediation, which was not yielding favourable results, Hezbollah increased its cooperation with local Iranian Revol-utionary Guards in order to regroup and strike effectively at its Shiite rival.[461] Amal and Israeli attacks on Hezbollah bases within a short time frame no doubt contributed to the pro-Iranian militia's paranoia and underlined the belief that the movement could be on the verge of extinction. For mainstream elements in the Iranian regime, their dis-pleasure with certain aspects of Syria's Lebanon policy compelled them (along with the more radical elements) to take decisive steps to prop up Hezbollah. At this point, Tehran was beginning to walk a fine line. Although it could not tolerate the elimination of Hezbollah, it was loath to jeopardize the partnership with Damascus.

In the first week in May, the Iranian team led by Jannati spent six days in Beirut trying to hammer out a compromise agreement. Amal continued to turn down requests to renew a Hezbollah presence in the south to conduct operations against the occupation.[462] The politi-cal deadlock perpetuated the charged atmosphere and led to renewed clashes. On the morning of 6 May, after an incident in which Hez-bollah killed three Amal members in the southern suburbs, Berri decided to deal a decisive blow by unleashing an assault on Hezbollah positions in Dahiya – Beirut's predominantly Shiite southern suburbs and slums.[463] Amal fighters (with Syrian logistical support) launched a ferocious attack, overrunning Hezbollah positions in the southern suburbs and outlying areas in the first 36 hours of fighting. The intensity of the Amal onslaught must have come as a surprise to Hezbollah and Iran. Both Amal and Syria seemed to have wrongly concluded that the Hezbollah defeats in the south and Maydoun had weakened and demoralized the movement, and that the opportune moment had arrived also to remove its presence from the Lebanese capital.[464] Moreover, they underestimated Iran's determination to hold onto its assets in Lebanon in the light of the diplomatic and military setbacks it was experiencing in the Gulf. Damascus calculated that Iran would concede certain of its privileges in the Levant in exchange for continued Syrian cooperation over a resurgent Iraq. In view of Tehran's weakness and isolation, the last thing Assad expected was such stiff resistance to his objectives.[465]

Besides failing to predict Iran's reaction, Syria and Amal also failed to grasp the complexity and gravity of the situation, particularly from Hezbollah's viewpoint. By mid-1988, Hezbollah was no longer an Iranian puppet, but a semi-autonomous organization with its own agenda that aspired to become a prominent force in Lebanese politics. Aside from Iran's concerns in Lebanon, Hezbollah interpreted events in April and May as a systematic and concerted effort to deny it a following among the Lebanese Shiites.[466] It is noteworthy that the southern suburbs of Beirut were now the only part of the country where Hezbollah could operate with relative freedom, for its activities in the Syrian-occupied Bekaa were closely monitored and intermittently controlled. As a result, resistance to the Amal incursion in southern Beirut was now considered imperative to avoid extirpation.[467]

On 7 May, as Amal wrested control from Hezbollah of much of the suburbs, a large contingent of Hezbollah fighters backed by several hundred Iranian Revolutionary Guards from Ba'albek, managed to slip into the Lebanese capital (undetected by the Syrians and Amal) to bolster Hezbollah's strength. The reinforced Hezbollah units immediately went on the offensive. In a well-planned and highly-disciplined attack on Amal positions, they quickly forced their foe to fall back and advanced in a methodical manner, capturing key areas of the southern suburbs.[468] As the clashes continued, the joint commission's calls for peace were ignored. There was a brief 16-hour ceasefire on the night of 7 May following a meeting between Iranian ambassador Dastmalchian and Amal and Hezbollah representatives, but it broke down the next afternoon. At the same time, Ghazi Kan'an arrived in Beirut to see Nabih Berri and later appealed to Sheikh

Fadlallah to rein in Hezbollah. Kan'an suggesed a ceasefire agreement and the deployment of Syrian troops in the southern suburbs to separate the rival militias. Iranian deputy foreign minister Sheikholislam also arrived from Iran in an attempt to negotiate a truce. By now, fighting had spread to most areas of south Beirut, with Hezbollah making significant inroads.

For the next few days, the fighting raged on, punctuated by short-lived ceasefires arranged by Iranian and Syrian mediators almost on a daily basis. Kan'an and Berri pushed for a cessation of hostilities followed by the withdrawal of all militiamen from the streets of the southern suburbs and the deployment of Syrian troops. But Hezbollah was reluctant to accept Syria's plan on two counts. First, a Syrian army presence in the suburbs would give Assad a strategic advantage in Hezbollah's domain. Second, Hezbollah managed over six days of intensive combat to expel Amal from almost 80 per cent of south Beirut.[469] Having gained the upper hand, it reckoned it would obtain better terms from the Syrians and Amal, in the quadripartite talks involving Iran, if it continued its advances. Its main goal was to reach a quid pro quo in which it would offer concessions in the suburbs in exchange for a renewed Hezbollah presence in southern Lebanon.[470] Iran, for the most part, was sympathetic with these aims. While it strove to be a valuable intermediary between the two sides, it was also keen to contain the bloodshed and ensure it did not cause irreparable damage to its bilateral ties with Syria.

By 11 May, after heavy fighting with more than 150 dead and 550 wounded, Hezbollah was indisputably on the ascendant. It had overrun the Amal headquarters in Bourj al-Barajneh (linking up with Arafat loyalists in the area) and consolidated its hold on the districts of Hayy Madi, Haret Hraik, Bir al-Abed and Hayy Muawwad.[471] Amal forces had been pushed into a narrow area on the western edge of the suburbs, only in control of the Chiyah district and parts of Ghubaryh. Frustrated by the inability to impose a truce and alarmed at the prospect of a complete Amal rout in the fighting, that same day, Kan'an threatened that unless calm were restored, Syrian forces would have to intervene to do so. Concerned about possible Syrian military intervention on the side of Amal and its implications, Iran's President Khamene'i immediately called his Syrian counterpart to discuss the intra-Shiite feuding and halting the violence. Afterwards, on the same day, the quadripartite committee met at the Iranian embassy in Beirut and reached a ceasefire agreement.[472] The parties agreed that the ceasefire would be followed by the evacuation of wounded, an exchange of prisoners and the withdrawal of fighters from the streets. As part of the agreement, a joint security force composed of Syrian soldiers, Iranian Revolutionary Guards and militiamen from Amal and Hezbollah began to patrol the southern suburbs in the early hours of 12 May to supervise and monitor the ceasefire. That evening, the quadripartite committee reconvened at the Iranian embassy to follow up matters.[473]

The committee tried to conclude a durable arrangement whereby Amal and Hezbollah could finally reach a *modus vivendi*. Assad was performing a delicate balancing act at this stage, for he and his Iranian allies were in a similar predicament. While he wanted to enhance his position in Lebanon, even if it meant curbing Hezbollah, the question of severing longstanding links with Iran did not enter his mind. In fact, both Syria and Iran were eager to resolve the crisis quickly, partly through fear that any fallout might have a harmful effect on their bilateral relations. However, they had divergent views on re-establishing the *status quo ante*. For Hezbollah and Iran, it meant returning to the situation prior to the April clashes in southern Lebanon, when Hezbollah had a sizeable presence in the region. In sharp contrast, Amal and Syria interpreted it as restoring the *status quo* in south Beirut only and steadfastly refused to accept a renewed Hezbollah presence in southern Lebanon.[474]

As the quadripartite negotiations reached deadlock, Syria's nightmare scenario began to unfold. Unable to persuade Amal to meet their demands, Hezbollah and Iran seem to have calculated that they could only obtain favourable terms by pressing the initiative and backing Amal into a corner. On 13 May, within 48 hours of the ceasefire, Hezbollah fighters resumed the offensive, pushing towards the outer perimeter of the suburbs and Beirut airport. They overran the Awzai district and, as Amal militiamen fell back, seized control of the highway connecting the airport to the capital. Close to a Syrian military camp they drew fire from Syrian troops stationed at a checkpoint guarding the highway and, in the ensuing mêlée, at least five Hezbollah fighters and one Syrian soldier died and others were wounded.[475] Brigadier Ali Hammoud warned that Syrian forces would 'eradicate any militia presence' in areas already under their control, while Sheikh Fadlallah asserted that it was up to Hezbollah's 5000 fighters to preserve an 'Islamic presence' in Lebanon.[476] To defuse tensions, Iranian deputy foreign minister Sheikholislam met Hammoud on 13 May. That evening, there was another lull in the fighting, but hostilities had resumed by the 15th, with Hezbollah making further gains. In Damascus, the Syrian leadership considered its options as its main Lebanese ally was on the verge of defeat.

As the situation seemed to be spiralling out of control, with Hezbollah advancing in the northern section of the southern suburbs and Amal facing certain defeat, Syria decided to prepare for military intervention in south Beirut, regardless of the reaction this could elicit from the Iranians or the Maronites. By now, six ceasefires arranged by Iran and Syria had collapsed, leaving Hezbollah in control of most of the 20 square kilometres that constituted the southern suburbs. More than 1100 people had been killed or wounded in eight of the bloodiest days in the Lebanese civil war.[477] Nevertheless, Berri continued to reject Hezbollah offers to relinquish control of certain areas to Amal in return for a foothold in southern Lebanon. His forces fell back south and west towards Syrian-controlled areas.

On 15 May, Ghazi Kan'an announced that Syria had no alternative but to enter the suburbs to protect their 600,000 inhabitants and impose law and order. Already, on the 14th, 5000 to 7000 Syrian troops under General Bairakdar's command and with armoured support had descended on West Beirut from the Shouf Mountains and were poised to enter the sprawling slums of Dahiya.[478] By now, Syria's main concern was to salvage Amal's position, while Iran was worried about the possibility of a full-scale confrontation between Hezbollah and the Syrian forces. Prior to Kan'an's announcement, as extra Syrian forces poured into West Beirut, Damascus sent a senior intelligence officer to Tehran for 24 hours to inform Iranian officials of the planned intervention and discuss the fate of the Western hostages held in Dahiya.[479] In effect, Assad had already decided to intervene without consulting Iran.

Tehran reacted immediately by sending two more envoys, deputy foreign minister Besharati and Revolutionary Guards minister Rafiqdoust, to Syria and Lebanon on 15 May to dissuade Syria from entering Dahiya.[480] The next day, while Sheikholislam was meeting Hafez Assad, Besharati had talks with Faruq al-Shara and Rafiqdoust saw other Syrian officials. The purpose of Rafiqdoust's mission was to work out mutually agreeable security measures to introduce and maintain a ceasefire. Besharati had visited Fadlallah in Beirut earlier to discuss the Syrian intervention. Meanwhile, a Hezbollah delegation had met Kan'an, who assured it that the Syrian move was not meant to curb Hezbollah and that both Shiite militias would be treated equally.[481] Although both Hezbollah and Iranian officials stated that in principle they had no objections to the Syrian entry, they were desperately trying to find a formula that would prevent, or at the very least delay, such action.[482] Iran was trying to win a valuable victory by ensuring Hezbollah's continued existence, and freedom to wage war on Israeli and SLA forces in the south, without jeopardizing its alliance with Syria. Damascus, on the other hand, was looking for a way to save its most important Lebanese proxy with a view to establishing a Pax Syriana, while at the same time keeping its links with its Iranian partner.[483]

There was intense Syrian and Iranian diplomatic activity between 14 and 17 May to prevent the planned deployment from turning into a confrontation with Iran's clients. It should be stressed that neither side wanted to precipitate a direct confrontation for fear of its broader implications. In fact, throughout the Amal–Hezbollah fighting, the two allies, especially Syria, emphasized how important they considered their 'strategic alliance'.[484]

It was evident that behind closed doors, the Iranian envoys were voicing their vehement opposition to Syria's planned intervention. Intense Iranian displeasure and the prospect of a costly confrontation with Hezbollah that could bleed the Syrians and endanger the lives of the Western hostages, eventually convinced Assad to hold back and try to find a political solution. Moreover, Hezbollah explicitly warned the Syrians that the hostages would be killed if their troops entered the southern suburbs.[485] Following a telephone conversation between Assad and Khamene'i, and consultations between Besharati and al-Shara on 16 May, Besharati rushed to Beirut and held talks that evening with Ghazi Kan'an at the Iranian embassy. Afterwards, they announced that they had agreed to reconvene the quadripartite committee, which met immediately to establish a ceasefire before holding further negotiations to make comprehensive arrangements to end the Amal–Hezbollah dispute. As a direct consequence of these developments, the seventh ceasefire went into effect that night.

The next day, fighting erupted again as Hezbollah pushed Amal even further back and the death toll mounted to more than 250.[486] Despite this setback, Besharati stated that a Syrian deployment would only complicate matters. He asserted they were 'in total agreement with the Syrian brothers ... desiring the implementation of the cease-fire, and withdrawal of militiamen from the suburbs'.[487] The Syrians, albeit reluctantly, seemed to have acceded to Iranian demands to give diplomacy a chance, for Kan'an also expressed his hope that peace and security could be achieved 'through political means'.[488] Implicitly acknowledging Syria's dilemma, Kan'an elucidated that Damascus 'has decided to postpone its entry into the suburbs to allow its political efforts to run their course ... we want to establish balanced relations with all parties'.[489]

As the clashes continued, Berri went to Damascus to beg Assad to intervene. Assad purportedly pledged that his forces would step in to rescue Amal and restore order. As Amal's position deteriorated, the political wrangling between Iran and Syria intensified, with Besharati maintaining firm opposition to Syrian plans to enter Dahiya. Furthermore, he insisted that if troops had to be deployed, their presence would need to be restricted to Amal-controlled neighbourhoods. Hezbollah also said it would not disarm as part of a ceasefire agreement. Both demands partially reflected concerns that Amal gunmen would return with Syrian peacekeepers and exploit their presence to settle scores with their Shiite rivals. From Syria's standpoint, that Hezbollah now controlled almost 90 per cent of the southern suburbs, and refused under any circumstances to disarm, made the Iranian demand for a limited deployment unacceptable.

As negotiations continued at a feverish pace, the Iranians sought guarantees that Syria would safeguard Hezbollah's institutions in Beirut, especially its social, religious and medical ones – the hallmarks of Tehran's influence on the Lebanese Shiites. Given Hezbollah's favourable situation on the ground, Iran and its client continued to put forth new proposals and extra demands to maximize their leverage and extract more concessions from Syria and Amal. In fact, this continued to be a recurrent pattern in the quadripartite negotiations for the next ten days, until the crisis was finally resolved on 26 May. After constant haggling, each time the parties seemed close to reaching a comprehensive agreement, the Iranians would insert new conditions, much to the dismay and exasperation of the Syrians.[490]

The renewed clashes on 17 May prompted Besharati and Kan'an to hold another meeting, with both parties agreeing on the need to end the fighting with a political settlement.[491] Iran asked for guarantees that 300 Revolutionary Guards in the suburbs would be given safe passage once the hostilities had ended. At a press conference after their talks, Besharati repeated that there was complete convergence in the positions of the two allies and a Syrian deployment was unnecessary.[492] At the same time, Amal's leaders grew increasingly disillusioned by their patron's conduct and feared that in the high stakes game of regional power politics, Damascus could well sacrifice Amal to preserve its relations with Iran. As Hezbollah continued to tighten the noose around Amal, on 18 May, Syrian defence minister Mustafa

Tlas hurried to Beirut for consultations with Ghazi Kan'an to assess the possibility for armed intervention. Frustrated by what he saw as Hezbollah and Iranian intransigence, Tlas struck a defiant note by declaring that Syria would 'not permit any gambling over Lebanon's Arab future'.[493] He also stressed that the decision to intervene made four days earlier was 'still in effect'.[494] Tlas inspected Syrian units in Beirut and called on them to 'remain fully prepared', for entry into Dahiya was only a question of time.[495] The Syrian defence minister had reportedly been predisposed initially to send in Syrian forces to halt the hostilities, but Kan'an persuaded him that that would only lead to a bloodbath that would tie down their forces in a costly and protracted conflict in Lebanon and possibly sound the death knell of the Syrian–Iranian alliance.[496]

Although fringe elements in the Syrian and Iranian regimes advocated advancing their respective agendas in Lebanon, even if ultimately at the expense of their nine-year alliance, the prevailing view in the ruling circles in Damascus and Tehran was that prudence dictated that a compromise would have to be reached to preserve their strategic ties. In essence, the Amal–Hezbollah crisis of May 1988 demonstrated beyond doubt that the Syrian–Iranian relationship had matured, and had evolved into a stable, durable, regional axis. It represented a major milestone, signifying the consolidation of the Tehran–Damascus nexus.

At this point, the stakes were quite high for Syria and Iran. Despite the critical situation in Lebanon, both players had to look at and evaluate their broader longer-term regional and international interests. Neither side wanted to precipitate a direct Syrian–Hezbollah confrontation.[497] With the USA and Maronites refusing to cooperate with Syria to establish a new order in Lebanon, and Amal's position in Beirut suddenly collapsing to expose the pro-Syrian movement's decrepitude and fragmented structure, Assad was left with few allies and no buffer through which to operate in Lebanon.[498] In fact, his room for political manoeuvre had become markedly restricted and he now needed Iranian cooperation more than ever to control events in his backyard. The Syrians knew that if vital national security interests were at stake, Hezbollah could probably be crushed if they committed at least 15,000 elite troops to such an undertaking.[499] On balance, however, Syrian interests militated against such a move.

Suppressing the pro-Iranian fundamentalists would not inevitably strengthen Assad's hand in Lebanon at this stage, and would definitely strain relations with Tehran. Also, Damascus knew that Tel Aviv and Washington would look favourably on a Syrian–Hezbollah confrontation in Beirut and elsewhere in Lebanon, for it would bog down their forces and bleed both sides.[500] In terms of regional power politics, the Syrians calculated that a rupture in their relations with Iran would leave them more vulnerable at a time when Iraq was beginning to reassert itself for the first time in more than six years and would seize any chance to mete out retribution for its Ba'thist rival's stalwart support of its Iranian foe.[501] Moreover, Assad realized that time was of the essence, and he had to act fast to end the intra-Shiite feuding before the Arab summit opened in Algiers on 7 June. He hoped to defuse the crisis to stabilize the situation in Lebanon and put relations with Iran back on a firm footing. The Syrian leader knew that his partnership with revolutionary Iran was a key asset in dealing with other Arab states and trying to gain their political and financial support. Assad was therefore keen to play his 'Iran card' in Algiers to obtain concessions and shore up his regional position.[502]

Tehran also wanted to preserve its strategic ties with Damascus. Though Lebanon had been important as a place to which to export the Islamic revolution, the clerical regime was conscious that, to date, its inroads there were only achieved through the Syrian government's active cooperation or acquiescence. Lebanon had become more important ideologically now that Tehran realized it could not topple the Iraqi regime; at a regional level, however, the alliance with Syria remained the most vital component in Iran's Arab policy. Overall, the Iranians believed that an accommodation would have to be reached with Syria over south Beirut that would leave Hezbollah either with some of its newly acquired gains or with its rights in southern Lebanon restored. This was preferable to adopting a rigid stance that could lead to an all-out Syrian–Hezbollah confrontation and possibly the latter's total eradication. Such an outcome would be a considerable waste of Iranian political, military and financial investment in the Shiite community since 1982 and would deal a devastating blow to Syrian–Iranian relations.[503] In sum, despite the importance Iran attached to its foothold in Lebanon as a way of ensuring the future of revolutionary Islam, its growing regional and international weakness and isolation meant that perpetuating the friendship with Syria figured first and foremost in the minds of Iran's leaders. Syria and Iran were both determined to maintain their strategic axis and present a common front, regardless of the obstacles they faced in resolving their differences. Hence, throughout the May crisis, as the two sides conducted long, arduous negotiations (marked by constant wrangling over details), for three weeks, they diligently pursued this painstaking process, almost on a daily basis and against a backdrop of the clashes and carnage only a few miles away.

As the fighting entered its second week, with casualties continuing to mount and Amal desperately trying to cling to its shrinking foothold in south Beirut, the quadripartite talks continued. Iran now began to soften its stance on the introduction of a Syrian force, but along with Hezbollah, argued that if a political solution could be reached, the deployment would be unnecessary. While Besharati and Kan'an continued to hope for a negotiated settlement, Berri insisted on immediate Syrian intervention to save the day for his battered militia. Besharati hinted that a Syrian entry would require 'further discussion', and 'preliminary steps' that would satisfy Iranian concerns.[504] In other words, Syria would have to meet certain Iranian demands and give specific guarantees on Hezbollah's future before a compromise could be reached. Syria and Hezbollah then both made conciliatory statements denying that the intra-Shiite feuding had caused a rift between them. In an interview with *Le Monde*, Kan'an praised Hezbollah's struggle against the Israeli occupation and emphasized that the fundamentalist movement was not an obstacle to Syrian efforts to find an equitable national solution in Lebanon.[505] Sheikh Fadlallah said Hezbollah would not resist Syria's entry into the suburbs if it received assurances it would not be disarmed. He stressed that the movement must continue to exist as a viable political and military force in the future[506] and pointed out that the Syrian army and Hezbollah coexisted peacefully in the Bekaa Valley.[507] A statement by Hezbollah reiterated that there was no dispute with the Syrians and 'the doors of the suburbs are not closed to them'.[508]

Intensive negotiations continued between the two allies as President Khamene'i sent another message about the crisis to his Syrian counterpart, which Besharati conveyed to Assad at a meeting on 19 May. It was apparent that something was afoot because Kan'an returned to Damascus that evening and deputy foreign minister Sheikholislam was sent to the Syrian capital the next day.[509] Sheikholislam met Assad on arrival and passed on another message from Khamene'i, while Besharati returned to Beirut to hold further talks with Amal and Hezbollah representatives. After discussions in Damascus, Kan'an and Sheikholislam proceeded to Beirut on 21 May where the quadripartite negotiations, which Besharati, Hammoud and the two militias' representatives also attended, now entered a new stage. The parties managed to forge a consensus on key issues and the ninth ceasefire went into effect.[510] As the fighting died down and Hezbollah temporarily eased some of the pressure on Amal, it became clear that Syria and Iran had agreed to allow Hezbollah to remain armed and continue to function as a political force in Lebanon, while the Western hostages would only be released if certain demands were met. However, as in the past, when the two sides seemed close to an understanding that would pave the way for the deployment of Syrian troops, Iran again raised the stakes by adding a new condition. At a six-hour meeting of the quadripartite committee on the night of 21/22 May in West Beirut, Iranian deputy foreign minister Sheikholislam – along with Hezbollah officials – insisted on creating a joint Syrian–Iranian security force for the southern suburbs, as opposed to only a Syrian peacekeeping contingent. Hammoud and Amal officials rejected the demand outright as being 'out of the question' and because the composition of the security force was non-negotiable.[511]

While Syria was keen to maintain its links with Iran, and cooperative ties with Hezbollah to help it control events in Lebanon, it was still determined to ensure that the lines it had drawn were not crossed and that if certain interests were at stake, other parties did not dictate terms in its backyard. Though willing to accommodate Iran and Hezbollah on key issues, it was unwavering in its insistence on being the ultimate arbiter in Lebanon. Vice-President Khaddam accurately articulated Syria's stance as follows:

> We greatly value our alliance with Iran, but our regional allies must respect our position ... our role [in Lebanon] is above all other considerations. In their operations, our allies should pay attention to our interests and to those of our [Lebanese] friends. The movements of some [Lebanese] have become a threat to the Syrian role. We shall not allow the creation of complications in the Lebanese arena.[512]

The quadripartite negotiations lasted two more days, but again reached deadlock because Syria refused to give ground on the composition of the peacekeeping force. Moreover, despite Syrian assurances that Hezbollah would be allowed to maintain a political presence in Beirut and its fighters keep their arms, there was no progress on the issue of allowing the pro-Iranian militia to resume guerrilla operations in the occupied south. On 24 May, the ceasefire broke down as Hezbollah resumed its assault. Iran calculated that further Hezbollah gains on the ground at Amal's expense would force Syria to rethink its position and grant Hezbollah's demands. As fierce fighting re-erupted, Amal, which now controlled about 10 per cent of Dahiya, lost more ground as it was pushed out of the Ghubaryh quarter and clung desperately to Chiyah, its only remaining foothold. Amal issued a statement acknowledging its losses in Ghubaryh and accusing Iranian Revolutionary Guards and PLO fighters of directing and assisting Hezbollah operations. The pro-Syrian militia was now in an extremely vulnerable and precarious position, controlling less than 10 per cent of the southern suburbs. Hezbollah forces now occupied seven of the eight quarters in south Beirut.[513]

With Amal on the verge of defeat in Beirut and the Iranian and Hezbollah position hardening, Assad decided to act swiftly and decisively to prevent a *débâcle* in Dahiya. The next day, 25 May, as Berri and Hoss were hurrying to Damascus to beg Khaddam to intervene militarily to end the violence, Assad received a high-ranking delegation of four Hezbollah representatives whom he had invited to his summer palace at the seaside resort of Latakia for direct talks. The mere fact that no Iranian representatives were present was a testimony to the growing independence of the Shiite movement. After three hours of negotiations, a five-point agreement was reached to let the Syrian army enter the suburbs while leaving Hezbollah assets intact. It stipulated that Syrian troops would be stationed throughout the suburbs, Hezbollah and Amal gunmen would be withdrawn from the streets, both Shiite groups could keep their political and information offices in the suburbs, Hezbollah fighters and Iranian Revolutionary Guards would withdraw to the Hayy Madi barracks, the pro-Iranians could only deploy fighters along the green line with East Beirut, and Lebanese gendarmes would replace Syrian troops in a few weeks.[514] Although not specified, there was an implicit understanding that Hezbollah would be allowed to resume guerrilla operations in the occupied south.[515]

The quadripartite committee in Beirut approved the deal the next day.[516] Syrian information minister Mohammed Salman officially announced the breakthrough. Iranian deputy foreign minister Sheikholislam expressed his pleasure that joint efforts with Syria to end the fighting had finally borne fruit, while Sheikh Fadlallah pointed out that the agreement had been 'crafted in a manner to save face for all parties concerned'.[517] Upon his return from Damascus on 26 May, a relieved Nabih Berri stated that the Syrians would start their deployment the very next day, Friday 27 May. Indeed, Ghazi Kan'an arrived in Beirut the same day to supervise the operation.

As news of the agreement spread, the fighting receded and militiamen from both sides disappeared from the streets. The Dahiya clashes had been some of the most vicious in Lebanon's 13-year civil war. In three weeks of gunbattles more than 300 people died, over 1000 were wounded and 400,000 civilians fled their homes in south Beirut.[518]

At 11 a.m. on the morning of 27 May, the first detachment of 800 Syrian soldiers backed by 100 Lebanese gendarmes entered the southern suburbs to enforce the ceasefire agreement, thus officially ending the 22-day Amal–Hezbollah confrontation. By now, all militiamen had disappeared from the streets. Consequently, the deployment went quite smoothly with local inhabitants warmly welcoming the peacekeeping forces.[519] At a Friday sermon in Beirut, Fadlallah called on his followers to cooperate fully to ensure the successful implementation of the new security plan, and the Iranian embassy issued a statement to the same effect.[520] The second and last phase of the deployment was completed by the second day as 3500 Syrian troops fanned out and took up positions throughout Dahiya without any major incident.[521] By 1 June, as a result of Iranian mediation, Hezbollah turned over 200 Amal prisoners it had captured during the fighting to the Syrian peacekeepers, and Amal freed 58 Hezbollah captives. Berri also promised to release all Lebanese and Palestinians in Amal custody.[522]

Assad had shown all sides his indispensability as final arbiter in Lebanese affairs.[523] In control of Dahiya in late May, Syria again tried to link its policy of limiting Hezbollah's power and securing the release of the foreign hostages to US diplomatic assistance in bridging the gap between Damascus's and East Beirut's positions on the presidential elections. As Syrian troops completed their deployment on 29 May and set up checkpoints around the pro-Iranian quarter of Bir al-Abed, the Syrian information minister indicated his government's disenchantment with Samir Geagea's Lebanese Forces and stressed that Syria would 'not tolerate the presence of parties that collaborate with Israel'.[524] He warned extremist elements on both sides of the fence that any party that tried to deepen divisions in Beirut would be 'removed from the arena'.[525] Assad's ability to cut a deal with Iran and Hezbollah that opened the way for Syrian control of the southern suburbs and simultaneously strengthened his hand in Beirut without endangering the Western hostages' lives, did not go unnoticed in Washington. In fact, the Reagan administration reacted positively and, following the superpower summit in Moscow, US secretary of state Shultz arrived in Damascus and held talks with Assad on 6 June. Although the Syrians and Americans both seemed to want the Lebanese army commander General Michel Aoun to succeed Amin

Gemayel as president, Geagea, who held enormous sway in the Maronite community, overshadowed all other contenders.[526]

Overall, the Amal–Hezbollah confrontation, and the crisis it precipitated, demonstrated the strength and maturity of the Syrian–Iranian relationship. Despite three long weeks of tortuous and painstaking negotiations marked by incessant wrangling over guarantees and conditions, and the prospect of a forceful Syrian entry to crush Hezbollah, neither Syria nor Iran seriously considered ending their alliance. Both sides continued to value their partnership and, moreover, displayed confidence in their ability to consult and negotiate continuously to find some common ground to resolve the crisis. Assad refrained from confronting Hezbollah not only for fear of sinking deeper into the Lebanese quagmire and jeopardizing the hostages' lives, but more importantly out of deference to Iran, whose influence and backing were needed to control events in Lebanon and contain Iraq at the regional level.[527] His conciliatory policy towards Hezbollah fed into his plans to secure its support for his future designs in Lebanon and to strengthen relations with Iran to thwart his regional rivals. Indeed, Assad's strategy paid off several months later, after the end of the Gulf War, when the struggle in Lebanon over Gemayel's succession intensified. The Syrians relied heavily on Iran and Hezbollah to crush Aoun's anti-Syrian rebellion in 1988/9, which received support from Iraq and Israel.

From Tehran's standpoint, despite its determination to boost its position in Lebanon, there was never any doubt that if it had to choose between this and the axis with Syria, it would abandon the former. Iran's support for Hezbollah during the crisis was a calculated move to enhance its position in the Levant and safeguard its proxy's future. The clerical regime never seriously contemplated severing its links with Damascus. With Iraq on the ascendant in the Gulf, and the Algiers summit approaching, Iran agreed to the Syrian intervention and Hezbollah relinquishing control of Dahiya as part of an overall understanding that guaranteed its continued influence in Lebanon and left Hezbollah's assets untouched. Iran needed Syria and was in no mind to challenge it in its own backyard.[528]

Diplomatic moves and the end of the Persian Gulf war

After the resolution of the Amal–Hezbollah confrontation in Lebanon, the Syrians prepared to take part in the Algiers summit to show their support for the Palestinian *intifada* (the main item on the agenda). At the same time, amid reports in the Western and Arab

news media during the May crisis that the Syrian–Iranian alliance was
at breaking point, some members of the pro-Iraq camp, most notably
Saudi Arabia and Kuwait, reckoned that the opportune moment had
come to try once more to prise Syria and Iran apart. Indeed, at the
heat of the May crisis, there had been reports that Hafez Assad and
King Fahd had spoken on the telephone on several occasions.[529]
Given Riyadh's decision to sever diplomatic links with Iran in late
April, intensify its propaganda war against Tehran and facilitate Iraqi
aerial attacks on Iranian assets in the Gulf, contacts between Syrian
and Saudi leaders had aroused suspicions that something was afoot.
Against a backdrop of what many had perceived as the most severe
crisis in Syrian–Iranian relations, Syria's political isolation in the Arab
world, Iran's inability to meet the combined US–Iraqi challenge in the
Persian Gulf and Iraq's string of battlefield successes in the land war,
many surmised that the Damascus–Tehran axis could collapse with
an appropriate push. However, this was not to be the case.

That Syria and Iran were able to manage the May crisis through
protracted negotiations over a three-week period and to reach a
mutually acceptable arrangement to end the Amal–Hezbollah clashes
signified that the alliance had matured and become consolidated.
Syria needed Iran to control events in Lebanon and, despite the
sudden resurgence of Iraqi power in the Gulf, a *rapprochement* with
Baghdad was not something that Damascus seriously entertained.
Furthermore, Syria and Iran had concluded another one-year oil
agreement in late April in which Damascus would continue to receive
a million tons of Iranian crude free of charge, which translated into
20,000 barrels a day.[530] It is important to note that by this stage, the
significance of Iranian oil deliveries was beginning to recede for
Damascus and no longer served as a bone of contention between the
allies. With the Dayr al-Zawr oilfields gradually coming on stream,
Syria was achieving self-sufficiency for its domestic oil requirements
during 1988 and was expected to have a comfortable surplus by
1989.[531] Consequently, foreign oil supplies – whether from Iran or
elsewhere – were no longer a major long-term consideration in Syrian
foreign policy, so the oil factor was not a prominent element in
Assad's calculations to maintain cooperative links with Khomeini's
Iran. Common political and strategic objectives and not economic or
financial considerations now maintained the alliance. Given the
relatively better economic outlook for Syria, the political importance
of the Palestinian *intifada* in the Arab world and the reduction of the
Iranian threat in the Gulf, the Syrian leader believed that he had more

room for manoeuvre at the upcoming Algiers summit and decided to attend personally to exploit the evolving regional situation.

In sharp contrast to the Amman summit, where the Gulf War had been the main topic on the agenda, when the Algiers meeting was convened seven months later, the eruption of the Palestinian uprising and Iraq's ability to reverse the situation and score notable gains in the Gulf theatre meant that the focus was shifting back to the Arab–Israeli arena. The Palestinian–Israeli conflict would be the most important item on the conference agenda. As a result, Assad was in a less precarious position and could make a convincing case for more Arab assistance in view of his stalwart opposition to Israeli policies in the Levant. Although the summit did not mark a major turning point in inter-Arab politics, as Amman had done with Egypt's *de facto* re-entry into the Arab fold, it was important symbolically, though not devoid of controversy. At the four-day summit, heads of state represented 18 of the Arab League's 21 members. Only the leaders of Somalia, Oman and Iraq failed to attend. Saddam Hussein sent Taha Yasin Ramadan in his stead, for he was still 'needed in the confrontation theater'.[532]

Because of Palestine's centrality on this occasion and Arafat's assertiveness, Hafez Assad and King Hussein avoided open confrontation with the PLO chairman. While the conference's first two closed sessions dealt with the Palestinian uprising, in the third session, on 9 June, developments in the Gulf region were also discussed. The Iraqi delegation tried to corner the Syrians, with Ramadan reiterating Iraq's dissatisfaction with Syria's stance and declaring that 'Iranian aggression is parallel to the Zionist aggression, is similar to it, and is its partner'.[533] As in the past, the Iraqis tried to portray the war as a pan-Arab conflict against Iran and, in the text of the final communiqué, moved for the inclusion of passages strongly critical of Iran. Syria, along with Algeria and Libya, tried to thwart these efforts. During the session, Assad objected to any anti-Iranian amendments, a move Ramadan later described as 'impudent'. However, after a bilateral meeting between the Syrian leader and King Fahd and further deliberations involving Assad and a number of other Gulf heads of state, Assad assented to their requests to go along with the passage of a final communiqué that condemned Iranian conduct and condoned Iraq's recovery of occupied territories in the Gulf War. Moreover, there were indications that the GCC states provided financial inducements for Syria's agreement as a frontline state against Israel. Some reports stated that Damascus was promised an aid package totalling $250 million, while others claimed that each donor would decide how much to contribute on its own. In the end, despite objections to the wording of the final statement, the Syrians neither expressed any formal reservations nor opposed its passage. The communiqué criticized Iran's 'intransigence' for continuing the hostilities, threatening the Gulf states, occupying Arab land and refusing to comply with UN Resolution 598. It went on to express 'full solidarity' with Iraq for its adherence to pan-Arab responsibilities, including its defence of 'pan-Arab security and Arab land'. The participants also reaffirmed their support for Saudi Arabia and Kuwait to take action to defend themselves against Iranian subversion.[534]

After the Algiers summit, Syria welcomed renewed Arab attention to the Arab–Israeli conflict and more support for the frontline states. It also emphasized that Syria had disagreed with the anti-Iranian sections of the final statement. Despite Damascus having gone along with the Arab League's condemnation of Tehran, it did not deviate from its previous policy of maintaining and expanding cooperative links with its non-Arab ally. Both in Amman and Algiers, Syria did not try to swim against the strong anti-Iranian current and paid lip service to the pro-Iraqi bloc by endorsing its position, but it refused to abandon its strategic relationship with Iran. In early July, the Emir of Kuwait sent his foreign minister, Sheikh Sabah al-Ahmed al-Jabir, to Baghdad and Damascus to hold talks with the leaders of both states in a bid to mend the Syrian–Iraqi rift, but, like previous mediation efforts, this initiative failed to bear fruit.

Two developments in July persuaded the entire Iranian leadership, including Khomeini, to sue for peace. On 3 July, the US navy cruiser USS *Vincennes*, operating near the Straits of Hormuz, entered Iranian territorial waters and challenged two Iranian gunboats. The *Vincennes* fired on them and, in the ensuing engagement, shot down a commercial airliner, Iran Air 655 (on a regular scheduled flight from Bandar Abbas to Dubai), mistaking it for an Iranian F-14 warplane. When two missiles fired from the US vessel struck the aircraft, 290 passengers and crew died.[535] While Washington expressed regret at the tragic incident, it defended its policy in the Gulf. Ronald Reagan described the event as an 'understandable accident' and argued that the USS *Vincennes* had acted in self-defence while under attack.[536] Washington immediately engaged in an extensive disinformation campaign to conceal the truth about the incident.[537]

While Tehran lashed out at Washington, angrily accusing it of 'premeditated murder', the incident came as a profound shock to the clerical regime, for it highlighted the formidable nature of the forces arrayed against it.[538] Furthermore, the mildness of the international reaction to the shooting down of the aeroplane was no doubt a bitter disappointment, for it exposed Iran's isolation and weakness. The Arab world's reaction was for the most part neutral, or critical of Iran. Only Syria and Libya harshly condemned the US government. Damascus called it a 'criminal act' and one of the 'ugliest forms of terrorism'. It expressed its condolences and solidarity with the Iranian government and families of the victims.[539]

The destruction of Iran Air 655, coupled with Iraq's military victories on land and US–Iraqi efforts to neutralize Iranian power in the Gulf, compounded the sense of helplessness already felt in Tehran. Iraq kept up the pressure in the ground war throughout the heightened tensions in the Gulf. On 12 July, within three weeks of the victory in the Majnoon islands, the Iraqi army launched a major offensive northeast of Basra near the Amarah oilfields to retake the last significant Iranian-held pockets of territory. The Iraqis quickly overpowered the Iranian defenders. In addition to recovering their territory, the Iraqis pushed into Iran and temporarily occupied 1500 square miles.[540] The next day, Baghdad threatened to invade Iran again unless it gave up its remaining footholds in Iraqi Kurdistan.

By now, Iran had lost virtually all the gains it had made in Iraq since 1984. With the loss of much of its heavy equipment in the recent fighting, Iranian morale was at an all time low. On 14 July, Tehran announced it would oblige and pull its forces back behind the international frontier. Three days later, Ayatollah Khomeini convened an extraordinary meeting of 40 senior political and military officials to discuss the future of the war. After eight hours of deliberations, the majority had convinced him and the remaining hawks that victory could not be attained on the battlefield and that Iran had no choice but to end the eight-year conflict.[541] The next day, 18 July, Ali Khamene'i sent a letter to UN secretary-general Perez de Cuellar formally accepting Resolution 598. In an address to the nation on 20 July, Khomeini, an uncompromising foe of Saddam Hussein and the Iraqi Ba'thist regime, indicated that the decision to end the war had been a difficult one – 'more deadly than drinking poison'. He admitted having finally accepted his military advisers' advice.[542]

Syria was surprised when Iran accepted Resolution 598, for it had been neither consulted nor informed prior to Iran's announcement on 18 July.[543] Nonetheless, Damascus welcomed Tehran's decision to end hostilities with Baghdad and again condemned its Ba'thist rival for having started the war in the first place.[544] Iran's sudden acceptance of a ceasefire caught Iraq off guard, although only a day earlier, in a speech commemorating the twentieth anniversary of the Iraqi Ba'th Party's seizure of power, Saddam Hussein predicted 'the enemy's total collapse this year'. In his address, he had expressed gratitude for the pan-Arab support he had received at the Amman and Algiers summits and condemned Syria's 'abominable crimes' in Lebanon and betrayal of 'Arab solidarity'.[545] Sensing that Iran was at its weakest and in a most vulnerable state, Iraq decided to bolster its negotiating position by invading it and seizing territory. It launched a series of offensives on the central and southern fronts between 22 and 29 July, capturing huge swathes of territory, men and *matériel*. Iran fought back desperately and recouped some of its losses in the closing days of July and early August. Ironically, Iran now appealed to the Security Council for support, with Iraq showing contempt for the UN body by ignoring repeated calls to end the fighting and withdraw its forces.

Throughout this period, Syria denounced Iraqi actions. It argued that Baghdad's refusal to sue for peace vindicated its stance and proved that the Iraqi regime was determined to 'wreak havoc' in the Gulf and divert Arab attention way from the Arab–Israeli theatre.[546] Under strong international pressure, Saddam Hussein finally accepted a ceasefire on 6 August. A UN observer force of 350 troops was hastily assembled and sent to the region. The UN Security Council met subsequently and decided that the ceasefire would officially come into effect on 20 August, with Iran and Iraq agreeing to start peace negotiations under UN auspices in Geneva on 25 August.[547]

As Iran and Iraq prepared for peace talks immediately after the Gulf War, there was heightened diplomatic activity in the region on both sides. A week after Iraq agreed to cease hostilities, Velayati left for Damascus and Tripoli to inform their leaders about recent developments and hold consultations with them. He first travelled to Syria to brief Assad and al-Shara on implementing UN Resolution 598 and discuss future bilateral cooperation in the emerging regional environment. Assad reportedly congratulated Velayati on deciding to end the war, describing it as an opportunity to stabilize the situation and improve their relations. In mid-August, King Hussein visited Baghdad with a high-level military delegation to congratulate Saddam Hussein on his triumph against Iran. The Jordanian monarch was presented with huge quantities of US and British-built tanks and armoured vehicles captured from the Iranians as a token of appreciation for his consistent support of Iraq during the war. He called Iraq's victory a 'brilliant chapter in modern Arab history'.[548]

Alongside the diplomatic moves on each side, there was an intensification of propaganda in some quarters, most notably with Baghdad
stepping up its attacks on Syria. In an interview with Egypt's *Al-
Akhbar* on 11 August, Iraqi deputy premier Ramadan commended
Egypt for its support during the war and claimed that Egyptian–Iraqi
relations served as a model for fraternal ties among Arab states. He
contrasted Cairo favourably against Damascus, which he accused of
betraying the aims and aspirations of the Arab nation by assisting
Iran, destroying Lebanon and massacring Palestinians. Ramadan
advocated Arab steadfastness against what he called Syria's treachery.
Even before the peace talks between Iran and Iraq had got underway,
Baghdad was signalling its determination to punish Syria for its
policies during the Gulf War. For example, an editorial on 14 August
in the Iraqi Ba'th Party's daily *Al-Thawrah* warned that the Syrian
regime would soon face the most difficult stage in its history now that
Iraq had emerged victorious from its 'holy defensive war'. It emphasized that Assad would pay dearly for his treasonous collaboration
with the Khomeinist and Zionist enemies of the Arabs.

Damascus was equally harsh in its ripostes. It continued to stress
how much Baghdad had harmed the Arab cause by initiating the Gulf
conflict and by trying to extend the hostilities into an Arab–Persian
conflict, thus deflecting attention away from the Palestinian issue.
With the cessation of hostilities, Syria now urged other Arab states to
follow its example by deepening Arab–Iranian cooperation to restore
unity and confront the 'common enemy'. The Syrian media predicted
that Saddam Hussein would find it difficult to maintain power under
peaceful conditions so he would manufacture crises to oppress the
Iraqi people and, to highlight the fabricated Arab–Iranian cleavage, he
would block a satisfactory resolution of its outstanding problems with
Iran. They intimated that Saddam Hussein's fallacy would ultimately
confirm what Syria had maintained all along since 1979, that 'the
Islamic Republic of Iran is a supporter of the Arab cause and not an
enemy of the Arabs.'[549]

Another sign of the continuing Syrian–Iraqi rift was the visit of a
high-level Iraqi opposition delegation to Damascus in late August,
composed of senior representatives from the ICP, Socialist Party of
Kurdistan, PUK and KDP. This was at a time when the Iraqi army had
begun a systematic campaign to crush resistance in the Kurdish
north, now that the guns had fallen silent on the Iranian front. It was
clear that, despite the end of the Iran–Iraq hostilities and the beginning of peace negotiations, the gulf between Baghdad and Damascus

remained as wide as ever. It looked as if the rivalry between the two Ba'thist regimes would continue unabated. Meanwhile, Iran's military weakness and diplomatic isolation, combined with the powerful Washington and Riyadh-backed Egyptian–Jordanian–Iraqi axis and the cooling of Syrian–Soviet relations, raised questions in the minds of many about the future viability of the Syrian–Iranian alliance. Many observers concluded that as Tehran turned inward to put its own house in order, Assad would have to reorder his strategic priorities and reformulate his foreign policy because of changing balances of power on both the regional and international stage.

Conclusion

By the summer of 1988, at the end of the third phase in the evolution of the Syrian–Iranian axis, the partnership between the two sides had become consolidated. It had survived numerous intra-alliance tensions and serious disputes between 1985 and 1988. The inherent wish of both regimes to perpetuate their special relationship was seen in their common ability always to consult one another, particularly when their interests diverged, and reach mutually agreeable arrangements. Their ability to withstand serious setbacks, find joint solutions and compromise on important issues in the Levant and Persian Gulf at an extremely turbulent time in Lebanese and Gulf politics, spanning more than three years, proved that the Tehran–Damascus axis had matured and become institutionalized. This was demonstrated in their successful handling of the February 1987 and May 1988 crises in Lebanon, and Syria's steadfast support for Iran in the aftermath of the Mecca incident and the Amman and Algiers summits.

While going through the motions of feigning solidarity with mainstream Arab states at the two Arab League conferences, Assad still supported his Iranian ally at a time when it was losing the initiative in the Gulf and becoming increasingly isolated in the Middle East and rest of the world. Furthermore, with Syria having boosted its oil production enough by 1988 to meet its domestic needs, the importance of Iranian oil shipments decreased, with only political and strategic considerations now paramount in maintaining close links with Iran. Damascus calculated that keeping Tehran on side would give it a better chance of controlling the volatile situation in Lebanon after the Israeli retreat in 1985 when the Maronites opposed Syrian policy, and Hezbollah was gaining prominence. Furthermore, Iran's war effort kept Iraq in check and neutralized Baghdad's potential to create problems for Syria in Lebanon or elsewhere. The Gulf War also gave Syrian foreign policy a new role. It could mediate between Iran and the GCC states to contain the hostilities, thereby bolstering its power and influence and ability to acquire financial and material benefits from both sides in return. Finally, as Gorbachev signalled his disapproval at Assad's quest to achieve 'strategic parity' with Israel, reduced arms supplies to Syria and began to diversify his relations in the Middle East by repairing relations with Israel and some of Syria's Arab rivals, the Syrian leader realized that he could no longer count on his superpower patron's support; he had to rely more on his own resources and those of his allies in the region, namely Iran and the Lebanese Shiites.

From revolutionary Iran's vantage point, the alliance with Syria was critical in several respects. In ideological terms, an alliance with the only true confrontation state against Israel, which was not only a key player in the Arab world, but also the cradle of modern Arab nationalism, allowed it to dismiss the pro-Iraqi propaganda that depicted Iran as an enemy of the Arab nation and the Gulf War as an Arab–Persian conflict. In practical terms, Iran's continued ability to stop Iraqi oil exports from the Gulf and to intercept shipping bound for its foe, along with Syria's refusal to reopen the IPC pipelines to the Mediterranean, served as a 'Syrian–Iranian pincer' to maintain a partial economic stranglehold on Iraq. This neatly fed into Iran's strategy of draining and paralysing Iraq economically and gradually bringing it to its knees through a war of attrition. Syria also gave Iran an important gateway into Lebanon. The activities it enabled Iran to carry out among the Shiite community were of both political and ideological value to the clerical regime. Syrian cooperation had allowed Iran to gain a large following among the Shiites and to mobilize them to resist the Israelis and their Lebanese allies. Despite intermittent squabbling with Damascus over the future of Lebanon from 1985 onwards, Tehran recognized that Assad was the final arbiter in Lebanon and that it would not serve Iran's long-term political interests to challenge him in his own backyard. In the final analysis, Syrian interests took precedence in Lebanon just as Iran's did in the Gulf and, even if Iran were unable to replicate its theocratic model in Lebanon, a modest foothold there (right at the doorsteps of the 'Zionist entity') was better than none. Between 1985 and 1988 the two allies were able to delineate the parameters of their cooperation, identify their vital interests and forge understandings on how to perpetuate their partnership for many years to come.

Chapter 4

Into the Twenty-first Century: The Syrian–Iranian Nexus Endures

In the two-year period between the cessation of the Gulf hostilities and the Iraqi invasion of Kuwait (August 1988 to August 1990), many observers predicted the imminent demise of the Syrian–Iranian alliance. However, the partnership still endures at the start of the twenty-first century. Why did the strategic relationship between Damascus and Tehran continue despite their inability to bring Saddam Hussein to his knees and to stabilize the situation in Lebanon by 1988? There were good reasons for the Syrian and Iranian regimes to continue their special relationship during the interwar years between the two Gulf conflicts and in the post cold-war era.

First and foremost, incessant speculation that the days of the Syrian–Iranian nexus were numbered proved unfounded: many analysts had failed to recognize that the two allies' continual consultations and ability to compromise on key issues, build mutual trust and maintain cooperative links during the troubled years of 1985–88 had consolidated the alliance. Their mutual ability over time to assess the evolving regional situation, to recognize the limits of their power and to set feasible goals lent stability to the alliance. Both Damascus and Tehran also understood that their activities in the other's sphere of influence had to be within certain limits and subject to the other's approval, particularly if vital interests were at stake.[1] Second, the environment immediately after the first Gulf War was such that they needed to preserve their ties to boost their regional positions and alleviate their security concerns. Indeed, two of the most important reasons to continue the Syrian–Iranian alliance during 1988–90 were the resurgence of Iraqi power and influence in the Middle East and the institutionalization of the pro-Iraqi Arab alliance that had gradually emerged during the 1980s through the formal creation of the ACC in February 1989.

As early as 1985, one Middle East scholar had predicted that 'even if the Iran–Iraq war were to end, so long as the present leadership remains in power in Iraq, Syria and Iran will in all likelihood cooperate to keep its influence in check.'[2] Indeed, not only had the Iraqi Ba'thist regime survived the eight-year war, but its massive foreign-assisted military expansion programme had enabled it to repulse Iranian offensives for six consecutive years and to regain the upper hand in the closing months of the conflict, thereby bolstering its power and prestige in the Arab world. By 1988, Iraq's well-equipped and battle-hardened army had become one of the five largest military establishments in the world. In addition, Iran's weakness and Syria's isolation magnified Iraq's political power and made it the prime contender for leadership of the Arab world. The regional situation instilled renewed confidence in Saddam Hussein, who felt flush with a sense of victory over Khomeini's Iran and now had a free hand to pursue an activist foreign policy and strike at his foes, most notably Assad's Syria.[3]

For two years before the Kuwaiti crisis, Iraq had been demonstrating its clear intention to play a pivotal role in the Arab world by providing military aid to Mauritania in its conflict with Senegal, by encouraging the two Yemens to unite, by backing the Sudanese Islamist regime's struggle against rebels in the south, and by becoming more outspoken and confrontational on issues to do with the Arab–Israeli conflict.[4] From the standpoint of Syria and Iran, however, two manifestations of Iraq's growing assertiveness in the winter of 1988/9 reinforced their resolve to continue their liaison. The deadlock over Amin Gemayel's succession, following the expiry of his term as president in Lebanon, had sparked a major political crisis, prompting armed forces commander General Michel Aoun to step into the political vacuum and challenge Syrian hegemony in that country. The confrontation between Syria and Christian Lebanese forces loyal to Aoun gave Baghdad an irresistible opportunity to punish Damascus on its very own doorstep for pursuing pro-Iranian policies during the Gulf conflict. So, in autumn 1988, Iraq began to deliver arms to anti-Syrian forces in Lebanon.[5] By 1989, when the conflict between Assad and Aoun had escalated, Baghdad used every available opportunity to thwart Syrian efforts to oust Aoun and regain control of the situation. Substantial quantities of weapons were sent to Aoun loyalists via Egypt and Jordan and, on the diplomatic front, the Iraqis tried to rally Arab support against the Syrian military presence in Lebanon and to seek condemnation of Assad's actions.[6]

No longer able to challenge Iraqi power effectively in the Persian Gulf, after the ceasefire, Iran turned inwards to revive its energies and focus on domestic reconstruction. Nonetheless, to restore unity to Shiite movements like Hezbollah and Amal and to mobilize them as part of a broad-based, pro-Syrian coalition that would eventually prevail over Aoun's supporters, in the latter part of 1989, Iran closely coordinated its policies in Lebanon with Syria. Besides Iraq's meddling in Lebanon, another worrying development for Iran and Syria only six months after hostilities in the Gulf had ended was the formation of an Arab alliance (the ACC) composed of Egypt, Jordan, Iraq and North Yemen. In essence, the ACC formalized the main Arab axis that had gradually emerged during the 1980s to contain Syrian–Iranian power in the region and, by this stage, it had undoubtedly become the dominant Arab political configuration. This new alliance not only marginalized Syria and Iran further, but it also caused deep consternation among some of Iraq's traditional Arab backers like Saudi Arabia, which rushed to conclude a non-aggression pact with Saddam Hussein in March 1989.[7] Syria was now the only key Arab state left out of the three existing alignments in the Arab world – the ACC, GCC and AMU.[8] Syria's status as an outcast in Arab politics, coupled with a gradual cooling of Syrian–Soviet relations, reinforced the logic of an alliance with Iran, which gave it valuable help in impeding Iraqi interference in Lebanon. Moreover, Syrian–Iranian cooperation against Aoun bore fruit that same year.[9]

Although Syria's participation in the Saudi-sponsored Taif accords in October 1989, which restricted Iranian access to Lebanon, and the Syrian–Egyptian *rapprochement* in the winter of 1989/90 had disenchanted Iran, there was no major shift in their bilateral relationship.[10] Saddam Hussein's growing boldness and hubris had begun to cause varying degrees of concern among some of his Arab supporters and, with the passage of time, this increased Syria's room for political manoeuvre.[11] When Damascus mended fences with Riyadh and Cairo in the year before the Kuwait crisis, the clerical regime in Iran could not do likewise because it did not have diplomatic relations with those countries. The stark reality was that, even had it wanted to, Tehran could not have found a viable alternative to its alliance with Damascus because most Arab governments had severed links with the Islamic Republic in the 1980s.[12]

The Kuwait crisis changed the entire political equation in the Middle East overnight and gave Syria and Iran opportunities to capitalize on the new situation and recoup their positions. Iraq's invasion and occupation of another Arab country vindicated Assad for having helped Iran during the eight-year war.[13] With the marked improvement in Syria's ability to control the situation in Lebanon, it subsequently opted to join the international coalition against Iraq, judging that it would help it both to neutralize Saddam Hussein and extract concessions from the Gulf Arabs and USA. Iran, with Khamene'i and Rafsanjani now in charge, was still weak militarily and decided to stay clear of the fray. However, its decision to remain neutral did not mean that it intended to be an idle bystander. Far from it, Tehran believed that by mediating between the two sides, it could gain leverage over them and exploit subsequent events. In fact, its ability in the initial phase of the crisis to thaw relations with Baghdad by breaking the two-year deadlock in the peace negotiations and by obtaining significant concessions from its foe alarmed the anti-Iraq camp, prompting Assad in September 1990 to undertake his first state visit to Iran since the 1979 revolution to seek clarification and gain assurances that Iran would not side with Iraq in the event of war. Again, analysts predicted the demise of the Syrian–Iranian alliance but, although they adopted divergent positions, the Kuwait crisis did not destroy the partnership. In fact, the two allies took a further step towards institutionalizing their bilateral relationship in November 1990 when they set up a Syrian–Iranian higher cooperation committee, which their vice-presidents and foreign ministers chaired. Its main purposes were to meet at regular intervals for consultations and to strengthen their cooperative links.[14]

Throughout the crisis, Iran held to the UN-imposed embargo on Iraq and maintained its neutrality. The fateful events of 1990/1 divided the Arab world. Iraq's annexation of Kuwait and the subsequent war that pitted Arabs against Arabs dealt a significant blow to Arab nationalism and to lingering notions of pan-Arab solidarity.[15] Such developments, coupled with the GCC's preference for a Western rather than Arab military presence in postwar Gulf security arrangements, made Assad's policy of perpetuating his alliance with non-Arab Iran acceptable in Arab political circles. This new regional environment of the 1990s was a stark contrast to that of the previous decade when backing a non-Arab actor against an Arab one was considered heresy in mainstream Arab politics.

Though the Syrian–Iranian alliance experienced a brief hiccup just after the second Gulf War when the prospect of a permanent deployment of Egyptian and Syrian troops in the Persian Gulf deeply alarmed Iran, tensions rapidly eased once it became apparent that the

GCC states preferred a continued US military presence in the area instead. In general, the conflict and its outcome were mixed blessings for the Syrian–Iranian axis. Both Damascus and Tehran took advantage of Iraq's aggression to mend fences with key Arab and Western governments and to break out of their regional and international isolation. They also derived considerable satisfaction from Saddam Hussein's military machine being cut down to size and from his regime becoming politically isolated for the remainder of the 1990s. The war reinforced Syrian and Iranian arguments that Ba'thist Iraq had been a revisionist power all along and had been the aggressor in both Gulf conflicts. Despite Iraq's removal from the immediate picture and the Bush administration's promise to craft an Arab–Israeli peace, the high-profile presence of US forces in the Gulf and subsequent failure of the incoming Clinton administration to break the impasse in the Syrian–Israeli peace process dashed expectations in Damascus and Tehran that they could benefit from the emerging 'new world order'. Assad later lamented that the 'main winners have been the Arabs' enemies', cautioning that the new environment was detrimental to Arab and Syrian interests.[16]

The collapse of the USSR meant that Washington was now virtually unassailable in the Middle East, both in the Persian Gulf and in the Arab–Israeli theatre. In the Gulf, it was free to establish a Pax Americana by isolating Iraq and Iran, maintaining large numbers of troops in the area and transferring billions of dollars worth of military equipment to the GCC states. In the Levant, Washington failed to end the Arab–Israeli conflict through its incapacity to resolve any outstanding issues, including the return of the Golan Heights to Syria. Despite wrapping up the 1994 Jordanian–Israeli peace treaty, progress on the Syrian or even Palestinian tracks of the peace process remained elusive. During its first term in office, the Clinton administration went to considerable lengths to try to prise Syria and Iran apart with its 'dual containment' policy in the Gulf, and by dispatching secretary of state Warren Christopher to Damascus more than 20 times between 1993 and 1997 to persuade Assad to distance himself from Iran and to sign a peace agreement with Israel.

Overall, Washington's pro-Israeli stance in the Arab–Israeli negotiations, its support for the emergence of a Turkish–Israeli alliance after 1996 to isolate Iran and cow Syria into submission, and its willingness to exploit Iran–Gulf Arab differences to justify its military presence and huge arms sales to its regional allies reinvigorated Syrian–Iranian cooperation in the period after the cold war.

Throughout the 1990s, Ba'thist Syria and Islamist Iran continued to collaborate and assist one another in various ways, both politically and militarily. On several occasions, Syria mediated between Iran and the Gulf states over differences that arose, most notably in the dispute with the UAE over Abu Musa and the Tunb islands after 1992 and in the row with Bahrain in 1995.[17] As in the past, Syria's strategy was to try to defuse Arab–Iranian tensions in the Gulf and prevent the USA exploiting volatile conditions to advance its own agenda. From Tehran's standpoint, Syrian intercession and political mediation was preferable in every sense to further Western intervention.[18]

In a similar vein, Iran and Hezbollah coordinated their moves with Syria in the early 1990s to restore stability and order in Lebanon, resolve the Western hostage issue and ensure that Israel paid a price for its continued occupation of the self-declared security zone. Hezbollah managed to become a viable political party in its own right by modifying its political platform and conforming to the realities on the ground. By toning down its Islamist rhetoric and recognizing the sectarian diversity of the country, it demonstrated its ability to operate within Lebanon's secular framework after 1992.[19] At the same time, with Syrian and Iranian backing, Hezbollah's increasingly effective guerrilla campaign throughout the 1990s against the IDF and SLA finally prompted Israeli prime minister Ehud Barak to announce that Israeli forces would be pulled out of southern Lebanon by July 2000. However, what was supposed to be an orderly, phased withdrawal over a two-month period turned into a rout in mid-May. The SLA collapsed and, by 24 May 2000, the IDF had hastily withdrawn. After many years of Syrian–Iranian cooperation, Lebanese resistance had finally borne fruit. It was the first time that Israel had given up territory and withdrawn to its international frontiers without any prior political agreement.

Since Iran and Syria had no reliable modern weaponry suppliers in the 1980s – the USA had cut off the flow of arms to Iran after the 1979 revolution and Gorbachev had significantly scaled back military aid to Assad – the two allies tried to diversify their sources of military hardware and develop indigenous arms industries. Unable to procure high-tech weaponry from the USA or western Europe, during the 1990s, the two relied primarily on the Russian Federation, Ukraine, China and North Korea for arms. Besides purchasing modern weaponry, Syria and Iran enlisted the support of these states to help them build arms factories and gain the necessary expertise to upgrade their weapons and develop new ones. Given the major impact of surface-to-surface missiles in the two Gulf conflicts, Iran and Syria focused most on acquiring the necessary technology and know-how to develop their own ballistic missile capability. Besides buying missiles from Russia, China and North Korea, they sought their assistance to design new ones. It is believed that as early as September 1991, during a visit to Tehran by Syrian chief of staff Hikmat Shihabi, a secret agreement was concluded for joint production of surface-to-surface missiles.[20] The two allies reportedly collaborated in developing a cruise missile, while Iran and North Korea participated in establishing production facilities for the manufacture of a missile similar to the Soviet-model Scud in Aleppo and Hama.[21] The primary motive for such programmes seems to have been to develop their own deterrent capability in the light of Iraq's willingness to use non-conventional weapons in two recent wars and Israel's overwhelming military superiority. Joint and independent development of ballistic missiles and possibly other non-conventional weapons were intended to diversify their capabilities and correct what Tehran and Damascus perceived as the major military imbalance in the region favouring their adversaries.

On the regional and international level, both Tehran and Damascus saw the continuation of their partnership as a useful way of maximizing their autonomy, keeping their local adversaries in check, diluting foreign (particularly US) power and influence in the Middle East and asserting themselves in their respective spheres of influence. While Syria had more room for manoeuvre than Iran in the regional and Arab state system, it also recognized the limits of the revived 'Arab triangle' (its alignment with Egypt and Saudi Arabia) in the post cold-war era. Both these Arab countries remained close political allies of the USA and were heavily dependent on it for their military and security requirements. Because they relied on US goodwill, Damascus recognized that it could not effectively use its contacts with Cairo and Riyadh to persuade Washington to modify its policies in the Arab–Israeli peace process to take Syrian interests and concerns more into account.[22] Hence, the alliance with Iran – a country with the capacity to neutralize Iraqi power and wield considerable influence in the Gulf and Lebanon – remained one of Syria's primary trump cards in the diplomatic tug-of-war to attain its objectives.

In the post-9/11 environment, George W. Bush's neo-conservative policies and adventurism in the Middle East have caused a great deal of consternation among ruling circles in Tehran and Damascus. Iran and Syria viewed the overthrow of Saddam Hussein's regime by US-led forces in April 2003 with ambivalence. On the one hand, both states welcomed the toppling of their long-time foe. On the other hand, the speed of the military victory in Iraq initially raised fears that they could become the next targets in the US-led 'war on terror'. However, once it became clear that the USA faced major difficulties and was becoming bogged down in the Iraqi quagmire, there was a degree of relief in Tehran and Damascus. Nonetheless, the two allies are still concerned about the prominent US military presence in Iraq and the possibility of encirclement by it and its allies. Iran has to contend not only with the US fifth fleet in the Persian Gulf and the presence of US troops in Afghanistan, but now also with US forces in Iraq. Similarly, Syria sees itself in a pincer between Israel and a US-occupied Iraq.

Since the beginning of the US occupation of Iraq, Syria and Iran have intensified their contacts and tried to coordinate their policies to meet the new challenge. High-level exchanges between the two allies have increased. In July 2004, Syrian President Bashar Assad made his third state visit to Iran since coming to power in 2000, while his Iranian counterpart Mohammad Khatami travelled to Syria three months later. US policy in the Middle East and the situation in Iraq were high on the agenda of their bilateral talks. More recently, while on a visit to Iran in February 2005, the Syrian prime minister Mohammed Naji al-Utri declared that the two countries were presenting a 'united front' against the challenges they faced in the region. There is little doubt that even if it is not official Iranian policy, at least some factions of the Tehran regime are giving material and financial support to the radical Iraqi Shiite cleric Muqtada al-Sadr and his followers in a bid to tie down the US-led coalition forces in Baghdad and southern Iraq. Moreover, even if Bashar Assad's government is no longer aiding and abetting the passage of Sunni Arab and Muslim volunteers from Syria to Iraq (as it did prior to and during the US-led invasion in 2003), it is at the very least looking at such movements with benign neglect. Both Washington and the Iraqi authorities have in the past accused Syria and Iran of facilitating the flow of foreign fighters into Iraq. The Bush administration, for its part, has been trying various means to exert pressure on Syria and Iran. In 2003, it imposed economic sanctions on Syria and in 2005, following the assassination of former Lebanese prime minister Rafiq al-Hariri, it brought enormous pressure to bear, leading to the Syrian troop withdrawal from Lebanon. At the same time, Washington has pushed the issue of Iran's nuclear activities centre stage – most notably at the

IAEA – in a bid to isolate it internationally. Furthermore, it is an open secret that since 2003, the USA has been supplying Kurdish Iranian separatists with arms (sent from Iraq) to engage Iranian security forces in the border regions. Neither Tehran nor Damascus want to see Iraq plunged into chaos and anarchy, but as long as the USA maintains a hostile stance towards them they would prefer the continuation of a degree of resistance in Iraq to pin down US forces and deflect attention away from them. For the foreseeable future, there is no indication that relations between the USA and the Syrian–Iranian camp will thaw. Hence, Tehran and Damascus will continue their partnership and may even bolster their cooperation depending on the challenges that lie ahead. For example, when the new Iranian president Mahmoud Ahmadinejad assumed office in August 2005, Bashar Assad was the first foreign leader to pay him a visit.

In conclusion, it is worth mentioning once more that to varying degrees the experiences and geography of the two states shaped the Syrian–Iranian alliance. However, one should not underestimate the role and impact of their political elite's ideologies and world views. Their leaders share some perceptions and their secular and fundamentalist ideologies overlap in certain respects. While Iran has tried to use its brand of revolutionary Islam to transcend nationalism, create Muslim unity in the region by surmounting Arab–Iranian political divisions and demonstrate its solidarity by actively participating in the Arab–Israeli struggle, Syria, as the self-proclaimed birthplace and heartland of Arabism, has striven to overcome the political fragmentation of the Arab world by acting as a vehicle for Arab unity. Hafez Assad, Ruhollah Khomeini and their successors have viewed the region as a strategic whole and regarded their alliance as a vital tool with which to further Arab–Islamic interests and increase regional autonomy by diminishing foreign penetration of the Middle East. As a result, to advance their common agenda over the years, both countries have put long-term interests before short-term gains. It is noteworthy that the USA has very little leverage over them today and that they have both staved off isolation in the post cold-war era. Although they have not always been successful in steering events in a desirable direction in the Middle East, their potential to thwart the ambitions of other actors like Iraq, Israel and the USA cannot be denied. In this respect, the achievements of the Syrian–Iranian alliance over the past quarter century have been quite remarkable. Irrespective of how much longer this partnership will endure, it has left its stamp on modern Middle Eastern politics.

Notes

Introduction

1. Here I adopt Stephen Walt's (1987: 1) working definition of an alliance as 'a formal or informal relationship of security cooperation between two or more sovereign states'.
2. Walt (1987: 150–1).
3. See Hirschfeld (1986: 105); and Hunter (1985: 30–1).
4. Hirschfeld (1986: 105). In Kashf al-Asrar, Khomeini (1942) criticized the contemporary international system and stated that the concept of the nation-state was inherently flawed. He saw modern states as 'the products of man's limited ideas' and instead advocated Islamic universalism, calling for the establishment of Islam on every corner of the earth. See also Ramazani (1983: 16–20).
5. Hirschfeld (1986: 10); and Hunter (1985: 31).
6. See also Ehteshami and Hinnebusch (1997: 64, 97–8).
7. Ehteshami and Hinnebusch (1997: 100–1).
8. See Fedder (1968: 83).
9. For more details, see Holsti et al. (1985: 21, 56–7).
10. See Dinerstein (1965: 599).
11. Liska (1962: 39–40); and Walt (1997: 159).
12. Liska (1962: 69) argues that consultations strengthen alliance cohesion since they reinforce solidarity and equality among the members. Loomis (1959: 305) posits that more communication enhances feelings of trust and brings about cooperation. Moreover, Haas and Whiting (1956: 178) state that the key factors in alliance maintenance are continuous consultation and adjustment of policies.
13. Liska (1962: 82).
14. See French (1941: 365–6).
15. Rothstein (1968: 119).
16. Kaplan (1957: 108–9).
17. See Walt (1987: 35–6, 206–12); and also Walt (1997: 163).
18. Iklé (1964: 236).
19. Dinerstein (1965: 592).

1. The Emergence of the Syrian–Iranian Axis: 1979–1982

1. Ramazani (1988: 176).
2. Conversation with former Ambassador Jafar Ra'ed, London, April 1994.

Ra'ed was a leading Arabist in the imperial Iranian foreign ministry during the 1960s and 1970s and later served as director of the CAIS in London.

3. Conversation with Abbas Sayghal, London, April 1994, a career diplomat who served in the imperial Iranian foreign service from 1931 to 1974. He was extremely knowledgeable about Arab–Iranian relations and was stationed for more than three decades in Syria, Iraq, Egypt, Jordan, Kuwait and Saudi Arabia.

4. Singh (1981: 102–3).

5. Ra'ed and Sayghal interviews, April 1994. See also Chubin and Zabih (1974: 15, 146); and Singh (1981: 119).

6. Eight Political Department (1976: 29); Institute for Political and International Studies (1995: 135–6). During the Six Day War Iran allowed Soviet transport aircraft to use its airspace to resupply the Arab combatants, and subsequently condemned Israel's seizure of Arab territory in the UN. Conversation with former Imperial Iranian foreign minister Ardeshir Zahedi, Montreux, Switzerland, November 2000. Also see Entessar (1993: 163).

7. Conversations with former Iranian foreign minister Zahedi, November 2000; and ambassador Ra'ed, April 1994. Zahedi said Tehran was determined to take decisive action to prevent the overthrow of King Hussein.

8. Ra'ed, April 1994.

9. SAVAK supported and financed Kzar's operation, intended to overthrow the Iraqi Ba'thist regime. Confidential conversation with former Iranian official with close links to SAVAK, London, March 1994. For more information, see Khoury (1982: 379); and Kienle (1990: 71, 85).

10. A group of wounded Syrian officers and soldiers were flown to Iran and treated in Tehran hospitals (Eight Political Department 1976: 31). During the fighting, Iran again let the Soviets use its airspace to resupply the Arabs, but reversed its position after pressure from the USA. Conversation with former Iranian foreign minister Ahmad Mirfenderski, Paris, December 1994; and confidential interview with a former Iranian official, London, March 1994. Ardeshir Zahedi explained that at the UN, Iran condemned the continued occupation of Arab territories captured by Israel in 1967. Conversation with former Iranian foreign minister Zahedi, November 2000. Also see Entessar (1993: 165).

11. Conversation with former ambassador Mohammad Poursartip, Iranian ambassador to Damascus 1973–77, Geneva, June 1997. Syria dispatched its own ambassador to Iran in 1974.

12. Emami (1997: 234–5). For details and in-depth analysis of the intensification of the Syrian–Iraqi rivalry between 1972 and 1975, see Kienle (1990: 61–86).

13. Seale (1989: 353).

14. Ramazani (1988: 176).

15. Hirschfeld (1986: 119); and Kessler (1987: 86–7).

16. Hirschfeld (1986: 120); and Baram (1986: 129–30).

17. Hirschfeld (1986: 119–20).

18. Kessler (1987: 86); Seale (1989: 334); and Kienle (1990: 135–6).

19. Kessler (1987: 86–7). According to Teune and Synnestvedt (1965: 189), disappointing historical experiences may prevent alliance formation with states associated with those experiences.

20. BBC SWB/ME/6041/i, 13 February 1979. For further details on Assad's message to Khomeini, see BBC SWB/ME/6042/A/5-6, 14 February 1979.

21. *Guardian*, 13 February 1979.

22. BBC/SWB/ME/6039/A/12, 10 February 1979.

23. Kienle (1990: 140).

24. Seale (1989: 352–3).

25. BBC/SWB/ME/6106/i, 2 May 1979. For full text of Iranian foreign ministry statement on the severance of diplomatic ties with Egypt, see BBC/SWB/ ME/ 6107/A/7–8, 2 May 1979.

26. BBC/SWB/ME/6145/A/7, 19 June 1979.

27. Seale (1989: 353).

28. Hunter (1985: 31).

29. Darius (1984: 38). Ayatollah Sadeq Khalkhali during a visit to the UAE in May 1979 declared that the Persian Gulf should be called the 'Muslim' Gulf. See *Kayhan*, 29 May 1979.

30. Hunter (1985: 32).

31. *Al-Ba'th*, 8 October 1980.

32. Darius (1984: 38); and Halliday (1986: 94–5).

33. Seale (1989: 355–6).

34. Seale (1989: 353); and *Kayhan*, 19 August 1979.

35. *Kayhan*, 19 August 1979.

36. *Middle East Contemporary Survey 1978/9*, pp. 440–1.

37. *Washington Post*, 17 November 1979.

38. BBC/SWB/ME/6238/A/6–7, 28 November 1979.

39. *Daily Telegraph*, 3 March 1980.

40. BBC/SWB/ME/6296/A/3, 13 December 1979.

41. BBC/SWB/ME/6272/A/10, 15 November 1979; and BBC/SWB/ME/6103/A/ 8, 28 April 1979. In reality, the Libyans had executed Musa Sadr during his visit to Libya the previous year. Moreover, Khomeini had had an indirect role in the elimination of Musa Sadr, whom he despised. As a pragmatic leader trying to mobilize and empower the Lebanese Shiites and change the political *status quo* in Lebanon, Musa Sadr had for years accepted financial assistance from radical states, and from other sources, including the Shah of Iran and the USAID, to improve conditions for his constituency. Khomeini resented what he interpreted as Musa Sadr's deviant conduct, and intentionally misinformed Qadhafi that Musa Sadr had used financial aid provided by Libya for his own personal gain. Confidential conversation with a former Iranian official intimately involved in Lebanese affairs.

42. *Middle East International*, 23 November 1979.

43. *Al-Watan al-Arabi*, 31 January 1980.

44. BBC/SWB/ME/6364/A/4, 7 March 1980.

45. *The Times*, 20 March 1980.

46. BBC/SWB/ME/6388/A/3–4, 4 April 1980.

47. BBC/SWB/ME/6390/A/4-5, 9 April 1980.

48. BBC/SWB/ME/6394/A/2, 14 April 1980. Iran claimed that King Hussein had arranged a secret meeting between US national security adviser Zbigniew Brzezinski and Saddam Hussein on the Iraqi–Jordanian border earlier in the year, resulting in the declaration of the Pan-Arab Charter by the Iraqi leader. For more details on Brzezinski's alleged secret visit to Iraq, see Karen Elliot House's article in *Wall Street Journal*, 8 February 1980; and Timmerman (1992a: 112–14).

49. *New York Times*, 26 April 1980.

50. At a press conference held in Beirut on 29 April 1980, Khaddam argued that 'We are all required to stand at the side of the Iranian revolution to face this US onslaught, which is aimed against the Arabs as much as it is aimed against Iran. This onslaught is aimed at eliminating the Palestinian issue and the Arab nation. It is also aimed at spreading full US control over the Arab world.' See BBC/SWB/ME/6409/A/4, 1 May 1980.

51. *Sunday Times*, 4 May 1980.

52. *Sunday Times*, 18 May 1980. According to the article written by Anthony Terry, Syrian elite troops had been sent to Iran to support the Iranian forces in border clashes against the Iraqis. However, the report seems suspect. Iran at the time did not need foreign soldiers to conduct operations and skirmishes against the Iraqis. A more plausible explanation for the Syrian presence is that they were there in an advisory capacity, for they were familiar with Iraqi tactics and the Soviet-made weaponry that the Iraqis used and the Iranians were trying to integrate in their armed forces. This is supported by Claudia Wright's (1980/1) account of the Syrian troop presence in Iran before the outbreak of the war.

53. *Middle East*, July 1980.

54. *Middle East*, October 1980.

55. BBC/SWB/ME/6523/i, 15 September 1980.

56. Interview with Kenneth R. Timmerman of the US Congressional Research Service (and author of two books on Western policy towards Iraq and Iran, *Fanning the flames*, and *The death lobby: how the West armed Iraq*) on the PBS *Frontline* television documentary programme, entitled 'The arming of Saudi Arabia', first aired on US television on 16 February 1993. Also see transcript of the *Frontline* programme, p. 5.

57. See Wright (1980/1: 281–2).

58. *Daily Telegraph*, 25 September 1980.

59. *International Herald Tribune*, 26 September 1980.

60. *Middle East Contemporary Survey 1979/80*, pp. 22–3.

61. Seale (1989: 357).

62. Hunter (1985: 32).

63. *Guardian*, 4 October 1980.

64. *Washington Post*, 8 October 1980; and *Middle East International*, 24 October 1980. According to former Iranian President Bani-Sadr, though Syria sent arms and military advisers to help the Iranian war effort, Syrian troops never participated in the fighting against Iraq. Conversation with Abolhassan Bani-Sadr, Versailles, France, December 1994.

65. *Daily Telegraph*, 7 October 1980; and *Guardian*, 9 October 1980.

66. *Washington Post*, 11 October 1980.

67. Seale (1989: 358).

68. *Financial Times*, 1 November 1980; *Daily Telegraph*, 7 October 1980.

69. Amos (1984: 66).

70. Amos (1984: 67).

71. *Daily Telegraph*, 7 October 1980. In a meeting with joint chief of staff Fallahi, Syrian ambassador Yunis informed him that according to their estimates, Iraq was depleting its ammunition stocks very quickly. This posed a major problem for the Iraqis, since the Kremlin had halted all military shipments to Iraq after the outbreak of the conflict.

72. *Daily Telegraph*, 29 October 1980; and O'Ballance (1988: 53).

73. BBC/SWB/ME/6546/A/1–2, 11 October 1980.

74. *New York Times*, 12 October 1980; and BBC/SWB/ME/6547/A/4–5, 13 October 1980.

75. BBC/SWB/ME/6547/A/5–7, 13 October 1980.

76. BBC/SWB/ME/6555/i, 22 October 1980; and SWB/ME/6564/i, 1 November 1980. In an address to a youth conference on 7 November Assad strongly attacked Saddam's conduct. Referring to the Iranian revolution, he posed the question, 'Is it not our right to ask why this revolution is under attack? Why was war suddenly launched against this revolution? Given the large, broad significance of this revolution and the huge gains achieved for us, the Arabs, by this revolution, is it not our duty to ask why war was launched against this revolution? If the matter is one of Arab rights, why were we not consulted? Are we not Arabs? Are we not concerned with every Arab right?' See BBC/SWB/ME/ 6571/A/4, 10 November 1980.

77. *Daily Telegraph*, 16 October 1980.

78. *Washington Post*, 14 November 1980.

79. *New York Times*, 13 November 1980; BBC/SWB/ME/6574/i, 13 November 1980.

80. *Guardian*, 20 November 1980. The defection of two Syrian air force pilots, who flew to Jordan at the time, aggravated the situation even more.

81. *New York Times*, 20 November 1980.

82. BBC/SWB/ME/6580/i, 20 November 1980.

83. BBC/SWB/ME/6582/i, 22 November 1980.

84. *Observer News Service*, 28 November 1980.

85. *The Times*, 26 November 1980.

86. *Middle East Contemporary Survey 1979/80*, p. 9; and *Neue Zürcher Zeitung*, 27 November 1980.

87. *International Herald Tribune*, 27 November 1980; and *Frankfurter Allgemeine Zeitung*, 28 November 1980.
88. *Middle East Contemporary Survey 1979/80*, p. 38.
89. *Frankfurter Allgemeine Zeitung*, 28 November 1980.
90. *The Times*, 28 November 1980.
91. See *The Times*, 28 November 1980; *Financial Times*, 28 November 1980; *Daily Telegraph*, 28 November 1980; BBC/SWB/ME/6588/A/2, 29 November 1980.
92. *Observer News Service*, 28 November 1980.
93. *Middle East Contemporary Survey 1979/80*, p. 9.
94. BBC/SWB/ME/6609/A/5, 24 December 1980. In the immediate aftermath of Iran's Islamic revolution, the Syrian Muslim Brotherhood appealed to Khomeini for support against the Syrian Ba'th regime. This overture to win Iranian support coincided with the Brotherhood's renewed efforts in spring 1979 to oust Assad from power. The Muslim militants initiated a widespread campaign of terror and violence against government and party officials. As it turned out, Iran ignored the Brethren's calls for help. Between 1980 and 1982, as the struggle between the Muslim Brethren and the Syrian government intensified, Iran's state-controlled media maintained a news blackout on events in Syria. Iranian officials rarely criticized the Muslim Brethren. However, after a massive uprising in Hama led by the *Ikhwan* in February 1982, which the Syrian army ruthlessly crushed, the Iranian government publicly condoned Assad's suppression of the revolt. The Iranian foreign ministry issued a statement officially condemning the *Ikhwan* for having become a functional ally of the 'Zionist entity and Hashemite Jordan'. It should be noted that since the late 1960s, the Syrian *Ikhwan*'s main source of support has been the Iraqi Ba'th. According to former Iranian president Bani-Sadr, there was never a serious debate among the Iranian leadership about backing the Syrian *Ikhwan*, for there was consensus that the movement had compromised its Islamic credentials by forging close links with Jordan and Iraq, and had become a 'stooge of the West'. Conversation with Abolhassan Bani-Sadr, Versailles, France, December 1994. See also Batatu (1982: 13); and Cottam (1986: 488–9).
95. *Tishrin*, 21 February 1981. Syria had initially hoped to use the Jordanian diplomat as a bargaining chip to seek the release of the Syrian agents in return for his freedom.
96. *Financial Times*, 3 February 1981.
97. BBC/ME/6660/A/10, 27 February 1981. During their meetings with the Syrian minister of religious trusts, Dr Mohammed al-Khatib, he declared his country's willingness to fight on the side of Iran against 'imperialism and Saddam's regime', if such a request were made.
98. *Observer News Service*, 8 April 1981; *Financial Times*, 1 April 1981. Damascus denounced Sadat's policy of aiding Iraq against the Iranian revolutionaries. See BBC/SWB/ME/6689/i, 2 April 1981.
99. Cordesman (1982: 84); and Staudenmaier (1983: 43).

100. Evans and Campany (1984: 31).

101. Hiro (1984: 7). Baghdad admitted to the loss of only one aircraft in the attack (see BBC/SWB/ME/6695/A/10, 9 April 1981), but the Iraqi Mujahedin estimated that 60 warplanes were destroyed (see BBC/SWB/ME/6704/A/6, 22 April 1981).

102. BBC/SWB/ME/6743/A/9, 23 May 1981.

103. *Financial Times*, 22 April 1981.

104. According to research associate at the IISS Dr Ahmed Hashim (conversation, London, August 1994), in the early stages of the war the Iranian air force had enough planes to fly air support missions and so did not need Syrian help in this respect. This is borne out by the confession of an Iranian pilot the Iraqis captured in May 1981 who said that the Iranians ruled out Syrian air cover for fear of confusing Soviet-made Syrian planes with those of Iraq – Syrian and Iraqi markings were similar, which increased the chances of the two being mistaken for one another. See BBC/SWB/ME/6731/A/9, 23 May 1981. Former Iranian president Bani-Sadr also confirmed that Syrian warplanes never participated in combat missions with the Iranian air force, although Syria allowed Iranian combat aircraft to use its airspace (conversation with Abolhassan Bani-Sadr, Versailles, France, December 1994).

105. The Iranian government's reluctance to condemn the *Ikhwan* officially could partly be attributed to a general perception among the public that the Syrian Brethren was a movement with solid and immaculate Islamic credentials. Therefore, the situation in Syria presented the Iranian clerics with something of a dilemma. In addition, not only did the Muslim Brethren use the same language against Assad as Khomeini had used against the Shah, but more importantly many of Khomeini's prominent aides, including former prime minister Mahdavi-Kani, and Islamic judges Sadeq Khalkhali, Mohammad Gailani and Assadollah Lajevardi were once members of the Iranian version of the Brethren, called Fadayeen-e Islam. Its founder, Navab-Safavi, had had close ties with the Brethren in Egypt and Syria during the 1940s and 1950s. See 'Syria Violence Seen Posing Dilemma for Tehran', London, statement released in English, Iran Press Service, No. 60, 25 February 1982.

106. BBC/SWB/ME/6704/A/6, 22 April 1981.

107. BBC/SWB/ME/6745/A/13, 10 June 1981.

108. BBC/SWB/ME/6745/A/14, 10 June 1981.

109. BBC/SWB/ME/6794/i, 6 August 1981. Former Iranian president Bani-Sadr was against a strategic partnership with Syria because of the nature and ideology of its regime, which was not unlike Saddam Hussein's; instead he favoured a limited relationship for tactical purposes. He agreed to cooperate militarily after the Iraqi invasion to safeguard national security. Furthermore, he believed that an alliance with Assad's dictatorship would discredit the Islamic Republic of Iran in the eyes of other revolutionary movements in the world. However, Khomeini was a

strong advocate of an Iranian–Syrian alliance to humble Iraq, and after Bani-Sadr was overthrown cooperative ties were expanded and eventually formalized in March 1982. Conversation with Abolhassan Bani-Sadr, Versailles, France, December 1994.

110. *Frankfurter Allgemeine Zeitung*, 8 October 1981.

111. See *Egyptian Gazette*, 6 October 1981. In fact, the INA claimed on 2 September that Iranian warplanes had again attacked the Al-Walid airbase. If so, fewer planes were probably involved and the Iraqis incurred smaller losses compared with the 4 April raid.

112. BBC/SWB/ME/6906/i, 15 December 1981.

113. See *Financial Times*, 21 December 1981; and *Guardian*, 21 December 1981.

114. BBC/SWB/ME/6912/A/10, 22 December 1981.

115. *International Herald Tribune*, 29 December 1981; *Guardian*, 28 December 1981.

116. *International Herald Tribune*, 21 December 1981.

117. O'Ballance (1988: 73).

118. *Neue Zürcher Zeitung*, 25 December 1981.

119. See *Guardian*, 17 December 1981; BBC/SWB/ME/6908/A/8, 17 December 1981; King (1987: 41); and Olmert (1990: 174).

120. *International Herald Tribune*, 30 December 1981.

121. BBC/SWB/ME/6918/A/3–4, 4 January 1982. In a news conference on 7 January 1982, Iranian President Khamene'i went so far as to deny that the topic of Syrian mediation and peace talks had come up during Velayati's visit to Syria. Also see BBC/SWB/ME/6932/A/7, 9 January 1982.

122. O'Ballance (1988: 69).

123. BBC/SWB/ME/6918/A/13, 4 January 1982.

124. Ibid. On 1 January, in response to reports about the Syrian–Kuwaiti mediation effort, Iranian deputy foreign minister Ahmad Azizi issued a statement that 'the recent victories in the battlefronts and the clear position of the Islamic Republic concerning the war gave Iran no reason to have any special talks with any country to end the war'. See BBC/SWB/ME/6918/A/4, 4 January 1982.

125. BBC/SWB/ME/6927/A/2, 14 January 1982.

126. See BBC/SWB/ME/6924/A/6, 11 January 1982. Ramadan addressed volunteers from eight Arab countries (Egypt, Syria, Palestine, Jordan, Lebanon, Tunisia, Morocco and the Sudan) leaving for the warfront 'to take part in the just pan-Arab battle Iraq [was] waging against the Persian enemy'.

127. *Al-Ba'th*, 29 January 1982.

128. *Guardian*, 1 February 1982.

129. BBC/SWB/ME/6942/A/4, 1 February 1982.

130. *Guardian*, 1 February 1982.

131. *International Herald Tribune*, 1 March 1982.

132. BBC/SWB/ME/6965/A/3, 27 February 1982.

133. *Le Monde*, 16 March 1982; *Neue Zürcher Zeitung*, 18 March 1982.

134. *Ettela'at*, 17 March 1982.

135. Ibid.
136. Ramazani (1988: 81).
137. Ibid.
138. *Middle East International*, 9 April 1982; and O'Ballance (1988: 79–82).
139. Heller (1984: 25). The pipeline was closed down hours after the arrival of the first tanker laden with Iranian oil in Banias. See *Middle East International*, 23 April 1982. The Iraqis claimed that Syria was losing $127.5 million in transit fees by shutting the pipeline. See BBC/SWB/ME/7003/A/4–5, 16 April 1982.
140. Chubin and Tripp (1988: 179–80); and Hirschfeld (1986: 108).
141. The plans to build an oil pipeline to the Jordanian port of Aqaba were later scrapped. The Iraqis responded to the Syrian action by asking the Arab states to impose sanctions on Syria. See Interview with Iraqi oil minister Tayih Abd al-Karim in the *Middle East Economic Survey*, 18 April 1982.
142. Chubin and Tripp (1988: 180); and Hirschfeld (1986: 107). Also see BBC/SWB/ME/7002/A/8, 15 April 1982; BBC/SWB/ME/7012/A/3, 27 April 1982; and BBC/SWB/ME/7041/A/3, 2 June 1982.
143. Chubin and Tripp (1988: 180).
144. Hirschfeld (1986: 107). In May 1981, Assad offered PUK leader Jalal Talabani commitments for arms and military advisers. In addition, the Syrians provided support for the Shiite opposition groups within Iraq. They created Shiite cells in the Iraqi Ba'th and infiltrated the *husseiniyahs*. The underground activities of such groups as al-Da'wa, the Iraqi Mujahidin, and the Movement of the Islamic Revolution in Iraq were partially financed by Damascus. See Hirschfeld (1986: 107); and Amos (1984: 53). For more details on Syrian–Iranian assistance to Iraqi Kurdish groups, also see Mortimer (1982: 368, 373).
145. Chubin and Tripp (1988: 180).
146. Hirschfeld (1986: 110).
147. This view is shared by Hazem Saghiyeh of *Al-Hayat*. He believes that immediately after the 1979 revolution Syria was keener to form close ties with Iran, but after the 1980 Iraqi invasion Iran became keener on cementing relations with Damascus (conversation with Hazem Saghiyeh, London, May 1994).

2. The Achievements and Limits of Syrian–Iranian Power, 1982–85

1. Ramazani (1988: 181).
2. In the Fatah al-Mobin and Quds operations, Iranians killed 30,000 Iraqi soldiers and captured 25,000. See O'Ballance (1988: 85); Cordesman and Wagner (1990: 140).
3. See Schiff and Ya'ari (1984: 98–100); and Evron (1987: 123–4).
4. Ramazani (1988: 180). According to Ze'ev Schiff and Ehud Ya'ari, Tel Aviv had informed senior officials in the Reagan administration (including secretary of state Alexander Haig) beforehand of its intention to invade Lebanon, and obtained their tacit approval.

5. Ramazani (1988: 180–1).

6. See *Guardian*, 8 June 1982; and *Financial Times*, 9 June 1982.

7. BBC/SWB/ME/7048/i, 10 June 1982.

8. After the SDC meeting, the speaker of the Iranian parliament and Khomeini's personal representative on the SDC, Hashemi-Rafsanjani, stated that Iraq should provide a route so 'we can speedily dispatch our armoured forces to Syria'. See BBC/SWB/ME/7052/i, 12 June 1982.

9. See *Financial Times*, 12 June 1982; and *Dawn*, 12 June 1982.

10. See *Financial Times*, 12 June 1982; *Le Monde*, 13 and 14 June 1982; and BBC/SWB/ME/7051/A/24, 14 June 1982.

11. See O'Ballance (1988: 95–6).

12. *Le Monde*, 15 June 1982; BBC/SWB/ME/7051/i, 14 June 1982. The first group was of 500 men. The airlift of three contingents seems to have been completed within four days. Iranian ambassador Mohtashami greeted the volunteers at Damascus airport. See *Guardian*, 15 June 1982; *Dawn*, 18 June 1982.

13. Liz Thurgood, *Observer News Service*, London, 16 June 1982; and BBC/SWB/ME/7051/i, 14 June 1982.

14. Foreign Broadcast Information Service, South Asia, VIII (118) I4, 18 June 1982.

15. Liz Thurgood, *Observer News Service*, London, 16 June 1982.

16. *DPA* report in *Dawn*, 19 June 1982.

17. BBC/SWB/ME/7058/i, 22 June 1982.

18. BBC/SWB/ME/7060/i, 24 June 1982.

19. According to former Iranian president Bani-Sadr, Khomeini was obsessed with creating a Shiite Islamic domain encompassing Iran, Iraq, Syria and Lebanon with him as the supreme leader. This was a primary reason for his insistence on continuing the Gulf War. His personal animosity towards Saddam Hussein contributed to his inflexible stance on the continuation of the hostilities. Conversation with Abolhassan Bani-Sadr, Versailles, France, December 1994. Also see Bani-Sadr (1991: 179, 183–4).

20. See O'Ballance (1988: 93); and BBC/SWB/ME/7065/A/15, 30 June 1982.

21. BBC/SWB/ME/7066/A/22, 1 July 1982.

22. BBC/SWB/ME/7066/A/26, 1 July 1982.

23. BBC/SWB/ME/7072/i, 8 July 1982. Also see O'Ballance (1988: 93).

24. *Kayhan*, 6 July 1982.

25. On the same day Saddam rejected Iran's demand for payment of Iraqi war reparations. See BBC/SWB/ME/7076/A/1, 13 July 1982.

26. See BBC/SWB/ME/7078/A/2, 15 July 1982; BBC/SWB/ME/7079/i, 16 July 1982.

27. *Frankfurter Allgemeine Zeitung*, 19 August 1982.

28. *Frankfurter Allgemeine Zeitung*, 19 August 1982.

29. *Al-Sharq Al-Awsat*, 20 July 1982. Kamal Hasan Ali stated that 'Syria's stand makes us wonder because it neither supports the Palestinian force

in Lebanon nor does it implement the Arab League Pact nor support Iraq in its war with Iran.'

30. BBC/SWB/ME/7079/i, 16 July 1979.
31. See Karsh (1988: 67); and Avi-Ran (1991: 138).
32. Avi-Ran (1991: 135).
33. *Middle East Contemporary Survey 1981/2*, p. 568.
34. *Daily Telegraph*, 21 June 1982.
35. Ibid.; and BBC/SWB/ME/7061/A/6, 25 June 1982.
36. *Daily Telegraph*, 29 June 1982.
37. Olmert (1990: 177).
38. *Middle East Contemporary Survey 1981/2*, p. 253; BBC/SWB/ME/7127/i, 10 September 1982; BBC/SWB/ME/7130/A/2, 14 September 1982. On the Gulf War, the resolution stated that 'the conference has decided to declare its commitment to defend all the Arab territories and to consider any aggression on any Arab country as an aggression on all the Arab countries'.
39. Olmert (1990: 177).
40. Ibid.; *Middle East International*, 17 September 1982; and BBC/SWB/ME/7128/i, 11 September 1982.
41. BBC/SWB/ME/7132/A/1, 16 September 1982.
42. Seale (1989: 396).
43. Seale (1989: 396); and Ramazani (1988: 183).
44. *Daily Telegraph*, 24 November 1982; *Guardian*, 24 November 1982.
45. According to some accounts, Islamic Amal militiamen fought along side the Iranian Revolutionary Guards during the attack on the Lebanese Army barracks in Ba'albek. After the clash, Syrian military helicopters flew the bodies of the dead attackers out of the area. See BBC/SWB/ME/7192/A/8, 25 November 1982; and *Middle East Contemporary Survey 1982/3*, p. 674.
46. *Middle East Contemporary Survey 1981/2*, p. 866.
47. From Tehran's viewpoint, to add insult to injury, at Fez II the Gulf Arab sheikhdoms agreed to provide Iraq with $6.5 billion to finance the war effort. By now Baghdad was receiving a generous sum of approximately $13 billion annually from the Gulf Arabs. Iraqi war expenditures were running at about $1 billion every month. *Middle East International*, 15 October 1982.
48. A few days later PLO chairman Arafat accompanied by the head of Fatah's foreign relations department Muhammad Abu Mayzar also visited Baghdad, much to Tehran's dismay. See BBC/SWB/ME/7150/i, 7 October 1982.
49. BBC/SWB/ME/7181/A/6, 12 November 1982.
50. BBC/SWB/ME/7181/i, 12 November 1982. The end of Operation Muharram al-Haram coincided with the GCC leaders' summit in Manama, Bahrain. In its final communiqué, the GCC expressed deep concern about Iran's recent moves, which it claimed posed an enormous threat to 'the safety and security of the Arab nation and the violation of its sovereignty'. It went on to say that the GCC 'affirmed its support for

Iraq in its endeavour to put an end to this war by peaceful means'. See BBC/SWB/ME/7182/ A/1, 13 November 1982.

51. BBC/SWB/ME/7205/i, 10 December 1982. At the end of the visit, a joint Iranian–Libyan communiqué was issued in which both parties declared support for Syria in the conflict with Israel. See BBC/SWB/ME/7209/A/1–2, 15 December 1982.

52. Karsh (1991: 40).

53. *Middle East Contemporary Survey 1982/3*, p. 815.

54. Karsh (1988: 80), and Karsh (1991: 156).

55. *Middle East Contemporary Survey 1982/3*, p. 815.

56. BBC/SWB/ME/7226/A/6, 8 January 1983.

57. See *Egyptian Mail*, 22 January 1983; and *Al-Sharq al-Awsat*, 22 January 1983.

58. *Middle East International*, 4 February 1983.

59. Hirschfeld (1986: 115 and 118).

60. *New York Times*, 23 January 1983. Also see *Neue Zürcher Zeitung*, 23 and 24 January 1983.

61. BBC/SWB/ME/7240/A/2, 25 January 1983; and *Guardian*, 24 January 1983.

62. BBC/SWB/ME/7240/A/1, 25 January 1983.

63. Ibid.

64. See *Middle East International*, 4 February 1983.

65. BBC/SWB/ME/7241/A/2. For further details on Iraqi and Jordanian statements on the communiqué see BBC/SWB/ME/7241/A/1–2, 25 January 1983; *Le Monde*, 25 January 1983; *Dawn*, 27 January 1983; *Neue Zürcher Zeitung*, 28 January 1983.

66. BBC/SWB/ME/7242/i, 27 January 1983.

67. *Middle East Contemporary Survey 1982/3*, p. 813. Under the terms of the barter agreement, Iran received 150 T-62 tanks, 400 artillery pieces, 1000 mortars, 600 anti-aircraft guns and 12,000 automatic weapons and ammunition from North Korea. See O'Ballance (1988: 103–4).

68. *Middle East International*, 4 February 1983.

69. O'Ballance (1988: 114–16). During the Wal-Fajr offensive, Major-General Hisham al-Fakhri, commander of Iraq's fourth army corps responsible for the defence of the Amara area, claimed that Iran was receiving military supplies from Syria and Libya. BBC/SWB/ME/7254/i, 10 February 1983.

70. BBC/SWB/ME/7251/A/6–7, 7 February 1983.

71. *Middle East Contemporary Survey 1982/3*, p. 815.

72. O'Ballance (1988: 121).

73. *Financial Times*, 7 April 1983.

74. *Middle East Contemporary Survey 1982/3*, p. 815. Syrian foreign minister Khaddam, Iran's ambassador to Damascus, and the Iranian undersecretary for Asian and African affairs also attended the high-level three-hour meeting. See BBC/SWB/ME/7307/A/11, 14 April 1983.

75. BBC/SWB/ME/7254/i, 10 February 1983; BBC/SWB/ME/7255/i, 11 February 1983.

76. Olmert (1990: 180–1). Also see Avi-Ran (1991: 171–3).

77. BBC/SWB/ME/7276/A/7, 8 March 1983.

78. Olmert (1990: 180); *Middle East Contemporary Survey 1982/3*, p. 674. In March, they are believed to have carried out an attack on a US Marine patrol that was part of the MNF supporting the Gemayel government in Beirut. See *Guardian*, 19 April 1983.

79. See *Observer*, 24 April 1983; and Woodward (1987: 245–7, 362–3). According to Ambassador Richard Murphy, who served from 1983 to 1989 as US assistant secretary of state for the Near East and South Asia, Washington was convinced of Iranian–Syrian involvement in the attack on the US embassy in Beirut. Conversation with Ambassador Richard Murphy, London, November 1995.

80. *Ettela'at*, 19 April 1983; BBC/SWB/ME/7312/i, 20 April 1983. Woodward (1987: 245–7, 362–3) states that the NSA had been intercepting and deciphering coded electronic messages from the Iranian foreign ministry in Tehran to its embassies in Damascus and Beirut. They were able to determine that an operation against a US target was being planned and a payment of $25,000 made in Lebanon for the purpose. They were convinced that at the very least Syrian intelligence must have known of the preparations for the attack. CIA director William Casey was certain that both Tehran and Damascus had a hand in the operation. See *Le Monde*, 18 May 1983 for more details. According to one account, the Soviets provided the Syrians with the intelligence about the scheduled, high-level CIA meeting in the US embassy. The Syrians subsequently shared the information with the Iranians, and then jointly proceeded to plan the attack. See Jaber (1997: 81).

81. Seale (1989: 406). Ambassador Richard Murphy confirmed that the death of Ames, an able and gifted man, was a major blow to Shultz, who had relied on his advice for Middle Eastern affairs. Conversation with Ambassador Richard Murphy, London, November 1995.

82. *Observer*, 29 May 1983.

83. For an excellent analysis of the Soviet military and political relationship with Syria during this period, refer to Eric Rouleau's article in *Le Monde*, 26 May 1983.

84. *International Herald Tribune*, 28 and 29 May 1983; also *Frankfurter Allgemeine Zeitung*, 31 May 1983. According to former US assistant secretary of state Richard Murphy (conversation, London, November 1995), Ariel Sharon and other senior figures in the IDF had basically dictated the terms of the 17 May accord. In essence, Washington went along with Tel Aviv's plan to impose humiliating terms on Beirut and bring Lebanon firmly into Israel's orbit.

85. *Guardian*, 31 May 1983. By the end of May 1983, 490 Israeli soldiers had been killed in Lebanon, while another 2951 had been wounded. See *Daily Telegraph*, 31 May 1983.

86. *Frankfurter Allgemeine Zeitung*, 14 September 1983.

87. Behamdoun's fall was a major setback for the Christian forces, for it enabled

the Druze fighters to link up with the Syrian forces positioned along the Beirut–Damascus highway. See *Financial Times*, 14 September 1983.

88. *Daily Telegraph*, 31 August 1983. The Shiites and Druzes resented the Gemayel regime's support for the Christian Phalangists and Lebanese forces, and US backing of the Lebanese army. Jumblatt in fact threatened to attack the US Marines and other MNF contingents if they did not remain neutral. He accused the USA of siding with the pro-Gemayel Lebanese army by providing it with logistical support and training. See *International Herald Tribune*, 2 September 1983.

89. *Guardian*, 14 September 1983. Souk el-Gharb was vitally important to both sides, for it lay between the Druze forward positions in the Shouf Mountains and the southern suburbs of West Beirut where the Shiite militias were concentrated. The fall of the town would have meant that the Druze and Shiites would be able to link up and threaten the Gemayel loyalists in East Beirut on three sides.

90. *The Times*, 12 September 1983; *International Herald Tribune*, 12 September 1983. Within a matter of a few days President Reagan authorized the use of air strikes to protect US Marine positions in the event of shelling. At the same time, the State Department said that Syrian soldiers disguised as Lebanese militiamen, and Iranian Revolutionary Guards were taking part in the fighting against the Lebanese army. See *International Herald Tribune*, 14 September 1983.

91. *Financial Times*, 19 September 1983.

92. Seale (1989: 414–15).

93. *The Times*, 28 September 1983.

94. *International Herald Tribune*, 5 October 1983.

95. *International Herald Tribune*, 18 October 1983. In total, two US marines and two Lebanese soldiers were killed, while seven US marines, three Italian soldiers, and one Lebanese soldier were wounded in the four days of fighting against the pro-Iranian Shiite militiamen. By now, the US, French and Italian MNF contingents had suffered 136 casualties; 113 of these were American or French.

96. Former US assistant secretary of state Richard Murphy admitted that US policy on Lebanon was misguided. He claimed that Washington was not trying to take sides, but unwittingly got caught in the crossfire by trying to prop up President Amin Gemayel, the Lebanese armed forces, and other vestiges of the Lebanese state. Conversation with Ambassador Richard Murphy, London, November 1995.

97. See Wright (1985: 70); and Wright (1989: 119).

98. For further details on initial US and French reaction to the bombings, see *Financial Times*, 24 October 1983; *International Herald Tribune*, 24 October 1983; and *Le Monde*, 25 October 1983.

99. *The Times*, 26 October 1983. According to Ambassador Richard Murphy, he later read an intelligence report pointing to Syrian–Iranian involvement in the bombing of the US marine compound. Furthermore,

the report indicated that the operation had required extensive preparations and sophistication. The bombing had been practised and simulated in the Syrian-controlled Bekaa Valley. Conversation with Ambassador Richard Murphy, London, November 1995.

100. *International Herald Tribune*, 31 October 1983.

101. See BBC/SWB/ME/7473/A/3–4, 25 October 1983; *Tishrin*, 24 October 1983; and *International Herald Tribune*, 25 October 1983.

102. *Daily Telegraph*, 24 October 1983. Within a few hours of the explosions the Agence France Press bureau in Beirut received an anonymous telephone call from a man speaking on behalf of Islamic Jihad. He explained that 'we are soldiers of God … we are neither Iranians, Syrians, nor Palestinians, but Muslims who follow the precepts of the Koran. … We said after that [embassy bombing] that we would strike more violently still. Now they understand with what they are dealing.' See Wright (1985: 73); and *Guardian*, 25 October 1983.

103. See *The Times*, 26 October 1983; and *International Herald Tribune*, 28 October 1983. It is interesting to note that the Syrians had previously occupied both buildings housing US marines and French paratroopers, so they had detailed knowledge of their structures and layouts. Furthermore, four days after the bombings, at a meeting with the French, British and Italian foreign ministers in Paris, US secretary of state George Shultz indicated that Washington was contemplating providing military equipment to Iran's main adversary – Iraq, and the bombing of Syrian strongholds in Lebanon in retaliation. See *International Herald Tribune*, 28 and 30 October 1983.

104. Woodward (1987: 275).

105. See *International Herald Tribune*, 1 February 1984; and *Middle East Contemporary Survey 1983/4*, p. 554.

106. Woodward (1987: 277).

107. See Olmert (1990: 181); *Middle East Contemporary Survey 1983/4*, p. 553.

108. Olmert (1990: 181); and Wright (1985: 87).

109. Wright (1985: 87).

110. Olmert (1990: 181).

111. Wright (1985: 89–90). Since the Israeli invasion of Lebanon in June 1982, a training camp on the outskirts of Zebdani had become the largest foreign base of operations for Iranian revolutionaries. An old dirt road connected the town to the Bekaa Valley in Lebanon. Throughout the Lebanon war, Syrians and Iranians made extensive use of this particular route to transport men and *matériel* for covert operations against the Israelis and MNF. During the mountain war, the Zebdani road was used to ferry Palestinian, Iranian and Syrian forces and arms to reinforce the Druze militia. Zebdani served as the primary base of operations for the Iranians in the eastern Mediterranean. The number of Revolutionary Guards stationed there at any given time fluctuated between 300 and 500, depending on their rotation in Lebanon. See Wright (1985: 80, 84).

112. Wright (1985: 88). Western intelligence agencies claim that Abu Haidar Musawi obtained a yellow Mercedes truck similar to the ones used in the Beirut airport cargo area for the bombing of the US Marine barracks, and a red van identical to one owned by a local vegetable vendor who catered to the French paratroopers. The available evidence clearly indicates the degree of sophistication in the preparations for seemingly simple operations.

113. *The Times*, 28 October 1983; and *Guardian*, 29 October 1983.

114. *Financial Times*, 2 November 1983.

115. *International Herald Tribune*, 7 November 1983.

116. *International Herald Tribune*, 8 November 1983. Within a short time, Syria's standing army of 220,000 men was beefed up to 350,000. Also refer to *Christian Science Monitor*, 18 November 1983.

117. BBC/SWB/ME/7493/i, 17 November 1983.

118. See Seale (1989: 415–16). Apparently, 15 Shiites were shot, resulting in at least two deaths. After the incident, the prominent Shiite cleric, Sheikh Mohammad Mehdi Shamseddin (head of the Higher Shiite Council) issued a religious edict (fatwa) proclaiming that armed resistance against the IDF to be a religious duty. In truth, this was tantamount to a declaration of war by the Lebanese Shiites. See *Middle East International*, 28 October 1983; and Wright (1985: 93 and 222).

119. BBC/SWB/ME/7493/i, 17 November 1983.

120. *International Herald Tribune*, 18 November 1983.

121. *Middle East International*, 25 November 1983. Reagan apparently authorized retaliatory air strikes against pro-Iranian Shiite targets in the Bekaa. But, following consultations and deliberations with Tel Aviv and Paris, once it became clear that the Israelis and French were about to undertake similar raids, the White House dropped plans for a US military riposte. See Woodward (1987: 287).

122. *International Herald Tribune*, 18 November 1983; *Le Monde*, 19 November 1983.

123. For further details on the debate within the US administration, see *Financial Times*, 17 November 1983; *Financial Times*, 23 November 1983; and *International Herald Tribune*, 19 and 20 November 1983.

124. *Financial Times*, 18 November 1983; *International Herald Tribune*, 18 November 1983; and *Le Monde*, 19 November 1983.

125. BBC/SWB/ME/7496/i, 21 November 1983. On 20 November, the speaker of the Iranian parliament (majles), Ali Akbar Hashemi Rafsanjani, informed a parliamentary session that 14 Iranians were killed in the attacks. Local Lebanese sources said that at least seven Iranians were also wounded. See *International Herald Tribune*, 19 and 20 November 1983.

126. *Financial Times*, 23 November 1983.

127. BBC/SWB/ME/7499/A/3, 24 November 1983.

128. BBC/SWB/ME/7500/i, 25 November 1983. On the same day the delegation left for Damascus, the Gemayel government severed diplomatic

relations with Iran. The move was justified as an appropriate action in the light of the Islamic Republic's refusal to withdraw the Revolutionary Guards in the Bekaa at the behest of the Lebanese government, and its continued silence regarding the nomination of a new Lebanese ambassador to Tehran. See BBC/SWB/ME/ 7501/A/5-6.

129. *Financial Times*, 7 December 1983.
130. Ibid.
131. *Middle East International*, 9 December 1983.
132. Ibid.
133. For further details, see *New York Times*, 5 December 1983; *Financial Times*, 7 December 1983; and *Washington Post*, 9 December 1983.
134. See *New York Times*, 5 December 1983; and *Financial Times*, 7 December 1983. The day after the US raids, Iranian foreign ministry spokesman Morteza Sarmadi praised the 'successful' Syrian military action and characterized the attack as aggression orchestrated by 'imperialism and Zionism'. Concurrently, an Iranian foreign ministry delegation headed by the director of the Afro–Asian Department, Lavasani, left for Syria to deliver a letter from Velayati to Khaddam and discuss recent developments. See SWB/ME/7510/A/4, 7 December 1983; and SWB/ME/ 7511/i, 8 December 1983.
135. *Washington Post*, 5 December 1983.
136. *Financial Times*, 5 December 1983.
137. *New York Times*, 5 December 1983.
138. *Washington Post*, 11 December 1983.
139. BBC/SWB/ME/7515/i, 13 December 1983.
140. *Washington Post*, 13 December 1983.
141. *New York Times*, 14 December 1983. In an interview a week earlier, Syrian foreign minister and acting information minister Faruq al-Shara had adopted a similar posture by explaining that 'Syria considers that the US Marines have become a party to the conflict, no matter what US officials say. ... The last air raid by the US Air Force against Syrian positions has increased tension in the region and constitutes a tangible proof of US involvement in Lebanon and the one-sided position taken by the marines.' On a more conciliatory note, he added that Damascus was still willing to continue the political dialogue with US special envoy Donald Rumsfeld. See *Financial Times*, 8 December 1983.
142. *Washington Post*, 15 December 1983.
143. Ghareeb (1981: 219). According to former US assistant secretary of state Richard Murphy (conversation, London, November 1995) in 1980, prior to the Iraqi invasion of Iran, Baghdad had signalled its readiness to restore diplomatic relations with Washington.
144. Axelgard (1986a: 50); Friedman (1993: 27). Richard Murphy (conversation, London, November 1995) explained that Ronald Reagan despised Iran more than the Soviet Union because of the 444-day hostage crisis and Iranian-backed attacks on US diplomatic and military outposts in

Lebanon. He believed that Iran was an implacable foe that had to be stopped. Consequently, the policy of tilting towards Iraq dovetailed neatly with containing Iran.

145. Axelgard (1986a: 51). According to Richard Murphy (conversation, London, November 1995) Iraq constantly wanted more US involvement in the Gulf conflict and a solid commitment to support Iraq.

146. Axelgard (1986a: 48).

147. *Washington Post*, 21 December 1983.

148. *International Herald Tribune*, 20 December 1983.

149. Ibid.

150. *Financial Times*, 20 December 1983; and *Daily Telegraph*, 21 December 1983.

151. Axelgard (1986b: 10).

152. *Financial Times*, 23 December 1983.

153. *The Times*, 23 December 1983.

154. *Washington Post*, 28 December 1983.

155. *International Herald Tribune*, 18 January 1984; BBC/SWB/ME/7544/i, 19 January 1984. The kidnapping of the Saudi consul was after France and Saudi Arabia had signed a major arms agreement worth $4.1 billion on 11 January. Many interpreted the deal as Riyadh's way of rewarding Paris for its steadfast support of Iraq in the Gulf War. See *Le Monde*, 17 January 1984; and *Al-Nahar Arab Report and Memo*, 23 January 1984.

156. See *International Herald Tribune*, 10 January 1984. In early January, Kuwaiti authorities disclosed that they had substantial evidence that responsibility for the December bombings lay with Musawi's followers. They claimed that several loose cells connected to Iran and Syria used the name 'Islamic Jihad'. According to one official, 'there is no doubt in our minds that the terrorists could not have carried out the attacks without the knowledge and probable support of Iran and, to a lesser extent, Syria'. *International Herald Tribune*, 7–8 January 1984.

157. Hezbollah leader Sheikh Fadlallah and Amal officials stated this. Hussein Musawi confirmed the dissolution of Islamic Amal in an interview with *Al-Shiraa* magazine on 29 November 1983.

158. According to an article in *Jeune Afrique* on 25 January 1984, Syria provided the logistics for Musawi's men. In addition to providing arms, supplies and financial support, Syrian army officers under the command of Rif'at Assad were responsible for training the recruits and familiarizing them with unconventional warfare in camps located in the Bekaa. Also see *Le Monde*, 21 January 1984.

159. *International Herald Tribune*, 23 January 1984.

160. Ibid. Suggestions by George Shultz that pre-emptive strikes might be carried out in Lebanon against terrorist strongholds, prompted Iranian President Khamene'i and parliamentary speaker Rafsanjani to caution the USA against new adventurism in the region. That same week, the Reagan administration put Iran on the list of states sponsoring

terrorism. Countries such as Syria, Libya, South Yemen and Cuba were already designated as sponsors of terrorism. See *International Herald Tribune*, 24 January 1984.

161. One of Assad's serious miscalculations in the winter of 1983/4 was his clumsy attempt to crush the PLO stronghold in the Lebanese port city of Tripoli in an effort to rein in Yasser Arafat, and prevent him from joining a US-led peace initiative, in conjunction with Jordan's King Hussein. His decision to lay siege on Arafat's last remaining base alienated many of his previous allies in the Steadfastness Front who sided with the PLO. These included Algeria, South Yemen, and to a lesser extent Libya; only Tehran stood by Damascus. The Tripoli affair proved to be a major blunder that contributed to the steady marginal-ization of Syria in mainstream Arab politics by early 1984. Although its immediate impact was to strengthen the Syrian–Iranian partnership, its power was diminished in the long run. See *Middle East International*, 27 January 1984; and *Financial Times*, 17 February 1984.

162. BBC/SWB/ME/7554/A/2, 31 January 1984.

163. *International Herald Tribune*, 9 February 1984; Avi-Ran (1991: 170).

164. *Financial Times*, 8 February 1984.

165. Ibid.

166. BBC/SWB/ME/7585/A/5, 7 March 1984.

167. Avi-Ran (1991: 171).

168. *Al-Ba'th*, 6 March 1984.

169. *Middle East Contemporary Survey 1983/4*, p. 131.

170. As many as 20,000 Iranians were killed, and another 20,000–30,000 wounded and captured. Iraqi losses consisted of 6000 dead, and 10,000–12,000 wounded. See Cordesman and Wagner (1990: 183); O'Ballance (1988: 147). According to the Iraqi daily *Al-Thawrah* of 1 March, Iraqi forces captured weapons from the Iranians built in the Syrian war factories. The arms were marked with the acronym Jim Ayn Sin, which stands for Jumhuriya al-Arabi al-Suriye (Syrian Arab Republic). The Stockholm International Peace Research Institute listed in its 1984 yearbook, *World Armaments and Disarmament*, that Syria continued to be a major supplier of arms to the Islamic Republic. Also see *The Times*, 7 April 1984.

171. The Majnoon islands contained seven billion barrels of oil – roughly a quarter of Iraq's proven oil reserves. Their capture allowed Rafsanjani to boast shortly after Operation Kheiber that 'we have now more than enough in terms of proven oil reserves to take care of the cost of reparations for the enormous damages we have suffered at the hands of the enemy'. *Le Monde*, 30 March 1984.

172. O'Ballance (1988: 148).

173. Cordesman and Wagner (1990: 191).

174. See BBC/SWB/ME/7587/A/7, 9 March 1984; and *Middle East Contemporary Survey 1983/4*, p. 133.

175. *Al-Thawrah*, 13 March 1984.

176. *Middle East Contemporary Survey 1983/4*, p. 133.

177. BBC/SWB/ME/7594/i, 17 March 1984.

178. *Middle East International*, 6 April 1984.

179. *Financial Times*, 24 April 1984.

180. *International Herald Tribune*, 18 May 1984; Cordesman and Wagner (1990: 194).

181. *International Herald Tribune*, 18 May 1984. Under the terms of the Syrian–Iranian oil deal, Damascus saved $365 million annually. Iranian oil accounted for 70 per cent of the oil refined in the Homs and Banias facilities.

182. BBC/SWB/ME/7618/A/4, 14 April 1984.

183. See *Al-Ba'th*, 4 April 1984.

184. *Middle East International*, 10 February 1984.

185. There was a noticeable upsurge in guerrilla activity in southern Lebanon. By the middle of May, Israeli casualties totalled more than 2700 since the beginning of the Lebanon war. Between March and May, there were over 120 attacks primarily carried out by Shiite militiamen. See *Middle East International*, 18 May 1984.

186. BBC/SWB/ME/7629/A/3–4, 28 April 1984.

187. BBC/SWB/ME/7637/A/7-8, 8 May 1984. Also see Rafsanjani's comments on Saudi–Iraqi collaboration after an SDC meeting in BBC/SWB/ME/7645/A/4, 17 May 1984.

188. BBC/SWB/ME/7647/i, 19 May 1984.

189. *Middle East Contemporary Survey 1983/4*, p. 134.

190. See *Middle East Contemporary Survey 1983/4*, p. 134; *Middle East*, June 1984.

191. BBC/SWB/ME/7652/A/1, 25 May 1984.

192. BBC/SWB/ME/7652/A/3, 25 May 1984. The bill permitted the oil ministry to sell five million tons of crude oil for a 12-month period at a $2.50 discount, and deliver an additional one million tons free of charge. With regard to the rescheduling of Syrian debts, the bill specified that monthly instalments of $20 million had to be made starting in May 1985 for four years. Afterwards 12 quarterly instalments would follow to pay off the remaining $500 million owed by Syria. See *Financial Times*, 24 May 1984; and *Le Monde*, 25 May 1984.

193. BBC/SWB/ME/7652/A/3, 25 May 1984.

194. *International Herald Tribune*, 24 May 1984; and *The Times*, 24 May 1984.

195. Earlier on 12 May, the pro-Iraqi Paris-based magazine, *Al-Watan al-Arabi*, published a report on Syrian military transport planes delivering weapons and war *matériel* to an Iranian military airbase near Tabriz. In addition, according to the magazine, Syrian military personnel had established a base of operations in Tabriz on Dr Ali Shariati street.

196. According to various reports, Iranian oil exports plunged from a daily average of 1.75 million barrels a day to as low as 500,000 or 700,000 a day in the spring. See *Middle East*, July 1984; and BBC/SWB/ME/7659/A/6, 2 June 1984.

197. See Khaddam's interview with *Al-Nahar al-Arabi wa al-Dawli* on 2 June. It

is highly unlikely that the Syrians were serious about possibly intervening in the Gulf against the Islamic Republic. They were well aware of Iranian concerns about sliding into greater regional isolation, and driving even more Arab states behind the Iraqis. The statements Khaddam and other Syrian officials made at the time were partially intended to pay lip service to the pan-Arab cause and deflect criticism from their detractors.

198. BBC/SWB/ME/7665/A/7, 9 June 1984. Afterwards Iranian warplanes concentrated their attacks on shipping in international waters in the southern parts of the Gulf and no more incursions were made into Saudi territorial waters.

199. See BBC/SWB/ME/7679/A/14-15, 26 June 1984; and BBC/SWB/ME/7687/A/ 6, 5 July 1984. In fact, as early as the beginning of 1984, the USA covertly sent shipments of chemical weapons to Iraq via a third country in Europe, taking great care to ensure that the deliveries could not be traced back to the USA. Confidential conversation with a US Department of Commerce official. Washington, DC, September 1993. Furthermore, in early July, a Congressional delegation led by Senator Bannerman of the Foreign Relations Committee visited Baghdad and held talks with Iraqi officials on matters of mutual interest. BBC/SWB/ME/ 7690/A/9, 9 July 1984.

200. *Frankfurter Allgemeine Zeitung*, 25 April 1984; *Al-Watan al-Arabi*, 7 July 1984.

201. In mid-August, elements of the Syrian eleventh armoured brigade commanded by Brigadier Hikmat Ibrahim entered Ba'albek and reassumed control of the city, in what turned out to be a peaceful transfer of power. The Syrians deployed their units throughout the former Iranian stronghold, and politely informed the Iranian Revolutionary Guards at various checkpoints to relinquish control to them. With the Lebanese government once again in the Syrian sphere of influence, and the IDF on the defensive in the south, Damascus calculated that the opportune moment had arrived to reassert control over the hotbed of Iran's Islamic revolutionary ferment in Lebanon. A smooth transition under the guidance of the imperturbable Brigadier Ibrahim was judged to be prudent to avoid straining relations with Iran, and alienating local Shiites with pro-Iranian sympathies. *The Times*, 15 August 1984.

202. *Financial Times*, 20 June 1984.

203. In August, US Congressman Stephen Solarz, an influential member of the House Foreign Relations Committee visited Baghdad.

204. See *Financial Times*, 25 August 1984; *International Herald Tribune*, 25 and 26 August 1984; and *Le Monde*, 26 and 27 August 1984.

205. At least one Iranian pilgrim was killed in the mêlée. Acting Iranian foreign minister Besharati and director of Arab and African affairs Lavasani summoned the Saudi chargé d'affaires to the foreign ministry and lodged an official protest, severely berating the Saudi authorities for their handling of the affair. BBC/SWB/ME/7737/A/10, 1 September 1984; and BBC/SWB/ ME/7750/A/1–2, 17 September 1984.

206. BBC/SWB/ME/7743/i, 8 September 1984.
207. *International Herald Tribune*, 19 October 1984.
208. BBC/SWB/ME/7773/A/5, 13 October 1984.
209. BBC/SWB/ME/7768/A/6, 8 October 1984.
210. See *Le Monde*, 19 October 1984.
211. *International Herald Tribune*, 21 November 1984.
212. BBC/SWB/ME/7805/A/2, 20 November 1984.
213. For the text of the interview broadcast on Radio France Inter, see BBC/SWB/ME/7805/A/7-11, 20 November 1984.
214. BBC/SWB/ME/7812/i, 28 November 1984.
215. According to Richard Murphy (conversation, London, November 1995), Tareq Aziz and Iraq's ambassador to Washington, Nizar Hamdoon were shrewd statesmen who managed to convince US officials that Iraq had become more moderate and changed its foreign policy orientation. They claimed that Washington could rely on Baghdad as a dependable partner in regional affairs and Gulf security.
216. It is interesting to note that following the Israeli government decision, in an interview on Shiite terrorism, Israeli chief of staff Lieutenant-General Moshe Levi admitted: 'The Shiite community has undergone processes – some of which ran parallel to the war ... the most prominent of which is so-called Khomeinism which originates in Iran. ... It is my assessment that through our continued presence in Lebanon we give the Shiites more reasons to go on attacking us.' BBC/SWB/ME/ 7851/A/1-4, 17 January 1985.
217. *Middle East Contemporary Survey 1984/5*, pp. 119–20; and *Middle East International*, 8 February 1985. Apparently, the Kuwaitis begged the Syrians to discontinue arms shipments to Iran, but to no avail.
218. *Financial Times*, 13 February 1985; and *Middle East International*, 8 March 1985.

3. Intra-Alliance Tensions and the Consolidation of the Syrian–Iranian Axis, 1985–88

1. See *Al-Thawrah*, 21 March 1985.
2. The aerial bombardment and missiles attacks reached a peak between 15–25 March and continued intermittently until 30 June.
3. BBC/SWB/ME/7911/A/3, 28 March 1985.
4. In an interview with the *Tehran Times* on 27 March, Iranian deputy foreign minister Ali Mohammad Besharati set out Iran's conditions for the cessation of hostilities: (1) identification and punishment of the aggressor, (2) reparation payments of $350 billion to Iran, and (3) the return of over 200,000 Iraqi expellees to their homeland.
5. Paradoxically, Iran's growing activism in Lebanon in the aftermath of the Israeli withdrawal from most occupied areas, its backing of the militant Hezbollah, which was rapidly gaining ground among the Shiite population, and its advocacy of the creation of an Islamic state, put it at odds with its primary Arab ally.

6. BBC/SWB/ME/7943/A/5, 6 May 1985.
7. Between 1984 and 1986, the Syrians arranged a series of secret negotiations between senior Saudi and Iranian officials to reconcile their differences, and thaw bilateral relations. See Claude van England's article in *Christian Science Monitor*, weekly international edition, 14–20 September 1987.
8. See BBC/SWB/ME/8014/A/2–3, 27 July 1985.
9. *Financial Times*, 29 July 1985; and *Guardian*, 30 July 1985.
10. *International Herald Tribune*, 12 August 1985. The communiqué also reiterated the Arab League's condemnation of Iran for prolonging the Gulf conflict and stated that the member states would reconsider their relations with Tehran, if it did not accept a negotiated settlement.
11. BBC/SWB/ME/8028/A/3, 13 August 1985.
12. BBC/SWB/ME/8040/A/1, 27 August 1985.
13. *International Herald Tribune*, 22 January 1987.
14. *The Times*, 18 June 1985.
15. Hiro (1992: 115). Only 48 hours after the Israeli army left Sidon 10,000–12,000 pro-Iranian fundamentalists poured into the city to take part in a massive demonstration denouncing Amin Gemayel and the Israelis, and demanding the establishment of an Islamic republic. The demonstrators, primarily Shiites from Beirut's poor Muslim suburbs, displayed placards with pictures of Ayatollah Khomeini and Lebanese religious leaders. See *Financial Times*, 19 February 1985.
16. *Middle East International*, 22 March 1985. During three incidents in February and March 1985 alone, Shiite guerrillas killed or wounded 23 Israeli soldiers.
17. BBC/SWB/ME/7918/i, 5 April 1985.
18. *Financial Times*; and *The Times*, 26 April 1985.
19. Some Hezbollah leaders explicitly stated that their main aim was to turn Lebanon into a theocratic state. In an interview with AFP, Hezbollah leader Abbas Musawi stated that his party's aim was to create an Iranian-style Islamic republic in Lebanon. See *International Herald Tribune*, 11 July 1985.
20. BBC/SWB/ME/7943/A/6, 6 May 1985. Upon his return to Tehran, in an interview, Karrubi asserted: 'Despite conspiracies of the Zionists' agents to create division between Shiite and Sunni brothers, the unity of the Shiite and Sunni ulema and solidarity of the followers of the two sects, are strong and foil conspiracies of the enemies of Islam.' See BBC/SWB/ME/ 7946/A/10, 9 May 1985.
21. *Financial Times*, 21 May 1985. Other estimates put the number of Palestinian fighters in Lebanon by then as high as 14,000, but this figure seems suspect. See Hiro (1992: 117).
22. BBC/SWB/ME/7958/i, 23 May 1985.
23. BBC/SWB/ME/7964/i, 30 May 1985.
24. *Middle East International*, 14 June 1985.
25. Ibid.
26. BBC/SWB/ME/7967/i, 3 June 1985.

27. BBC/SWB/ME/7970/A/1, 6 June 1985. This was one of the earliest indications that some Iranian leaders recognized that they could not overstep certain bounds in Lebanon, and would have to defer to Syria.

28. *Middle East International*, 14 June 1985.

29. See *Middle East International*, 14 June 1985; BBC/SWB/ME/7964/i, 30 May 1985.

30. *International Herald Tribune*, 24 June 1985.

31. Ibid.

32. In a disparaging statement, Ayatollah Montazeri referred to Berri's followers as 'renegades'. See *Le Monde*, 25 June 1985.

33. See *Le Monde*, 25 and 26 June 1985.

34. See Jim Muir's article in *Middle East International*, 12 July 1985, pp. 3–4.

35. Amal lost over 500 fighters in clashes with the Palestinians. Hiro (1992: 118).

36. For more details, see *International Herald Tribune*, 24 June 1985; *The Times*, 5 July 1985; and *Le Monde*, 7 September 1985.

37. *Middle East International*, 23 August 1985. Abu Musa posited, 'It is the first time that a non-Arab Muslim nation has received us with so much warmth and enthusiasm.'

38. *Frankfurter Allgemeine Zeitung*, 24 August 1985; and *The Times*, 26 August 1985.

39. *Frankfurter Allgemeine Zeitung*, 6 September 1985.

40. See BBC/SWB/ME/8066/i, 26 September 1985; and *Le Monde*, 27 September 1985.

41. *Middle East International*, 8 November 1985.

42. See Jim Muir's excellent analysis in *Middle East International*, 11 October 1985, p. 11.

43. *Financial Times*, 7 October 1985.

44. *Middle East International*, 11 October 1985.

45. *The Times*, 6 November 1985. Two months after the end of the confrontation between Tawheed and Syria, Sheikh Shaban visited Iran to discuss the situation in Lebanon with Iranian leaders and coordinate their policies. See BBC/SWB/ME/ 8132/i, 12 December 1985. Shaban had a series of high-level meetings with Revolutionary Guards minister Rafiqdoust, *Majles* speaker Rafsanjani, president of the supreme judicial council Musavi-Ardabili, and Ayatollah Montazeri. He told Montazeri: 'Today Islamic Iran has turned into the only source of hope for the deprived of the world and for the struggling nations and also for Islamic movements.' Ayatollah Montazeri responded by declaring: 'We have always supported Islamic movements and shall continue to do so, and in the case of Lebanon, since the categorical majority of its people are Muslims, it is necessary that through strengthening the Islamic movement in that country, Islamic rule shall soon be established in Lebanon. ... It is the duty of all Muslim strata and groups [in Lebanon] whether Shiite or Sunni, to put aside minor religious and sectarian

differences and not to permit Israel and its undercover lackeys to take advantage of these differences for purposes of weakening Islam and Muslims.' BBC/SWB/ME/8136/A/3–4, 17 December 1985.

46. *Middle East International*, 8 November 1985.

47. Ibid. Another editorial elucidated that Syria's actions 'to preserve the balance of forces in Lebanon in favour of pro-Israeli tendencies and the moderate leaders of the Amal movement [were in harmony with] the policy of Moscow and Washington to control the wave of militant Islam and to minimize the threat to Israel'.

48. BBC/SWB/ME/8088/i, 22 October 1985.

49. On 4–5 September, armed clashes occurred between Amal and the PSP. *Le Monde*, 7 September 1985.

50. Hiro (1992: 119–21); and *Guardian*, 21 December 1985.

51. See *Le Monde*, 26 September 1985; and *International Herald Tribune*, 26 September 1985.

52. *International Herald Tribune*, 26 September 1985; and *Guardian*, 28 September 1985.

53. O'Ballance (1988: 171); and *Guardian*, 28 September 1985.

54. See *Le Monde*, 31 October, 3 and 4 November 1985.

55. Cordesman and Wagner (1990: 212–13).

56. BBC/SWB/ME/8060/i, 19 September 1985.

57. BBC/SWB/ME/8060/A/4, 19 September 1985.

58. Musavi stated that Syria was at the forefront of the struggle against Israel, and by bolstering their relations, Iran and Syria now played a prominent role in Middle Eastern politics, and were a force to be reckoned with in international politics. BBC/SWB/ME/8060/A/4, 19 September 1985.

59. BBC/SWB/ME/8060/A/5, 19 September 1985; and *Financial Times*, 23 September 1985. An editorial in the Iranian daily *Jomhuri Eslami* of 19 September, reflecting the official Iranian position on the Syrian–Jordanian talks, advocated a firm Syrian stand on the Palestinian issue as long as the 'cancerous Zionist growth' had not been removed from the region, adding that the bilateral dialogue with Amman should be a means to 'tear Jordan away from the bosom of Zionism'.

60. BBC/SWB/ME/8060/i, 19 September 1985.

61. On 24 October, an editorial in the Persian-language daily, *Ettela'at*, warned about the implications of a Syrian–Iraqi *rapprochement*, calling it a 'dangerous' development that could possibly lead to Syria's loss of its 'anti-Zionist ally', Iran.

62. See *Le Monde*, 27–28 October 1985; BBC/SWB/ME/8094/A/3, 29 October 1985.

63. BBC/SWB/ME/8094/A/3, 29 October 1985.

64. BBC/SWB/ME/8128/i, 19 November 1985.

65. BBC/SWB/ME/8124/A/3, 3 December 1985. Velayati and al-Shara, met again the next day, 2 December, to discuss bilateral cooperation. See BBC/SWB/ME/8125/ A/3, 4 December 1985.

66. BBC/SWB/ME/8126/A/2, 5 December 1985.

67. *Middle East International*, 20 December 1985. *The Financial Times* on 5 December 1985 stated that Iran was believed to have acceded to Syria's request to resume oil deliveries, but this runs contrary to the available evidence.

68. *Middle East International*, 20 December 1985.

69. BBC/SWB/ME/8131/A/3, 11 December 1985.

70. BBC/SWB/ME/8132/i, 12 December 1985; and *Middle East International*, 20 December 1985.

71. BBC/SWB/ME/8133/i, 13 December 1985.

72. *Middle East International*, 20 December 1985; and BBC/ME/8132/i, 12 December 1985. The cessation of Iranian oil deliveries had also prompted Libya to send Syria some oil shipments.

73. See *Middle East International*, 20 December 1985; *The Times*, 27 December 1985.

74. BBC/SWB/ME/8142/A/4, 24 December 1985.

75. *The Times*, 18 December 1985.

76. *Le Monde*, 28 December 1985. Also see *International Herald Tribune*, 31 December and 1 January 1985/86. In his speech in November, King Hussein explained that a 'minority group had deliberately undertaken destructive activities in Syria in the guise of religion'.

77. BBC/SWB/ME/8146/i, 2 January 1986.

78. *Middle East International*, 10 January 1986. In the days leading up to King Hussein's visit, the Iranian news media depicted the forthcoming meeting as a successful outcome of Assad's attempts to persuade the Jordanians to modify their stance on the Arab–Israeli problem, and a victory for the radical states in the region. At the same time, the Majles rejected a bill the government submitted to renew the oil agreement with Syria. The previous arrangement had stipulated annual deliveries of six million tons to Syria, one million for free and five million at discounted prices – with the Syrians actually selling the surplus on the international market for a $200 million net profit.

79. Cordesman and Wagner (1990: 219–20).

80. *Financial Times*, 24 February 1986.

81. BBC/SWB/ME/8191/i, 24 February 1986.

82. In an interview with the Kuwaiti daily, *Al-Siyasah*, 1 March, King Hussein characterized Iran's recent military moves 'as an aggression against the whole Arab nation', and went on to describe the hostilities as 'an Arab–Iranian war'. He expressed dismay at Arab support for Iran in some corners, lamenting 'it is very painful not to see the Arab nation place its entire potential at the disposal of Iraq'.

83. Ayatollah Montazeri lashed out at those who had orchestrated this 'oil conspiracy', arguing: 'They sell oil which belongs to the Muslims and the oppressed, God-given wealth at bargain prices. They pour it into the pockets of the Superpowers at cheap prices in order to defeat revolutionary Iran.' See Chubin and Tripp (1988: 173); and BBC/SWB/ME/A/2, 12 March 1986.

84. See BBC/SWB/ME/8216/A/9–10, 25 March 1986.

85. Chubin and Tripp (1988: 145); and BBC/SWB/ME/A/4, 28 March 1986.

86. To minimize awareness of the growing Arab–Iranian rift, the Iranian media played up events that showed Arab–Iranian solidarity. For example, on 22 April, the Iranian media claimed that Iraqi refugees in Syria were flocking to five registration centres that had been recently opened up by the Iraqi opposition to sign up as volunteers for combat against the Iraqi army in the Gulf War.

87. The intra-Maronite fighting resulted in 800–1000 casualties (Hiro 1992: 121).

88. In the words of one observer, 'the speed, ferocity, and effectiveness of Maronite repudiation of the accord clearly caught the Syrians by surprise' (*Middle East*, March 1986, p. 41).

89. *Christian Science Monitor*, weekly international edition, 29 March–4 April 1986.

90. See Seale (1989: 480–2); *Middle East*, June 1986, pp. 9–10; and Glass (1992: 313–19).

91. *Daily Telegraph*, 16 May 1986.

92. *International Herald Tribune*, 15 May 1986.

93. See *Le Monde*, 3, 4 and 5 May 1986.

94. BBC/SWB/ME/8251/A/5, 6 May 1986.

95. Also see *Le Monde*, 17, 18 and 19 May 1986.

96. Al-Shara defended these actions, stating that Syria was seeking neither military superiority nor a conflict with Israel, but was determined to achieve parity with Tel Aviv. *Guardian*, 26 May 1986.

97. *Le Monde*, 15 June 1986.

98. *International Herald Tribune*, 17 June 1986. In the same period, clashes occurred in the Bekaa once more, this time pitting Hezbollah fighters against those of the pro-Syrian SSNP in the town of Mashghara. The fighting raged on for four days, until Syrian troops intervened and restored order. For more details, see *Le Monde*, 14 and 17 June 1986; and *International Herald Tribune*, 15 and 17 June 1986.

99. *Daily Telegraph*, 22 July 1986.

100. *International Herald Tribune*, 5 August 1986.

101. *Le Monde*, 6 August 1986.

102. For a detailed analysis, see Claude van England's article in *Christian Science Monitor*, weekly international edition, 3–9 May 1986.

103. *Middle East International*, 16 May 1986.

104. See *Al-Siyasah* and *Al-Mustaqbal*, 17 May 1986; and BBC/SWB/ME/8262/i and A/4, 19 May 1986.

105. BBC/SWB/ME/8256/i, 12 May 1986; and BBC/SWB/ME/8258/i, 14 May 1986.

106. BBC/SWB/ME/8258/i, 14 May 1986.

107. See the extremely thorough analysis of the situation by Judith Perera in *Middle East*, June 1986, pp. 9–10.

108. *Le Monde*, 25–26 May 1986.

109. *Financial Times*, 2 June 1986.

110. *The Times*, 26 May 1986; and *Le Monde*, 27 May 1986.

111. BBC/SWB/ME/8268/i, 26 May 1986; and *Le Monde*, 27 May 1986.

112. *Le Monde*, 29 May 1986; and *Financial Times*, 29 May 1986.

113. BBC/SWB/ME/8272/i, 30 May 1986.

114. *Le Monde*, 4 June 1986.

115. *International Herald Tribune*, 12 June 1986.

116. *Guardian*, 3 June 1986.

117. BBC/SWB/ME/8267/A/6, 24 May 1986.

118. In the absence of Iranian oil deliveries, Syria was forced to purchase oil on the spot market and from Libya. Algeria had also stepped in and promised to provide about 130,000 barrels a day to Syria on favourable terms. See *Le Monde*, 5 June 1986.

119. *Frankfurter Allgemeine Zeitung*, 14 June 1986. Quote taken from an interview with Assad by the Lebanese *Al-Shiraa* weekly magazine.

120. BBC/SWB/ME/8280/A/4, 9 June 1986.

121. Ibid.; BBC/SWB/ME/8285/A/2, 14 June 1986; and *Middle East International*, 27 June 1986.

122. BBC/SWB/ME/8280/A/4, 9 June 1986; *Middle East International*, 27 June 1986.

123. *Le Monde*, 15 and 16 June 1986; *International Herald Tribune*, 19 June 1985.

124. *Middle East International*, 27 June 1986, *Financial Times*, 16 June 1986.

125. See John K. Cooley's account in *International Herald Tribune*, 18 June 1986; *Al-Ittihad* of Abu Dhabi, 16 June 1986; and *The Times*, 24 June 1986.

126. *International Herald Tribune*, 19 June 1986.

127. Kuwait's *Al-Siyasah* carried a report to this effect on 16 June. See also *Financial Times*, 16 June 1986; and *Guardian*, 24 June 1986.

128. *Middle East International*, 27 June 1986. Aziz revealed that as early as March 1986, at the USSR'S behest, a secret meeting of Iraqi and Syrian intelligence officials had taken place, but the negotiations broke down.

129. See text of Tareq Aziz's interview in *Al-Siyasah*, 28 June 1986; and BBC/SWB/ ME/8298/A/2–3, 30 June 1986.

130. Also see *Guardian*, 25 June 1986.

131. The French reportedly made a commitment not to enter into any new arms agreements with the Iraqis and only honour the existing ones. The level of Arab concern was such that in June, the GCC's general-secretary, Abdullah Bishara was sent to Paris to clarify recent French moves. Bishara was assured that despite certain concessions to Iran, France would continue to provide support for the Iraqi war effort. See *Middle East International*, 27 June 1986.

132. BBC/SWB/ME/8304/i, 7 July 1986; *Le Monde*, 8 July 1986; and *Guardian*, 8 July 1986. The delegation also included oil minister Ghazi al-Durubi, and industry minister Ali al-Tarabulsi.

133. Al-Imadi also declared that 'the economic talks should have a positive effect on bilateral ties and reduce the impact of the conspiracies hatched by the two countries' enemies'. See *Guardian*, 8 July 1986.

134. *Le Monde*, 11 July 1986; and BBC/SWB/ME/8308/i, 11 July 1986.

135. For a comprehensive analysis of the economic problems facing Iran, Iraq, Syria and other concerned states, see David Hirst's article in *Guardian*, 17 July 1986.

136. *Middle East International*, 11 July 1986.

137. BBC/SWB/ME/8323/i, 29 July 1986.

138. *Middle East International*, 8 August 1986.

139. *Frankfurter Allgemeine Zeitung*, 26 August 1986.

140. *Middle East*, September 1986, p. 8. It should be noted that Iraqi warplanes attacking Iranian oil loading terminals and installations in the southern Gulf region were actually refuelled in the air by Saudi air force tankers. Confidential conversation with US government consultant and military aviation specialist, Washington DC, August 1993.

141. *Guardian*, 23 August 1986; *Le Monde*, 29 August 1986; Cordesman and Wagner (1990: 230); and O'Ballance (1988: 184).

142. *Guardian*, 23 August 1986.

143. Ibid.

144. *Frankfurter Allgemeine Zeitung*, 26 August 1986.

145. *Frankfurter Allgemeine Zeitung*; and BBC/SWB/ME/8347/i, 26 August 1986.

146. Chubin and Tripp (1988: 136–7).

147. *Financial Times*, 4 October 1986.

148. Ibid.

149. *Middle East International*, 12 September 1986.

150. *The Times*, 10 October 1986.

151. *The Times*, 16 October 1986.

152. BBC/SWB/ME/8392/A/3, 17 October 1986.

153. *Guardian*, 29 October 1986.

154. For an example, see the Iraqi daily, *Al-Thawrah*, 12 November 1986, on Israel's role in the Iran–Contra affair. At a ceremony marking the birth of the Prophet on 13 November Iraqi vice-president Taha Muhyi al-Din Ma'ruf delivered a fiery speech denouncing the 'fanaticism and rancour harboured by the Persians against the Arabs', and their attempts to 'falsify and distort' Islam in order to implement 'their evil political designs' under the garb of religion at the expense of 'the Arab nation' and Iraq since it represented 'the radiant centre of a civilizing renaissance'. He underlined that to carry out 'their racist and shu'ubi plot', they had cooperated with the 'enemies of Arabs and Islam, particularly the Zionists' throughout history. In a thinly-veiled attack on Syria, Ma'ruf highlighted that Iran's collaboration with the Zionists 'exposed and refuted the arguments of those who claim to be Arabs and who are cooperating with them, justifying such cooperation by citing the bragging by the rulers of Iran about liberating Jerusalem and regaining Palestine'. BBC/SWB/ME/8417/A/2, 15 November 1986.

155. BBC/SWB/ME/8439/A/2, 11 December 1986.

156. In mid-December, Tehran was somewhat relieved, but at the same time some of its worst fears were confirmed, when veteran journalist Bob Woodward broke the story in the *Washington Post* on 16 December about the CIA having provided Iraq with satellite intelligence since 1984. Despite initial denials, the Reagan administration subsequently confirmed the verity of the report. Immediately, the day after the new revelations, on 17 December, the Iranian foreign ministry issued a strongly-worded statement condemning US backing of Iraq and emphasizing that Iran was undeterred in its aim to eliminate 'the tyrannical regime ruling over Iraq'. BBC/SWB/ME/8446/A/2, 19 December 1986.

157. See Robert Fisk's article in *The Times*, 20 November 1986. Also refer to *Financial Times*, 19 December 1986; and O'Ballance (1988: 170).

158. Winslow (1992: 260). Furthermore, in southern Lebanon, armed Palestinians made their way back to refugee camps on the outskirts of Tyre and Sidon, and virtually controlled the port city of Sidon itself.

159. *Frankfurter Allgemeine Zeitung*, 26 November 1986; and *Christian Science Monitor*, weekly international edition, 8–14 December 1986.

160. *Le Monde*, 7–8 December 1986.

161. *International Herald Tribune*, 9 December 1986.

162. See *Financial Times*, 9 and 11 December 1986. During a temporary ceasefire arranged by the Iranians, Hezbollah ambulances transported casualties out of Maghdousheh. *Guardian*, 12 December 1986.

163. *International Herald Tribune*, 13 and 14 December 1986; *Guardian*, 15 December 1986. Estimates of casualties vary throughout this period.

164. See *Middle East International*, 19 December 1986.

165. See *Guardian*, 30 December 1986. Ali Khamene'i had called for an end to the bloodshed in the closing days of December, while Iranian envoy, Issa Tabatabai had remained in Rashidiyyah for three weeks, vowing not to leave until a satisfactory solution had been formulated.

166. In November 1987, Iran achieved a significant breakthrough when it convinced the two main Iraqi Kurdish opposition groups, the KDP and PUK, to put aside their rivalry and join forces with Tehran in the war against the Baghdad regime. Reportedly, this move received the blessing of Syria also. See *Guardian*, 19 November 1986; and *Frankfurter Allgemeine Zeitung*, 29 November 1986.

167. BBC/SWB/ME/8440/i, 12 December 1986.

168. Cordesman and Wagner (1990: 248–9).

169. According to some sources, Iranian and Iraqi losses may have been as high as 62,000 and 21,000 respectively. See O'Ballance (1988: 196); Cordesman and Wagner (1990: 253).

170. One military analyst described Karbala 5 as Iran's 'Verdun'. Conversation with IISS research associate Dr Ahmed Hashim, London, August 1994.

171. *Guardian*, 27 February 1987; and *International Herald Tribune*, 28 February–1 March 1987.

172. See the excellent analysis by Bernard Trainor in *International Herald Tribune*, 20 July 1988.

173. See *Middle East International*, 6 February 1987; and BBC/SWB/ME/8481/ A/1–3, 2 February 1987.

174. For further details, or the English translation see BBC/SWB/ME/8476/A/1– 8, 27 January 1987.

175. Throughout the winter of 1986/7, Syria continued to be a conduit for the procurement and transhipment of weapons on the international arms market for Iran's war effort, including munitions and shoulder-held anti-aircraft missiles from the Swedish arms manufacturer, Bofors. The Iranians used the latter during Karbala 5 to devastating effect, bringing down 50–60 Iraqi aircraft – 10 per cent of the Iraqi air force. See *Guardian*, 12 February 1987; BBC/SWB/ME/8496/A/9, 19 February 1987; *Washington Post*, 10 March 1987; and Stork (1987: 4).

176. See BBC/SWB/ME/8478/i, 29 January 1987.

177. See the analysis of Mary Curtius about the outcome of the Islamic summit in *Christian Science Monitor*, 30 January 1987.

178. Cordesman and Wagner (1990: 255).

179. See Claude van England's article in *Christian Science Monitor*, weekly international edition, 16–22 March 1987.

180. Hiro (1992: 126); and O'Ballance (1988: 172).

181. *Financial Times*, 14 February 1987; and *International Herald Tribune*, 14 and 15 February 1987.

182. O'Ballance (1988: 172–3). The Iranian embassy's political adviser Mohammad Hassan Sattari oversaw the delivery and distribution of food. Ambulances were allowed to take away the wounded, and sick women and children. See *International Herald Tribune*, 16 February 1987.

183. *International Herald Tribune*, 16 February 1987; and O'Ballance (1988: 173).

184. O'Ballance (1988: 174); *Financial Times*, 23 February 1987; and *Guardian*, 24 February 1987.

185. See the superb analyses in the *Financial Times* by Nora Boustany on 23 February; and by Richard Johns on 24 February.

186. O'Ballance (1988: 174); and *International Herald Tribune*, 27 February 1987.

187. See O'Ballance (1988: 174); and *Le Monde*, 25 February 1987; and *International Herald Tribune*, 25 February 1987.

188. See BBC/SWB/ME/8359/i, 9 September 1986; and *Middle East Contemporary Survey 1986*, p. 485 for details on the Amal–Hezbollah clashes. The fighting ended after the intercession of Iranian embassy personnel and members of the Amal–Hezbollah joint committee that had been formed earlier under Iranian auspices.

189. Ranstorp (1997: 98).

190. *Financial Times*, 2 February 1987; and BBC/SWB/ME/8482/i, 3 February 1987.

191. See Robert Fisk's fascinating piece in *The Times*, 20 March 1987.

192. See *Daily Telegraph*, 26 February 1987; *International Herald Tribune*, 27 February 1987; and *The Times*, 3 March 1987.
193. BBC/SWB/ME/8502/i, 26 February 1987.
194. *International Herald Tribune*, 26 February 1987; *Le Monde*, 27 February 1987; and *Middle East International*, 6 March 1987.
195. *Le Monde*, 27 February 1987; and BBC/SWB/ME/8503/i, 27 February 1987.
196. BBC/SWB/ME/8502/i, 26 February 1987.
197. See Robert Fisk's article in *The Times*, 25 February 1987.
198. BBC/SWB/ME/8501/i, 25 February 1987; *Financial Times*, 7 March 1987.
199. *The Times*, 3 March 1987.
200. *Middle East International*, 6 March 1987; and *International Herald Tribune*, 7 and 8 March 1987.
201. *Guardian*, 27 February 1987.
202. *International Herald Tribune*, 28 February–1 March 1987.
203. See BBC/SWB/ME/8505/A/3–4, 2 March 1987.
204. *Middle East International*, 6 March 1987.
205. *Guardian*, 27 February 1987.
206. *Middle East International*, 20 March 1987.
207. BBC/SWB/ME/8511/i, 9 March 1987.
208. *Middle East International*, 20 March 1987.
209. See *Financial Times*, 7 March 1987.
210. Ibid. On the same day, while addressing a Friday prayer sermon at Tehran University, President Khamene'i again officially exonerated Assad and the Ba'thist leadership, but blamed elements within the Syrian military for the Basta killings. He also warned against trying to disarm Hezbollah, arguing that 'if these young, pious forces were to be deprived of their weapons, who would defend Lebanon and the Islamic forces against Israeli aggression?' Khamene'i stated that such a move would damage Syria's prestige, underlining that, after all, Hezbollah had been responsible for dealing 'the most blows against the forces of Zionism and arrogance'. Furthermore, he reiterated previous demands for the punishment of the culprits. See *Guardian*, 7 March 1987; *International Herald Tribune*, 9 March 1987; and BBC/SWB/ME/8511/i, 9 March 1987. In response to Khamene'i's remarks, the next day Damascus radio justified the Syrian military intervention arguing that those who carried firearms in Beirut under the pretext of fighting the Israelis had killed Lebanese civilians instead. It went on to lambaste 'foreign powers' that were opposed to the Syrian security measures in West Beirut.
211. *Middle East International*, 20 March 1987; and *International Herald Tribune*, 11 March 1987.
212. *Middle East International*, 20 March 1987; and *International Herald Tribune*, 11 March 1987.
213. BBC/SWB/ME/8512/i, 10 March 1987.
214. For the full text of the interview broadcast on Tehran radio, see BBC/SWB/ME/8513/A/4-6, 11 March 1987; and also *Jomhuri Eslami*, 12 March 1987.

215. *International Herald Tribune*, 11 March 1987.

216. BBC/SWB/ME/8516/i, 14 March 1987.

217. Many Amal militiamen who defected to Hezbollah also felt betrayed by Syria's handling of the Basta affair.

218. See Karsh (1988: 86–7). In mid-1987, Syria was facing its worst financial crisis in 16 years. Its hard currency reserves had shrunk to $20–40 million, and it had defaulted on $60 million in payments to the World Bank, prompting the latter to stop disbursements to Syria. The USSR and most GCC states had discontinued financial assistance to Syria. Only Saudi Arabia contributed about $540 million annually. By now, its was unofficially estimated that domestic inflation was running at about 125 per cent. See the articles by Nora Boustany in *International Herald Tribune*, 18 and 19 July 1987; and *Financial Times*, 23 July 1987.

219. *Le Monde*, 10 March 1987; and *Financial Times*, 18 March 1987.

220. See *Le Monde*, 17 April 1987. It was even claimed that as of January 1987, Iran had discontinued oil deliveries to Syria altogether to signal its displeasure with Syrian policies in Lebanon and the Gulf.

221. Freedman (1991: 241, 247).

222. *Middle East Contemporary Survey 1987*, p. 123.

223. Karsh (1991: 166–7).

224. Karsh (1991: 170).

225. *Frankfurter Allgemeine Zeitung*, 25 April 1987; *Le Monde*, 28 April 1987; and Karsh (1991: 170–1).

226. Freedman (1991: 264); Karsh (1991: 171–2).

227. *International Herald Tribune*, 4 May 1987.

228. *Al-Qabas*, 4 May 1987; *Frankfurter Allgemeine Zeitung*, 9 May 1987; and BBC/SWB/ME/8564/A/7, 11 May 1987.

229. *Financial Times*, 5 May 1987; and *Le Monde*, 6 May 1987.

230. *Le Monde*, 6 May 1987; and *Middle East Contemporary Survey 1987*, p. 121.

231. See *Guardian*, 5 May 1987; *Le Monde*, 6 May 1987; *Al-Qabas*, 7 May 1987; BBC/SWB/ME/8564/A/8, 11 May 1987. Consequently, a scheduled meeting of Iraqi opposition organizations in Damascus was cancelled. See *Le Monde*, 6 May 1987.

232. It was only two months later that Jordanian prime minister al-Rifai confirmed that King Hussein had hosted the secret meeting between the Syrian and Iraqi presidents. BBC/SWB/ME/8614/ A/13, 8 July 1987; and *Middle East International*, 11 July 1987.

233. Hafez Assad publicly revealed that he had indeed met his Iraqi rival during an interview with the *Washington Post* published on 20 September, asserting that he had refused to comply with Saddam Hussein's demand to break with Iran.

234. Al-Shara was subsequently quoted by the news media: 'Syria will never tread the path of compromise. Since the first day, Syria has welcomed the revolution as an anti-Zionist bastion. ... The most grave events in the region after the creation of the Zionist entity were the compromise

by the Egyptian and Zionist regimes, and the launching of Saddam's war against the Islamic revolution of Iran, which has had the worst consequences.' BBC/SWB/ME/8549/A/11, 23 April 1987.

235. *Le Monde*, 28 April 1987; and *Middle East Contemporary Survey 1987*, p. 123.

236. BBC/SWB/ME/8566/i, 13 May 1987. *Le Monde*, 13 May 1987.

237. BBC/SWB/ME/8567/i and A/5-6, 14 May 1987. Al-Shara reiterated Syria's solidarity with Iran, and later described the outcome of his visit as 'successful and positive'. See BBC/SWB/ME/8566/i, 13 May 1987; and *Le Monde*, 14 May 1987.

238. Already in March, Tunisia severed diplomatic relations with Iran, accusing its diplomats of 'flagrant violations of diplomatic norms' through the recruitment of religious extremists to create 'chaos and ideological sedition'. BBC/SWB/ME/ 8527/i, 27 March 1987. Several weeks later on 13 May, Egypt announced its decision to close down the Iranian interests section in Cairo, denouncing the conduct of its staff as unacceptable, and giving them seven days to leave the country. See BBC/SWB/ME/8567/i, 14 May 1987; and BBC/SWB/ME/8571/A/11-12, 19 May 1987.

239. Hunter (1990: 66–7).

240. See also Hunter (1990: 69); Chubin and Tripp (1988: 217–18).

241. For a good analysis of Soviet efforts to reconcile Syrian–Iraqi differences, and the convergence of Soviet, Saudi and Jordanian interests in this respect, see Jim Muir's article in *Christian Science Monitor*, weekly international edition, 18–24 May 1987.

242. See BBC/SWB/ME/8566/A/2, 13 May 1986; and BBC/SWB/ME/8567/A/4-5, 14 May 1987.

243. For an excellent analysis of US policy, see Sick (1990: 223–7).

244. BBC/SWB/ME/8565/i, 12 May 1987.

245. See Charles Krauthammer's superb piece on the motives behind the reflagging effort, 'The real US mission in the Gulf', in *Washington Post*, 29 May 1987; and Freedman (1991: 269).

246. Freedman (1991: 271–2); and Sick (1990: 231–2).

247. See the excellent analysis by Sick (1990: 241–2).

248. *Le Monde*, 26 June 1987; and *Middle East Contemporary Survey 1987*, p. 418.

249. On 29 June, Mauritania broke off diplomatic ties with Iran, citing Tehran's 'continuous rejection of any negotiations' to end the Gulf War in order to restore stability and security of the Gulf region as the determining factor in its move. France followed suit on 17 July. See Hunter (1990: 152–3); Ranstorp (1997: 122); and BBC/SWB/ME/8607/i, 30 June 1987.

250. See BBC/SWB/ME/8585/A/1–2, 4 June 1987.

251. *Le Monde*, 26 June 1987; and *Middle East Contemporary Survey 1987*, p. 419.

252. *Middle East International*, 27 June 1987.

253. See *Guardian*, 23 June 1987; and *Middle East International*, 27 June 1987.

254. BBC/SWB/ME/8599/i, 20 June 1987.

255. *Le Monde*, 23 and 26 June 1987.

256. BBC/SWB/ME/8604/A/8-9, 26 June 1987.

257. BBC/SWB/ME/8608/i, 1 July 1987.

258. See *International Herald Tribune*, 13 July 1987; and *Le Monde*, 14 July 1987.

259. According to an article by Robert Fisk in *The Times* of 14 July the Syrians had snubbed the Iranian prime minister to show their displeasure with Iran. On the other hand, another report in *Le Monde* on 26 June indicated that the visit had been postponed due to the poor health of Syrian prime minister al-Kasm, who had to be hospitalized.

260. *Guardian*, 13 July 1987; and *Le Monde*, 14 July 1987.

261. *Financial Times*, 13 July 1987. According to the Lebanese daily, *Al-Safir*, al-Shara asked for Tehran's assistance to gain the release of all foreign hostages in Lebanon. Also see *Guardian*, 23 July 1987.

262. See *Guardian*, 13 July 1987; and BBC/SWB/ME/8619/A/1–2, 14 July 1987.

263. BBC/SWB/ME/8620/A/3, 15 July 1987.

264. BBC/SWB/ME/8620/A/2, 15 July 1987.

265. *Middle East Contemporary Survey 1987*, pp. 646–7.

266. Iraq's *Al-Thawrah*, 29 July 1987. Also see BBC/SWB/ME/8634/i, 31 July 1987.

267. *Al-Thawrah*, 29 July 1987.

268. Cordesman and Wagner (1990: 301); and *Guardian*, 6 August 1987.

269. *Le Monde*, 4 August 1987. Assad reportedly promised Sheikholislam that he would contact the Saudis to facilitate the return of dead Iranians from Mecca. *Middle East Contemporary Survey 1987*, p. 646.

270. According to IRNA, while expressing sympathy for Iran's plight, Khaddam asserted, 'Undoubtedly, the first fruit of this incident will be reaped by the Americans.'

271. *Le Monde*, 8 August 1987; and *Middle East Contemporary Survey 1987*, p. 126.

272. *Le Monde*, 8 August 1987.

273. *Middle East Contemporary Survey 1987*, p. 126; and *Frankfurter Allgemeine Zeitung*, 19 August 1987.

274. *Middle East Contemporary Survey 1987*, p. 126.

275. BBC/SWB/ME/8640/i, 7 August 1987. Another envoy, President Khamene'i's chief adviser, Mir Salim, had been dispatched a few days earlier to Islamabad and Ankara to secure Pakistani and Turkish support.

276. *Le Monde*, 7 August 1987; and *Frankfurter Allgemeine Zeitung*, 19 August 1987.

277. *Le Monde*, 8 August 1987; BBC/SWB/ME/8640/A/11-12, 7 August 1987.

278. BBC/SWB/ME/8640/A/12, 7 August 1987.

279. *Al-Thawrah*, 11 August 1987.

280. BBC/SWB/ME/8649/i, 18 August 1987; and BBC/SWB/ME/8652/A/2–3, 21 August 1987.

281. *Middle East Contemporary Survey 1987*, p. 127.

282. BBC/SWB/ME/8654/i, 24 August 1987. Going into the meeting, Tunisian foreign minister Hedi Mabrouk candidly admitted that the Arab League would seriously consider 'a rupture in relations with Tehran'. See *International Herald Tribune*, 25 August 1987.

283. *Daily Telegraph*, 25 August 1987.

284. *Financial Times*, 25 August 1987.

285. *Financial Times*, 25 August 1987.

286. *Financial Times*, 26 August 1987. During the second day of the deliberations, al-Shara asserted that the hostilities could not be brought to an end 'except within the framework of a unified Arab stand and a comprehensive, cohesive strategy that does not seek to turn Iran into an enemy of the Arabs. Rather, efforts to end the war should be joined with efforts to establish good-neighbourly relations and cooperation with Iran.' BBC/SWB/ME/8656/i, 26 August 1987.

287. *Middle East Contemporary Survey 1987*, p. 127; *Financial Times*, 26 August 1987.

288. *Middle East Contemporary Survey 1987*, p. 127.

289. BBC/SWB/ME/8655/i, 25 August 1987; and *Middle East Contemporary Survey 1987*, p. 127.

290. See *International Herald Tribune*, 25 August 1987; and *Middle East International*, 28 August 1987.

291. *Middle East International*, 28 August 1987.

292. BBC/SWB/ME/8657/A/3-5, 27 August 1987.

293. *Middle East International*, 28 August 1987; and *Middle East Contemporary Survey 1987*, p. 128.

294. *Middle East Contemporary Survey 1987*, p. 128; and BBC/SWB/ME/8658/A/1, 28 August 1987.

295. BBC/SWB/ME/8659/A/11, 29 August 1987.

296. *Financial Times*, 2 September 1987. *Le Monde*, 4 September 1987.

297. In a speech commemorating Syrian Navy Day on 30 August, defence minister Mustafa Tlas condemned the growing presence of NATO warships in the Gulf, describing it as a plot by Washington to open a new front against the Arabs and the Iranian revolution. He reaffirmed Syrian backing for Iran, while denouncing Saddam Hussein as an 'agent' of US imperialism, and 'the butcher of Iraq'. BBC/SWB/ME/8661/A/5, 1 September 1987.

298. For details on Libya and South Yemen distancing themselves from Iran, see *The Times*, 11 September 1987; *Frankfurter Allgemeine Zeitung*, 11 and 12 September 1987; and *Le Monde*, 12 September 1987.

299. *Financial Times*, 26 August 1987.

300. *Middle East Contemporary Survey 1987*, p. 128.

301 Cordesman and Wagner (1990: 309–11).

302. Cordesman and Wagner (1990: 311–12). Kuwait responded by protesting to the UN Secretariat and the Security Council, and expelling five Iranian diplomats.

303. Cordesman and Wagner (1990: 312). In essence, Iran was willing to

accept an informal ceasefire followed by identification of the party responsible for starting the conflict, and only then observe a formal ceasefire and comply fully with Resolution 598.

304. *The Times*, 14 September 1987; and *Daily Telegraph*, 18 September 1987.

305. *Frankfurter Allgemeine Zeitung*, 19 September 1987.

306. *International Herald Tribune*, 21 September 1987.

307. Ibid.

308. *Guardian*, 22 September 1987.

309. *Middle East International*, 26 September 1987. According to one Western observer, 'The Arabs are forced to wait on events at the UN, hoping that someone else will pull the chestnuts out of the fire.'

310. BBC/SWB/ME/8679/i, 22 September 1987.

311. Ibid.

312. *Guardian*, 21 September 1987; and *Financial Times*, 25 September 1987.

313. BBC/SWB/ME/8679/i, 22 September 1987; *Financial Times*, 25 September 1987.

314. See *Guardian*, 21 September 1987; *Middle East International*, 26 September 1987.

315. *Guardian*, 25 September 1987; and BBC/SWB/ME/8682/i, 25 September 1987.

316. BBC/SWB/ME/8685/i, 29 September 1986. Iranian radio greeted the Libyan and Syrian announcement, commenting on 28 September that 'the coordinated stand of Libya and Syria, which are among the friends of the Islamic Republic of Iran in the Arab League, casts doubt on the fate of the extraordinary Amman summit'.

317. *Middle East International*, 7 November 1987; and *Middle East Contemporary Survey 1987*, p. 128.

318. BBC/SWB/ME/8698/i, 14 October 1987.

319. See Cordesman and Wagner (1990: 318–19). The authors concur with Rafsanjani's subsequent assertion that the USA deliberately timed the raid to divert attention from the Iranian initiative at the UN.

320. See *Al-Sharq Al-Awsat*, 22 September 1987.

321. See *Al-Ba'th*, 23 September 1987.

322. US Navy SEAL units subsequently captured two other boats and six personnel (Cordesman and Wagner 1990: 325–6).

323. Cordesman and Wagner (1990: 328–9); and Sick (1990: 226).

324. *Financial Times*, 19 October 1987.

325. *Middle East International*, 24 October 1987; *Financial Times*, 19 October 1987.

326. *Middle East International*, 24 October 1987. In the autumn of 1987, Italian authorities discovered that two major Italian armaments firms, Brescia and Valsella (both partly owned by Fiat) were shipping weapons and mines to Iran via Syria. See *The Middle East*, November 1987, p. 18.

327. *Middle East International*, 24 October 1987.

328. *The Times*, 5 November 1987.

329. Ibid.

330. *Middle East International*, 24 October 1987.

331. Cordesman and Wagner (1990: 330); and El-Shazly (1998: 248).

332. BBC/SWB/ME/8704/i, 21 October 1987.

333. Ibid.

334. Ibid.; and BBC/SWB/ME/8704/A/10, 21 October 1987.

335. BBC/SWB/ME/8704/A/10-11, 21 October 1987. Also see *Al-Ba'th* and *Al-Thawrah*, 20 October 1987.

336. BBC/SWB/ME/8705/A/3–5, 22 October 1987.

337. *Financial Times*, 22 October 1987.

338. Cordesman and Wagner (1990: 332); and Ramazani (1990: 43).

339. See Godfrey Jansen's excellent analysis of the situation in *Middle East International*, 7 November 1987.

340. *Middle East*, December 1987.

341. *Frankfurter Allgemeine Zeitung*, 5 November 1987. At the same time, there were promising signs that Syria's economic woes and dependence on foreign oil would be eased by the development of the Dayr al-Zawr oil field. Already in 1987, the field was producing 60,000 barrels a day of high-quality light crude, and production was expected to increase by another 40,000 in early 1988, thereby significantly decreasing dependence on Iranian oil imports. During 1986, oil imports had contributed $54 million to the country's total fiscal deficit. See *Le Monde*, 28 October 1987.

342. *The Times*, 5 November 1987; and *Financial Times*, 7 November 1987.

343. *International Herald Tribune*, 4 November 1987; and *Guardian*, 7 November 1987.

344. *Guardian*, 7 November 1987; and *Le Monde*, 8 and 9 November 1987.

345. By the end of 1987, Egypt had emerged as a key supplier of arms to Iraq, having sold over $2 billion worth of war *matériel*, and sent tens of thousands of workers and military volunteers to assist the Iraqi war effort. *International Herald Tribune*, 6 November 1987.

346. See *Financial Times*, 9 November 1987; and *Guardian*, 13 November 1987.

347. *Guardian*, 13 November 1987.

348. *Financial Times*, 9 November 1987; and *International Herald Tribune*, 11 November 1987.

349. *Le Monde*, 10 November 1987.

350. *International Herald Tribune*, 9 November 1987.

351. *Financial Times*, 10 November 1987; and *Le Monde*, 11 November 1987.

352. *Middle East Contemporary Survey 1987*, p. 130.

353. *Financial Times*, 11 November 1987.

354. *Middle East Contemporary Survey 1987*, p. 130; and BBC/SWB/ME/8722/A/9, 11 November 1987.

355. *Guardian*, 12 November 1987.

356. *Financial Times*, 10 November 1987.

357. BBC/SWB/ME/8722/A/9, 11 November 1987; and *International Herald Tribune*, 11 November 1987.

358. BBC/SWB/ME/8722/A/9-10, 11 November 1987; and *Middle East Contemporary Survey 1987*, p. 130.

359. *Middle East Contemporary Survey 1987*, p. 131.

360. See article by Lamis Andoni in *Jordan Times*, 11 November 1987; and also BBC/SWB/ME/8723/A/9-10, 12 November 1987.

361. Article by Lamis Andoni in *Jordan Times*, 11 November 1987; .

362. *Financial Times*, 11 November 1987; BBC/SWB/ME/8723/A/11, 12 November 1987; and *International Herald Tribune*, 11 November 1987.

363. *Middle East Contemporary Survey 1987*, p. 131.

364. *Middle East Contemporary Survey 1987*, p. 131; *Jordan Times*, 11 November 1987.

365. *Middle East Contemporary Survey 1987*, p. 131.

366. For more details, see *Financial Times*, 12 November 1987; *Le Monde*, 13 November 1987; *Middle East International*, 21 November 1987; and *Middle East Contemporary Survey 1987*, pp. 131–2.

367. *Financial Times*, 12 November 1987; *International Herald Tribune*, 12 November 1987; and *Le Monde*, 13 November 1987.

368. *Middle East Contemporary Survey 1987*, p. 131.

369. Ibid. Also see *Middle East International*, 21 November 1987.

370. *Middle East Contemporary Survey 1987*, p. 131.

371. *Guardian*, 13 November 1987.

372. Also see *The Times*, 13 November 1987.

373. *Financial Times*, 12 November 1987; *International Herald Tribune*, 12 November 1987.

374. *International Herald Tribune*, 12 November 1987; and *Frankfurter Allgemeine Zeitung*, 1 December 1987.

375. *Le Monde*, 11 November 1987; and *Financial Times*, 12 November 1987.

376. See *Middle East International*, 21 November 1987; and *Financial Times*, 1 December 1987.

377. See also *Guardian*, 13 November 1987; and *International Herald Tribune*, 14 and 15 November 1987.

378. *Middle East International*, 21 November 1987.

379. *Financial Times*, 13 November 1987.

380. *International Herald Tribune*, 13 November 1987.

381. *Middle East International*, 21 November 1987.

382. *International Herald Tribune*, 11 November 1987; *Guardian*, 13 November 1987.

383. See Godfrey Jansen's accurate analysis in *Middle East International*, 21 November 1987.

384. *Middle East International*, 21 November 1987.

385. At this juncture, only Oman, Jordan, Somalia and Sudan had normal relations with Egypt. See *International Herald Tribune*, 13 November 1987.

386. *Middle East Contemporary Survey 1987*, p. 132.

387. *Middle East Contemporary Survey 1987*, p. 134.

388. BBC/SWB/ME/0001/i, 16 November 1987. In a poignant statement broadcast on Damascus radio on 12 November, partially reflecting a volte-face, a Syrian official elucidated that the government 'has not approved any phrase which harms or provokes Iran. It has not bargained nor has anyone bargained over this relationship. Syria has always emphasized its good relations with Iran and its keenness on the continuation and constancy of this relationship. Syria considers its relationship with Iran a force for Syria, the Arab nation, and Iran.'

389. See also BBC/SWB/ME/0002/A/7, 17 November 1987. In an interview in December, Vice-President Khaddam refuted King Hussein's assertions that both Israel and Iran coveted Arab land. He asserted: 'Iran is an Islamic state. There are differences between Iran and some Arab states. We believe that these differences can and must be settled. Iran has no designs on the Arab homeland. ... The matter is different with the Israeli enemy. The Israeli enemy has designs on our territory.' See BBC/SWB/ME/0033/A/2, 23 December 1987.

390. *Middle East International*, 21 November 1987.

391. *Daily Telegraph*, 18 November 1987.

392. *Middle East Contemporary Survey 1987*, p. 134. See also *Daily Telegraph*, 23 November 1987.

393. According to the Kuwaiti daily *Al-Watan*, of 14 December, the head of Syrian military intelligence Colonel Ali Duba met a senior Iraqi security official on the Syrian–Iraqi frontier in mid-December to discuss normalization of bilateral relations.

394. BBC/SWB/ME/0014/A/2, 1 December 1987.

395. In a subsequent interview on 18 December, Prime Minister Musavi bitterly criticized those Arab leaders in Amman whom he described as 'reactionary' and 'obsessed with racism'. He stated that Iran's strong relations with Libya and Syria disproved the 'propaganda of the Ba'thist–Saddamist system on the Arab versus Persian nature of the war'. See BBC/SWB/ME/0029/A/3, 18 December 1987.

396. See *International Herald Tribune*, 26 November 1987; Cordesman and Wagner (1990: 359). The authors support the view that the devastating losses suffered by Iran during Operation Karbala 5 had led to a decline in morale and hampered the government's mobilization effort.

397. Sick (1990: 227).

398. *Middle East International*, 21 November 1987.

399. Cordesman and Wagner (1990: 337, 359).

400. See *Financial Times*, 30 December 1987; *Le Monde*, 31 December 1987; and BBC/SWB/ME/0036/i, 30 December 1987.

401. *Le Monde*, 31 December 1987.

402. Al-Shara delivered messages from Assad to Khamene'i on both his visits to Tehran on 22 and 29 December. On his first stopover he also held

talks with Velayati and Musavi. For more details, see *Financial Times*, 24 December 1987; *Le Monde*, 30 December 1987; BBC/SWB/ME/0034/i, 24 December 1987; and BBC/SWB/ME/0036/i, 30 December 1987.

403. *The Times*, 4 January 1988; and Sick (1990: 235).

404. BBC/SWB/ME/0044/i, 9 January 1988; and *Financial Times*, 8 January 1988.

405. See Godfrey Jansen's article in *Middle East International*, 23 January 1988, p. 12; and *International Herald Tribune*, 8 January 1988.

406. *Financial Times*, 8 January 1988; and *International Herald Tribune*, 9 and 10 January 1988.

407. See *International Herald Tribune*, 8 January 1988; and *Middle East International*, 23 January 1988.

408. *Guardian*, 11 January 1988; *The Times*, 12 January 1988; *International Herald Tribune*, 13 January 1988.

409. *Financial Times*, 13 January 1988.

410. *Guardian*, 9 January 1988. Reportedly, Egypt had already received about $1 billion from the GCC in the period prior to Mubarak's visit.

411. *The Times*, 12 January 1988.

412. *Le Monde*, 14 January 1988.

413. *Financial Times*, 16 January 1988.

414. Cordesman and Wagner (1990: 362–3). Two days before the offensive, Iran's ambassador to Syria held a meeting with Faruq al-Shara, and handed him a note from his Iranian counterpart concerning developments in the Gulf conflict. See BBC/SWB/ME/0051/A/8, 18 January 1988.

415. *Financial Times*, 18 January 1988; *International Herald Tribune*, 27 January 1988.

416. Sick (1990: 235).

417. Cordesman and Wagner (1990: 363).

418. *Financial Times*, 20 January 1988.

419. See BBC/SWB/ME/0057/A/4-5, 25 January 1988. On 21 January, the Baghdad-based radio, Voice of the National Alliance for the Liberation of Syria, in one of its commentaries depicted the Gulf conflict as an 'Arab–Persian war' in which the Arab people from 'the Atlantic Ocean to the Arabian Gulf' would participate. It emphasized that Iraq had been defending the entire Arab nation for seven years and deserved Arab support to protect the Arabs against the 'Persian danger'. It went on to conclude that 'regional peace cannot be ensured if Iraq is not safe, proud and victorious'.

420. See BBC/SWB/ME/0060/A/2-3, 28 January 1988. Tareq Aziz implicitly blamed Syria's deviant stand for Iran's insistence on prosecuting the war. He stated: 'No country, not even the backward and bigoted Iran, can continue aggression if it finds in its face a brave and capable resistance.'

421. *Le Monde*, 29 January 1988.

422. *International Herald Tribune*, 4 February 1988. Besides describing Syrian

moves as 'treacherous', Iraqi officials were worried that Syria's actions in the Gulf were undermining the UN Security Council debate on imposing an arms embargo on Iran.

423. See *Al-Ba'th*, 28 January 1988; and BBC/SWB/ME/0064/A/6, 2 February 1988.

424. BBC/SWB/ME/0066/A/3–4, 4 February 1988.

425. See BBC/SWB/ME/0063/i, 1 February 1988; and BBC/SWB/ME/0065/A/4, 3 February 1988. Al-Shara expressed dismay at Iraq's 'trouble-making' in the region, and asserted that Iran and Syria were in agreement on the need to exert efforts to reduce tensions in the Gulf, and establish amicable relations between Tehran and the Arab sheikhdoms. *Le Monde*, 2 February 1988.

426. Cordesman and Wagner (1990: 368); and Sick (1990: 237).

427. Sick (1990: 236); and Freedman (1991: 280).

428. Sick (1990: 238).

429. See Cordesman and Wagner (1990: 363–8); and Sick (1990: 238–40).

430. See also *International Herald Tribune*, 3 March 1988.

431. Cordesman and Wagner (1990: 367–8).

432. *International Herald Tribune*, 8 March 1988.

433. Cordesman and Wagner (1990: 370–2); and Sick (1990: 239–40).

434. Cordesman and Wagner (1990: 372–3). In response to the Halabjah massacre, the UN sent a team of experts to investigate the matter in greater detail.

435. Hiro (1992: 130); and *Middle East Contemporary Survey 1988*, p. 630.

436. *Middle East International*, 25 July 1987.

437. For further details on these events, see *Le Monde*, 2 September 1987; *The Times*, 9 September 1987; and O'Ballance (1988: 180).

438. BBC/SWB/ME/8715/A/10, 3 November 1987. Also refer to Robert Fisk's piece in *The Times*, 14 November 1987; and Jim Muir's article in *Middle East International*, 19 December 1987, p. 7. In addition, with Iranian assistance, Hezbollah set up a television and radio station in the Bekaa (Hiro 1992: 130).

439. BBC/SWB/ME/8719/i, 7 November 1987.

440. See also Hiro (1992: 131).

441. Ibid.

442. Hezbollah accused Higgins of being a CIA operative. Higgins had previously served as an aide to US defence secretary Caspar Weinberger during 1985–87.

443. Ranstorp (1997: 101) actually argues that Sheikh Abdul Karim Obeid, the local leader of Hezbollah's military wing, and Mustafa al-Dirani masterminded the kidnapping.

444. BBC/SWB/ME/0106/A/8, 22 March 1988.

445. Hiro (1992: 132); *Middle East Contemporary Survey 1988*, p. 630; and Winslow (1992: 265).

446. BBC/SWB/ME/0121/i, 9 April 1988.

447. See BBC/SWB/ME/0122/i, 11 April 1988; and BBC/SWB/ME/0126/i, 15 April 1988.

448. See also Winslow (1992: 266).

449. Cordesman and Wagner (1990: 373–4).

450. Cordesman and Wagner (1990: 375–7).

451. The very next day, on 19 April, the daily *Al-Thawrah* lambasted US policy, accusing Washington of escalating tensions and pursuing hegemonic ambitions to turn the Gulf into a 'US lake'. It argued that by becoming a 'direct party' in the war, the Reagan administration was now revealing its conspiracy against the Arab nation and its allies. See also BBC/SWB/ ME/0131/A/2–3, 21 April 1988.

452. *Le Monde*, 26 April 1988; and BBC/SWB/ME/0135/A/2, 26 April 1988.

453. See BBC/SWB/ME/0164/i, 30 May 1988; Cordesman and Wagner (1990: 383). In a speech the same day, Saddam Hussein boasted that Iraq had achieved military superiority over its foe, asserting 'time favours us rather than the Iranians'.

454. Cordesman and Wagner (1990: 387). See also BBC/SWB/ME/0161/i, 26 May 1988.

455. For details of the operation, see Cordesman and Wagner (1990: 388–9); and BBC/SWB/ME/0188/i, 27 June 1988.

456. Cordesman and Wagner (1990: 389).

457. BBC/SWB/ME/0134/ia, 25 April 1988.

458. *Le Monde*, 7 May 1988; and Winslow (1992: 266).

459. BBC/SWB/ME/0140/i, 2 May 1988.

460. The Israelis later claimed that eight Iranians were among the dead at Maydoun. BBC/SWB/ ME/0147/i, 10 May 1988.

461. Ranstorp (1997: 101).

462. *Le Monde*, 7 May 1988.

463. *Financial Times*, 7 and 8 May 1988; BBC/SWB/ME/0146/i, 9 May 1988; and O'Ballance (1988: 182–3).

464. See Michael Jansen's excellent analysis of the situation in *Middle East International*, 14 May 1988, p. 3–4.

465. Ibid.

466. See also Hiro (1992: 132).

467. For a good overview of the situation, see *Financial Times*, 12 May 1988.

468. *Middle East Contemporary Survey 1988*, p. 631; O'Ballance (1988: 183); *Middle East International*, 14 May 1988. Iranian Revolutionary Guard instructors reportedly coordinated and supervised the operations. See *Financial Times*, 9 May 1988.

469. *Financial Times*, 14 and 15 May 1988; and *International Herald Tribune*, 14 and 15 May 1988.

470. *Le Monde*, 15 and 16 May 1988.

471. Much to Syria's consternation, PLO fighters in Shatila and Bourj al-Barajneh overpowered pro-Syrian dissidents, and subsequently threw their weight behind Hezbollah's effort to oust Amal from the suburbs.

See *Financial Times*, 17 May 1988; and *International Herald Tribune*, 17 May 1988.

472. BBC/SWB/ME/0150/i, 13 May 1988. Iranian deputy foreign minister Sheikholislam, Syrian brigadier Ali Hammoud and representatives from the two Shiite militias arranged the truce.

473. The joint security force included 72 Iranian Revolutionary Guards and 36 Syrian soldiers.

474. *Middle East Contemporary Survey 1988*, p. 632.

475. *Financial Times*, 14 and 15 May 1988; *International Herald Tribune*, 14 and 15 May 1988; and *Le Monde*, 15 and 16 May 1988.

476. *International Herald Tribune*, 14 and 15 May 1988.

477. *Financial Times*, 16 May 1988. At the time, there were major discrepancies in the figures given for the number of casualties.

478. *Financial Times*, 16 May 1988; and *International Herald Tribune*, 16 May 1988. The Syrian force included 60 tanks. See *Le Monde*, 17 May 1988.

479. BBC/SWB/ME/0154/i, 18 May 1988; and *Guardian*, 20 May 1988.

480. *International Herald Tribune*, 17 May 1988; *Financial Times*, 18 May 1988.

481. BBC/SWB/ME/0154/i, 18 May 1988.

482. For example, Sheikh Fadlallah said there was 'no obstacle' to Syrian entry into Dahiya, but mentioned earlier that a direct Syrian presence was not necessary to stop the bloodshed. See text of a Radio Monte Carlo interview with Fadlallah in BBC/SWB/ME/0152/6–8, 16 May 1988; and BBC/SWB/ ME/0153/i, 17 May 1988.

483. *International Herald Tribune*, 17 May 1988.

484. For more details, see *Le Monde*, 7 and 13 May 1988; and *Financial Times*, 19 May 1988.

485. *International Herald Tribune*, 19 May 1988; and BBC/SWB/ME/0156/i, 20 May 1988. During a brief visit to Damascus on 21 May the US ambassador to the UN, Vernon Walters, expressed concern about the fate of the hostages during a meeting with Hafez Assad and cautioned against a forceful Syrian entry into the suburbs. See *Middle East International*, 11 June 1988.

486. *Financial Times*, 18 May 1988.

487. See *International Herald Tribune*, 18 May 1988; *Le Monde*, 18 May 1988; and BBC/SWB/ME/0155/i, 19 May 1988.

488. *Le Monde*, 18 May 1988.

489. *Le Monde*, 20 May 1988.

490. Also see Jim Muir's excellent analysis of Iranian tactics in *Middle East International*, 28 May 1988, p. 4.

491. See BBC/SWB/ME/0156/i, 20 May 1988. In a radio interview later that day, Kan'an posited that Syria had decided to delay entry into Dahiya 'to give an opportunity for the success of the ongoing political efforts'.

492. After a meeting with Lebanese prime minister Selim al-Hoss, Besharati explained that the issue of a Syrian troop deployment had 'ceased to exist'. BBC/SWB/ME/0156/i, 20 May 1988.

493. BBC/SWB/ME/0156/i, 20 May 1988.

494. *Financial Times*, 19 May 1988.

495. BBC/SWB/ME/0156/i, 20 May 1988.

496. See the thorough analysis by Harvey Morris in the *Independent*, 25 May 1988.

497. *Financial Times*, 19 May 1988.

498. *Middle East Contemporary Survey 1988*, pp. 632–3.

499. See Jonathan Randal's article in *International Herald Tribune*, 25 May 1988.

500. See John Cooley's article in *International Herald Tribune*, 19 May 1988.

501. Olmert (1990: 184).

502. *Financial Times*, 19 May 1988; and *International Herald Tribune*, 25 May 1988.

503. Olmert (1990: 184).

504. *Financial Times*, 20 May 1988; and BBC/SWB/ME/0157/i, 21 May 1988.

505. See the text of the interview by Françoise Chipaux in *Le Monde*, 21 May 1988.

506. *Guardian*, 23 May 1988.

507. BBC/SWB/ME/0158/i, 23 May 1988. Later, Hezbollah information officer Ali Hashem added that they had no problem with Syria and, in fact, they were strategic partners in the struggle against the USA and Israel. He explained that a political disagreement had arisen with Amal because of the latter's attempts to impede the Islamic resistance to the occupation in south Lebanon and to annihilate Hezbollah. Hashem left the door open to political dialogue to resolve intra-Shiite differences. *Le Monde*, 24 May 1988.

508. BBC/SWB/ME/0161/i, 26 May 1988.

509. Kan'an held talks with Besharati in Damascus.

510. See *Guardian*, 23 May 1988; *Financial Times*, 25 May 1988; and BBC/SWB/ ME/ 0158/i, 23 May 1988.

511. *Financial Times*, 24 May 1988; *International Herald Tribune*, 24 May 1988; *Independent*, 25 May 1988.

512. *Al-Safir*, 27 May 1988. Also see Hiro (1992: 133).

513. *Independent*, 25 May 1988; *International Herald Tribune*, 25 May 1988; *Financial Times*, 25 May 1988; *Le Monde*, 27 May 1988.

514. See BBC/SWB/ME/0163/A/4, 28 May 1988; Hiro (1992: 133); and *Middle East Contemporary Survey 1988*, pp. 632–3.

515. Ranstorp (1997: 125).

516. *Daily Telegraph*, 27 May 1988.

517. *International Herald Tribune*, 27 May 1988; and *Financial Times*, 27 May 1988.

518. *Daily Telegraph*, 27 May 1988; and *International Herald Tribune*, 27 May 1988. Other sources claim that there were more than 400 or 500 dead, and 2000 wounded. See *Financial Times*, 28 and 29 May 1988; *Independent*, 30 May 1988; and Hiro (1992: 133). There were also conflicting

figures on the number of displaced people ranging from 60,000 to 600,000. In addition, there was extensive collateral damage during the fighting. See also *Financial Times*, 27, 28 and 29 May 1988; *International Herald Tribune*, 28, 29 and 30 May 1988; and *Guardian*, 30 May 1988.

519. BBC/SWB/ME/0163/i, 28 May 1988; *Le Monde*, 28 May 1988; *International Herald Tribune*, 28 and 29 May 1988; and Winslow (1992: 266).

520. BBC/SWB/ME/0164/i, 30 May 1988.

521. Ibid.; *Middle East International*, 11 June 1988; Hiro (1992: 133); and *Middle East Contemporary Survey 1988*, p. 633.

522. BBC/SWB/ME/0167/i, 2 June 1988; and BBC/SWB/ME/0168/i, 3 June 1988.

523. See Hiro (1992: 133).

524. See *Guardian*, 30 May 1988; and *Le Monde*, 31 May 1988.

525. BBC/SWB/ME/0164/i, 30 May 1988.

526. See Jim Muir's analysis in *Middle East International*, 11 June 1988, pp. 5–6.

527. See also *The Times*, 28 May 1988; and *Independent*, 30 May 1988.

528. See *The Times*, 28 May 1988; and *Middle East International*, 28 May 1988. In an interview towards the end of the crisis, Iranian foreign minister Velayati dismissed reports on the imminent collapse of the alliance with Syria as completely baseless. He pointed out that the two sides had shown restraint and that relations remained on a firm footing. Velayati stated: 'Our ties with Syria are friendly and fraternal, and God willing, will remain so.' BBC/SWB/ME/0164/A/4, 30 May 1988.

529. *Le Monde*, 26 May 1988.

530. Ranstorp (1997: 125).

531. See Tony Walker, 'Syrian oil industry gets into gear', *Financial Times*, 21 October 1988. By now, Syria was producing 250,000 barrels a day.

532. *Middle East Contemporary Survey 1988*, p. 144.

533. *Middle East Contemporary Survey 1988*, p. 147.

534. *Middle East Contemporary Survey 1988*, pp. 148–9.

535. See Cordesman and Wagner (1990: 390–4).

536. See Entessar (1988: 1447); and *New York Times*, 5 July 1988.

537. For more details on the cover-up and subsequent revelations, see the transcript of a special ABC news *Nightline* programme, 'Sea of lies', broadcast on 7 July 1992, and the *Newsweek* cover story with the same title published on 13 July 1992. The programme and the article were the result of a special joint ABC–*Newsweek* investigation conducted over a four-year period. Further revelations were made on the BBC World two-part television programme, *Correspondent*, entitled 'The other Locker-bie', shown in April 2000.

538. See *Kayhan*, 5 July 1988.

539. BBC/SWB/ME/0196/A/7-8, 6 July 1988.

540. Cordesman and Wagner (1990: 395–6).

541. Cordesman and Wagner (1990: 396–7); Entessar (1988: 1450); Sick (1990: 240–1).

542. Cordesman and Wagner (1990: 397).

543. *Middle East Contemporary Survey 1988*, p. 740.

544. See *Al-Thawrah*, 19 July 1988.

545. BBC/SWB/ME/0207/i, 19 July 1988.

546. See BBC/SWB/ME/0214/A/2–3, 27 July 1988; and BBC/SWB/ME/0224/A/ 6-7, 8 August 1988.

547. Cordesman and Wagner (1990: 398–9); and Sick (1990: 241).

548. BBC/SWB/ME/0233/A/4, 18 August 1988.

549. BBC/SWB/ME/0233/A/3, 18 August 1988.

4. Into the Twenty-first Century: The Syrian–Iranian Nexus Endures

1. See also Agha and Khalidi (1995: 31 and 119–20).

2. Hunter (1985: 34).

3. *Middle East*, November 1988, p. 11.

4. Stork and Lesch (1994: 21). It is interesting to note that during this period, for the first time, joint Jordanian–Iraqi military exercises were held by their air forces in Jordan near Israel and Syria. Saddam Hussein also denounced Israel on a number of occasions and, in April 1990, promised Yasser Arafat that Iraq would confront Israel to liberate Jerusalem. See Baram (1994: 26).

5. For early accounts of Iraqi political interference and arms shipments to anti-Syrian forces in Lebanon, see *Frankfurter Allgemeine Zeitung*, 19 August and 11 October 1988; and *Independent*, 27 September and 22 October 1988.

6. See *Washington Post*, 26 May and 9 July 1989; and *International Herald Tribune*, 8 June 1989.

7. For a good analysis of the ACC, see Ryan (1998: 386–401).

8. Ryan (1998: 391).

9. See also, Agha and Khalidi (1995: 26–7).

10. Ehteshami and Hinnebusch (1997: 104–5).

11. See Chubin (1994: 1–22) for an excellent overview of the regional situation and Iraqi policies during 1988–90.

12. Ehteshami and Hinnebusch (1997: 45–6).

13. Agha and Khalidi (1995: 30).

14. *Middle East International*, 9 November 1990.

15. Ehteshami and Hinnebusch (1997: 105).

16. Hinnebusch (1994: 178).

17. See Agha and Khalidi (1995: 73 and 86).

18. Agha and Khalidi (1995: 87).

19. Agha and Khalidi (1995: 78–9).

20. *Middle East Contemporary Survey 1991*, p. 684. For more details on the Syrian and Iranian missile programmes see Timmerman (1992b).

21. *The Times*, 12 November 1993; Agha and Khalidi (1995: 106).

22. See also Hinnebusch (1994: 177).

References

Books, Chapters in Books, Articles and Government Publications

Agha, H. J. and A. S. Khalidi (1995) *Syria and Iran: rivalry and cooperation*, London: Pinter Publishers for the Royal Institute of International Affairs

Ahrari, M. E. (1984) 'Implications of Iranian political change for the Arab world', *Middle East Review*, XVI (3) Spring

Amos, J. W. (1984) 'The Iran–Iraq war: conflict, linkage, and spillover in the Middle East', in Robert G. Darius, John W. Amos II, and Ralph H. Magnus (eds) *Gulf security into the 1980s: perceptual and strategic dimensions*, Stanford, CA: Hoover Institution Press

Avi-Ran, R. (1991) *Syrian involvement in Lebanon since 1975*, Boulder, CO: Westview Press

Axelgard, F. W. (1986a) 'The United States–Iraqi rapprochement', in Z. M. Szaz (ed.) *Sources of domestic and foreign policy in Iraq*, Washington, DC: American Foreign Policy Institute

(1986b) 'War and oil: implications for Iraq's postwar role in Gulf security', in F. W. Axelgard (ed.) *Iraq in transition: a political, economic, and strategic perspective*, Boulder, CO: Westview Press

Bani-Sadr, A. (1991) *My turn to speak*, Washington, DC: Brassey's Inc

Baram, A. (1986) 'Ideology and power politics in Syrian–Iraqi relations, 1968–1984', in Avner Yaniv and Moshe Ma'oz (eds) *Syria under Assad: domestic constraints and regional risks*, New York: St Martin's Press

(1994) 'Calculation and miscalculation in Baghdad', in Alex Danchev and Dan Keohane (eds) *International perspectives on the Gulf conflict 1990–91*, Basingstoke: Macmillan Press Ltd

Batatu, H. (1982) 'Syria's Muslim Brethren', *MERIP Reports*, November/ December, pp. 12–20

Chubin, S. (1994) 'Regional politics and the conflict', in A. Danchev and D. Keohane (eds) *International perspectives on the Gulf conflict 1990–91*, Basingstoke: Macmillan Press Ltd

Chubin, S. and C. Tripp (1988) *Iran and Iraq at war*, Boulder, CO: Westview

Chubin, S. and S. Zabih (1974) *The foreign relations of Iran*, Berkeley, CA: University of California Press

Cordesman, A. H. (1982) 'Lessons of the Iran–Iraq war: part two', *Armed Forces Journal International*, June, 68–85

Cordesman, A. H. and A. R. Wagner (1990) *The lessons of modern war: the Iran–Iraq war*, Boulder, CO: Westview Press

Cottam, R. (1986) 'Iran: motives behind its foreign policy', *Survival*, 28 (6) 483–95

Darius, R. G. (1984) 'Khomeini's policy toward the Mideast', in R. G. Darius, J. W. Amos II and R. H. Magnus (eds) *Gulf security into the 1980s: perceptual and strategic dimensions*, Stanford, CA: Hoover Institution Press

Dinerstein, H. S. (1965) 'The transformation of alliance systems', *American Political Science Review*, 59 (3) 589–601

Ehteshami, A and R. A. Hinnebusch (1997) *Syria and Iran: middle powers in a penetrated regional system*, London: Routledge

Eight Political Department (1976) *Relations of the imperial government of Iran with West Asian countries and Egypt*, Tehran: Foreign Ministry (in Farsi)

El-Shazly, N. (1998) *The Gulf tanker war: Iran and Iraq's maritime swordplay*, Basingstoke: Macmillan

Emami, M. A. (1997) *Politics and government in Syria*, Tehran, Iran: Institute for Political and International Studies (in Farsi)

Entessar, N. (1988) 'Superpowers and the Persian Gulf security: an Iranian perspective', *Third World Quarterly*, 10 (4), October, pp. 1427–51

(1993) 'The lion and the sphinx: Iranian–Egyptian relations in perspective', in H. Amirahmadi and N. Entessar (eds) *Iran and the Arab world*, Basingstoke: Macmillan Press Ltd

Evans, D. and R. Campany (1984) 'Military strategy: the lessons of conflict', *The Atlantic Monthly*, 254 (5) November, 26–34

Evron, Y. (1987) *War and intervention in Lebanon: the Syrian–Israeli deterrence dialogue*, London: Croom Helm

Fedder, E. H. (1968) 'The concept of alliance', *International Studies Quarterly*, 12 (1) 65–86

Freedman, R. O. (1991) *Moscow and the Middle East: Soviet policy since the invasion of Afghanistan*, Cambridge: Cambridge University Press

French, J. R. P. (1941) 'The disruption and cohesion of groups', *Journal of Abnormal and Social Psychology*, 36 (4) 361–77

Friedman, A. (1993) *Spider's web: Bush, Saddam, Thatcher and the decade of deceit*, London: Faber & Faber

Ghareeb, E. (1981) 'Iraq: emergent Gulf power', in H. Amirsadeghi (ed.) *The security of the Persian Gulf*, London: Croom Helm

Glass, C. (1992) *Money for old rope: disorderly compositions*, London: Picador

Haas, E. B. and A. S. Whiting (1956) *Dynamics of international politics*, New York: McGraw-Hill

Halliday, F. (1986) 'Iranian foreign policy since 1979: internationalism and nationalism in the Islamic revolution', in J. R. I. Cole and N. R. Keddie (eds) *Shi'ism and social protest*, New Haven, CT: Yale University Press

Heller, M. A. (1984) *The Iran–Iraq war: implications for third parties*, Tel Aviv: Jaffee Center for Strategic Studies

Hinnebusch, R. A. (1994) 'Egypt, Syria and the Arab state system in the new world order', in H. A. Jawad (ed.) *The Middle East in the new world order*, London: Macmillan

Hiro, D. (1984) 'Chronicle of the Gulf War', *MERIP Reports*, July/September, 3–14

(1992) *Lebanon: fire and embers*, New York: St Martin's Press

Hirschfeld, Y. (1986) 'The odd couple: Ba'thist Syria and Khomeini's Iran', in A. Yaniv and M. Ma'oz (eds) *Syria under Assad: domestic constraints and regional risks*, New York: St Martin's Press

Holsti, O. R., P. T. Hopmann and J. D. Sullivan (1985) *Unity and disintegration in international alliances*, Lanham, MD: University Press of America

Hunter, S. T. (1985) 'Syrian–Iranian relations: an alliance of convenience or more?', *Middle East Insight*, June/July, 30–4

(1990) *Iran and the world: continuity in a revolutionary decade*, Bloomington: Indiana University Press

Iklé, F. C. (1964) *How nations negotiate*, New York: Harper & Row

Institute for Political and International Studies (1995) *Syria: a country study*, Tehran: Foreign Ministry (in Farsi)

Jaber, H. (1997) *Hezbollah: born with a vengeance*, London: Fourth Estate Ltd

Kaplan, M. A. (1957) *System and process in international politics*, New York: John Wiley & Sons

Karsh, E. (1988) *The Soviet Union and Syria: the Asad years*, London: Routledge

(1991) *Soviet policy towards Syria since 1970*, London: Macmillan

Kessler, M. N. (1987) *Syria: fragile mosaic of power*, Washington, DC: National Defense University Press

Khoury, N. A. (1982) 'The pragmatic trend in inter-Arab politics', *Middle East Journal*, 36 (3) 374–87

Kienle, E. (1990) *Ba'th versus Ba'th: the conflict between Syria and Iraq 1968–1989*, London: I.B.Tauris

King, R. (1987) 'The Iran–Iraq war: the political implications', *Adelphi Papers*, No. 219, Spring, London: IISS booklet

Liska, G. (1962) *Nations in alliance: the limits of interdependence*, Baltimore, MD: Johns Hopkins University Press

Loomis, J. L. (1959) 'Communication, the development of trust and cooperative behavior', *Human Relations*, 12 (4) 305–15

Marr, P. (1985) *The modern history of Iraq*, Boulder, CO: Westview Press

Mortimer, E. (1982) *Faith and power: the politics of Islam*, New York: Vintage Books

O'Ballance, E. (1988) *The Gulf War*, London: Brassey's Defence Publishers Ltd

(1998) *Civil war in Lebanon, 1975–92*, London: Macmillan

Olmert, Y. (1990) 'Iranian–Syrian relations: between Islam and realpolitik', in D. Menashri (ed.) *The Iranian revolution and the Muslim world*, Boulder, CO: Westview Press

Ramazani, R. K. (1983) 'Khumayni's Islam in Iran's Foreign Policy', in A. Dawisha (ed.) *Islam in Foreign Policy*, Cambridge: Cambridge University Press

(1988) *Revolutionary Iran: challenge and response in the Middle East*, Baltimore, MD: Johns Hopkins University Press

(1990) 'Iran's resistance to US intervention in the Persian Gulf', in N. R. Keddie and M. J. Gasiorowski (eds) *Neither east nor west: Iran, the Soviet Union and the United States*, New Haven, CT: Yale University Press

Ranstorp, M. (1997) *Hizb'allah in Lebanon: the politics of the Western hostage crisis*, New York: St Martin's Press

Rothstein, R. L. (1968) *Alliances and small powers*, New York: Columbia University Press

Ryan, C. R. (1998) 'Jordan and the rise and fall of the Arab Cooperation Council', *Middle East Journal*, 52 (3) Summer, 386–401

Schiff, Z. and E. Ya'ari (1984) *Israel's Lebanon war*, London: Allen & Unwin

Seale, P. (1989) *Asad of Syria: the struggle for the Middle East*, Berkeley, CA: University of California Press

Sick, G. (1987) 'Iran's quest for superpower status', *Foreign Affairs*, 65 (4) Spring, 697–715

(1990) 'Slouching toward settlement: the internationalization of the Iran–Iraq war, 1987–1988', in N. R. Keddie and M. J. Gasiorowski (eds) *Neither East nor West: Iran, the Soviet Union and the United States*, New Haven, CT: Yale University Press

Singh, K. R. (1981) *Iran: quest for security*, New Delhi: Vikas Publishing House Ltd

Staudenmaier, W. O. (1983) 'A strategic analysis', in S. Taher-Kheli and S. Ayubi (eds) *The Iran–Iraq war: new weapons, old conflicts*, New York: Praeger

Stork, J. (1987) 'Reagan re-flags the Gulf', *MERIP Reports*, September/October, 2–5

Stork, J. and A. Lesch (1994) 'Background to the crisis: why war?', in H. H. Blumberg and C. C. French (eds) *The Persian Gulf war: views from the social and behavioral sciences*, Lanham, MD: University Press of America

Teune, H. and S. Synnestvedt (1965) 'Measuring international alignment', *Orbis Journal of World Affairs*, 9 (1) Spring, 171–89

Timmerman, K. R. (1992a) *The death lobby: how the West armed Iraq*, London: Bantam Books

(1992b) *Weapons of mass destruction: the cases of Iran, Syria and Libya*, Los Angeles, CA: Simon Wiesenthal Center

Walt, S. M. (1987) *The origins of alliances*, Ithaca, NY: Cornell University Press

(1997) 'Why alliances endure or collapse', *Survival*, 39 (1), Spring, 156–79

Winslow, C. (1992) *Lebanon: war and politics in a fragmented society*, London: Routledge

Woodward, B. (1987) *Veil: the secret wars of the CIA 1981–1987*, New York: Simon & Schuster

Wright, C. (1980/1) 'Implications of the Iran–Iraq war', *Foreign Affairs*, 59 (2) Winter, 275–303

Wright, R. (1985) *Sacred rage: the wrath of militant Islam*, New York: Simon & Schuster

    (1989) *In the name of God: the Khomeini decade*, New York: Simon & Schuster

Newspapers and Periodicals

Al-Adwa (Sudan)

Al-Ba'th (Syria and Iraq)

Al-Hayat (UK and Lebanon)

Al-Jazirah (Saudi Arabia)

Al-Nahar (Lebanon)

Al-Nahar Arab Report and Memo (Lebanon)

Al-Safir (Lebanon)

Al-Shiraa (Lebanon)

Al-Thawrah (Iraq and Syria)

Al-Watan Al-Arabi (France and Lebanon)

Daily Telegraph (UK)

Egyptian Gazette (Egypt)

Ettela'at (Iran)

Frankfurter Allgemeine Zeitung (Germany)

International Herald Tribune (USA)

Jomhuri Eslami (Iran)

Kayhan (Iran)

Mardom (Iran)

Middle East Contemporary Survey, vols 3–15 (1978–91) Moshe Dayan Center for Middle Eastern and African Studies, Shiloah Institute, Tel Aviv University, Boulder: Westview Press

Observer (UK)

Sunday Times (UK)

The Times (UK)

Wall Street Journal (USA)

Al-Ahram (Egypt)

Al-Dustur (Jordan)

Al-Ittihad (UAE)

Al-Mustaqbal (Lebanon)

Al-Nahar al-Arabi wa al-Dawli (Lebanon)

Al-Qabas (Kuwait)

Al-Ra'y Al-Amm (Sudan)

Al-Sharq Al-Awsat (UK and Beirut)

Al-Siyasah (Kuwait)

Al-Watan (Kuwait)

Christian Science Monitor (USA)

Daily Mail (UK)

Dawn (Pakistan)

Egyptian Mail (Egypt)

Financial Times (UK)

Guardian (UK)

Independent (UK)

Jeune Afrique (France)

Jordan Times (Jordan)

Le Monde (France)

Middle East (UK)

Middle East Economic Survey (Cyprus)

Middle East International (UK)

Neue Zürcher Zeitung (Switzerland)

Newsweek (USA)

New York Times (USA)

Sunday Telegraph (UK)

Tehran Times (Iran)

Tishrin (Syria)

Washington Post (USA)

Transcripts and Summaries of Radio Broadcasts

BBC Summary of World Broadcasts – Middle East (UK)

Foreign Broadcast Information Service – Near East and South Asia (USA)

Formal Interviews

Bani-Sadr, Abolhassan (president, Iran), Versailles, December 1994

Hashim, Ahmed (IISS), London, August 1994

Hiro, Dilip (August 1994) London

Mirfenderski, Ahmad (ambassador, Iranian foreign minister), Paris, December 1994

Murphy, Richard (ambassador, US assistant secretary of state for Near East and South Asia), London, November 1995

Poursartip, Mohammad (Iranian ambassador to Damascus 1973–77), Geneva, June 1997

Ra'ed, Jafar (ambassador, Imperial Iranian Foreign Ministry), London, April 1994

Sayghal, Abbas (Imperial Iranian Foreign Ministry), April, March 1994

Sagiyeh, Hazim (*Al-Hayat*), London, April 1994

Zahedi, Ardeshir (ambassador, Iranian foreign minister), Montreux, November 2000

Index